Clarissa's I

Clarissa Dickson Wright found fame alongside Jennifer Paterson as one half of the much-loved TV cooking partnership *Two Fat Ladies*. She is the author of the bestselling memoir *Spilling the Beans* as well as many cookery books including *The Game Cookbook* and, most recently, *Potty* – her one-pot cookbook. She is also a passionate supporter of the Countryside Alliance and of rural life. She lives a little in London but mostly in Scotland.

Clarissa's England

CLARISSA DICKSON WRIGHT

HODDER

First published in Great Britain in 2012 by Hodder & Stoughton
An Hachette UK company

First published in paperback in 2013

1

A CIP catalogue record for this title is available from the British Library

ISBN 978 1 444 72911 5

Printed and bound by Clays Ltd, St Ives plc

Hodder & Stoughton policy is to use papers that are natural, renewable
and recyclable products and made from wood grown in sustainable forests.
The logging and manufacturing processes are expected to conform to the
environmental regulations of the country of origin.

Hodder & Stoughton Ltd
338 Euston Road
London NW1 3BH

www.hodder.co.uk

To Mark and Delia Merison whose
hospitality inspired this book.

Contents

Introduction

The idea for this book came when I was sitting on the veranda of the house belonging to some friends just outside Devizes, with the Kennet and Avon Canal at my back and a side of Roundway Hill, the site of Oliver Cromwell's gun battery in that part of the world, which I had never seen before, watching the sun set. It was very beautiful and I suddenly thought that I wanted to write a book about my England. This is not an exhaustive book; some counties are longer than others because I have spent time there or I am very fond of them and some are shorter because I haven't had the experience of them. It is a personal book, although it contains history and references to food and all the things that you would expect from any book by me, but it is really my love affair with my country. I had been to almost every country in the world by the time I was forty when I got sober and those that I haven't been to I have no particular desire to visit; moreover I have seen the destruction that mass tourism can bring in its wake in places like the Costa del Sol and the Costa Blanca and even parts of Italy. But until then I hadn't really started looking at my own country. Since that date I've spent hours driving thousands of miles around England for filming or for pleasure or for field sports or to support field sports. I've been to rural shows and I've been to great conurbations.

Some of the counties reach right back into my childhood and some of them I only discovered as an adult. I hope you will enjoy travelling them with me, either in the comfort of your own armchair by your own fire, or perhaps as some sort of guide for holidaying at home and not going abroad. Many of you, having read your county, will turn round and say why didn't she mention this or why did she leave out that. The answer is probably because I haven't been there or because there wasn't room or because, as with some places, there's not a lot to say however beautiful they may be. So enjoy this and don't be too unkind to me when you see me at one of the shows because I've left out your bit. Indeed I have left out both Surrey and Middlesex because to me they form part of Greater London and I may one day write that book.

Clarissa Dickson Wright
Inveresk

Kent

Historically, it seems, everybody comes from Kent. One of the many Roman invasions came through Dover; Hengist and Horsa, those two Jutes of unforgettable names, came to Kent. It is in Kent that they were offered a piece of land that could be covered by an ox hide, and by cutting the hide into infinitesimally thin strips they consequently managed to enclose a fairly sizeable area of land.

Christianity, in the form of St Augustine of Canterbury, came through Kent inspired to convert its people. Indeed rather entertainingly, St Augustine came to Ebbsfleet, which is one of those places that you have probably never heard of, where he landed and was welcomed by King Ethelbert and Queen Bertha. Queen Bertha was the first person in Britain to be baptised by Augustine, who was sent to this country by Pope Gregory I, because he had seen fair little Saxon children in the slave markets in Rome and had made the comment, '*Non angli, sed angeli*': not Angles but angels. Augustine went on to Canterbury and to glory.

William the Conqueror missed Kent by a hair's breadth, landing at Pevensey Bay near Hastings in East Sussex, of which more later, but people continued make landfall in Kent. In 1216 there was a landing by a French fleet to support the rebellious barons against King John. In 1457 the Marquis de Brézé sacked the town of Sandwich in order to support Margaret of Anjou, the wife of poor, mad Henry VI. It is said that Margaret actually gave de Brézé, who was a personal friend of hers, the plans of the Bay of Sandwich in order to help him. The Mayor of

I

Sandwich to this day still wears a black robe to commemorate the murder, by the de Brézé landing force, of John Drury the then mayor. In 1255 the first elephant in captivity in England landed at Sandwich as a gift from the King of France, Louis IX, to Henry III. To this day most of the immigrants coming into England still arrive in Kent on the ferries, some of them attempting to enter illegally by hanging on to the undercarriages of lorries, or indeed hiding inside the lorries themselves, where they run the risk of suffocating. The Eurostar travels through Kent and I understand that one of the simplest ways for illegal immigrants from those parts of Europe not in the EU to enter the UK is to get on the Eurostar, buying a ticket from Lyon to Paris, and just stay on board. Kent may be the gateway to England but it is rather an insecure one.

People worry about Kent. In the 1930s there was a great deal of anxiety that Kent would become the 'Black Country' of the south due to its extensive coal mining and the subsequent industries that arose around it. In the 1960s people worried that the Channel Tunnel would turn Kent into a suburb of little houses. People also worried because imports of Golden Delicious apples from France and apples from the Antipodes were leading to the grubbing up of the Kent orchards. Kent, which since Tudor times had been known as the Garden of England, was home to a great many apple and pear orchards, along with plums and cherries and of course the Kentish cobnut.

But Kent seems to survive everybody's worries. The oast houses that were built for drying the hops have now been converted into homes for the professional classes and, far from the county becoming a suburb of little affordable houses, those houses that remain fetch extremely good prices due to the easy commuting time to London. The growth of interest in home-grown food produce is seeing the replanting of the fruit orchards. New methods of storage – chillers and the application of gas – are increasing the length of time for which pears can be kept and they are beginning to come back into fashion. Previously the problem with pears, probably our native fruit rather than the apple, was that their shelf-life was very short, and they went off after only a couple of days of perfect ripeness. Perry, the pear equivalent of cider, once one of our very common national drinks, is likewise coming back into fashion. In the second series of *The Great British Food Revival* on TV, in which I took part in 2011, Michel Roux Jr was championing the pear and was filmed in Kent, while Yotam Ottolenghi, another chef, was talking about the revival of the Kentish cobnut. This is eaten when it is green and soft and you can just peel off the skin with your fingers, but then as it matures a nutcracker is needed to reach the kernel. Now even nut oil is being produced from it, which gives an interesting flavour to salads and suchlike dishes. Nobody, as far as I know, is as yet producing milk from it. Nut milk in the Middle Ages and Tudor times was a popular alternative to milk from ruminants and I would have thought could be particularly good for people who are allergic to dairy products; perhaps it will come one day.

Since the Middle Ages, hops were an essential ingredient in the production of beer, which had replaced ale as the nation's drink, and the Kentish hop fruit had to be picked by hand. Charabancs of cockneys would pour out of London for the hop picking, staying in the same huts that their parents and grandparents had used for generations. The children would play about and generally have a splendid time in the fresh air. Food would be provided by the hop farmer, and when the day's work was done there would be singing round campfires and no doubt the sampling of some of the previous year's produce in the form of beer. A nice time was had by all and it was probably a lot healthier than flogging off to the Costa del Sol and risking horrendous stomach upsets and sunstroke, to say nothing of skin cancer. Most of the hop fields have now gone and most of those that remain are picked by machinery, but looking at those old pictures and listening to the stories of the hop pickers one cannot help but regret the passing of a different age. The side shoots of hops are pruned off in the spring to help the fruit to grow more intensely, but can be eaten as a vegetable. I was sent some hop shoots few years ago to try – and very good they were too. Chefs who are forever seeking new delicacies to adorn their menus might well look to hop shoots, which nowadays are mostly just burned.

Oddly enough, Kent is also a county that has produced a great number of rebels. Whether this is because of the continual changes in population with the different waves of immigrants, or its proximity to London, or a combination of both, I don't know. Although the revolts of 1381 started in Essex, Wat Tyler's Kentish revolt began shortly after with the sacking of Rochester Castle. The rioters, let by Wat and his colleague John Ball – a failed priest who was responsible for their theme tune 'When Adam delved and Eve span, who was then the gentleman?' – marched for London where they encamped at Blackheath. They broke into the Tower of London and killed Simon Sudbury, the Archbishop of Canterbury of the day. The revolt came to an end when the young King Richard II rode out with the Lord Mayor of London and others to placate the rioters and he promised them a better world. The Lord Mayor, a fishmonger, stabbed Wat Tyler who he thought was attacking the King. His dagger can be seen to this day in Fishmongers' Hall in London. The rioters believed the King and, cast down by the loss of their leader, returned to their homes where they were heavily persecuted.

The second rebellion, in 1450, was an outburst against Henry VI and his unpopular Queen, Margaret of Anjou, and was led by another man from Kent, Jack Cade. The rebels set off for London, which they looted, but were defeated in a battle on London Bridge. The King had fled to Warwickshire, but issued pardons for the rebels. Jack Cade also called himself Mortimer and received his pardon in that name, which particular untruth allowed him to be hunted down and killed as Jack Cade. Margaret was so angry with Kent that she said that she would turn the county into a deer park so that no people could live there.

The gentry of Kent were fairly rebellious too. One family in particular, the Wyatts of Allington, were deemed treasonous for three consecutive generations, the first of which was Sir Henry Wyatt's. In the reign of Richard III he protected the treatment of the little Princes in the Tower, quite rightly, so it would seem with the benefit of hindsight, and was thrown into the Tower where it was decreed that he should starve to death. Sir Henry was particularly fond of cats and he befriended a cat that was walking the lead roof outside his room of incarceration. The cat would bring him, so the story goes, pigeons, which he would pluck and cook over the fire that he was allowed, and he and the cat would share the birds. This was what kept him alive until Richard or perhaps Henry Tudor released him. His son, Thomas the poet, was imprisoned for his supposed involvement in the shenanigans with Anne Boleyn; he was reputed to be one of her lovers and certainly was one of her familiars. Finally Sir Henry's grandson, Thomas Wyatt the Younger, was also imprisoned in the Tower for treason and executed. After that the Wyatts went into soldiery and carried on their campaigns abroad. It is possibly the same rebellious streak that had led to the appointment of the Dutch scholar Erasmus as the incumbent vicar of Allington. This may have caused some difficulties, as Erasmus spoke very few words of English and, while he could conduct his services, I doubt he was much of a pastor to his parishioners.

One of the other great families in Kent was, of course, the Boleyns who lived at Hever Castle, now carefully restored with American money in the twentieth century. Anne Boleyn is one of those examples of how even in our historic times, when men totally dominated, a woman could still alter the course of history. Had she been allowed by Wolsey to go off and marry the future

Earl of Northumberland, she would probably have ended her days quite happily lording it over the north, but as it was the steel entered her soul. We might never have had the transference from Rome to the Anglican Church without Henry's determination that he would have the one person who refused him. We certainly wouldn't have had the greatest Queen that England has ever known and arguably one of its greatest monarchs. The curious outcome of the whole Boleyn story is that her sister Mary, set aside by Henry VIII after having delivered him two living children, a boy and a girl, was then allowed to marry for love and retired to be the wife of an Essex squire. As we know, Anne and her brother George both went to the block and the Boleyn fortune went to the only remaining sibling, Mary. I don't know why I love that story but I do.

If we travel north to the Thames-side towns that were once such an important site for the shipbuilding industry and for tending to the vessels that traded in and out of the Thames, we come to another story of a strong woman whose life ended tragically. Buried at Gravesend, so called because it was the last place where you could put people ashore to bury them if you were on the outward journey and they died suddenly, or you buried them on the inward journey, is Pocahontas, the daughter of the Red Indian chief Powhatan, who fell in love with the early English settler John Smith. According to the story, he was due to be clubbed to death at Powhatan's order by the braves of the tribe when Powhatan yielded to his daughter's entreaties and saved his life. Twice more Pocahontas saved the lives of colonists: once when they were starving and she persuaded the tribe to give them food, and once when she ran through the woods at night to warn them that there was going to be an attack and this allowed them to prepare and fight it off. John Smith returned to England having suffered injuries as a result of an explosion, and the settlers, not wanting to lose the support of Pocahontas who was probably their only advocate, told her that he had died.

In her grief and despair she was persuaded to marry another of the settlers, just to keep her onside, one suspects.

Eventually James I said he would like to meet her, so she was brought to England. She arrived at court to discover John Smith alive and well and burst into floods of hysterical tears: 'They told me you were dead.' History doesn't relate what happened between John Smith and Pocahontas during her visit but when she was being shipped back to America she died before the ship had left English waters. I often think that this was as a result of a broken heart, and I always think that it is one of the saddest stories. I remember my father taking me down the river and explaining to me the former importance of the various towns along that stretch of the river and finally coming to Gravesend and showing me Pocahontas's grave. Those towns on the river are rather uninspiring, it has to be said. Chatham, once the site of the mighty naval dockyard, with the remains of the biggest rope walk – that is a building in which you twisted your ropes for the hawsers for the ships and for other rigging and so forth – was destroyed by fire in the eighteenth century, and it is now mostly a rather depressing suburb.

What does Kent mean to me, personally? One of the parts of it that I love very much is the Romney Marsh. I knew nothing of the Romney Marsh until towards the end of my drinking career in the 1980s, when I was working for an agency that sent people out for one or two weeks at a time to act as cook/housekeeper to clients whose cook was perhaps on holiday or for some reason needed extra help. In this case it was an elderly gentleman whose wife had been taken into hospital and he really couldn't cook and look after himself, for no other reason than that he was a man of his generation. He lived just down the road from Sissinghurst Castle. Every day for a fortnight we would go in the morning for him to visit his wife in hospital, and while he was there I would do some provision shopping for the evening; afterwards we would set forth into the Romney Marsh. It was an area in which he had spent most of his life and loved very much and he took me to various places which I could share through the eyes of someone who was not only knowledgeable but caring. I remember going to New Romney, which I thought would be something like Harlow New Town so I wasn't particularly keen, and was astonished to discover that the church was Norman and that the town was very old. On the pillars of the church you could see the rope marks from ships that had tied up in medieval times during periods of flood and very high water.

The Romney Marsh is the home of the Romney Marsh sheep, a breed supposed to have been brought to England by the Romans and which has the advantage of not getting foot rot when living in wet and marshy areas. These sheep taste delicious as they graze on the marsh herbs, which give them a distinct and unique flavour. With the coming of the railways the sheep, which would have been shipped to the London markets or sold locally, suddenly became a much more valuable asset and could be put on the train and sent up to Smithfield much more quickly and were much sought after in Victorian times for the quality of their mutton. Today we eat lamb rather than mutton and very often we eat hogget which is a beast that is between one and two years old and to my mind doesn't have an awful lot of flavour, not even the sweetness of lamb. Good quality mutton properly cooked is a delicious thing. Prince Charles has tried hard to promote it and bring it back, but in order to cook mutton properly it requires long, slow cooking, which is really an anathema to the chefs who pervade our food scene today. Mutton is only appreciated and bought by the West Indian, Indian and Pakistani communities. So the Romney Marsh sheep crop out their days happily waiting for a revival of mutton.

The other great food associated with the Kent marshes was wildfowl. In the spring and autumn the marshes are alive with migrating ducks and geese of all different varieties and the wildfowlers would go out and build decoys and lay nets and gather them up. They would be shipped mainly to Leadenhall market, where they would be hung in their hundreds for people to buy. To this day great swathes of the Kent marshes are owned by the various Kent wildfowling groups who look out for the birds, ensure that their habitat is secure and protected and take what is now a very small percentage of the huge number of wild birds that come in and out. It is quite fascinating when you go shooting on the marshes on the north Kent coast because on the other side of the Thames is the huge oil refinery at Thamesport and you see the birds coming in against its lights which makes for very good night-time shooting. There is a large heronry in the north Kent marshes which is the only bit that is owned by the Royal Society for the Protection of Birds (RSPB). Heron is not now, of course, part of our diet, although it was a popular feature on medieval and Tudor tables, and as the RSPB refuses to control the birds, they are proving to be something of a nuisance, taking the rare wild carp that have lived in the streams of the marshes since time immemorial. There is also a new migrant, the strange frog from the Camargue region of France, which trills like a night bird and is busy populating the marshes, probably, as is so often the case, to the detriment of our native newts and frogs.

There is an area of the north Kent marshes called the Isle of Grain where it is believed that the Romans grew substantial amounts of grain to feed their troops. When, after the Second World War, the Ministry of Agriculture, Fisheries and Food (MAFF) tried to reintroduce grain crops to the area, two problems were discovered. The first was that the area was riddled with ergot. This is a fungal parasite which you will sometimes see if you look in the hedgerows; it looks rather like mouse droppings attached to the stalks of grain, and is a dangerous hallucinogenic. St Vitus's dance, that odd disease that led people to dance themselves to death, is supposed to be ergotism, and the reason for the strange case of the *Mary Celeste* is reputed to be because ergot got into the flour used for making the bread and the crew just went mad and leapt over the side. The second problem was that generations of flooding had affected the flocculation, the process whereby the molecules of earth are held together, so that when they took heavy machinery on to the marsh the ground just gave way and the tractors and harvesters sank up to their engines.

The marsh also contains the remains of gunpowder works which were in active service until the second half of the nineteenth century. But most famous of all in the area are the fever graves that appear so poignantly in Dickens's *Great Expectations*. These are where whole families of tiny children are buried with their parents in these curious little graves, marked by small gravestones beside the parents' larger one. Marsh fever was malaria and it is a curious thing that Johnny Scott and I helped save the Isle of Grain from becoming the third London airport quite by accident. When we were filming *Clarissa and the Countryman* there we came across a man in a barn collecting something, and being nosy we went and asked him what he was doing. He told us he was looking for the larva of the anopheles mosquito which historically had caused the marsh fever. The mosquitoes were still in evidence but due to the fact that there was no malarial blood available for them to transfer the malaria virus from one person to another, there was no longer any malaria. We filmed this because we found it interesting. The people who were campaigning to stop John Prescott putting the third London airport there recognised at once that having people coming in from countries where there was malaria would have started the whole cycle all over again, and they built a successful case against the presence of the airport. It felt good to have helped in some small way to protect this unique part of England.

On the landward side of Romney Marsh stands the Lympne Escarpment. The sea would have reached this point and the marsh would have been submerged. Where once you would have looked over the rolling waves, today you look over the beauty of the Romney Marsh, a strange, wild place where in Edwardian times people came to appreciate Port Lympne House, built by the dilettante and very rich Sir Philip Sassoon, a relation of mine by marriage. In an age where it wasn't acceptable he was openly gay and hosted lavish and extremely elegant parties at the house, which was designed by Sir Herbert Baker. A little to the north, near Canterbury, is another house which I believe was also commissioned by Philip Sassoon called Howletts. Howletts is now a zoo which respectably fronts the children's television series *Roar*. In its heyday it was the home of the well-known gambler John Aspinall, who kept a private zoo there and was leader of a debauched, extremely rich, set of friends such as Mark Birley, who founded Annabel's and various other night-clubs, and Lord Lucan, 'Lucky' Lucan. There are rumours suggesting that the reason Lucan has never been found was that he died there, possibly of a heart attack, and the lions devoured him. Also part of the set was Jimmy Goldsmith, the millionaire entrepreneur and founder of the Referendum Party. Aspinall made his money from his ownership of the Claremont Club, a celebrated and very select gambling club where huge amounts of money changed hands. In my youth an aura of sinister glam-our hovered over the whole group. The animals were not as well controlled as they might have been, however. Mark Birley's son, Robin, nearly lost his life and certainly was badly injured from a contretemps with a tiger when he was a young boy, and there were various reports of models being injured by some of the primates. Today, as I said, an aura of respectability envelops the entire zoo, but it is not the Howletts I remember.

Much of the historic wealth of Kent came from the fact that four of the five Cinque ports were located in the county. The Kentish Cinque ports are New Romney, Hythe, Dover and Sandwich, with Hastings being the one in the adjoining county of Sussex. In return for maintaining ships for the use of the crown should they be required, they were allowed to levy tolls for themselves, and were exempt from paying various Saxon taxes to the crown, a dispensation that continued into Norman times. Their levies had wonderful names such as infangtheof and outfanghtheof, pillory, soc, tol and team, blodwit and fledwit. These allowed the ports to levy heavy fines on criminals caught within their boundaries, as in infangtheoth, or who had committed crimes within their boundaries but were apprehended beyond them, as in outfangtheof. It proved a lucrative way of raising money because anyone who could afford to chose to pay off their fines, rather than suffer imprisonment or the death penalty, both of which probably resulted in the same outcome.

The post of Warden of the Cinque Ports was a prestigious appointment that brought a lot of wealth, together with the residence of Dover Castle. Sandwich received its original charter from King Canute and it is supposed to be on the beach here that King Canute made his abortive attempt to turn back the tide to convince his courtiers that he was not more powerful than God or the sea.

Kent is a county rich in history and beautiful buildings, such as Leeds Castle and Sissinghurst Castle, the home of diplomat Harold Nicolson, husband of the author Vita Sackville-West. I once went to Leeds Castle with a party of American fundamentalist Christians who spent the entire journey not talking to me because I had made the improper suggestion that Jesus Christ was Jewish. Even their bad temper didn't ruin the beauties of Leeds. My only visit to Sissinghurst was when I stayed the night with Adam Nicolson and Sarah Raven prior to doing a demonstration at Sarah's cookery school, where just wandering around the gardens, which were influenced by the work of Gertrude Jekyll, was a joy and a delight. Another joy and delight is the tomb of William the baker at Rochester, who was murdered by his adopted son. William was a pilgrim who came from Perth and, as described on his tomb, used to give away one in ten loaves he had made to the poor and needy. He is the patron saint of pilgrims and, of course, of bakers.

To me, however, the very special reason I have for visiting Kent is that this is the place where, in 1987, I got sober. I was a morally, physically and spiritually destitute drunk when I attended Robert Le Fevre's Promis Recovery Centre at Nonington, not far from Canterbury. We used to be bussed into AA and Narcotics Anonymous meetings in Canterbury itself and I rather liked the fact that I was trying to re-start my life and look for some sort of miracle in that great centre of Christian faith in England. I'm not particularly fond of places of pilgrimage, they tend to be overcrowded and full of shops selling tat, but even I could not fail to be moved by the centuries of faith that the town represented and, of course, the spot where Thomas Becket was martyred on the instructions of an irascible king. It does place a slightly different context on the 'Will nobody rid me of this turbulent priest?' line when you realise that William de Tracy, who was one of the four assassins, came from a long line of royal hitmen who continued on that particular road until after the Battle of Copenhagen in 1801. Becket's killers were clearly professionals, as all but one of them died in their beds. But Becket's death established the independence of the Christian Church in England and so it remained until at least Henry VIII.

Sussex

If we go west through the chalk hills of Kent we will come to the county of Sussex. Sussex is a very special county to me as it is where I spent many of the happiest days of my childhood and it is where I learned about the country and the countryside. One of the most famous towns in Sussex is Hastings and it is here, as every schoolchild knew in my generation, although what they know now is another matter, that in 1066 William the Conqueror, the Duke of Normandy, landed with his assembled rather motley army made up of a great many of the sort of people who would have been transported to Australia in later generations. If you say you have a Norman escutcheon, the odds are that your ancestor was a crook, but a crook who could wield a sword. Hastings Castle, the Conqueror's castle in England, dominates the town and is part of a line of Norman castles that he established right around the countryside.

William moved inland to take position at Battle, as it is now called, and Harold Godwinson, the King of the English, came by forced marches down from Yorkshire where he had won the Battle of Stamford Bridge and defeated the Viking invasion led by Harald Hardrada. I have often wondered why he felt it necessary to engage the Norman landing force immediately and not give his troops time to recover, but we all know the story that on that October morning it was a lucky arrow that found its way into Harold's eye and changed the course of English history. The remains of Harold's housecarls, his private bodyguard, those who had not died with him, fled ashamed and dishonoured abroad where a great many of them ended up in Constantinople forming a regiment as part of the Sultan's bodyguard. With the death of Harold, the much loved and duly elected last Saxon King, there was nobody to rally or to regroup them to fight another day. The Norman invasion was a particularly brutal and all-changing one and is magnificently catalogued by the Bayeux Tapestry, which was commissioned by the Conqueror's half-brother Odo, Bishop of Bayeux, who had ridden into battle wielding a massive battle axe. As a cleric, of course, he was not allowed to draw blood.

I first came to Sussex through Brighton, or indeed through Hove, that discreet suburb of the rather racy town of Brighton, when I was sent to boarding school there at the age of ten and a half. A friend of mine said of Brighton in the late 1950s and early 1960s: 'Queen Anne is dead but if she lived in Brighton no one would have noticed the difference.' I think, with hindsight, that that is probably unfair: it was not the town that was boring as much as the school. Every weekend there were clashes in the streets and along the seafront, between the 'mods', who wore anoraks and rode scooters with foxes' tails flying from their aerials, and the 'rockers' who wore leather and chains and rode proper motorbikes. Brighton was full of little antique shops where in those days it was quite possible still to find bargains, quite unlike the rather polished rip-off area that the Lanes have perhaps become. The town had cafés and even a Wimpy Bar, which was regarded as very recherché by those of us who sneaked off to go there on an exeat from school. Looking back on it now, the treats of packet chicken soup and pre-made hamburgers are maybe a strange beginning to my fascination with restaurant food, but they seemed awfully good at the time fed, as we were, on a rather dreary school diet.

Brighton boasted two piers then which were full of strange gaming machines and 'What the Butler Saw' machines which, of course, we were not allowed to look at but which seemed very risqué at the time. But the town's real glory was and still is the Royal Pavilion. What caused the Prince Regent, later

George IV, to choose the fishing village of Brighthelmstone as his seaside retreat I have never really been quite sure, but certainly he transformed it. His favourite architect John Nash built the elegant terraces of Brighton and Hove and, rather surprisingly for Nash, who seems to have been an architect of extreme elegance, also built the oriental pavilion, a weird and wonderful construction of perceived Chinese interior, where no two rooms are the same, and an Indian-influenced exterior. All the rooms are gorgeous, lavish and vulgar, and the lighting and artefacts are amazing in their own way. Sir Walter Scott called it a sort of Chinese stables, while William Cobbett thought it was like half a turnip with four small ones at the corners. It was so expensive that Byron wrote of it:

> Shut up – no, not the King but the Pavilion,
> Or else 'twill cost us all another million.

The dome of the Pavilion is 130 feet high and whole front of the pavilion is 375 feet long. The rooms are decorated with hanging bells and flowers and the ceiling in the saloon is like a sky with a gilded star from which the chandelier is suspended. The windows have massively gilded canopies springing with dragon's heads. The music room is extravagantly decorated with serpents and dragons at the windows, on the walls and on the gilded columns. On the walls are Chinese scenes on a crimson background. The artist, who spent two years painting them, died a pauper in an Islington workhouse, presumably not having been paid. The Chinese gallery is 160 feet long and has Chinese lanterns moved there from Buckingham Palace, and its walls are hung with canvasses painted with rocks, birds, trees and shrubs. The banqueting room has a ceiling like an eastern sky with a dragon hanging from the centre, holding in its claws a shining chandelier of glittering glass and dazzling stone weighing, I believe, a ton. The magnificent kitchen has a lantern roof supported on columns with spreading leaves of copper giving the illusion of palm trees.

It was here that Prinny brought the French chef Antonin Carême, with a CV that included the kitchens of Marshal Talleyrand and the Tsar. Carême introduced a change in the way we ate. Up until his coming all the dishes had been put on the table in removes, which included both sweet and savoury dishes. Now he brought in *service à la Russe*, which is what we have come to know today, that of having a meal served in individual courses. Carême had, as a boy, been employed as a pot washer in Paris where he obtained access to the Architectural Library at the Bibliothèque Nationale and he copied the various architectural designs which he used in the precision of his magnificently created dishes. The English didn't like Carême and Carême certainly didn't like the English. His use of the word *quelquechose* was translated by the English squirearchy to 'kickshaws', with a proviso that they were not having any on their table. After only a few years Carême returned to the Continent, leaving us to our own devices.

The French Revolution had brought in its wake an invasion not only of refugees, but also of chefs who could no longer find employment in France and who, to my mind, really ruined English food for ever. When you consider that in the mid-eighteenth century the Venetian Ambassador had written, 'The food of the Inns of England is the stuff of which heaven is made,' referring to the food served mostly in the great political taverns that littered the south of England, you can perhaps see my point.

Attached to the Pavilion is the Dome, which was its private theatre and was where, when I was at school, we used to be taken to see some really very fine productions, the highlight for me being Sir Ralph Richardson as the best Shylock I have ever seen in *The Merchant of Venice*. The Pavilion Art Gallery contains not only the famous Thomas Lawrence portrait of the Prince of Wales, but also the astonishing mosaic of George IV made from about half a million pieces of stone. There is also a rather charming portrait of a woman called Martha Gunn who died in 1815, having been one of the best known women in Brighton. There is a charming story of how, when stealing a pound of butter from the royal kitchens, she met the Prince of Wales, who kept her talking for so long that the butter melted in her pocket. Also in the gallery is a portrait of a woman called Phoebe Hessel who died at the age of 108 in 1821. It was said that she saw the reigns of all the Georges and obtained a pension from King George IV. In order to be near her lover she had dressed as a man and served in the British Army for seventeen years, being wounded at the Battle of Fontenoy. A well-known character in the town, she used to keep a stall near the gardens that Brighton calls the Steine, and she was the muse behind Tennyson's poem 'Rizpah'. She was also responsible for the conviction of a notorious villain called Rooke for highway robbery.

It was while I was at school in Sussex that I met my lifelong friend, the poet and writer Christine Coleman, whose family lived in the village of Selmeston under the line of the Downs at Firle Beacon. To this day the screen saver on my laptop is the road up to the Beacon. I look at it now and remember that there was once a time when I used to walk up there happily with my friend to watch the sunrise or just for a stroll before breakfast. Now I think I could barely get to the foothills. The road up to the top rises to the chalk pit of Bopeep and this road was once, in my youth, a great place for hill starts and for racing vintage Bentleys up the very steep incline. When I was young, Bruce Shand, father of Camilla, Duchess of Cornwall, was the Master of the Southdown Hunt and Johnny Scott's father, Sir Walter Scott, was chairman, and it was a great place for hunting, especially the Point that ran from Firle Beacon at one end along the line of the Downs. The five-mile gallop along here had the most wonderful views on a very clear morning as we picked our way up through the village of Firle to the top of the Downs by the Beacon and then the hounds found a fox in the gorse bushes there.

It was also the road by which we used to walk to the beach at Seaford, quite some miles distant. Once you were up on the top you could walk the whole way along the tip of the Downs and then drop down into Seaford and hope that somebody would pick you up and drive you back to Selmeston. It was on this ridge that I was sitting one morning with my friend, looking over the mist in the valley below, and we saw the sun come up and burn holes through the mist. You could see, as in little cameo pictures, a barn here, some cows there, some chickens over there. I must only have been about eleven years old at the time but I remember thinking that this was a land that was very different from the world I knew in my comfortable well-to-do London home, and one that I didn't understand. I vowed then that I would learn more about it and so I have over the years. This makes me realise that you don't have to be born in the countryside to understand how it works, you just have to be willing to learn.

This part of the Downs has now been declared a National Park and I don't know whether I am glad or sad about this. I am glad that it won't be built on and will be preserved but, from my experience, National Parks are rather crowded with people who feel permitted to go there rather than to other bits of the countryside, and they sometimes engage in activities that to my mind are not always in the best interests of the countryside. Still, it is better than a three-lane motorway I suppose, and the site of that motorway, would have been the A27 which runs from Lewes to Eastbourne. It is strange because it is an ordinary A road and I can remember the first time I was driven down it saying in my rather pompous London way, 'Oh, I love these little English country lanes,' and everybody fell about laughing because it was one of the two main roads in that bit of the county.

If you approach Lewes from Rodmell on the Downs side it looks much as it must have looked in the Middle Ages, with the castle standing there and the houses scrambling up towards it. Lewes was another of the Conqueror's castles and the Church of St Pancras and the abbey were built by the Conqueror's fifth daughter Gundrada and her husband William de Warenne, who are buried in the church there. An old stained-glass window shows a picture of Gundrada with golden hair, and indeed when her grave was opened in the nineteenth century, the golden hair was there to be seen.

Lewes is perhaps most redolent of Simon de Montfort who, given his early background, you could perhaps have told was going to be something of a nuisance. He married Henry III's sister and then had to go and obtain papal dispensation for the marriage, which was an ecclesiastical offence, as Eleanor had taken a vow of perpetual widowhood. He quarrelled repeatedly with his brother-in-law about debts over his rights to various governances arising out of the earldom of Leicester, which he had inherited from his English grandmother. De Montfort fought repeated battles in Gascony, both on behalf of Henry III and indeed of the French King and, finally, on 14 May 1264, having raised an army of barons, he defeated Henry III at the Battle of Lewes and took him prisoner. The virtual governor of the kingdom and certainly governor of the King, he called a parliament that consisted not only of churchmen, barons and knights but also two citizens from every borough in England. He was not the creator of the House of Commons nor indeed the inventor of the representative system, but he was a champion of righteousness and it was Edward I who, having killed Simon de Montfort in 1265, went on to form the first proper parliament.

Lewes is particularly famous for its Bonfire Night, where an awful lot of effigies other than Guy Fawkes are burned. The valley of the Sussex Ouse, which runs from Lewes to Newhaven, is divided into Catholic and Protestant villages, or certainly was in my youth, on either side of that road. As a Catholic I would go with my friends to attempt to tear down the 'No Popery' banner that hangs across Lewes High Street on Guy Fawkes night where the Pope is burned in effigy along with the effigies of the local Member of Parliament, the Prime Minister and anybody else who the town feels like burning. It's a great night and the only time any real trouble ensued was when an effigy of a caravan chickies, as gypsies are called in that part of the world, was burned and the representatives of the gypsy communities caused the most terrible furore. In my youth the Protestant/Catholic divide was almost worthy of Northern Ireland. Protestant children living in Catholic villages or Catholic children living in Protestant villages were bussed across the A27 to go to school on whichever side provided a Protestant or a Catholic school.

Curiously the area between Lewes and Jevington was colonised after the First World War by the Bloomsbury set. Virginia Woolf lived at Rodmell, where she wrote most of her great novels and the Rodmell Pottery, which was still going when I was at school, was started as part of the Bloomsbury movement. Further down the road lies Charleston Farmhouse, which is now open to the public. It was once the home of Duncan Grant, Vanessa Bell and her husband Clive, and was regularly visited by Lytton Strachey and the playwright Roger Fry. When I consider that even in my youth in the 1950s and 1960s that part of Sussex was still very rural, populated by agricultural labourers with wonderful bucolic names like Puttock and Pilbeam, who lived in houses in great disrepair and had hens that picked around everywhere and produced eggs that were almost square, the Bloomsbury set and their bohemian ways and rampant homosexuality must have made quite an impact. Even when I was young in the early 1960s, young lads were told that if Duncan Grant offered them a lift on no account were they to accept it, however bad the weather. Moreover in a county that had sent many brave men to die in the trenches of the First World War, a hotbed of pacifists and conscientious objectors must have caused a lot of displeasure. It was Lytton Strachey who, when asked by the board that passed judgement on conscientious objectors what he would do if he saw a German soldier raping his sister, replied, 'I would interpose my body.'

Duncan Grant became intimate with Vanessa Bell and

fathered a daughter, Angelica, which must have been a great shock to both of them. While it is worthwhile going to Charleston Farmhouse to see the curious place, decorated much as it was when the Bells and Duncan lived there, due to the fact that after Vanessa's death Duncan lived there alone and changed nothing, it is to my mind more interesting to go on to the church at Berwick Village where Duncan and Vanessa painted a modern 'doom' painting, with many local inhabitants easily recognisable as the people being assumed to heaven or cast down to hell. There are several other paintings of theirs too, as well as some by Vanessa and Clive's son Quentin. It caused a great deal of disapproval at the time, as I believe Charleston Farmhouse held the advowson on the church, but it is a lasting legacy and worth visiting.

On the other side of the road from Charleston Farmhouse, but also worth visiting, is Middle Farm, Firle, which is one of the few farm shops that I know of in the British Isles licensed to sell unpasteurised milk, and believe me if you have ever made a rice pudding with unpasteurised milk, life is never the same again. Continue along the road towards Eastbourne and you will pass the village of Alciston where Elizabeth David grew up. She came to hate the land of her birth so much that, following the Second World War, she imbued us all with a love of continental, Mediterranean and French provincial cooking with her exquisite writing. I always think that the people who rush off to buy casa colonica in Tuscany and farmhouses in France and villas on the Mediterranean coast are actually looking for a land that Elizabeth David created in her own mind but that actually does not exist outside it.

A little further on is the turning to Alfriston with its fine church, which has been there since Saxon times and is known as the Cathedral of the South Downs. The village is a great place for tourists, with a very good bookshop and a slightly over-exaggerated history of smugglers. Next you will come to the

Long Man of Wilmington on the right-hand side, a magnificent and early chalk cutting. The figure of a man stands 226 feet high and is outlined in white bricks on the green turf of Windover Hill, which rises 600 feet above sea level. The man is facing away from you so there is not the usual rampant penis. He is holding a stave in each hand, a little taller than himself. He is believed to represent the Celtic god of rain who, perforce, was also a god of fertility and is flinging open the gates of the Rain. It was traditionally a site where women went to entreat the god to give them a child. Even when I was young, women would go up there with such requests and leave their knickers on the chalk slope. Possibly they took their boyfriends with them to make the outcome a little more likely.

Still travelling on towards Eastbourne, you pass the village of Jevington off to the right, where the restaurant the Happy Monk in the 1970s created the now famous dessert known as banoffee pie. I was actually there the day they launched it. Banoffee pie is banana, coffee and *dulce de leche*, which is condensed milk boiled and boiled in the tin for about four hours until it becomes a sticky toffee substance. The road continues onward to the rather suburban delights of Eastbourne. This part of Sussex is known for the birthplace of cricket, which is supposed to have been the village of Dicker, so it is appropriate that it was in Sussex that I learned my skills as a cricket umpire. It is a particularly fine county in which to watch cricket, because when the clouds and the barometric pressure they cause come off the ridge of the Downs, conditions are unpredictable; I have stood and watched six balls in one over do completely different things. The story I like concerns the church at Wiston Manor and the brass of Sir John de Braose in armour, dated 1426, in which he appears to be wearing cricket pads. One Sunday a young man sitting in the church, enduring the sermon no doubt, and suffering from sore shins from a cricket match the day before, looked at this brass and decided that if he could have something similar made out of canvas and dowelling, it would preserve his legs and shins. He went to the local saddler and the first cricket pads were produced.

The Tudor house at Wiston is worth seeing and was the home of three well-known Elizabethan brother adventurers of the Shirley family. Sir Anthony Shirley, the middle brother, who received a French knighthood for his services against the Spaniards, so enraged Elizabeth I that she said, 'I will not have my sheep marked with a strange brand nor suffer them to follow the pipe of another shepherd,' and threw him into prison. On his release he became a buccaneer and held Santiago on the Cape Verde Islands with 280 men against 3,000 Portuguese. Leaving Cape Verde he sailed across to the other side of the world and took possession of Jamaica. When returning, unsuccessful, to England, he was then sent to bring the Shah of Persia into agreement with the Princes of Europe against the Turks. The Shah took a shine to him and made him a Persian Prince, the first Christian to receive an oriental title, and agreed to trade with the European dominions. Sir Anthony eventually died in Madrid an impoverished outcast. The youngest brother, Sir Robert, who had gone to Persia with Anthony, remained there after his brother's departure and married a Circassian Princess. There is a famous portrait of the couple in Persian dress. He settled in Europe but eventually he returned east and died in Kazveen. The eldest brother, Sir Thomas, fought in the Low Countries and was imprisoned for two years in Constantinople. On returning to England he found that his estates had fallen into rack and ruin and he was thrown into the Tower on a charge of conspiracy to trade with the Levant. He retired to the Isle of Wight where he died overwhelmed by debt.

I have always had a passion for castles, and Sussex does well in the way of castles. Christine and I, when we were seventeen going on eighteen, decided one summer that we would visit some of the ruined castles by night. I remember going into Pevensey Castle, the magnificent ruins of both the Roman and the Norman castle, which stands overlooking the Pevensey marshes. It is a wonderful building, one that I had seen regularly in the distance when I used to go beagling on the frozen marshes with the Pevensey marsh beagles. I had a car by this time, a little Renault Dauphine known as the dustbin because its number plate was BIN and my cars are seldom tidy, and we drove down and crept into the castle in the middle of the night. We stood there grasping each other's arms at the sound of this terrible rattling noise, which we were convinced must be the ghost, until we found a very old and asthmatic sheep that had found its way into the castle ruins.

The other castle that we successfully visited at night was Bodiam. This was the castle of its age. It stands moated by the River Rother and was given to the nation by Lord Curzon. The castle is rectangular in shape with a round tower at each corner and a square tower in the middle at the side and rear walls. The moat, which is heavily carpeted with water lilies, covers three acres. We made a dashing but abortive attempt to cross the moat in a small inflatable dinghy, but were stopped by the water lilies. We eventually entered by climbing the gate. The castle was built by Sir Edward Dalyngrigge, who was a great warrior and was custodian of the Tower of London and Governor of the City of London in 1392. However, he lost his post when Richard II seized its liberties, imprisoning him and the sheriffs because, in Richard's opinion, they were too lenient with the Londoners. Although there are the remains of a mutilated fragment of Dalyngrigge's tomb in Lewes, he is generally regarded as being under a rather magnificent but unnamed brass in the village of Fletching, recognising that his tomb would probably be desecrated by Richard.

The other great Sussex castle is, of course, Arundel, the historic home of the Dukes of Norfolk. It was built in 1068 by Roger de Montgomery with the permission of William the Conqueror, and passed into the Fitzalan-Howard family in the sixteenth century when it was given to Thomas, Duke of Norfolk, Henry VIII's powerful warlord. His son drew up the regulations for coursing, the favourite sport of Elizabeth I, at her request. The large church in Arundel, now a cathedral, is and always has been Catholic. The Norfolk family was so powerful that they managed to maintain their Catholic faith throughout every adversity. I am happy to say that this is one of the castles that I entered by invitation. The story I particularly like about the family is the one of the Duke of Norfolk who, in Victorian times, kept owls which he named after his friends. There is a delightful account of the butler coming in at breakfast and saying to the Duke, 'May it please Your Grace, Lord Thurlough has laid an egg.'

If you go north-east you will come to Ashdown Forest, that ancient and venerable woodland with its verderers who still preside over the forest laws. One of the villages that fringes the forest is Hartfield, and in its shingled fifteenth-century church lies the grave of Beggarman Smith. The story is that Nicholas Smith, a very rich man of Sussex, resolved to find out the nature of Sussex folk by disguising himself as a tramp. As a wandering beggar he made his way from village to village and met with no kindness until he came to Hartfield, which he then remembered in his will. To this day, on Good Friday afternoon, a group of villagers gather about his grave to receive his bounty from the rector and the church wardens.

To the west you will, sooner or later, come to Petworth; as all the traffic passes through Petworth (they have never built a bypass), you will get a good view of the gates of Petworth House. The house had originally belonged to the Percys of Northumberland, but in the seventeenth century it came into the possession of the Duke of Somerset. It was he who transformed it into the magnificent mansion that it now is. There is a carved room where the Duke gave Grinling Gibbons a free hand, and he created a masterpiece. It is almost impossible to describe the magnificence of Gibbons's carving. There is an eagle holding bouquets of sprigs of British oak, there are flowers and cherubs and bay trees, festoons of ivy and doves beneath the roses. It is something you really should visit. Petworth passed to the Earls of Egremont and it was the third Earl who laid down the magnificent collection of paintings which are another of the great glories of the house. Here you will find the largest collection of Turner oil paintings to be found together anywhere. There are works by Romney and Lely, by Reynolds and Hoppner. Even foreigners get a look in, with works by Van Dyck, Holbein, Frans Hals, a Rembrandt and many early primitive masters. The park, which was laid out by Capability Brown, is one of his earliest and more splendid pieces. It is a perfect example of what can be done when money is no object and the families in question possess a great deal of taste. For me Petworth is almost and always reminiscent of marmalade tasting of onions as I had packed all the sandwiches together.

Hampshire

If you carry on westward along the A272, one of the slowest but most charming of roads in the south of England, you will come to Hampshire, a county in which I have spent a lot of time over the years and of which I am very fond. When I was growing up, my friend Carrots's parents lived in a charming rural village called Upham. The village church may have been thirteenth century but there was nothing of much interest in it except for a reference to the cost of cleaning out the chancel after Cromwell's horses had been stabled there. The family lived in Upham because it was near Bishop's Waltham, where Carrots's father was a solicitor. In Bishop's Waltham, about ten miles from Winchester Cathedral, Henry of Blois built a castle with a park of 1,000 acres which was finished as a palace by William of Wykeham, the founder of Winchester College and Bishop of Winchester. The palace ruins are fairly sumptuous, with one wall pierced with five great windows with embattled transom, part of the old hall. Still there too are the remains of the abbot's pond, an old stewpond that was made by damming the River Hamble. Bishop's Waltham has narrow streets of delightful, old-fashioned houses and nothing very much happens there, but it was from there that Carrots's father gave me my first ever brief when I was a young barrister. It was the safest undefended divorce you were ever likely to find; the couple had been separated for over twenty years, there were no children, no property and no costs. It took me a whole weekend to go down and enjoy myself and conclude the case on the Monday so that my clerk remarked, 'I hope, madam, that all your undefended divorces aren't going to take quite so long!'

In their garden, which abutted a property owned by the Pakenhams, better known by the title of their earldom, Longford, and where the pheasants used to take refuge when there was a shoot on next door, I would attempt to pot-shot pheasants with an air rifle with no success whatsoever. It was at their house, too, that I learned from Carrots's mother to make the steak and kidney pudding that I make to this day.

One of the particular attractions of Bishop's Waltham was its proximity to Winchester, that most magnificent of towns and the former Saxon capital of England. You do not really need the huge bronze statue of Alfred that dominates the town to be reminded that this is Alfred's town. Alfred, King of the Saxons, the founder of England through his grandson Athelstan, a man who had a dream of universal literacy, of a united England and, despite a life spent battling the Normans, a man to whom we have reason to be indebted; one of the few historical characters and probably the only King recorded as a truly bad cook! The story goes that, while in hiding, the farmer's wife left him to watch the cakes (a sort of drop scone) cooking on the bakestone in her kitchen. He was so busy dreaming of the future that he let them burn and, so history says, had his ears soundly boxed.

The old minster in Winchester was begun in AD 642 by King Cenwalh of Wessex, and King Alfred was laid to rest there, although his body was removed to the new minster when the church was founded in the early eleventh century. Excavations on the north wall of the present cathedral have exposed the foundations of the old minster. Legend goes that Walkelin, a kinsman of William the Conqueror, pulled down the Saxon church that was on the foundations and asked the King for as much oak as he could cut in four days and four nights from Hampage Wood. He then set an army of men to work, who removed virtually the entire forest. He was responsible for the transepts. William Rufus, that wicked king, is buried at the cathedral under a very plain, straightforward tomb. He died in the New Forest, shot with an arrow by a man called Walter Tyrell, which may or may not have been an early royal assassination. I remember when I was a tour guide sitting in Winchester Cathedral listening to two old girls talking about William Rufus as they cleaned. One of them said, "'E were a terrible man 'e were. 'E was an homosexual and the Church condemned him and it's a good thing that 'e died when 'e did. 'E brought no good to the country.' The other one went on polishing the brass inscription then looked up and said, 'I don't know, Ethel, all I can say is 'e's awfully easy to clean.' Ever since, in my mind, William Rufus has gone down as 'awfully easy to clean'.

Bits and pieces went on being added to the cathedral until William of Wykeham, undoubtedly the greatest Winchester man who ever lived, Lord Chancellor of England, from the nearby village of Wykeham, cut back the Norman work, facing it with new stone and raising the cathedral half as high again. It is the longest cathedral in Europe. It measures 185 yards from east to west and its walls contain about an acre and a half of space. It is the result of five centuries of human labour, but the real hero of Winchester Cathedral is a man called William Walker, a diver who saved the cathedral. Unfortunately the Conqueror's cousin set his cathedral on a bog. It was found to be sinking badly and cracks were appearing; using machinery to underpin the building would have been impossible as it would simply have fallen down. For six years William Walker spent his time under the cathedral, grovelling about in the dark just beneath the graves of kings. He excavated and cleaned the flooded trenches, filled the cracks with cement and laid down four layers of bags of concrete. Then water was pumped out and the walls were underpinned by bricklayers. From pit to pit, beneath the cathedral the heroic Walker went like a rat until, at last, with his unaided hands, he had remade the bed of Winchester

Cathedral and set it on solid ground. A small statue of him in his diving suit, holding his helmet, stands in the cathedral.

Winchester still has very much the feel of a medieval town, with its old medieval houses and of course the presence of the cathedral and its nearby college, which prevents any destruction of these buildings and of that atmosphere. The motto of Winchester College, given by William of Wykeham, its founder, is 'Manners Maketh Man' and certainly all the Wykehamists I have met in my life have extremely good manners.

Slightly away from the centre of Winchester are the church and almshouses of St Cross, built to house thirteen pensioners, with a hall known as the 'hundred men's hall' where one hundred people were fed each day; in a rather charming tradition they were issued with bread, beer and candles, and at Christmas they were given extra candles. This was because they were only allowed to drink until the light of the candle failed, and this extra allowance allowed them to go on partying for longer. The inhabitants of St Cross wear a gown very like a cassock, although it is not a religious order. When I was young I used to think it must be a wonderful place to end your days, but of course unfortunately they did not take women. We used to go, as a great wheeze, to claim the 'Wayfarer's Dole', which was issued at eleven o'clock in the morning and consisted of a glass of beer and a piece of bread. How daring we felt at seventeen having a glass of beer at eleven o'clock in the morning; *sic transit gloria mundi*.

Winchester boasts probably the finest farmers' market in England, held weekly and supplied by producers from all over the county. It is well worth a visit.

If you travel nor-nor-east out of Winchester you will come eventually to Basingstoke. It is a Hampshire legend that the weather always changes at Basingstoke, whether you are leaving or entering the county. Try it: you might find that it is true. Basingstoke is now one of those rather horrible modern towns that consist of nothing but roundabouts and shopping malls selling nothing out of the ordinary, and there is nowhere to stop. Some years ago the Duke of Westminster endeavoured to open a farmers' market there that would take place at the edge of one of the shopping centres on four days a week. However, while the inhabitants of Hampshire are quite happy to travel long distances to the farmers' market in Winchester, they actually couldn't face going to Basingstoke, so unattractive is it.

It was not always thus. The nearby Basing House, which is incredibly difficult to find, was the home of the Marquess of Winchester and one of the greatest houses in the land. It was destroyed after a very long and terrible siege redolent of treachery and double-dealing during the English Civil War. The Marquess, a Royalist, suffered a crushing blow when he discovered that his brother Edward Paulet was in treacherous communication with Waller, the Parliamentary general, with a view to surrendering. The traitor's punishment was dreadful, for he was made to act as a hangman to his confederates, while himself being spared to live on with his guilt. The defenders suffered from smallpox and starvation and, on May Day 1645, some 500 men deserted, leaving the remainder to fight on. Nonetheless, Waller was unable to break through and Cromwell himself arrived and finally took possession of the house with much use of cannon and overwhelming forces. The remaining defenders lost 100 men and 300 prisoners were taken, among them Inigo Jones, Queen Henrietta Maria's architect. Cromwell set the house on fire and gave orders that anyone might carry away the stones, but he spared the life of the old Marquess, committing him first to the Tower and then allowing him to leave the country. You can visit the ruins and gardens.

If you go nor-nor-west out of Winchester you will come to another rather unpleasant modern town consisting of roundabouts and supermarkets and with nothing really to recommend it; this is the town of Andover. However, if you go to the museum you will discover that it wasn't always like this. There have been settlers on the banks of the River Anton since the Stone Age, buried in long barrows; there are also remains of Roman villas and ancient roads. It was once the site of Witenagemot, the Saxon 'parliament', and in AD 994 Ethelred the Unready entertained a Viking king who was converted by Bishop Alphage and promised never to return to England as a foe. Andover, incidentally, was responsible for changing the social laws of the country because conditions in the Andover workhouse were so appalling that the government had to sit up and take notice and as a result rewrote the Poor Laws.

Hampshire is a county of rivers. The great Izaak Walton, who served at Winchester Cathedral before the Civil War, is widely regarded as the father of English fly fishing from his amazing work *The Compleat Angler,* and he couldn't have found a better place to practise his passion than the chalk streams of Hampshire. The two great chalk streams of the Test and the Itchen, with their large tributaries such as the Dever and the smaller tributaries and bourns and aquifers that feed them, make it one of the most sought-after fishing areas in the country. Trout fishing on a chalk stream is a very different kettle of fish from fishing elsewhere. The water runs gin-clear and you stalk the fish upstream trying to ensure that no shadow or heavy footfall will spook it. The fish can see you much more successfully than you can see it. The other great feature of the Test and its tributaries is of course the mayfly season. The mayfly lives but a single day before it mates and lays its eggs and dies, and they all hatch in early May. It is an amazing sight to see the dance of the mayflies as they swirl up into the air around the trees, where they may mate and lay their eggs, and see them over the water where the fish go bananas gorging themselves on this great treat. I remember once when I was trying to catch a particular trout and suddenly there was a hatching of mayfly on either side of my trout, which hadn't shifted an inch. Two other trout hurled themselves in the air and performed complete somersaults, like synchronised swimmers, and fell back into the water again having had a mouthful of mayfly. The National Rivers Authority monitors the rivers, taking water to test its purity and requiring riparian owners to report on suitable fish food to be found in the river. Cutting the weed is now strictly regulated so that it is all cut around certain dates and then shifted down by dint of the current to a particular point where it hits a grid and is collected. In the old days it used to be dried and used for thatching.

One of the nicest, unspoilt towns of Hampshire stands at the heart of the Test valley, and this is Stockbridge, so named because there was a bridge across the Test over which livestock were brought to market. Stockbridge has proper shops and an extremely good butcher in the form of Robinson's. I once spent a delightful morning ferreting on a frosty cold down just outside Stockbridge, and we must have taken the best part of fifty rabbits. You knew they would all be sold through the butcher's shop in the coming week. The town also now has an extremely good fishmonger in a part of the delicatessen and there is a well-stocked Co-op. There is furthermore a proper greengrocer that sells locally produced goods. Everything you could wish for in a small town is there, with its long street, Tudor and Georgian houses, a good baker with a tearoom and a number of perfectly acceptable pubs. In the heart of it lies the old coaching inn which, when I saw it, had seen better days but still housed the private members' room of the Houghton Club. This club, which has fishing rights on the Test at Stockbridge, used to be the crème de la crème of fishing in the Test valley, but has somewhat brought itself into disrepute in recent years by introducing rainbow trout into the waters of the Test. The natural British trout is of course the brown trout. The rainbow trout is, like the grey squirrel, an American import and, curiously, I discovered the other day that the Americans have imported Scottish loch trout, which are brown trout, into their waters. Supposedly it is to give them better fishing.

Just outside Stockbridge is Marsh Court, which is unique in

that it is a chalk house with mantelpiece and other interior features made of chalk and was built by Sir Edwin Lutyens. It is, I believe, the only chalk house to be found in Britain. Stockbridge has a real feel of Jane Austen about it. You can easily imagine her heroes and heroines driving up the main street in a curricle or a phaeton and going to parties around the town by the light of the 'parish lantern', as she so eloquently described the full moon. Jane Austen is Hampshire's most famous daughter; born at Steventon she lived for the last eight years of her life at Chawton, where her house is open to the public. I always find it delightful that in this day and age, with all our modernisms, Jane Austen is the author that the media return to time and time again. Alton was the scene of a dramatic Civil War battle, where Lord Crawford, who commanded a troop of the King's Horse and a small company of infantry under a certain Colonel Bolle, sent to Waller, the Parliamentary general, and suggested he should exchange a butt of wine for an ox. Crawford further suggested that he should bring the ox in person, to which the answer was that he need not trouble as General Waller would fetch it himself. The general marched upon Alton and took them by surprise. Crawford fled, leaving Bolle to fight a valiant rearguard action. In an attempt to confuse the Parliamentarians he set fire to his own house and withdrew to the church where, eventually, he was killed at the foot of the pulpit's steps, crying aloud the name of the King.

One more great Hampshire writer was the naturalist Gilbert White, who is to be remembered at Selborne, where he was the vicar, as his grandfather had been before him. He was under the patronage of the Earl of Selborne, who allowed him to get on with his naturalistic writings, possibly to the detriment of his duties as vicar. Gilbert White's book on nature still thrills when you read it. Also in Selborne is to be found the Oates Collection, in memory of Captain Oates, the man who died on the Scott Expedition to Antarctica and whose famous words, as he walked out of the tent and into the ice, 'I am just going outside and may be some time,' have passed into history.

Hampshire has its great houses too, the most famous of which at the moment is undoubtedly Highclere, the setting for Julian Fellowes's successful television series *Downton Abbey*, which is filmed there. It is the home of the Earls of Carnarvon, best known for the fifth Earl who financed the discovery of the treasure of Tutankhamun and who died soon afterwards, giving rise to tales of a curse connected to the Pharoah's tomb. Highclere used to have a large rabbit warren, providing food for the household and surrounding villages. A man of my acquaintance told me that when his father was keeper there they would bring in bucks as breeding stock in the spring and turn them out first of all into an enclosure in the vegetable garden. Then they would turn them out into the warren where the most terrible and bloody battles apparently took place. Rabbits, one often forgets, are very fierce creatures.

Another of Hampshire's great houses is the Queen Anne mansion that a grateful nation gave the Duke of Wellington at Stratfield Saye. Wellington was not too keen on the property and declared that it was a bad investment that would have ruined almost any man, but he did use it as the site of the tomb and monument to the horse Copenhagen, which had carried him for sixteen hours at the Battle of Waterloo. The epitaph reads: 'God's humbler instrument, though meaner clay, should share the glory of that glorious day'. Copenhagen lived out the last ten years of his life on the estate and was buried there with full military honours. Nearby, at Stratfield Turgis, is the grave of John Mears, Wellington's groom, who served the Iron Duke for thirty-five years. The Duke was a very keen hunting man, as indeed his family have remained until the present day. I remember seeing this lovely contemporary cartoon of a yokel in a smock locking a gate which the Duke of Wellington with his entourage was trying to go through. The yokel is saying, 'Master says thou shalt not pass', and underneath was the inscription,

'The man who stopped the man the French could not'. I used to hunt over Stratfield Saye and there was a lovely moment at a Purdey Awards when I found myself on the same platform as the Duke, Valerian, who kept looking at me. This was a time when *Two Fat Ladies* was at its height and he came up and nudged me in the ribs and said, 'I know who you are.' I said, 'Oh yes,' expecting him to say that he knew me from television and he replied, 'You were that skinny girl on that ex-steeplechaser you couldn't stop.' I smiled and said, 'Yes, that's right.' He nudged me in the ribs again and said, 'You could stop it now!'

Worthy of a mention among the great houses is Titchfield Abbey, now ruined, once home to the Earls of Southampton, and Shakespeare's great patron Henry Wriothesley, the third Earl. One of the proofs that Shakespeare must have visited is found in the records that in 1593, three years before *The Merchant of Venice* was published, one Augustine Gobbo was buried there. His rather unlikely name is to be found in the characters of Old Gobbo and his son Launcelot Gobbo in that very play.

If Hampshire has the feel of a Saxon kingdom, which indeed it was, and the feel also of the Regency era, one must not forget the people who left one of the biggest stamps on the county, the Romans. The A30 and the A303 are both the sites of the old tin roads that led down to the West Country and were the roads up and down which the Romans carried their convoys of tin. Remember, the Romans invaded England largely for its mineral wealth. In parts of Hampshire it is scarcely possible to put a spade in the ground without turning up some fragment of Roman remains. You will also find the sites of various marching camps such as the one at the Andyke near Barton Stacey. Off the Roman road at this point is the village of Wherwell, which is believed to be a corruption of the word Whoreswell, and one wonders if indeed this was a site of an ancient brothel set up to entertain the Roman troops. At Barton Stacey, whose excellent jazz band played all day at the last Parliament Square protest

against the hunt ban, they discovered when they went to conse-
crate a field to enlarge the churchyard that they needed to have
an archaeological dig because they had found such an array of
Roman artefacts.

Silchester marks the lost Roman city of Calleva, which once
boasted an amphitheatre that held 10,000 spectators; most of the
remains of the great city are now under agricultural fields. If you
go to Reading Museum nearby you will see the result of forty
years of excavations with models of the site as it must have been
at the time. You will notice when driving about Hampshire that
a lot of the roads are very straight and this is the legacy of the
Roman road system that ran throughout the county. Five large
roads radiated out from Winchester for example. Portchester,
overlooking Portsmouth's bay, is the most extensive and complete
remnant of Roman architecture in the British Isles. The castle
and defensive works that the Romans built there, although now
only a shell, enclose approximately nine acres and set up
Portsmouth Bay as the headquarters of the Britannic Fleet, the
first organised navy in the British Isles. Portsmouth has remained
one of the Royal Navy bases ever since. The Normans saw the
benefit of the site at Portchester too and built defence works and
a castle there. For anybody interested in the military history of
our islands, it is one of the most valuable sites to visit.

The Test runs into the Solent in Southampton, one of the
oldest ports in the country, with extensive ancient and medieval
walls to defend it. It was the chief port for Winchester when it
was the capital of England in Saxon times; the Crusaders sailed
from there; and Philip II of Spain arrived there for his wedding
to Mary Tudor in Winchester. The *Mayflower* and the *Speedwell*
sailed to America from here. It is curious to think that if Charles
I had not exercised the prerogative writ of *ne exeat regno* and
removed Oliver Cromwell and John Hampden from their ships
sailing to America, the entire history of the English Civil War
and the future of England might have been very different today.

Sail into the Solent and turn sharp left and you will come to the great naval port of Portsmouth, which faces across its channel the equally important naval town of Gosport. Here you have very much the history of the British navy, and you will find moored at Portsmouth Nelson's flagship *Victory*, the ship on which he died at the Battle of Trafalgar. Across the Solent is the Isle of Wight, a county in its own right. Until 2010 I had never been inland on the Isle of Wight and had only visited Cowes for the famous Regatta week organised by the Royal Yacht Squadron.

In 2010 I was invited by a man called Colin Boswell to open the Taste and Historic Centre at the Garlic Farm at Newchurch in the middle of the Isle of Wight. I fell in love with the incredible beauty of the island; once you get away from the sea it has the most stunning views and high ground that give you a perspective of the countryside. The Garlic Farm produces dozens of tonnes of garlic each year, growing all the varieties from elephant garlic, which is native to the British Isles, through Solent Wight, which originated from garlic from the Auvergne, flown in by Lysander during the Second World War because the Free French, who were billeted on the island, complained that the food was so dull. It was later discovered that the variety thrived in the island climate. The Garlic Farm has been in existence for over thirty years and now exports garlic to Spain, Italy and even to France. It is a fascinating place, well worth a visit, and it is so much nicer to eat English garlic than stuff that has been imported from the Far East. Even the Chinese admit that English garlic tastes better.

The Garlic Farm produces all sorts of weird and wonderful additions to its garlic bulb range which are sold in its shop: you can buy garlic ice cream, garlic chocolate, garlic fudge and, rather more excitingly, all sorts of delicious chutneys and pickles. There is also a very good café where you can sample the wares before going out on the motorised tour of the farm to see the process of actually growing the garlic. I returned there to film for *The Great British Food Revival*, having chosen garlic as my ingredient. The BBC in its wisdom said, 'Oh, garlic isn't British,' until I pointed out that the name actually meant Spear Leek in Saxon, and how much more British could you get?

While on the island I also went to East Cowes to visit Osborne House, the seaside home and long-time residence of Queen Victoria. It was built by Albert and Victoria and after Albert's death, when Victoria went into a decline, she retired to Osborne where she lived isolated from the world for a number of years. It is, we are led to believe, only the consolations of John Brown, her Highland gillie, who coaxed her away from the island to return to her public duties. She was spending Christmas at Osborne as usual, but later fell ill and died; her body was taken on the yacht *Alberta* across to the mainland for her funeral. I managed to visit Carisbrooke Castle too, which was where King Charles I was imprisoned after being captured at the end of the Civil War. He attempted to escape from the castle and it was, of course, that attempt that led finally to his trial and execution.

Hampshire has a great tradition of horses, with a number of successful hunts in the county, even one on the Isle of Wight. It is surprising that it has no racecourse of its own until you look back and discover that up to Victorian times there were two sizeable racecourses, one at Andover and the other at Stockbridge. At that time there were more trainers in that area of Hampshire than there were at Newmarket. It was while following the Tedworth Hunt in the run-up to the hunt ban that I understood that the idiots in Westminster could never really win because I saw a woman trotting up, slightly red in the face, to the meet and I said to her, 'Having a good blow?' She smiled at me and moved on. I then realised that she had no arms and that she controlled her horse entirely by using her toes on reins attached to her feet. She was a Thalidomide victim and so determined to hunt, coming as she did from a hunting family, that she had overcome every adversity to do so.

Heading south-west from Southampton you pass through the

area known as the New Forest. 'New' once again is illusory, as it refers to the Norman hunting forest that was set up here. It is a sizeable area of forest in the old meaning of the word, which meant somewhere where deer were kept for hunting; there are trees but there are also open areas of scrub and moorland. A pack of buckhounds were kept in the New Forest until well into my lifetime. The centre of the New Forest is at Lyndhurst and there you can see the strange stirrup, dating from the time of William Rufus, that was used for testing the size of a dog's foot. If the dog's foot would not go through the stirrup, the dog was deemed to be large enough to hunt deer and therefore it had to have one of its toes removed before it would be allowed to live in the forest. There are still quite stringent regulations about what can and cannot be done in the forest, and various forest landholders are responsible for the wellbeing of the New Forest ponies that run wild, supposedly the descendants of the ancient British chariot ponies. The landholders also look after the well-being of the deer. Charles II was responsible for re-regulating the order and running of the forest and it is said that if he hadn't planted his plantation of oaks, Nelson would not have won the Battle of Trafalgar, because there would not have been enough trees to build the ships for the English navy.

Wiltshire

Turn north-west out of Hampshire and we come to the county of Wiltshire. I always feel that the lands around Salisbury Plain, once one moves on to the Wiltshire chalk, are older than time. I once drove across the plain on a summer's night under a full moon and you could almost feel the ghosts of the Druids and other early peoples moving towards some great gathering at Stonehenge. When I was a child it was possible to walk into the middle of Stonehenge and even to lie on the Killing Stone and pretend that one was a sacrificial victim. I am always slightly taken aback that in this politically correct age we live in, people deny that there were ever human sacrifices, or that the Druids and the older Windmill Hill folk actually killed humans as an offering to their gods, and insist that it was all Roman propaganda. Nobody denies that the South American people committed human sacrifice. Nobody denies that ritual cannibalism still occurs in South America and parts of Africa and that the Caribs and the inhabitants of Papua New Guinea ate human flesh, but for some reason there is a complete denial of the fact that it might have happened in our own country.

Whatever you believe, there is no doubt as to the ingenuity, magnificence and endeavour that created Stonehenge. When I was younger, and had cause to drive to the West Country, I would always get up early and, taking a sandwich and a Thermos flask with me, I would try to get to the field opening where you could pull off the road in those days and look across at Stonehenge before the sun came up. We know that the Henge is over 3,500 years old and while we don't know the exact reason for its construction or its purpose we can only marvel at the people who brought the huge stones, anything from eight to twenty-two feet high, six feet broad and three feet thick, the tallest weighing about thirty tonnes, and set them up in two immense circles with two gigantic horseshoes in the inner circle, covering an area almost equal to the inner dome of St Paul's. There are thirty such stones, in pairs, with a ten-foot slightly curved stone placed on top of each pair and burrowed out to receive the shaped knob from the end of the upright stone. The inner circle numbers about forty stones and there are five separate pairs with crossbeams above them. A circular earthwork around the outside circle measures about 1,000 feet and beyond the whole circle there is a Sighting Stone on the north-eastern side over which the sun would rise as viewed from the flat Altar Stone on the morning of the summer solstice. Four other stones are symmet-rically placed so as to serve a similar purpose at sunrise and sunset on other days.

All this arrangement has astronomical precision at its founda-tions. The Sighting Stone does not exactly fit the sun's rising at the summer solstice now, but astronomers say that 3,500 years ago it would have done. Most of the stones are of local origin but the Altar Stone and the single upright stones have been brought from Pembrokeshire and there are aerial photographs that show the track by which they were brought up from the river at West Amesbury. We have evidence of the flint axes and rounded hammer stones and heavy mauls used in shaping the stones and in smoothing their surfaces to perfection. Also found are the picks of stag horn used to make the holes in the chalk into which the stones were lowered. This construction, made at the end of the Stone Age and the very beginning of the Bronze Age, is an amazing feat of heavy labour, faith and precision.

All around on the plain are tumuli, the burial sites of the people who presumably held some position in the Druidic world, either as warriors or Druids, and were allowed to be buried in the vicinity of Stonehenge, rather like a burial site allocated in Westminster Abbey. It would seem that Stonehenge is the final hurrah, for the construction at Woodhenge nearby and the stones at Avebury to the north are both older than Stonehenge itself.

Nowadays Stonehenge is so regimented that unless you go very early there are always people wandering about outside the wire that keeps the general public from having any access to the stones. Nearby you will find the strange construction, again from the same period at the end of the Stone Age and the early Bronze Age, of Woodhenge, discovered in 1925 as a result of an aerial survey. Woodhenge consists of a large number of stone pits which excavation has shown held wooden posts, since replaced by modern ones to give an impression of what it looked like. There are standing stones after every third or fourth wooden erection so that this whole combination of Silbury Hill, Avebury, Stonehenge and Woodhenge marks a not yet understood religious triumph for early man.

Avebury is best approached from Silbury Hill, which is itself an amazing place, the largest artificial mound in Europe, 1,660 feet round at the base, 300 feet round at the top and 130 feet high. It is an astonishing monument covering five acres, a task comparable to building one of the pyramids, and the mightiest piece of labour put forth by prehistoric man in Europe. We still don't understand the vast plan that led to the construction of the hill, and all the various stones standing on the plain, but the large circle of stones at Avebury, about one hundred in total, are sunk two feet into the chalk and stand some twenty feet high and weigh about sixty tonnes. Within the circle of chalk there are two small rings of upright stones. All around the great circle is a deep trench, dug into the solid chalk for some thirty feet. One can walk round this immense mound, which is twenty-nine acres in extent and nearly a mile around. The stones at Avebury don't stand in splendid and dignified isolation like those at Stonehenge. They are much cosier, in a way more intimate, intruding as they do into the village life. You can walk around the stones, you can touch and see where broken stones have been used in building construction in the village and then sit down in the café and have cup of tea and look at them. On the other side of Silbury Hill is Windmill Hill, which was the home of the earliest civilisation known in England.

The Elizabethan Manor House at Avebury has just been the subject of a BBC programme when Paul Martin and Penelope Keith led a project to restore the Manor House to different periods of its inhabitation. It has never really had one family living there for any length of time. The thing that fascinated me about the programme, which I watched intermittently, was why the researchers would have thought that anybody in a manor house of that size would have washed up in the kitchen. The kitchen is represented as in the 1920s and there are piles of what are presumably the remains of a dinner party with newly washed dishes. What do they think the scullery was for?

Maybe it is because Wiltshire contains 40 per cent of the world's – yes, I did say the world's – chalk downland, a material that always gives off the most extraordinary light, such as in a pool, especially when reflecting the light of the full moon, that it has inspired its inhabitants over several millennia to raise magnificent religious edifices. The splendid cathedral of Salisbury stands not far from the stones. Salisbury was an important Roman garrison town, which they called Sorbiodunum, where four or five roads converged. The Saxons took it over and fortified it as Searesbyrig and Alfred dug the outer ditch; then came the Normans who renamed it Seresberi from which it merged into the modern Salisbury. The cathedral is 473 feet from north to south covering an area of 55,000 square feet, and the imposing spire, which you can see from miles around, soars to a height of 404 feet. In the capstone of the spire is a small box that contains, so it was believed when it was put there in 1375, a relic of the fragment of the Virgin's veil; now the capstone also contains the nose cone of a rocket. When the spire needed to be restored they could think of no way to support it until some bright spark suggested the nose cone; it was therefore inserted and so the spire continues to point to heaven.

The cathedral Chapter House holds the best preserved copy of Magna Carta anywhere in the kingdom, appropriately so, for below it in the cathedral is the superb tomb of William Longespée in full armour as he would have been at the sealing of the great document of rights. The arches around the tomb supporting his effigy are made of oak and still gleam with a silvery sheen. He was the illegitimate son of Henry II, became the Earl of Salisbury and married Countess Ela in 1196, who was a power in the land in her own right; we will come to her when we reach Devon. He was the first man to be buried in the newly consecrated cathedral. Particularly outstanding is the Chapter House with its wonderful Early Perpendicular pillars and its enchanting carvings. When I was young I always wanted to be taken to see the one of Noah's Ark. The peaceful cloisters contain two magnificent cedars of Lebanon which, when we were in our teens, a couple of friends and I used to climb, quite illicitly of course. We would then throw acorns down on the people wandering around below who, when they looked to see what they had been struck by, were slightly mystified as to why there should be acorns coming from a cedar tree!

The Cathedral Close at Salisbury is especially remarkable, with buildings ranging from the medieval to the Georgian. You will also find in the little museum there the charter granted to the Earl of Salisbury's truffle hunters, together with the tools of their trade, licensing them to dig truffles in the county. The last truffle hunter in England, who also worked in Wiltshire, went down with the *Titanic*. His sons endeavoured to sue the White Star Line for loss of profits because all his secrets died with him. I always find this place to be a monument to the fact that in

England you can rise from the lowest origins, because a house in the Close was where Prime Minister Edward Heath once lived. Edward Heath's mother was a parlour maid in domestic service and he rose not only to be Prime Minister of the country but also to live in this magnificent house.

About a mile from Salisbury Cathedral stands Wilton House, which is certainly worth a visit. It was built on the site of an ancient nunnery, one of the four most important of such in England, the other three being in Berkshire, Shaftesbury and Winchester; their abbesses were automatically made Peeresses of the Realm, though being women they didn't have a seat in the House of Lords. The house was given to the Herbert family by Henry VIII after the Dissolution of the Monasteries and the Herberts were made Earls of Pembroke. The third Earl is believed to be the Mr W.H. of Shakespeare's sonnets; certainly Shakespeare's Folio was dedicated to his patron William Herbert. It is believed that the first performance of *As You Like It* was staged in the Great Hall in the presence of James I. One of the best rooms in the house is the Hunting Room, decorated with scenes of early seventeenth-century hunting, but it is not open to the public as the family use it as a private drawing room. The family still own Wilton House and it is open to the public.

The town of Wilton itself was of course famous for Wilton Carpets, which exists to this day and made use of the wool from the sheep that thrive so well on this good farmland. It is a mystery to me why the Wiltshire Wildlife Trust, which is endeavouring to restore the chalk uplands, would populate them with Herdwick sheep to crop down the grass so that wild flowers can come through when the Wilton Horn is one of our oldest known breeds of sheep.

Salisbury Plain is still very much the home of the British Army and you see tank tracks and warnings about tanks everywhere. It was the army who in the 1920s restored Stonehenge by lifting the stone lintels that had fallen from their supports back into place. I also remember a rather entertaining picture of a Land Rover that had been hoisted on to the top of one of the lintels at Stonehenge after rather a good night out in the Officers' Mess. Cavalry and Horse Artillery reviews used to be held on Salisbury Plain and my father, who had been a horse gunner before joining the Royal Flying Corps, described how on one occasion the officer riding ahead of the mounted battery realised that the battery had bolted, so he spurred on his horse, unable to wheel round in front of the review stand, and he and the battery just kept on going and disappeared, past a rather astonished royal, far out into Salisbury Plain.

The plain has long been a thriving ground for both hunting and beagling. The beagles are in fact still called the Royal Artillery Beagles and wear, for some obscure reason, sky-blue cotton socks. One of the more interesting projects in the area has been the return of the Great Bustard to Salisbury Plain. This strange running bird, which once inhabited the plain, had become completely extinct in the UK and attempts to reintroduce it appear to be successful. I was, in fact, invited by a charming man to come and inspect the Bustard project and lest I should think he was one of the fluffy bunny brigade he said that to prove his street cred perhaps I would like to go shooting with them. I said, 'Surely not Bustards!' and he said no, they had a black powder shoot (which is shooting with muzzle-loading firearms). I didn't quite like to tell him that my great interest in the Bustard is that I would dearly like to eat one to see what it tastes like, as it was a great feature of medieval and Tudor menus. When I did raise the question he said that he had in fact eaten one in Hungary and that it had seemed rather like a tough turkey, but he hinted that perhaps I could cook it better. However, I think it will be quite a long time before there are sufficient Bustards on Salisbury Plain, so I don't think I will ever get to taste one.

One of the more realistic food delights of Wiltshire is the existence at Malmesbury of the set-up that is Tracklements, which makes sauces, mustards, jellies and relishes. This is a small private family business that has grown during my adult lifetime, and one of their latest projects has been to redeem the medlar. The medlar is this curious medieval fruit that nobody quite knows what to do with because you can only eat it once it has bletted, in other words rotted. It has a strange taste rather like a compote of apples, redolent of the spices that you would normally add to it. The family are going round people's gardens in the area, where medlar trees are fairly numerous, picking the fruit and giving the owners a couple of jars of medlar jelly in return. Medlars make very good jelly, as they are full of pectin, but it is quite difficult to get the balance right. I once had a friend who would dump her entire medlar crop, in a black plastic bag, on my doorstep, so I have had a lot of experience.

Malmesbury itself is well worth a visit. Quite apart from Tracklements it is home to a magnificent Norman abbey, and here lies a later tomb dedicated to Athelston, Alfred's grandson, the man who united England as one country after the Battle of Brunanburh in AD 937, the most bloodthirsty of battles, but after which England became one country. Athelstan is in fact buried in the vicinity of the Norman abbey and the tomb that bears his name is a later creation. The common here is called King's Heath after him as he donated 500 acres where every freeman of the borough was entitled to an allotment. There has been a church here and indeed an abbey since the year AD 640 when an Irish man called Mailduib came from Iona to set up a school and a church. The outer doorway of the abbey has eight depths of carving with the most magical figures. There are hundreds of them: Eve taking the apple from the serpent, a man turning a somersault, an angel, a peacock and the tree of knowledge. There is also a monument to Eilmer, the Saxon monk who flew from the church tower having created a strange construction of wings. He survived to tell his tale but broke both his legs. Most importantly the abbey was the home of the medieval chronicler and scholar William of Malmesbury. My mother, while staying at the Old Bell Hotel at Malmesbury, had a very unpleasant experience. Those of you who have read my work know that my mother was psychic and on this occasion there had been excavations in the abbey site for which the Old Bell had been the hospitality wing. They had found a nun who had been walled up, presumably for adultery. My mother had the most terrifying experience when she saw this face in total agony in the window, and it was only the quick intervention of a friend of hers who was staying there that broke the spell, so to speak.

If Wiltshire raises monuments to different gods, the house at Longleat can only be said to be raised to Mammon. The builder, Sir John Thynn, took thirty-seven years to build it. He had made his fortune in the service of the first Lord Vaux of Harrowden and then of the Duke of Somerset, the Lord Protector to Edward VI, and he was the perfect epitome of an Elizabethan new man. The house remains in the Thynne family – the present Marquess of Bath is a direct descendant of Sir John – although over the years they added an 'e'. The estate was saved by the father of the present Marquess, a man who was reputed to be the best looking and most devastatingly attractive man of his generation, and although I only met him in old age, I could see why you would think he merited the description. It was he who decided that the best course of action was to open an animal safari park on the estate, which he duly did, and most of my youth was taken up with spotting labels on the backs of cars saying, 'I have seen the lions of Longleat'. It was perhaps an old family tradition, because in the early eighteenth century one of the daughters of the house was killed by a tiger. The safari park attracts hundreds of thousands of visitors and is the subject of a television series presented by Kate Humble and Ben Fogle, and there is no doubt that it has restored the fortunes of the estate. The present Marquess, who is wonderfully eccentric and a great example of 1960s hedonism, was known for his 'wifelets', a number of young women who lived with him. He has also altered the interior of the house in various rooms by covering it with paintings and sculpture which I leave to your own taste to decide whether you like or not.

One of my favourite towns in England is in Wiltshire and that is Devizes. It is still a proper town with lovely buildings, real shops and some very good pubs where you can get an excellent meal, including the regular appearance of crayfish from the Kennet. The museum there contains the Marlborough Bucket, which is the remains of an early Celtic funerary vessel. The wooden part has been replaced but the bronze handles are the most beautiful early work. Devizes was one of the important stopping places of the Bloody Assizes, Judge Jeffreys' progress through the country after the Monmouth Rebellion, and I remember reading in my legal studies that the inhabitants of Devizes took to the hills and abandoned the town leaving Judge Jeffreys with nobody to try. The Kennet and Avon Canal passes through Devizes by means of twenty-nine locks, a magnificent feat of the early 1800s, which thus linked the port of Bristol to the Thames and to London. The canal fell into disuse with the coming of the railways and then the motorways, but in the 1960s it was lovingly restored, mostly by volunteer work, and is now a thriving holiday attraction for narrowboaters and canal lovers alike. If you are going to take a boat up the locks make sure that you have several strong young men with you as it is a fairly exhausting feat to go through the sixteen locks in the stack up Caen Hill. You can travel eighty-seven miles along the canal's length either by boat or by bicycle on the towpath and it was actually while sitting looking at the sun going down behind Roundway Hill, an ancient Celtic fortification and the site of one of Cromwell's more unpleasant battles, that I had the inspiration to write this book. So I hope you will feel kindly towards Devizes as well.

In the north of the county lies Wootton Bassett. If you were to look up Wootton Bassett in a book written, say, thirty years ago, you would find nothing much said about it apart from the fact that it was a peaceful market town in the north of Wiltshire. However, by its own quiet displays of respect and reverence to the dead military of Iraq and Afghanistan who, by force of circumstance, were driven through the town in their hearses on the way to burial, it has become a royal borough. It will have a place in this generation that will long be associated with the young who laid down their lives for a series of bloody, and to my mind unnecessary, wars. Well done, Wootton Bassett.

Dorset

Once there was a Flanders and Swann song called 'The Slow Train' and if you look at the village names of Dorset you are reminded of that song, places with such wonderful names as Sturminster Newton, Castlemaine, Cerne Abbas, Winterborne Stickland and Gussage All Saints. However what Dorset really brings to mind is Thomas Hardy, who made the county so memorable. As you drive through Dorset and you stop somewhere you immediately think of some place in Hardy's novels and then, of course, you realise that is exactly where you are and that he has just changed it slightly. The most notable of these places is Dorchester, which is Casterbridge in *The Mayor of Casterbridge*, and until about fifteen years ago Dorchester was much as Hardy would have remembered it. It still boasts Maiden Castle, the Stone Age earthworks that date back to 2000 BC – although occupation of the hilltop began in the Neolithic period, over 6,000 years ago – with its reinforced fortifications, its signs of being heavily palisaded at its weaker points and a pit that contained something like 2,200 sling stones; iron spear heads and other weapons have been found too. There are graves there, possibly sacrificial, of two children and a young man. The hill was held until AD 44 when it was taken by the Roman Army under Vespasian and fairly soon afterwards the remaining Durotriges, the local tribe who occupied it, were moved to what became the Roman city of Dorchester.

On the other side of Dorchester is Poundbury Camp, a rather lesser known and less impressive Celtic fortification, where some twenty years ago Prince Charles decided to build his dream of what rural habitation should be. It is really, I suppose, just another urban development built on rural land and in this case on land owned by the Duchy of Cornwall. Such was Prince Charles's passion that architects were employed and the houses were built to emulate the styles of different centuries so that the whole looks like a proper English town. It is not the Victorian philanthropist's dream as found at Saltaire or Port Sunlight, but it is a very beautiful addition to the town of Dorchester, although one does wonder what the Mayor of Casterbridge would have made of it. This is a development for the upper middle classes and has brought good restaurants, shops and lovely building to this part of the world, but thank God that the Prince of Wales does so much for the poor with the Prince's Trust, otherwise one would be very cynical indeed.

I love Hardy and his creation of the rural world in which he lived, changing very little from the original; it is not so much his stories as his description of contemporary habits that appeals. In *Tess of the d'Urbervilles*, for instance, we find a unique description of the dairy maid linking her arms and using them to create butter in the tub rather than using some plunger as we normally assume was the case. If you go to Bere Regis you will find the tombs of the Turbervilles, so slightly removed from the d'Urbervilles of Tess's story. You will remember that her father discovers that though he is an agricultural labourer, he is of ancient lineage, and it turns his head. Hardy describes the canopied tombs of the d'Urbervilles, their carvings defaced and broken, their brasses torn from their matrices, the rivet holes remaining like sand martin holes in a sand cliff, and that is exactly how these tombs are at Bere Regis. The Turbervilles came over with the Conqueror but they never made any particular mark, although they remained major landowners in Dorset; their fall from even minor prominence came with a spell in the Tower for the Turberville of the day for refusing to swear an oath to a

Protestant sovereign. The family probably would have seeped into dust and disinterest but for Thomas Hardy's creation of the fictitious descendant, the Dorset dairy maid, which brings people to Bere Regis on the Hardy trail.

Dorset seems to remain very much as Hardy left it, something of a rural backwater, without much benefit of railway or major roads and all the more charming for that. It is very easy to forget that it was a centre of quite considerable importance in the country: Wimborne 1,300 years ago was a major centre for the education of women, not something that was vastly popular in those days. St Cuthburga and St Quinberga, sisters of the ruling King Ine of Wessex, founded a nunnery and focused on the education of women, who were then sent out as missionaries, taking the word of Christ all over Europe. Their convent was the Girton of the day and people came from all over the country in order to attend it. Such was its repute that when Ethelred, the elder brother of Alfred, fell in battle against the Danes, it was decided to bury him in Wimborne Minster. Edward the Confessor was one of the benefactors of the minster and its accompanying nunnery, as was William the Conqueror, and it is perhaps appropriate that Margaret Beaufort, the mother of Henry VII, founded a chantry and endowed a priest, interestingly to teach grammar to all-comers. A hundred years later her great-granddaughter founded the grammar school as part of the great buildings that are as we see them today.

Ethelred had fought nine battles against the Danes and eventually died in the last of them, leaving his twenty-year-old brother Alfred to stand in Wimborne Minster to take the oath of sovereignty. A plaque to Ethelred reads: 'In this place rest the body of Ethelred King of West Saxons, Martyr, who within the year of our Lord 873 on the 23rd day of April felled by the hand of the pagan Danes'. The brass is not over his grave, but he is buried somewhere in the building.

Also buried here in a rather charming tomb are John Beaufort,

Earl of Somerset, and Margaret his wife, who were the parents of Margaret Beaufort, the mother of the Tudor dynasty who lies, of course, in Westminster Abbey. The Earl of Somerset lies in full armour with his gauntlet in his left hand and his bare right hand lovingly holding that of his wife. She has rings on her fingers and a carving of a fine jewel on her bosom and her veil is held by a simple coronet and falls about her shoulders. Death mellows all things because nearby is the tomb of the widow of Henry Courtney who was beheaded by their great-grandson, Henry VIII, for having rather too close a claim to the throne. Outside the minster is a rather charming clock with a wooden figure that strikes the quarters with a hammer and is known as Quarter Jack. It is an orrery, or astronomical clock, nearly 700 years old, and may be by Peter Lightfoot, the monk of Glastonbury who made two or three other such clocks to be found in the West Country.

Rather more modern is the home of the Shaftesbury family at nearby Wimborne St Giles. The Shaftesburys have always been great eccentrics and reformers and the first Earl, Anthony Ashley Cooper, was the most public-minded man of his day, standing up for the right of Parliament to rule against both the King and the Commonwealth. He was a rich young man when war broke out and he turned out for the King but, finding that he thought that Parliament was right, he changed sides, still maintaining the right of Parliament to rule and deploring the influence of Cromwell's army as the dominant power in the realm. On Cromwell's death he stood by General Monck in his campaign to restore the monarchy and, when it was restored, used his influence to prevent Charles II from being too revengeful on those who opposed him. Charles made him a peer and Chancellor of the Exchequer. I suspect that it was more his refusal to finance payments to various of Charles's mistresses rather than his political activities against the Roman Catholics that led to his being sacked, and his principles allowed him to refuse both an offer of a dukedom and 10,000 guineas from King Louis of France and become the leader of the Protestant opposition. He keenly supported the Duke of Monmouth's claim as the Protestant successor to the throne and was thrown into the Tower of London and tried for high treason. So popular was he that the jury threw out the charge and the case was dropped; his subsequent plotting came to nothing and he escaped to Holland, finally dying in exile in Amsterdam.

Six generations later his descendant, the seventh Earl of Shaftesbury, showed the same energy, enthusiasm and independence. He hated the Reform Act and opposed it strenuously, while encompassing reforms far more dramatic than those provided. He feared to trust democracy to the ballot box and yet toiled to gain emancipation for slaves and political liberty for the Poles. He was the friend to all Jews, which was unusual in the aristocracy of those days. Every bill that he promoted or called to Parliament or proposed bettered the lot of the working man, and it was entirely due to him that the manufacturing towns were forbidden from employing children under the age of seven and working them fifteen hours a day, beating them with sticks, straps and rollers or immersing them in cold water to keep them awake. Before his legislation, the children crippled at work numbered thousands in a single day. They had no intervals for breakfast and were often required to walk twenty or thirty miles a day. He travelled tirelessly visiting mills, factories and the homes of the poor, noting their conditions. Those who praise the House of Commons over the House of Lords should look to Lord Shaftesbury, for without his legislation the horrendous conditions that made the fortunes of the Industrial Revolution would have continued. It was entirely due to him that the use of children as young as four for sweeping chimneys was abolished. If you have ever read Charles Kingsley's *The Water Babies*, you will see what a clever man Shaftesbury was, utilising PR long before the days when 'spin' became so fashionable. He was a strong man who feared, as it was said, neither cabinets nor caucuses, and was a true reformer in an unfashionable age for such reforms. One must remember all these other realities when thinking of Dorset as the bucolic county of Hardy's works.

Perhaps the most important part of Dorset is its coastline running from Poole in the east to Lyme Regis in the west. I have spent a number of years holidaying in Lyme Regis; it is a quiet, charming town and the absence of the railway has preserved it as such. It is beloved of Jane Austen, who describes the Cobb so evocatively in *Persuasion*. The Cobb is a quay, 600 feet long, and there has been a similar construction on the same spot for 700 years, frequently rebuilt after great storms. In fact on one visit I watched in fascination as workmen offloaded more stones to protect it further. Part of the popularity of Lyme Regis, which lies on what is now known as the Jurassic Coast, was started by a woman called Mary Anning, who was fascinated by the fossils that were found so readily in the rock in this area. She took a few months to uncover the skeleton of the first ichthyosaurus in its entirety. This fish lizard fossil is seventeen feet long and she sold it for £23 to a local collector, who some years later sold it to the British Museum. It was an age when people were fascinated by archaeology and the study of fossils and other natural phenomena. She opened a shop, Anning's Fossil Depot, which was visited by all manner of people hoping to meet her, among them the King of Saxony, who handed her a book in which to write her name and address. She gave it back to him saying, 'I'm quite well known throughout the whole of Europe.' To this day fossil tours run regularly from the centre of Lyme Regis and they have great cause to be grateful to Mary Anning.

The other famous name associated with Lyme Regis is that of Thomas Coram, who was born in the town in 1668, the son of a ship's captain, who, despite his well-recorded irascibility and difficult temperament clearly had a big heart. In an age when such things were almost unthought of, he was greatly moved by the little waifs that were abandoned, homeless and unwanted, on London's streets. He brought together a number of rich people to set up homes for these children and after twenty years obtained a charter for the Foundling Hospital, which was opened in 1745, a matter of tremendous interest in a day where life was really very cheap indeed. Hogarth painted a portrait of Coram and donated it to the Foundling Hospital.

A more recent name to add to the history of Lyme Regis is Keith Floyd, who died in nearby Bridport some hours after enjoying a good lunch at Mark Hix's restaurant. I say a good lunch, but I think I would have been rather cross if my last meal, when I had ordered grouse, was merely one of red-legged partridge, as was the case. Since the restaurant stands on an impossibly steep hill with nowhere to park, or indeed nowhere to stop legally, walking away from it after a good lunch would kill the strongest of us. Keith Floyd was a wonderful example of early television cooking and thought nothing of demeaning himself in his efforts to entertain. Few of us will ever forget the scene where he shows his *pipérade* to an elderly French woman who wrinkles her face and says, '*C'est dégoûtant.*' Remarkably the clip was left in. He unfortunately never found recovery for his alcoholism and his life was full of ups and downs, but he made great television.

Looking across the bay at the wonderful headlands, such as Golden Cap which, when it catches the setting sun, is a lovely sight, one sees Portland Bill. Four hundred years ago this was a simple sheep run with a fort and a prison. It was Inigo Jones who was so impressed by the suitability of Portland limestone for building that he adopted it for the Banqueting Hall of the new Whitehall Palace, and Christopher Wren used it for his new St Paul's. The fashion spread so that at one time as much as 100,000 tonnes of Portland stone had been quarried in a year. London University is built out of Portland stone and wherever you look in London you will see it. It is said that if you sleep in one of the villages on Portland Bill you will be lulled to sleep by the snoring of the sea at Chesil Beach, that great bulwark of stones that runs for eighteen miles along the coast from Portland, with the Channel pounding on one side of it and the still backwater of the Fleet Lagoon on the other.

Behind it is Abbotsbury. The foundation of the abbey was laid down by Orc, who was in the service of King Canute, so it is very old indeed. All that is left now, apart from a few stone pillars, is the Great Tithe Barn of the abbey, which remains a magnificent sight. You will still find swans in the swannery on the Fleet, where monks harvested 2,000 swans a year in the Middle Ages to be sold for the table. When Henry VIII granted the manor at Abbotsbury to the Strangways family there was a separate grant of the swannery so that they could continue to harvest and sell them. We don't eat swans now, except on rare ritual occasions, although it was interesting when a vast number of Poles came over to Britain in the last decade and started to eat swans. Having done so myself, let me tell you it is very much an acquired taste and certainly not one that I favour. I have eaten swan three times in my life and that was really three times too many.

It is strange to think, isn't it, that in this land of rural idyll are to be found the foundations of the trade union movement and hence, I suppose, of the Labour Party which is its child. Tolpuddle up near Bere Regis is a very quiet corner of the world today, but in 1834 the names of the brothers George and James Loveless, the father and son pair of Thomas and John Standfield, James Hammett and James Brine shook the world. They were unlikely kindling to set off an inferno. Most of them were faithful Methodists, while the Loveless brothers were village preachers. They all decided that they were not satisfied with the wages they were being paid for their agricultural labouring and, under the sycamore, now known as the Martyrs' Tree, they met and decided to make an issue of it. A labourer's wage at that time was seven shillings a week and the men had in effect joined a trade union in the hope of getting ten shillings a week. In the early hours of one morning, as is always the way with arrests, they were taken from their homes and sent to Dorchester to answer a charge of conspiracy. After the guilty verdict they were sent in chains to Australia for a sentence of seven years. Their families were turned out of their cottages, refused parish relief and had to live on the charity of their neighbours. So great was the public outcry that Parliament announced that they would be pardoned and brought home. Of course in those days there were no wirelesses or telegraphs and very few steamships, so it took six months for the pardon to reach Australia. The Governor wrote back to say the release was illegal and it was another eighteen months before the government finally secured freedom for these six men. Eventually they were brought home to England and the government gave them money in order to rebuild their lives, but the men had started something very important indeed. In 1934, a hundred years later, the Trades Union Congress built six cottages as a tribute to the Tolpuddle Martyrs to house retired agricultural trade unionists. The cottages stand as a memorial to events that moved this land of England a little closer to justice and liberty.

I gather from a friend who follows the 'Twitterati', which I hasten to add I do not, that one of the things that turns up repeatedly is my talking in one of my books about Pidd the god of rain who was responsible for such words as piddle and puddle and so forth. If Pidd has a kingdom there is no doubt it is in Dorset, for if you go to the villages on the River Piddle, such as Piddletrenthide or Puddletrenthide as it was previously known, you will find that the word piddle or puddle occurs all around Dorset and ends where the River Piddle runs into the bay at Poole Harbour. However, the dominant god of the Dorset chalk is not Pidd in the sense of the Long Man of Wilmington but the Giant at Cerne Abbas, although he may of course be Pidd because we really don't know who he is. He is a chalk cutting carved into the hill above the Sherborne road and his height is half that of St Paul's; he equals thirty tall men standing one on top of the other. Each of his fingers measures seven feet and the club in his hand is forty yards long. I don't actually have a measurement for his most famous feature but there is no doubt that if the club is forty yards long, his wedding tackle is something similar.

There are some sights, aren't there, that always attract a conglomeration of religion. Long after the Cerne Abbas Giant was carved, an abbey was built, and the Franciscan Order set up the first of their homes for young vagrants in the early 1920s. Followers of St Francis are sworn to poverty, but they befriended the young men who roamed the country, maddened by the years of war, and set up their homes, where they provided the men with meals, keep and pocket money in a peaceful environment. They taught the men to work as housemen, gardeners and labourers. In the days before the welfare state it was a very necessary and worthwhile thing to do.

It was Dorset that saw the successful escape of one Stuart monarch and another unsuccessful attempt by a would-be such. The then Prince Charles (later King Charles II), fleeing to the Continent, tried to get out through Bridport but the town was full of Cromwell's men who were hunting for him. He managed to escape and went to Charmouth where, disguised as a servant of Lord Wilmot and a woman called Juliana Coningsby, who claimed to be eloping lovers, they all took rooms at the Queen's Arms. A boat was arranged under a skipper called Limbry. He came ashore at ten o'clock, two hours before the rendezvous, to pick up his clean linen and his wife, who had heard a declamation in the streets denouncing any who concealed Charles or his followers, took matters into her own hands and locked him in his bedroom. No summons came for Charles to take ship, but nonetheless once again he evaded capture and eventually got clean away to the Continent. The unsuccessful Stuart was of course the Duke of Monmouth, who was captured and later executed.

In the north of the county is the Blackmore Vale. Like most of

Dorset this is wonderful hunting country with great thick double oxers into which it is said you can lose yourself and your horse for the best part of the day, and people have to come and get you out of it. I always remember when Johnny Scott and I, at the beginning of the *Clarissa and the Countryman* years, were called on to Ned Sherrin's *Loose Ends* radio programme and I, thinking of Ned as a charming London puff, said to him, 'Ned, you know, be kind to us, give us a chance,' to which he replied, 'A chance! I asked for you specially. Blackmore Vale man me.' That most witty, urbane and erudite of London presenters came from a farming family in the Blackmore Vale. He apparently sent large donations to the hunt which kept them going quite happily. I always liked that story so I am pleased to find a place for it.

Let us exit Dorset through the port town of Bridport, famous for centuries for the quality of rope that it made. In fact the hangman's noose, historically, was known as the Bridport Dagger, and it was said that the felon would die stabbed by the Bridport Dagger.

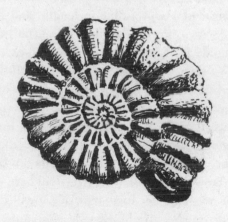

Devon

If one was to dream seamlessly of the most beautiful agricultural country, one would conjure up Devon. Everything about Devon looks lush and appealing: the soil is a stunning dark red colour, the grass seems to be particularly green and the red cattle of Devon match the soil. It has dramatic windswept moorland and fine harbours along its coast. The only trouble is that in the twenty-first century, British agriculture is not a productive occupation. The government does not support British farmers and there isn't an awful lot of shipping going out of the West Country now, but let us ignore all that and concentrate on Devon.

I usually come into the county through Honiton, down the A30, the old Roman tin road. The central street of Honiton is an old Roman road, about a mile in length, and is one of the straightest and widest streets of its kind in England, with a stream running alongside it. If you come to the summer fair, it starts when the town crier walks down the street with flowers and a glove attached to the top of them. People cry, 'The glove's up,' and no one will be arrested until the glove is down. I think, however, that that tradition is no longer with us, as with the old one of throwing a handful of hot pennies into the street from the inn for the children to burn their fingers on to the amusement of the throwers. Health and Safety will have put a stop to that. Honiton was a highly successful lace town, its lace much sought after. Even after machine-made lace came into fashion with the Industrial Revolution, it continued to be made by hand there. Queen Victoria had her wedding dress made of

Honiton lace and Princess Diana incorporated it when she married Prince Charles, as did Kate Middleton when she married their son.

You get a fine view of the county from the town, looking down on the valley of the River Otter below. The Otter lends its name to various villages in the area, the most charming of which is probably Ottery St Mary, with its extremely beautiful church built by John Grandisson, Bishop of Exeter. What is particularly interesting about Ottery St Mary is that it was the birthplace of Samuel Taylor Coleridge, whose father was vicar and schoolmaster in the village and who, at the age of nineteen, wrote, 'And while old Otter's steeple rings . . .,' referring to this miniature cathedral. His father had thirteen children by two marriages and Samuel was the youngest of them all. He became heavily addicted to opiates which he was prescribed for his asthma. His West Country origins do perhaps explain why he should have been interrupted in the dream that produced 'Kubla Khan' by a visit from a 'Person from Porlock'.

In more recent years I have come to this part of Devon for the Devon County Show, which is one of those shows that has its own standing showground which, during the rest of the year, is used for other events. It is still a very rural show with animals and packs of hounds of all varieties from the county's numerous hunts. I remember an old beagler talking about the fact that they had only had one problem with the antis and I asked him what had happened. His faded blue eyes stared into the hills and a smile spread over his weather-beaten face and he quietly remarked, 'That were a great day,' and that was all he said. The nicest of the shows in that area is the Honiton Hound Show, which is the west of England hound show on a par with Ardingly or Peterborough or Builth Wells in other regions. Here packs of hounds from all over the west of England, and indeed further afield, come to be judged on their merits. I remember sitting there on a rather cold and damp day signing books and being plied with Cornish pasties as packs of hounds and huntsmen on horses trotted past me on their way to the various rings; every so often I would go down and look at the hounds and smile at the enthusiasm and passion that still remain in these dark days for hunting. Opposite me was the stall of the firm that had made my last pair of hunting boots, which I shall come to in Northamptonshire, and on other stalls people were selling hunting clothes and whips and such like. It could have been almost any time during the last 300 years and I was very happy.

Honiton is not far from the cathedral city of Exeter, the capital of Devon. Although Exeter has been much modernised and is full of those rather nameless, 'samey' shops that you so often get, if you step back from the shopping centre and you go to Southerhay, where they burned the heretics, or Northernhay, or into the Cathedral Close, you are back in the Middle Ages. The cathedral itself was started by Athelstan but it is a magnificent medieval construction. There is a marvellous war memorial to the 958 dead of the First World War, sculpted by an Exeter man, John Angel, and cast in the workshops of William Morris, and no doubt those workshops had something to do with the design of the strange beast that Victory is trampling on.

What I have always loved best in the cathedral are the misericords, some of the earliest known. The misericord is the bit below the flap-down seat in the choir stalls, which the monks or the members of the choir could prop their bottoms on after hours and hours of standing for devotions. In many churches these are beautifully carved. Here there are fifty of them in all, mostly thirteenth century, and there are quite extraordinary scenarios. There is a crocodile swallowing its prey, an elephant set between a monk and a Crusader, a knight attacking a leopard, a mermaid holding a fish, a minstrel playing his pipe, a man being drawn in a boat by a swan, a king sitting in a cauldron of boiling water as penance and a carving of the first African elephant known, or perhaps the first carving of an African elephant known. Misericords can be hard to spot but the ones in Exeter really repay the effort of crawling around the choir stalls. More prominent is the magnificently carved Bishop's Throne, made on the orders of Bishop Stapledon in 1316 for the sum of what would now be about £3,000. It stands fifty-nine feet high and is covered with hundreds of little faces, both wise and foolish. The whole is carved with exquisite foliage, with the small heads of oxen, sheep, pigs, dogs, monkeys and other animals enriching the corners of the pinnacles. Its construction is remarkable, as not a single nail has been used, and it is all held together by wooden pegs.

The cathedral requires more than a day's visit to appreciate it properly. One of the things you should look out for is the Exeter Book, the *Codex Exoniensis*, given to the cathedral by Leofric twenty years before the Norman Conquest. Most of the book is devoted to the poetry of Cynewulf and written in the English language before the Danes and the Normans swept over the land. The poem is in the West Saxon dialect. There are ninety-five riddles in the book, which pre-date Christianity and are totally charming. There is, for instance, the poet's image of an iceberg as a charging Viking, laughing and shouting as he breaks the ships of a foe into pieces. Also in the library is a Devonshire Domesday Book. All the country's Domesday Books have been transcribed, but I do wish somebody would pay more attention to Leofric's book and undertake a translation.

When I was in early recovery I used to come to Alcoholics Anonymous meetings in Exeter and some of them were held in the seventeenth-century Church of St Thomas the Apostle, which was the only church in the country where a vicar was hanged, in 1549, from his own tower. I used to look with interest, too, at the gravestone of Gordon of Khartoum's grandfather which Gordon had come to visit when he was given the telegram recalling him to London; from there he left for Khartoum, never to return.

As we leave Exeter on the Exmouth road, spare a thought for Countess Ela, whom we encountered before, if you remember, at Wimborne, and her continual battle with the citizens of Exeter, who objected to the tolls she was charging shipping coming up the River Exe to unload. Finally, in a fit of rage, she built a new port at Topsham, further down the river, which meant that shipping didn't get as far as Exeter, and so we have the charming town of Topsham. In the late eighties and early nineties it was where I went to spend my week's annual holiday. I used to stay in this light tower built at the end of a house called Rikadon, which in Russian means River House, and had been built by a Russian sea captain. His wife would place a light in the tower to welcome him home and to guide shipping coming up the river to Topsham. I stayed in the flat at the top of this tower; it was on two floors, the first of them containing a bedroom, kitchen and bathroom, and then above it was the light. This was just one room with 360 degrees of glass, so that you could look behind you at the green Devonshire hills and ahead towards the estuary of the Exe. This was tidal, and little wading birds would come in and out with the tide, and you could sit for hours just mesmerised by the changing of the light and the movement of the water. There was a Japanese gentleman who used to take the flat for two days a year and come all the way over from Tokyo simply to meditate.

This treasured accommodation had been discovered by a dog. It came into my life because a very old, wise and Confucian mongrel called Digger was being walked through the town by his owner one day and he shot through a gate and up these stairs. The owner chased after him to find Digger being confronted by a very large and angry-looking Alsatian. Digger being a Confucian dog, as I have said, the anger seemed to fade, and my friend made friends with the couple who owned the house. The tower was available for rent and consequently I would go there on my holidays. I came to love Topsham, a delightful town with one or two good restaurants and a very good second-hand and antiquarian bookshop run by a man called Joel. He had a band called Spinach for Norman which was a klezmer/ceilidh band. He was Jewish and his band was moderately successful in this country, but was all the rage in Outer Mongolia. I would spend hours sitting in the bookshop talking to him and buying books and just generally having a nice time.

At that point Trevor McDonald, the newsreader, had a flat in the town and I would see him from time to time, his black face being very out of the usual in such a quiet rural Devonshire town. Joel's partner Lily and I would go out in a rowing boat to see the wading birds, but the tides were somewhat unpredictable, or we didn't read the tide-tables right, for many times we found ourselves plopping through the mud dragging the boat behind us to get back to shore. I was not a child, I was forty then, and I would go back to my tower and wash off the mud, then cook delicious fish and look out across the estuary to Powderham Castle, the home of the Earls of Devon. There was a rhyme left by the Duke of Monmouth that ran:

> Topsham thou art a lovely town
> Oh Topsham thou art pretty
> And when I come into my own
> I'll make of thee a city.

Monmouth of course, probably fortunately for Topsham, did not come 'into his own' and so the town remains unspoiled. I never had the heart to tell Lily that the avocets we strained so hard to go and find would practically jump into the car with you, nearer where I live, if you simply drove across the causeway to Holy Island at the right time of year.

Topsham fell out of use as a port when a canal was built by the Earls of Devon on the far side of the estuary, which enabled shipping to go up and down to Exeter, thus flouting the memory of Countess Ela. If you continued on down the road to Exmouth, where I used to go to buy fish, you would come to the curious building called A La Ronde built by the two Parminter cousins. The Parminters were wealthy Devon merchants and Jane became guardian to her orphaned cousin Mary, who was slightly younger. In 1784, on her father's death, Jane went off to do the Grand Tour, after which she and Mary decided to set up home together in Devon. They bought fifteen acres of land near Exmouth, built their house and enjoyed a sheltered and unconventional existence until Jane's death in 1811. The house is most unusual, apparently based on the Basilica of San Vitale, and comprises twenty rooms. Those on the ground floor radiate out from an octagon shape and were originally separated by sliding doors, the spaces between the principal rooms being filled by triangular closets with diamond-shaped windows. Wine cellars and other offices are situated in the basement. The octagonal gallery on the upper floor is decorated with an elaborate hand-crafted frieze. A lot of the interior decoration was done by the two cousins themselves, so there are amazing friezes of shells and feathers and silhouettes and all the handicrafts that occupied genteel ladies of the day, but carried out to some excess. When Mary died, her will stipulated that the property could only be inherited by unmarried kinswomen. The condition was met until 1886, when the house went to a male relative, who put in such luxuries as a water tower, a laundry and central heating.

The two women also set up a chapel and almshouses and rather curiously the deeds for the almshouses specified that any Jewess who converted to Christianity would take precedence over any other candidate for a place. The oaks planted on the estate are protected to this day by a will left by the Parminter cousins declaring that the oaks 'shall remain standing until Israel returns and is restored to the Land of Promise', the implication here being that the oaks would then be cut down and the wood used to build ships to return to the Promised Land. It is a most strange and singular place and much deserves a visit. Such little enclaves were, throughout history, places where women who were determined enough could overcome the mores of the day and establish their independence, even if in a way that to us in the twenty-first century may seem slightly unwarranted, but it showed they had the ability to survive on their own away from society.

Follow the Exe to its mouth and turn right down the Devon coast past the mouth of the River Teign and various other little rivers and you come to Brixham, a town that has three memorable comings and goings to mark its history. The first was when Francis Drake sailed into its harbour with the first prize he had captured at the Armada, the ship *Capitana*, which he had plundered of its powder and shot in time to turn it to fire at other of the Spanish galleons. Drake was a local man, as we shall see, and much rejoicing must have welcomed him in. Slightly less uproarious would have been the welcome extended to Prince William of Orange, the future Protestant King, who ended the Stuart dynasty in England when he landed at Brixham quay in 1688. There is a rather pompous statue of him carrying his hat and saying, 'The liberties of England and the Protestant religion I will maintain'. The third of these memorable comings and goings was the curious moment in 1815 when on 7 August the *Bellerophon* stopped at Brixham, carrying the Emperor Napoleon Bonaparte en route to his exile and death on St Helena. When Napoleon surrendered after Waterloo, he had hoped that he could come to live in England, and brought with him his little camp bed, his travelling library, a huge suite of followers, £4,000 in gold napoleons; he also wanted to embark six carriages and forty-five horses for his life in England. He longed to meet the Prince Regent and set up as an English country squire. In the event the nearest he ever got to England was Brixham harbour.

Perhaps the most enduring association is the fact that the hymn 'Abide With Me' by Henry Francis Lyte, the vicar of All Saints Church in Brixham, started life in that town. He wrote many hymns but the most famous, partly due to football crowds, is no doubt 'Abide With Me'.

Continue along the coast and you come to the mouth of the River Dart, the river that starts its life on Dartmoor, as so many of them do in the north of the county. Dartmouth is, quite rightly I think, dubbed the home of the English navy. Devon is the prime county for the English navy: it gave us Raleigh and Drake, it has provided seamen for every major battle and it was Edward VII, at a time when the British Empire was at its height, when the navy hadn't suffered any of the shortcomings that had beset the British Army since Wellington's day, with losses in Afghanistan and in the Boer War, who opened Dartmouth Naval College. My generation's walls are hung with pictures of young men in their naval uniforms, young men of thirteen years or so, looking very young and vulnerable. The war memorial of the 153 Dartmouth men who lost their lives in the Great War reads:

> No Saint or King has tomb so proud
> As he whose flag becomes his shroud.

Dartmouth was a home for naval and sailing endeavours long before the Naval College was founded and the town has a very fine castle where a chain used to be run across the mouth of the river at night. In St Saviour's Church is the grave of John Hawley, a man who was Mayor of Dartmouth fourteen times and built the chancel where they laid him some 600 years ago. He is shown in armour, his two wives on either side, holding the hand of the one on his right. And he it was who owned so many ships and sailed so many seas that it was said of him:

> Blow the wind high, blow the wind low,
> It bloweth good in Hawley's Hoe.

Carry on and you come to the charming fishing port of Salcombe, with the town of Kingsbridge hovering above it like a golden eagle poised on a mountain crag. I came to Salcombe and Kingsbridge for the first time in 1975, following the death of my mother, at the beginning of my drinking career, with my best friend from school, Christine, who was heavily pregnant with my goddaughter, and I always remember – and I don't know why I obtained such consolation from it – the little verse on a plaque outside the priest's doorway in the church at Kingsbridge which reads:

> Here I lie at the Chancel door,
> Here I lie because I'm poor,
> The further in the more you'll pay
> Here lie I as warm as they.

Keep going on and you come at last to the great haven of Plymouth, great in so many senses. On Plymouth Hoe there stands the only memorial anywhere to the most remarkable sailor who ever lived in England, Sir Francis Drake. It is difficult now to understand the power that Drake held over the sailing community, of Devon in particular and of the British Isles in general. He was a man who broke the power of Spain almost single-handed. He hated Spain with an intensity that is almost impossible to imagine. The Spanish had broken their word to naval explorer John Hawkins when he spared the Spanish treasure fleet by attacking Drake's ships; he and his companions very nearly died, but Drake managed to limp home to the West Country. Many others were tortured and did die. Drake went back in revenge and captured the Spanish treasure fleet, which carried immeasurable wealth, and brought the rewards back to England and to Elizabeth I who was always glad of a bit of extra money.

Then he set off on his circumnavigation of the world in 1577. He was not the first man to do it, as Magellan had already done it, but he was certainly the first Englishman to sail into the Pacific and to carry on going despite every danger and eventuality. When he went through the Straits of Magellan he would have seen the gallows that Magellan had set up to hang his would-be mutineers; Drake very nearly had the same problem with his men who wanted to turn back. However, he persevered, and in a year returned once again to Plymouth laden with gold, the ship falling apart from the ravages of the worm. When news spread that his little flotilla had been sighted, all the churches emptied and the people flocked to Plymouth Hoe. The *Golden Hind* was taken up the Thames to Deptford, where Elizabeth went on board and knighted him, and he then returned to Devon. It was not terribly long afterwards that Philip of Spain brought his great Armada to land on English shores and to invade the country. In my day every schoolchild knew that the might of the Armada was defeated by the smaller and unprepared English fleet, which sent fire-ships in among the bigger galleons and set them alight. The weather, of course, helped. The weather as we all know is always on the side of the English. That is why we spend so much time talking about it, no doubt.

Many expeditions set sail from Plymouth, the most famous, especially if you are an American, being the voyage of the *Mayflower*, which took the Pilgrim Fathers to America. Where they landed is known as Plymouth Rock. I spoke in a debate once on the motion 'This house wishes that the Plymouth Rock had landed on the Pilgrim Fathers'. One forgets that Captain Cook also set sail from Plymouth on his way to discover Australia. Even before the Romans established their tin mines, Plymouth was a port trading with the Phoenicians, and it may have been that some Phoenician, casting aside the contents of his luncheon, was responsible for the establishment of elephant garlic which grows wild in the West Country and is native to England.

In the Plymouth Guildhall there is a series of fourteen stained-glass windows which shows the whole story of Plymouth better than anything really. There is the Black Prince embarking with his followers for Poitiers on a quaint little ship, the *Breton*. There is a window depicting the attack on the town by the Bretons in 1403, where they burned 600 houses before being driven off. The Drake window curiously illustrates Drake bringing water to Plymouth, and workmen are seen opening the water hatch, while in the distance is the waterwheel of one of Drake's mills, and of course Drake is there in his mayor's robes surrounded by the town officials. The Armada window shows the famous game of bowls and Drake's wonderful remark when the Armada was sighted that there was still time to finish his game of bowls and defeat the Armada. The Raleigh window depicts Sir Walter Raleigh being arrested, worn and broken, and carted off to die in the Tower for his failure in the Americas. There is the pottery window in memory of William Cookworthy, the first maker of porcelain in England and the founder of the china clay industry that is so important to the West Country. A very unusual window called the Opening Window portrays Edward VII in a frock coat and morning dress with a top hat. There is the Catherine of Aragon window where she is arriving as a young bride to Prince Arthur, Henry VIII's elder brother. A William window represents the landing of William of Orange at Torbay; the Pilgrim window illustrates the departure of the Pilgrim Fathers; the Siege window shows the siege in the Civil War and the battle in Freedom Field, the trained arms of the town advancing to meet the Cavaliers; and the Napoleon window shows Napoleon on *Bellepheron*.

Of course there is also the memorial to another of Devon's sons, Robert Falcon Scott. Given that Amundsen made it to the South Pole as if he were taking a stroll in the park, it is perhaps only the English who would make such a hero out of Scott. Walt Whitman wrote: 'Did we think victory great? . . . Now it seems to me . . . that defeat is great.' Certainly the Scott expedition was a testament to courage, faith and devotion and failure from a lack of organisation, but given that it was the eve of the First World War and England badly needed a hero, Scott came in very handy.

It is also from Plymouth that John Hawkins started the slave trade to the West Indies travelling with his cousin Sir Francis

Drake. He enslaved up to 1,400 Negroes, carrying them into bondage and selling the best of them at £160 a head. When eventually he received a grant of arms from Elizabeth I, he included in it a kneeling Negro in chains – so another first for Plymouth.

The huge stretch of Tor Bay is known for its sea bass fishing. Historically, a lad would be placed on the headland overlooking the bay and when he saw the shoals coming into the bay he would signal and wave and the boats would put out their nets and set off in the right direction. I have been bass fishing in the bay, and certainly it is very good fishing although, of course, nowadays, with the aid of the various radar devices that allow you to see where the fish are, it is a much more secure industry.

Travel north-west into the heart of Devon and you will come to the magnificence that is Dartmoor. The horror stories that have been written about Dartmoor, such as *The Hound of the Baskervilles*, are all perfectly believable when you get on to the excesses of the moor. When I stayed at Topsham I used to go to Chagford, which is a peaceful little town at the foot of the moor, and go to the hotel there where, in those days, Shaun Hill was the chef, in order to eat his beautiful food. Shaun Hill is to my mind the finest chef in the country. Single-handedly he turned Ludlow into a food town and now is to be found at the Walnut Tree in the Brecon Beacons, but in those days I would save all my pennies and go to the moor. Dartmoor is a splendour of towering rock structures and high tors and not somewhere you would want to get lost in the dark. In the heart of it stands Dartmoor Prison, which must be an alarming place indeed for those prisoners who are taken to it from the sink estates of London. I once had a brother-in-law who was incarcerated there for various felonies; he enjoyed being there. He ran the library and I think he found the peace and tranquillity of the moor quite enlivening. However, he said that when the mists came down those prisoners who wanted to escape would look out and know that if they tried their chances of making it were slight. They would get lost on the moor with the klaxons blaring to announce that somebody had escaped and eventually they would be rather grateful to be picked up. It is probably the toughest prison in the country and manages to cow even the hardest prisoners.

North of the moor is lush Devon farmland, good hunting country, with little fields to make it interesting.

Cornwall

Travelling into Cornwall is to enter a different country. Cornwall is almost completely cut off from the rest of England by the River Tamar, which rises in the north of the county near Launceston and flows into the southern coast at Plymouth or Saltash on the Cornish side. The Tamar was a very successful salmon river until the foot and mouth outbreak of the 1960s led to the farmers ploughing up the old pasturage on the fields on the slopes above the river. Subsequent soil slippage into the river has caused the Tamar at times to appear an almost chocolate-brown colour. This silted up the breeding beds for the salmon and led to a decline in salmon stocks. That excellent institution, the Westcountry Rivers Trust, persuaded farmers to give up part of their flat land nearest the river so that it could be used as a filter for escaping soil, which has done much to address this problem. That and the efforts to prevent netting at the river mouth and on the coast have helped, but it is still not restored to anything like its former glory.

The name of the Tamar is of Celtic origin and means darkly flowing, and is the same derivation as that of the River Thames on the far side of the country. Until the opening of Isambard Kingdom Brunel's Royal Albert Bridge across the Tamar in 1859 by Prince Albert, after whom the railway bridge was named, the only way you could get into Cornwall except by boat was to go to the very north of the county and cross over there. The bridge, which was started in 1854 and finished in 1859, is 2,187½ feet in length and is an amazing wrought-iron construction. An interesting medical statistic for the early 1800s shows that Cornwall had the highest proportion of insanity of any county in the British Isles, which was attributed to genetic inbreeding as a result of its isolation.

Cornwall is another county that has the feeling of being old. At various times in its history it has been one of the wealthiest areas of the British Isles. The Phoenicians came here to trade tin and its mineral wealth was one of the main reasons for the Roman invasion of Britain. My mother's father's family were of Cornish origin, having gone out to Australia for the mining. A Cornish friend of mine once said that the Cornish character has been dictated by the fact that tin seams are notoriously unpredictable, so that one day you will be trucking away quite happily on a wealthy seam and the next day the seam would drop without any warning to some enormous depth. You would have no idea where it had gone to and so you went from riches to struggling near-poverty almost overnight. There is no doubt in my mind that there is a strong pragmatic streak of survival in the Cornish nature, whether it is following the tin seams or the tourists.

Cornwall has beautiful light, which inspires so many artists to go and join the St Ives school and explore its 300 miles of coast-line. The north and south coasts of Cornwall are very different, with the south focusing on shipping and fishing and nautical activities, while the much starker, more dangerous, north coast is given over to mining and, nowadays, to the surfing beaches where the Atlantic rollers provide a great playground for such sport. The county is in fact an isthmus, very nearly an island, and is 50 per cent fuller during holiday times than it is for the rest of the year, with tourists flocking into Cornwall to enjoy its clotted cream, its hog's pudding and its Cornish pasties. People will be jumping up and down in Devon because I didn't mention cream teas in their county and of course clotted cream is common to both, but from my own experience in recent years, it isn't easy to find a cream tea in Devon. But when I was young every little farmhouse offered cream teas in their garden almost everywhere you went. In Cornwall, however, financial pragmatism makes sure that cream teas are widely available. Hog's pudding is a white pudding with groats, which are crushed oats, in the mix, and very good it is indeed, and readily found on breakfast menus in Cornwall.

The pasty is of course designed to be a portable food taken down a tin mine, and there is a theory that the nature of the pastry is such that you could actually drop it from the top of the mine wrapped in a cloth and it wouldn't shatter. This must have been a lot tougher than any I have ever made. My Cornish pasty recipe was given to me by a Cornish Druid called Jack Treleaven, who taught me criminal law in London. What is almost certainly true is that the thick roll of pastry round the upper edge was designed for the worker to hold while eating the pasty; it would get dirty from the grime on his hands so he wouldn't want to eat that and he could just throw it away. Which is why I say to you, if you complain about that thick ridge of pastry, remember it is not actually there to be eaten, but goes back to the medieval idea of pastry being a cooking pot rather than, necessarily, an edible substance. The great delight to me is that a true Cornish pasty does not contain carrots, although try telling the commercial manufacturers that. I have an intense dislike for the carrot. The reason for them not being in the recipe is in fact quite genuine. The carrot fly flies all the year round in Cornwall and you do not have the gap that comes between the first hatching and the second that you get in the rest of England, so that the Cornish have never traditionally grown carrots.

Falmouth, with its adjacent Carrick Roads, is the third deepest natural harbour in the world and facing as it does towards both Europe and the Atlantic, is therefore easily accessible to trade with the Americas and the West Indies. It was one of the most successful ports of the country until a Cornishman called Richard Trevithick, focusing on the tin mining industry, invented the steam pump, which really kick-started the Industrial Revolution. This meant eventually that shipping was not subject to the prevailing winds and could sail straight on to London and that railway trains could carry produce that was unloaded in Falmouth up country. Should you go to Falmouth you should be able to see the *Curlew*, the last remaining, I think, quay punt. These little punts were lighters specifically built for unloading cargo from the ships that put into port. They are immensely stable and quick because the first to the job would get the work. They are so stable that the *Curlew* was actually sailed to Antarctica by the couple who had restored it and sailed all over the world, although it was eventually brought back on a transport.

A few years ago I opened the Falmouth Oyster Festival. The Falmouth oyster is a native oyster and therefore only to be eaten when there is an 'R' in the month, because May, June, July and August are the months when they breed. The festival took place in October and was a great pleasure. I was taken across by boat from St Mawes, where I stayed at the Tresanton Hotel. When I was young the Tresanton was a family holiday hotel, where we used to take great delight in going back and forth on the St Mawes ferry. It has become a designer hotel now, very elegantly presented with lavish furnishings and smart food, rather than sandy wellingtons and buckets and spades in the hall. St Mawes stands on the western tip of the Roseland peninsula. The word Roseland comes from the ancient Celtic 'rhos' meaning green and lush, while St Mawe was an ancient Celtic saint not heard of elsewhere. That is not difficult in Cornwall because the county has, I think, 362 saints that are not found anywhere else. It is believed that when Christianity came to Cornwall, one of the arguments against it was that the members of the ruling household automatically become demi-gods on their deaths, so the Church cut a deal whereby they became saints instead. No doubt that was at a time when the Church still argued that any Christian was automatically a saint by being a member of that particular religion. Certainly you get some very strange saints such as St Winwaloe and St Gunwalloe, as well as an awful lot more.

My favourite hotel anywhere outside London is the Nare at Veryan in Roseland. Some years ago now I was sitting at the Royal Cornwall Show when a nice young man with a healthy crop of blond hair came up and introduced himself and gave me his card which showed a picture of the hotel set back from the most beautiful white beach. He said, 'Something that might recommend me to you is that I said no to the Blairs.' Apparently they had tried to go and stay there and first of all the secretary rang, then Tony Blair himself rang, and Toby Ashworth, the young man in question, when asked when he might have room said, 'For you, Mr Blair – never!' I was so delighted by the story that I determined to go and stay there and I have done so regularly ever since. I have never had cause to regret it.

One of the delightful places on the Roseland peninsula is St Just, and particularly its church, where the local inhabitants, believing that the dead would all rise on the last day together in some form of corporeal re-embodiment, are buried in families lying on top of each other. The result is that the churchyard has been built right up and the church nestles in the dip below it. You can be buried there by the water because the church is down at the harbour bar. It is all very peaceful and one thinks that one would quite like to lie in rest waiting for the resurrection there. I, and the friend I visit with, will often go to St Mawes and pick up an excellent pasty just by the ferry and then go down to the bar and park on the hard-standing to eat them and enjoy the view. It is altogether a very lovely place to visit.

The best way out of the Roseland to get to Truro is to my mind to go across on the King Harry ferry, which is something I have loved doing all the days of my life. It is a chain ferry and it clunks backwards and forwards across the river there, causing sailing boats and even china clay ships, quite large ones, to have to wait for its passage. The river and all its surrounding creeks were the gathering point for the landing craft for the D-Day invasion, and the Cornish smugglers of former years could have told them that the creeks are very all-concealing and it would have been difficult for the Germans to spot them even if they had had an inkling of where they were starting from.

On the far side of Truro, which is a pleasant town with some good shops and a Victorian cathedral, you will drop down to Restronguet Creek. I once nearly bought a cottage along the headland from this but, fortunately, as it was in my drinking days, I did not because you have to turn very sharply right to avoid going into the river down what is, I think, the steepest hill in Cornwall. The Pandora Inn is worth a visit, if only to see the large model of the sailing vessel of that name which was constructed by the landlord who was the man sent to try to find the *Bounty* mutineers and bring them back to justice under the command of Captain William Bligh himself, which must have been something of a nightmare. Incidentally, naval records show that far from Bligh being a flogging tyrant, he was among the most moderate of the captains of the day, and this was considered a weakness by his crew so he was someone to be taken advantage of. He was the most fantastic navigator and had been Captain Cook's sailing master and was in turn the man who took the ships up the Quebec River so that Wolfe could storm the Heights of Abraham. When he was put off the *Bounty* in an open boat with nothing but a compass, some food and water, and brought those who had chosen to go with him safe to land, having navigated his way across 400 miles of open ocean, it was the most amazing feat of navigation. The captain of the *Pandora* failed to find the missing mutineers and was brought back, and Bligh demanded that he be kicked out of the navy for his failure. He returned to his native Cornwall and opened the pub. Another interesting thing about the Pandora Inn is that at the high spring and autumn tides the lower bar, in my day, was under water, and you would stand around in your wellington boots drinking your beer.

If you head north-east to St Austell you will come to what is known as the Cornish Alps, great white towering mountains which are the slag heaps of the china clay works. Kaolin, or china clay, of very good quality, was discovered by Thomas Cookworthy in 1746, and the largest deposits of this material in the world are here. There is enough still remaining to last at least another one hundred years. Thomas Cookworthy started his own Plymouth porcelain company and began exporting the china clay not only to other potteries in the United Kingdom, but later abroad. At the industry's height they were mining 1 million tonnes of china clay a year, and for every one tonne dug you have five tonnes of spoil, which explains the towering slag heaps. Kaolin is also used in the finishing of good quality paper, and in fact these days more is used in the paper industry than in the china industry. When the sun is reflecting off their bright whiteness, the heaps make an amazing sight.

As you go north the land gets harsher and you come to the wildness of Bodmin Moor. Bodmin Moor houses Daphne du Maurier's famous creation *Jamaica Inn*, which is a story of smuggling and wrecking and all the evil practices that the pragmatic side of the Cornish nature led them to when things went wrong. It is up here in the north of Bodmin Moor that you find the town of St Breward, where the granite came from for building Tower Bridge in London and also Sydney Harbour Bridge. It is here that I find my direct ancestry on my mother's father's side, for Thomas Bathe was vicar here for over thirty years during the time of upheaval with Henry VIII and Mary I and Edward VI and Elizabeth I, and he survived the lot. I didn't know about this until I received, out of the blue, an email from a cousin of mine in Queensland, Australia, which is where my grandfather came from, telling me about this and sending me a copy of the work that had been done on constructing the family tree.

So the next time I was in Cornwall I went to St Breward and there, in this quiet, high church – I mean high above the moor as opposed to high Anglican – I found his name on the list of former rectors and, much to my surprise, I cried. My family on both sides, but especially on my mother's father's side, is so much a history of violence and alcohol and wildness (my mother's father died of the drink when she was two), and here I like to think that somewhere along the line it was not like that and that this man was a good parson. Then of course I thought, most likely as the real villain of *Jamaica Inn* is a smuggler and a wrecking parson of that date, how am I to know that he was a good man, but I like to think he was. We went back the next day to attend a service and, as we arrived at the church, the North Cornwall Hunt rode past on a hunt rite, it being the summer, and I stood outside the church and watched them and felt very much at peace.

St Breward is only about four miles from Padstow, where I go whenever I am in the area to make a pilgrimage to Rick Stein's restaurant. Padstow is very much the creation of Rick Stein, so much so that the rather more hostile natives call it Padstein, and there he has not only the restaurant but a cookery school, a fish and chip shop and a deli and all of them, rather remarkably in the career of a celebrity chef, are very successful; not only that but excellent to boot. One year when I was at the Royal Cornwall Show and the B & B I was staying in was four miles from Padstow, for three of the four nights I went to eat on my own at the restaurant, and not on any one of those nights, or on subsequent visits, have I ever been disappointed. It is Rick Stein's first wife, from whom he is divorced, who keeps it all going. He is not often there because he films in fairly remote parts of the world, and in any event his second wife, an Australian, encouraged him to open a restaurant in an area south of Sydney which

I gather is not quite so successful. Rick Stein started his television career the same year as Jennifer and I did and it is amazing that he is still going. In fact, so successful has Padstow become, and so attractive to the tourist trade, that it is virtually impossible even in mid-September to find a parking space. Fortunately, however, Rick has now opened a tapas bar and fish and chip shop in Falmouth. Not only is this a vitally necessary addition to a town not very blessed with places I would want to eat in anyway, but also it is by the quay where there is ample parking. The fish is all locally sourced and with adequate descriptions on the menu of where it comes from. There is a breeding programme for lobsters that has been set up in Cornwall to strip the eggs, rather as they do with trout or salmon and, when they are hatched, to return them to the area where they would have been born. I understand that this is entirely due to the demands made by Rick Stein's Padstow.

Leave Padstow and drive south along the north coast of the Cornish peninsula and you will see what a hard, stark and ruthless land it is in comparison to the south. All the way along you will see the remains of tin mines with their distinctive chimneys rising out of the granite. The tin is no longer commercially mined in Cornwall, although with the rising price of base metals who knows what may happen, but it was, as I have said, the dominant industry and export of the area from Phoenician times until the 1990s. The last mine to close was the South Crofty in 1998. Most of the mines have been given women's names over the centuries, I believe because of the fickle nature of a tin seam. This leads to some curious anomalies. My favourite one is called Bessie Beneath which refers to the mine rather than the local whore! Huge fortunes have been made out of tin and it was said that the home of the Godolphin family stood on a mountain of silver; this was not referring to the silver seam underneath, but to the fact that their entire fortune was based on this silvery metal. It was the

Godolphin Arabian that was one of the three sires from which all English thoroughbred racehorses are descended.

Keep going on through the tough granite landscape and you will come, eventually, to Land's End. I have to admit I have always found Land's End an enormous disappointment. One gets terribly excited about the idea, and thinks that it is going to be wonderful, but there is nothing very much in the way of entertainment in the Visitor Centre. All you know is that somewhere out there, stretching far away, is no longer the flat edge of the earth over which you might fall but simply America. I was at law school with the man who owned Land's End and who sold it, but unfortunately at the time I didn't realise that so there was never any opportunity to tell him quite how dull I thought it was.

We filmed the first *Two Fat Ladies* programme at Mevagissey in Cornwall. I wonder if any of you know that the streets of the City of London were once lit by Mevagissey pilchard oil and that Mevagissey had various tax breaks as a result of this provision. If you go to the town, in the basements of some of the houses, you can still see the old stone pilchard presses which are very like the old olive presses that you find in Italy. An enormous amount of oil comes out of a pilchard. Somebody asked me when I was writing this book what they did with all the detritus left over after the pressing. I can't imagine that there was an awful lot left but I suspect that the answer is fertiliser. On the first day we were unable to begin because we woke up to thick fog and the one thing you can't film in is fog. And neither can you record sound because the fog muffles and deadens it, and if you laid it over other material it would sound very strange. We were filming at a hotel in Mevagissey and there was nothing whatsoever we could do; it wasn't a kitchen day so we couldn't film in the kitchen and the scallops, an ingredient in one of Jennifer's recipes, had not in any event been brought down from Scotland.

So we were sent off to amuse ourselves by looking at the Lost Gardens of Heligan, which at that point had only just begun to be restored. Jennifer decided to go to sleep in the car – she didn't like walking much anyway – and I set off to look round the whole area. I have been back since then and they have done a magnificent job and it is quite fascinating, but even more interesting was my trip when it was in its very early days. They had just begun clearing back the vegetation that had grown up around the fern trees and clearing out the various houses, such as the pineapple house and the mushroom house, and you could see how the heating had worked because it had all been stripped back to basics. It really is worth a visit if you find yourself in Cornwall – unlike, in my view, the Eden Project, which is a rather strange creation where they try to grow everything in or around glass bubbles. Its main disadvantage to my mind is that it smells of cheap cooking fat from all the franchises that have been set up to feed the masses who go there. Heligan, on the other hand, has a very pleasant café.

When I was a child we used to go to Cornwall every Easter because my father, who was President of the St Mary's Hospital Rugby Society, would take a team down to Cornwall to play various Cornish clubs. We stayed at the Tregenna Castle Hotel, just outside Penzance which is not, I think, what it once was, but it was exciting and very nice for a small child. I was, like so many of my generation, brought up on the legends of the Arthurian Cycle and of course one of the places firmly connected to Arthur is Tintagel on the north Cornish coast, which was supposed to be Uther Pendragon's castle and where Arthur was born. It is also rumoured to be the place, where Merlin was born. I prefer to think of Arthur in the Somerset Levels but certainly Tintagel is an extraordinary and exciting place especially when you are young. It seems unlikely to me now that Arthur, who was busy fighting off the invading Saxons, would have placed himself quite so far away from any prospective battlefields. Even more so given the difficulties of getting in and out of Cornwall at the time, but it is nice to dream about such a great legendary hero and certainly I did at Tintagel when I was young.

There was also, I remember, among the monoliths that occur all over Cornwall, something called the Crickstone, which was a circular stone, and if you climbed through it nine times it was supposed to cure you of various ills such as scrofula and a bad back. As a small child it was quite easy to go in and out nine times and I didn't have a bad back then. I do now, but I don't think I'd manage to make it through once!

I have a great affection for Cornwall. I remember when I was twenty-one that I joined the Mebyon Kernow which is the political party in favour of Cornish independence. The last person living to speak Cornish as her first language was a woman called Dolly Pentreath, another great Cornish name. She died in 1777. What is it that they say? 'By Tree, Poll and Pen you will know the Cornishmen.' It must have been rather frustrating for her as she would have had no one else to converse with. When shooting *Clarissa and the Countryman* in Cornwall we filmed with the Devon and Cornwall Mink Hounds, who hunt for mink on the Tamar. It was a really happy programme. I am told that our use of my Kelly Kettle, which I had received for my fiftieth birthday as a present, actually saved the Kelly Kettle from extinction. A Kelly Kettle is a very useful thing to take on picnics because you can boil water very quickly, just by stuffing its base with newspaper or twigs, and make a fresh cup of tea, which is so much nicer than one from a Thermos flask.

ISLES OF SCILLY

At the end of Cornwall there is a series of lethal little islands called the Isles of Scilly. Today they are a visitors' centre for bird-watchers for birds flown in from the Atlantic, and a safe place for children to play because there are almost no cars on the islands. However, it was not always so tranquil. The Isles of Scilly have seen the destruction of so many ships over the centuries, from when Sir Cloudesley Shovell's flagship, returning with him on board, smashed on to the rocks here in 1707, to the last in the long line, the *Torrey Canyon* disaster in 1967, which polluted the Cornish coast with oil for quite a long time. Some people believe that, because this is the burial place of so many ancients, King Arthur was brought here, and this is the Island of Avalon referred to in the old stories. However, anybody who has stayed for any time on the Isles of Scilly will discover that 'where blows not rain nor hail nor any snow' is not a description of these islands. When I was staying there in Hell's Bay Hotel the storms were very impressive indeed.

Somerset

The name Somerset is believed to have come from the fact that during the winter the water meadows were flooded to produce fine pasture for the summer months and therefore most of the county was only really accessible in summer. On the matter of Arthur, I consider it far more likely that the island valley of Avalon is the water meadows of Somerset. I believe, along with Mortimer Wheeler, who excavated the site back in the 1950s, that if Camelot was anywhere it was most likely to be at South Cadbury. The area abounds with hill forts and earthworks, and South Cadbury is the largest of these. Excavations show the bones of dead Celts who presumably died fighting the Saxons and also show the remains of a Roman pay chest containing 20,000 coins, probably left behind when the Romans departed, because if Arthur existed it would be at that period. The novelist Bernard Cornwell had cast Queen Guinevere as a priestess of the old religion, from before Christianity, which was of course a matriarchal religion, and so she took Sir Lancelot to her bed because Arthur was unable to father a child on her. It's a nice argument, and he gives the reason why Arthur does not appear in the monastic chronicles as because he was a pagan and never joined the Christians. Certainly there is no doubt that the old religion persists in this part of the world, and of course within sight of Cadbury Hill is Glastonbury Tor, a place of pre-Christian worship.

The Somerset Levels, which occupy the area I am referring to, between the Quantock and the Mendip Hills, are famous for their elver runs. Elvers are baby eels. In the early seventeenth century, a woman was burned as a witch because the witch finder, who came from another county, saw her with a bucket of water which she had over a fire. She was dipping her ladle into it and pulling out little fish. These were the elvers which are quite transparent when alive. Since the licensing of elver fishing there has been a huge eruption of poaching on the Levels. Legal fishermen use a hand-held net which they are allowed to dip into the water and take elvers. Poachers go out before the tide turns and place static nets in the mud which then fill with, in some instances, as much as thirty-three pounds of elvers on a single tide, to a value of approximately £3,000. Elvers are not much eaten in England, and so the bulk of those caught are either shipped to Spain and Italy for eating or sold live to such areas as Lough Neagh in Northern Ireland. Here they are released into the water system and grow to maturity and are then caught either by fishermen on the lough or by the eel traps that mark the entrance to the lough. The poachers go out in gangs and I believe that the fights that erupt, territorially, between the gangs are very bloody indeed. Eels breed only in the Sargasso Sea near Bermuda; they migrate from wherever they have reached maturity back to the Sargasso Sea, to the great hanging weed pads; in their turn the elvers set off on their huge journey across the ocean to return to the rivers where their parents lived before them. The elver migration up the Bristol Channel and the River Severn and into all the little rivers of the Levels is one of the largest, although in recent years for a variety of reasons eel stocks have dropped by as much as 95 per cent.

If the Severn and its tributaries are the domain of the Sargasso eel, then the Bristol Channel used to be the kingdom of the conger eel and, like Cornwall, Somerset made large sums of money selling dried conger eel to the Continent for use during days of abstinence and Lent. Because the tides on the Bristol Channel have an unusually high rise and fall, the congers would lie up in the little rock hollows along the shoreline when the tide went right out and they just waited for it to come back in again, there being enough moisture to keep them alive during the turns of the tide. One of the ways of catching the eel at low tide used to be with terriers. This practice, called glatting, was not only entertainment for the fishermen but also very effective. The terrier flushes the eel out of its rock space and the eel then sets off at full pelt towards the sea, with everybody chasing after it, and it is caught and killed.

When we were filming *Clarissa and the Countryman*, we were determined to film this as part of the programme. We had to persuade the BBC to film terriers at work and Johnny succeeded in finding the last man in England who still did this, hunting along the shoreline with his collie. Tug, Johnny's terrier, had probably never been on a beach and had certainly never seen a conger eel before but, being a very good and natural terrier, on seeing the conger eel lying in its niche he grabbed hold of its tail and pulled. The conger eel did in fact shoot out, but Tug was rather too quick for it and, grabbing it like a rat, killed it stone dead on the spot. What the BBC did not film is Tug happily sitting there eating its head while I barbecued the rest of it on the beach! It is a very good meat to barbecue, and in fact it's a very good meat all round, but in this country it seems that only the West Indians or those of Afro-Caribbean stock eat it. The fishing of conger eels along the edge of the Bristol Channel is much reduced now, because again the ploughing up of the old pasture-land after the foot and mouth epidemic in the 1960s led to the little cavities in which the eels hung out being filled up with silt.

The most famous food product to come out of Somerset is of course Cheddar cheese. If only the inhabitants of the area had been able to register Cheddar to its local origins, rather like the French did in Champagne or we did in Melton Mowbray with the pies and Stilton, then the heritage of this famous cheese, which is now made all over the world but none better than in Cheddar itself, would have been maintained. The centre of the cheese industry now is based around Shepton Mallet, which ironically has a name derived from 'sheep town', and Cheddar is made with cow's milk, but real proper mature Cheddar cheese as dreamed of by Ben Gunn in *Treasure Island* is a wonderful ingredient. Cheddar cheese, as I have said, is now made everywhere, and I was delighted to discover that the couple who started Isle of Mull Cheddar, a very good cheese actually, made their way to that part of the world as hippies from Somerset. Being native to Somerset, the only skill they really knew was how to make cheese. They started hand-making it in a bucket and now it is produced on a much larger scale but still by hand.

Connected with the cheese industry and totally worth seeing in its own right is the Cheddar Gorge. Water and wind have cut away the rocks into a fantastic gorge; the only trouble is that you have to get up very early on a summer's morning to get the real feel of it before all the tourists arrive. Man has lived in these caves since the Stone Age and an enormous amount of archaeological artefacts have been found there. The caves are the property of the Marquess of Bath, and over the centuries various enlargements have been made so that you could enter into the caves more easily, and very impressive they are. They would have made a safe place to live, if perhaps a rather damp one, as there is the constant sound of running water. One of the most curious of the remains, found at the beginning of the twentieth century, was of a Stone Age man who had become encased inside a stalagmite.

In Somerset, as in North Devon, people hunt the red stag; there are the Quantock Staghounds and the Devon and Somerset Staghounds who hunt on Exmoor. Stag hunting is the oldest of our hunting traditions and it is bathed in history. The Harbourer goes out and watches the deer on a constant basis. Before a hunt, he brings the fewmets or faeces of what he considers a suitable stag, or indeed hind if it is the hind season, and shows them to the Master. When it is agreed, they send in two tufters, who are older, wiser hounds, to flush out the deer. The deer is flushed, the tufters are leashed and the younger hounds are set after it until it turns at bay, not because it was run to exhaustion, but simply because that is what stags do. At this point the huntsmen would shoot it with a bow and arrow, or cut its throat; nowadays it is shot with a humane killer pistol. Those who disapprove of stag hunting have never done it. Not only is it, as is all hunting, an exciting experience, but it is also very well organised and you have to be incredibly fit. Going up and down the steep coombs of Exmoor, or indeed Quantocks, you really need a horse that is designed for the job. I have never followed staghounds on a horse but I was taken out by the chairman of the Devon and Somerset and we followed in his old Volvo and he, having hunted all his life on the moor, knew where to position us so that we got the best view of events. The stag is taken away and eaten and the umbles, which are the innards of the stag and which used to be the perk of the huntsman, are now given to the hounds, with the exception of the liver and the kidneys.

When Johnny and I were writing our *Game Cookbook*, I thought it would be nice to have a recipe to honour the fact that he always wrote in every book he signed 'Bollocks to Blair', so I devised a recipe for roe deer testicles with a green peppercorn sauce. Testicles, known in France as white kidneys or *rognons blancs*, are very good eating but even I would be slightly anxious about eating the testicles of the much stronger flavoured red deer. However, I did meet a couple up on Exmoor who had collected sufficient testicles from the huntsmen to provide for their engagement breakfast. I asked them what the dish was like when made with red deer appendages and they smiled sweetly and said they weren't getting divorced any time soon and you only had one engagement party! Stag hunting, which still continues within the law, brings in a large and very welcome income to the hotels and livery stables of the area during a time when tourists are rather scarce. Quite honestly, the hunting community spends its money rather more lavishly than the rambler or the birdwatcher. I say this advisedly, not because I'm pro-hunting, which I am as everybody knows, but because I have spent much of my lifetime in the catering industry.

In the south of the county lies Glastonbury, which is an ancient and magical place. Long before Joseph of Arimathea, the man who buried Christ, there was a famous settlement of priestesses of the old religion, and people would come to consult the Oracle there. The legend goes that Joseph of Arimathea came to bring the teachings of Christ from Galilee to the Britons and he thrust his stave into the ground on Wirral Hill where it burst into bloom. The thorn that still flowers at Glastonbury is said to be a direct descendant of this. Joseph is supposed to have buried the Holy Grail on Glastonbury Tor, where he built a church of wattle and daub, and now there stand at Glastonbury the ruins of a noble Norman abbey. Glastonbury is known as Avalon the Isle of the Blessed. It is believed that Arthur lies here, as do the bones of St Patrick, as indeed do those of Joseph of Arimathea, although of course these are only old legends. The abbey that was set up under a charter of King Ine, long before Arthur, was really begun by Dunstan over 1,000 years ago. He was a local boy who rose to be the most powerful man in England and Archbishop of Canterbury. He was only twenty-one years of age when King Edmund charged him with the building of Glastonbury Abbey. The story goes that King Edmund, a Saxon king, was hunting his hounds along the cliffs here when his horse nearly went over the edge and he felt himself being pulled backward, as if by the grip of an invisible hand, and so that is why he appointed Dunstan to become Abbot of Glastonbury and enlarged the abbey here.

Nowadays, when people hear the name Glastonbury, their minds are immediately carried to the pop festival that is held here annually. Every year we see on our television screens young people, and the not so young, floundering about in the mud listening to famous groups and bands. The festival has got very

large and the farmer who started it has made a small fortune out
of it. Nowadays it is not just the young or the hippies but the
great and the good who attend. Recently a Member of
Parliament was found dead in the toilets. I have never been
attracted to large crowds wallowing under the smoke of mari-
juana and altered by other class B drugs; when I went to
Glastonbury it was where you went to see the beautiful medieval buildings, St Joseph's thorn and to climb the Tor for the
view. Visit when it is not the festival or the school holidays and
it still remains a wonderful place.

Somerset forms a crescent shape, from Devon in the south
with the Bristol Channel and the mouth of the Severn border-
ing one flank of it, and the counties of Devon, Dorset, Wiltshire
and Gloucestershire surrounding it. At its heart lies the cathedral city of Wells, which has another magnificent Norman
cathedral. I remember going there as a child to watch the swans
that swim in the moat ringing the bell in order to be fed. It is
a peaceful and lovely place with glorious architecture and carvings. Keep going to the north-east and up on the Wiltshire/
Gloucestershire border you will come to what is probably the
pride of Somerset, the town of Bath. Bath is endowed with
natural hot springs that come out of the ground. This must
have delighted the ancient Romans who built there and called
it Aquae Sulis, probably the most splendid of all Roman cities
in England, and with no parallel on this side of the Alps. There
was a temple, a forum, immense baths and fine houses. After
400 years the Romans left and at the end of the sixth century
the Saxons, with their passion for religious buildings, founded
an abbey at Bath. Roman Bath was buried and eventually the
Norman abbey fell into ruins, until it was rebuilt at the end of
the fifteenth century.

It was not until the eighteenth century that a Cornishman
called Ralph Allen, who had made a fortune out of the Post
Office by carrying mail, decided to buy stone quarries and made

another fortune supplying Bath stone for what we think of as Georgian Bath. The workmen came upon Saxon coffins and, as they removed them to bring them out to the light, hot springs came gushing out from the Roman masonry. It is almost unbelievable that nothing had been done for many hundreds of years in Bath. Gradually the remains of the Roman city began to be unearthed, with the most fantastic Roman treasures. The Roman baths are filled with hot water coming into them straight from the ground. One of the baths has a floor that is sixty feet long and half as wide with a platform running all the way round it. There are six steps down into the water with recesses for the patrons to recline in around the sides of the pool. The water still runs away down the original culvert. Lead, which the Romans mined in the Mendip Hills, was used a great deal, and set all around the baths are magnificent Roman carvings showing the seasons of the year and busts of various gods and goddesses as well as ordinary people. Among all those magnificent carvings there was found in the rubble a nest with an intact egg of either a coot or a teal which had obviously been frightened off its nest before the egg was hatched. It is a memory of the years when the city lay as a wilderness.

When Georgian Bath built the Grand Pump Room and the fashionable Assembly Rooms, the Roman baths still lay uncovered, because it wasn't until 1869 that a proper survey of the ruins was carried out and the great baths were discovered. Bath became the fashionable assembly point for the rich who were suffering from the diseases of Georgian excess. The hot springs were obviously good for the treatment of rheumatism, but more commonly the people came to drink the waters for their gout and to give their livers a rest. The arbiter of fashion for Georgian Bath was Beau Nash, and you look up at the top of the hill to the exquisite Royal Crescent which is for ever connected with his vision. The life of Regency Bath is well described by Jane Austen and everybody came here: Clive of India, Oliver

Goldsmith, Fanny Burney, Mrs Thrale, Jane herself of course, Mrs Siddons the actress, even David Livingstone, the African explorer, and so many others. As some Victorian wrote: 'These rooms are filled no more with the wastrels, half-wits, gamblers, drunkards and simpering Misses who kowtow to Beau Nash and his successor, but who would not be thankful for the chance of seeing the elegant throngs of decent people massing through these rooms and the Pump Room down below.' I go most years to Bath, not to drink the waters, but to record books for the BBC, and when my busy working day is finished I can go and promenade the streets of the city, less elegantly but as enthusiastically as any Georgian.

Somerset remains very much a rural county and, not far from the delights of Bath, you will find the permanent showground of the Bath and West Show, a big agricultural show held every summer, and one where it is guaranteed to rain on at least one day. The last time I was there I was delighted to be able to witness an amazing feat. The SolaRolas are a group of paraplegics led by Annie Maw, who had broken her back hunting when Master of the Mendip Farmers. They travelled by solar-powered vehicles, provided by a remarkable man called Malcolm Moss, from the Houses of Parliament, where we all saw them off, to the Bath and West Show. It would have been a great achievement for people fully in possession of all their physical faculties, but they had to contend with terrible weather and yet they made it. It really was the most moving event and raised money for disabled charities.

Fortunately they did not arrive on the day of what was known as the Bath Tsunami, where six inches of rain fell in twenty minutes, completely blocking all the drains into the showground, so that it took everybody an enormous amount of time to get out of the showground at the end of the day. The following day the Health and Safety people, completely oblivious, it seemed to me, that perhaps they should have been checking the drains before the show, were going round bullying people in their normal manner. I went to buy a pair of waterproof trousers from a stall holder who just had a little stall with a grass floor. This had become a puddle and he was putting down straw in order to soak it up so that people could actually stand in his stall to look at his goods when the Health and Safety people appeared. 'You can't do that,' they said, 'you're creating a fire hazard.' He looked at them in amazement and then, whipping out a petrol cigarette lighter from his pocket, he said, 'A thousand pounds to anyone who can succeed in setting fire to that straw.' I think they would probably have nicked him but for the fact that I was standing there, roaring with laughter, and most people know who I am. I said, 'That's my column for the week, gentlemen,' then, turning to the Health and Safety officers, asked, 'Can I have your names please?' at which point they made a hurried escape. It was a fine show with a very good food tent of local produce, as well as some from surrounding counties.

If we leave the county by Bath in a northerly direction we will find ourselves in Gloucestershire.

Gloucestershire

When I was young I used to go frequently to Gloucestershire with my mother who had a lot of friends there. My recollections of it are lots of sheep, beautiful stone walls and large houses full of excellent Georgian furniture and old paintings of horses brown with aged varnish. The people who lived in these houses spent most of their time outdoors either racing or hunting or in the stables and saw very little need to install central heating in their houses. There was a range in the kitchen and a fire in the library and one used to run between the two and dread having a bath because there was never enough hot water and the bathroom was always freezing. The houses were rather scruffy round the edges and full of riding boots and crops and so forth, but the stable yards and the horse boxes were always immaculate. My mother spent many happy hours leaning on posts and rails and looking into the paddocks with friends and discussing the potential of the mares and their foals and what stallion they should go to next and other such lovely horsey things. I think it was Sellar and Yeatman who said that the art of riding was talking about the horse when off it. This wasn't true in this case because everybody hunted and point-to-pointed and the young men were very dashing.

The Cotswolds were full of villages of beautiful golden local stone with delightful vistas, the fields cropped to the smoothness of a croquet lawn by centuries of sheep. Today the sheep are pretty well gone and the dry stone walls are covered in brambles and breaking down in places. The children of my mother's friends have, in a lot of instances, sold the large cold houses and moved into something warmer, but there is still a huge horse culture in Gloucestershire. The large houses are now occupied by people with an awful lot of money to spend, most of it, it seems to me, on interior designers. They are all very comfortable with too many scatter cushions but with excellent central heating and it is not really much of a place for me any more.

Nonetheless, racing and hunting are still very much the rage in Gloucestershire, supplemented by polo, as to be found in the pages of a Jilly Cooper novel. Rather curiously I owe my life to hunting in Gloucestershire because, just after the Second World War, a Master of Hounds, who had had a very good war, came back to spend the rest of his days hunting and drinking. He had an enabling wife and an even more enabling butler and a lot of money, so really he had no incentive to change his lifestyle until he had a nasty shock. He woke up one morning and could not remember the names of his hounds. This so shook him that he went to America to find out about Alcoholics Anonymous which had started there but thirteen years before, and he and a friend of his, an Irish peer, brought it back to England and set up the first ever AA meeting. This was held in the ballroom of the Grosvenor House Hotel in May 1947, which was about a month before I was born; you can see a little plaque there by one of the windows. The only paper at the time that would take their advertisement was the *Financial Times*, but like Topsy 'it just growed'. So forty years later it was there for me when I needed it. I have always felt very kindly disposed to the North Cotswold Hunt for a lot of reasons, but in particular for that.

Many years later I went to talk in Gloucestershire on behalf of a friend of mine who had just become the High Sheriff. She was a great hunting girl so I assumed that I would be addressing the hunt. I would be talking before lunch, as sometimes happens, and I was nearly late in getting there, and so without time for any prior chat I stood up and spoke; it was only when I sat down and looked at the menu that I realised that I was actually talking to the Association of North Cotswold Churches. I leapt back to my feet and apologised if I had offended anybody but they should be grateful because I knew considerably more about hunting than I did about North Cotswold churches. This caused much mirth and I think they were quite happy with my speech anyway.

At the hub of racing culture is of course Cheltenham, known nowadays as the home of steeplechasing. There is no doubt that the March meeting contains the very best you can expect from both amateur and professional racing, with the Cheltenham Gold Cup at its heart, the Champion Hurdle and the Foxhunter Chase, the most important ride for amateurs in the country. When I was in my early teens I used to go with my mother to Cheltenham. In those days there was no television in the bars and I wasn't allowed in them anyway because I was under age. My mother was magnificent in her beaver skin coat, which she wore to go racing and which was so heavy it would stand up on its own. It was so warm, as I came to know later, that really the chilliest wind off Cleeve Hill could not penetrate it. She would give me her binoculars and say, 'There you are, Clarissa, go and stand outside and come and call me when you see the horses appear over the brow of the hill.' I can remember standing there with snow reflecting off the hill, my hands so cold I could barely hold the binoculars, and the snow blowing into them so that I could barely see, waiting for the greasy excitement and anticipation of the first sight of the horses. I would then nip inside into the warmth and say, 'Ma, they're coming,' and she and all her friends and everybody else would flock outside to watch the horses come down the hill and go through to the finish. I would lurk inside the door of the bar, hoping that nobody would notice me, and try to thaw out. A tweed coat, however thick, didn't have quite the same effect as furs.

In those days it was a meeting where all the English people knew each other and that bonhomie was supplemented by the infusion of the Irish who came across in great numbers, as they still do, to cheer on their champions, and in those days you would get amazing stories about the Irish horses. Horses such as Arkle or Flying Bolt, the first of which was rumoured to be the result of an accident where a stallion had jumped the fence, and the second of which was found in the back hills in a field in western Ireland. Cheltenham remained a delight to me into my thirties, when the races were my last outing with my dear Clive, and really it was the last thing we did together before he went into hospital with the viral infection that took his life. He had been told to go in the week before, but there was no way he was going to miss Cheltenham, and very possibly he knew that his days were numbered. By that time in 1982 there was already the beginning of the plethora of hospitality tents, and I remember that we had an invitation to a Christie's tent and would go there to thaw out. It had become much more crowded and harder to get from the paddock to the rails to watch the race, but it was still possible. People were starting to stay in the hospitality tents and watch the races on the television screens, which made me wonder why one would bother to attend, but the journey down on the train was still full of like-minded people exchanging impossible tips.

There is a lovely story of when Clive was in the stands, next to an elderly Irish priest, and he had put rather a large sum of money on the horse that he favoured. His horse and the priest's were neck and neck at the finish, and it was announced that the priest's horse had won. So Clive, being the gentleman he was, turned to the priest and said, 'I hope you had a good bet, Father,' and the priest beamed at him and said, 'I did, my son, I did. I had £2 each way,' at which Clive had to smile rather ruefully.

As was always the case when the Irish came to party, to say nothing of the English racing folk, there was a great deal of drinking, and after the last race a lot of dancing jigs around your hat, all huge fun and most enjoyable. After Clive died I could not face going for a number of years, and as my drinking got worse I could not really have afforded it or got it together anyway. When I did return I was somewhat horrified: it was now called the Festival of Racing, not that I have any objection to that title, and the hospitality tents had spread and spread and spread and it was impossible really to do almost anything except stay in your hospitality tent and watch the races on television. Consequently I never went back and I think the only thing that would ever persuade me to return would be if I had an interest in a horse, and perhaps not even then. It is curious how nowadays people go to events in which they have no particular interest, and probably would not even watch on television, but they go for the hospitality, whether it is at Wimbledon or the Derby or Cheltenham. I stay at home nowadays to watch Cheltenham and cheer on my contenders and actually probably pocket rather more money than I would have done if I had been there. It is still, however, a great racing event with brilliant races. They have now extended it to four days which, personally, I think is a mistake, but I suppose they have so many people who want to have horses running there. They say you are getting old when you think that things were so much better when you were younger; well, probably I am getting old, but in some instances things were definitely better when I was younger.

Cheltenham is another of those beautiful Georgian towns with lovely buildings, and well worth a visit when there are no race meetings. There was an old girl I knew called Adriana Bethel, now long since dead, who came from a well-to-do Irish family and used to keep one of those Georgian houses in Cheltenham simply to open for the racing. I first met her in London when she used to come clad in the most beautiful but dreadfully scruffy old tweeds with exquisite, unsuitable hats which she came over to Fortnum and Mason's to buy. She always carried a little Fortnum's bag at her wrist because she was a very heavy drinker, and when she was thrown out of various places, as she sometimes was, or was refused another drink, she would open the bag, which always contained a small bottle of whisky, pour herself that last drink, throw it back with an·eldritch shriek then leave to go somewhere else. The parties in her house at Cheltenham were astonishing, and used to go on all night, and everybody would go off to the races next morning and keep on going. Her one ambition was to die out hunting, which she achieved with her beloved Meath Hunt. Hounds were going away up the valley and she was sitting on her horse watching them. Her groom realised that she had actually died but was held in place by her side saddle. He simply led her home quietly – they don't stop a day's hunting in Ireland just because somebody dies.

The county town of Gloucestershire is of course Gloucester, and a place worth visiting if only for the cathedral, which stands on the River Severn. People coming to it from the north will approach it through the beauties of the Wye valley. As the name indicates, Gloucester was a Roman camp, but it was inhabited long before the Romans got there. It remains a pleasant county town with interesting shops as well as the conglomeration of chain stores. Wherever you walk in the city, whether you are looking across the river or up narrow lanes, everything is dominated by the tower of the cathedral, which is the birthplace of the style of architecture known as Perpendicular, with its wonderful lace-like fan structures. The cloisters hold what was the first ever fan-vaulting in the world, and there is no finer example of the Perpendicular style. The cathedral contains the tomb of King Edward II, which for centuries was a site of pilgrimage and made the cathedral very wealthy indeed.

Edward II, you may remember, was murdered in Berkeley Castle nearby and was buried with great pomp in 1327, his tomb being set up by his young son King Edward III. The murder, which allegedly gave the Earls of Berkeley their earldom, was carried out on the order of Edward's wife Isabella, She-wolf of France, and her lover Roger Mortimer. It is a particularly horrible piece of English history because in order to leave the body unmarked, they inserted a cow's horn up his rectum into which they pushed a red-hot poker, so he died by having his intestines burned out. The screams apparently could be heard for many miles. Isabella might have considered this an appropriate death for her husband, who neglected her because he was a homosexual, and spent his time and a lot of the country's money on his favourite, Hugh Despenser, who suffered an almost equally brutal death, having his appendage cut off and stuffed into his mouth and being left to bleed to death. It is an incestuous little area in a curious way, because Edward II was the man who lost to Robert the Bruce at the Battle of Bannockburn. The Bruce was married to Hugh Despenser's sister and she is buried fairly close by in Tewkesbury Abbey with a number of the rest of her family.

Berkeley Castle, over towards Wiltshire, is like that other great house of Gloucestershire, Badminton, the home of the Dukes of Beaufort and the family that gave us the Tudor dynasty through Henry VII's mother Margaret of Beaufort. She was a most amazing woman, the supporter of Caxton and his printing press and the patron of Wynkyn de Worde who followed him. She was an educator of women who completed Henry VI's two masterpieces, Eton and King's College, Cambridge, and founded Christ's College, Cambridge. The Beauforts are a great hunting family and, in my mother's generation, the then Duke of Beaufort, who was known as Master in reference to his being Master of Hounds, would hunt his hounds when he could for four days a week and was the author of that wonderful expression, 'I have two passions in life, hunting and ratting, and I don't know which I loves the most.' When Master died the antis dug up his body and cut off his head, which they then impaled on a spike and put it up to view.

In my day the hounds were hunted by a man called Ian Farquhar, who was undoubtedly one of the finest huntsmen of that generation. Johnny Scott and I spoke to the hunt supporters in Badminton House and were invited to dinner afterwards. I found myself sitting between Ian Farquhar and the present Duke, two of the most handsome men in hunting, so that was a very pleasant evening for me. The house is not open to the public and the present Duke has done very well in the City, and so manages, literally, to keep it as his castle. The family has produced many interesting eccentrics including, in the reign of Charles I, the Duke of Somerset, as he then was, known as the Wizard Earl because he invented among other things the first ever hydraulic press, which must have seemed like magic in the seventeenth century but which was never put to any use. The Wizard Earl threw his fortune at the feet of Charles I and virtually bankrupted himself. Fortunately Charles II was restored to the throne and restored to his fortunes as well and he made him a Duke. It was at this time that the present Badminton House was built. It has a dining room beautifully carved by Grinling Gibbons and with its cupolas and turrets the house is a perfect example of seventeenth-century architecture. The avenue that leads to Badminton is approximately five miles long and is lined by thousands of trees, well husbanded and strengthened by generations of the family, and is a most impressive sight. The estate covers about 15,000 acres and is nearly ten miles round. It contains the village with its trim cottages of stone, the church and Badminton House. Badminton is, of course, best known nowadays as the site of the three-day event that takes place annually, and to which riders flock from all over the world.

One of the great providers of wealth for the county is the port of Bristol, which stands on its western edge. Bristol had long been a successful port, trading with the Continent, but the port's real wealth came from its position facing the Americas. It was from Bristol, on a May morning in 1497, that John Cabot set sail at the diktat of Henry VII to try to follow the route taken by Columbus some five years earlier. The deal was that Cabot would pay all the expenses and the King would share the profits. They were back in August having placed North America on the map. Cabot found Cape Breton and Nova Scotia, for which he was given £12 down and a pension of £20 a year. On his second voyage he vanished from history and his son Sebastian, rather better known, sailed to Brazil and founded a colony, but failing at this and being banished by Spain, he returned to England, where he was made Inspector of the English navy. Thereafter trade with the Americas thrived and the most famous imports into Bristol, and which earned it the most money, were tobacco, chocolate and cocoa, their industries employing 5,000 people in the city. Originally, of course, one of the main imports was slaves. Before Liverpool became successful as a port, Bristol was the main slaving port for the country and the heart of what was known as the 'triangular trade'.

Bristol was very heavily bombed during the war and a lot of its historic buildings were destroyed, but one that was spared was the first ever Methodist chapel, started by John Wesley himself, who called it the New Room. It is in the Horsefair and has been restored by the Wesleyan Foundation. Here you will find a magnificent bronze of Wesley and the chair that he used to sit in.

Bristol also has a large Anglican cathedral, but the church that I like best is the Church of St Mary Redcliffe, which was founded by wealthy Bristol merchants but particularly by one called William Canynges, who was described as the richest merchant in the town. He is buried here in a tomb showing a tall scholastic man, but it is not his tomb that is my favourite, or even that of Admiral Penn who, when the Dutch Admiral van Tromp fixed a broom to his masthead to say that he would sweep the Channel of the English fleet, fixed his riding crop to his own masthead as a sign that he would thrash the Dutch. He succeeded in doing this in three days, and he too is buried here. The tomb I go to touch my hat to is that of William Canynges's cook, who lies on the floor of the south transept with his knife and his colander. Not many cooks are quite so valued.

Gloucestershire abounds with beautiful churches, and all the little villages have rather larger churches than you would expect to find in such places, which were mostly as a result of the sheep industry. I don't know what it is between sheep men and God, or what they do that in such counties where sheep are farmed you get these amazing churches put up to 'redeem' perhaps 'their immortal souls', to quote George Bernard Shaw. The sheep industry was huge in Gloucestershire at one point. Stow-on-the-Wold market would turn over 2,000 sheep in one day and this was not unusual. It brought a lot of wealth to the county which remains heavily agricultural. Quite appropriately, the main agricultural college for England is to be found in Cirencester, where a lot of my friends studied and thoroughly enjoyed their time there.

I don't go much to Gloucestershire since the Chief Constable of the county told me during the *Clarissa and the Countryman* years that he could not guarantee my safety if I went to Stroud market. We had been about to film a farmers' market in Stroud when a rather foolish woman, having been told that all we wanted to do was film a farmers' market, determined to turn it into a beano and sent out invitations to all the local councillors. Unfortunately word got out to the antis and as a result of threats of violence to my person and other such goings-on I received this call from the Chief Constable. I thought, Whoopee, let's go and film that – dying on camera after all would be a first – but the BBC lost its nerve and was not prepared to go there. In the end we filmed at Perth's farmers' market which is magnificent.

On another occasion Johnny and I arrived in Cirencester to speak at the Waterstone's Bookshop, which had formerly been a bank, and the antis came and banged their knees against the windows while we were speaking, windows that they knew were made of unbreakable glass. The bookshop called the police, the police arrived, but they refused to intervene in any way and so we fought on regardless. I went out and spoke to the police and said, 'Well, you could at least stand between them and the window,' and they said, 'No.' Then I suggested that I could go and stand between them and the window, at which point they said that they would have to arrest me for my own safety. It got very loud and very unpleasant. One girl, perhaps about ten or eleven or even younger, turning up late with her father, was so abused by them that she arrived in tears. I remember speaking to her and saying, 'You know you mustn't let people like that persuade you by that sort of behaviour against what you believe in.' I had then dubbed her 'the brave girl', and some years later she came up to me at a Game Fair and said, 'You dubbed me "the brave girl" and I just wanted you to know that I am still hunting.'

One of the glories of the Gloucestershire/Berkshire border is the Highgrove Estate, the official residence of the Prince of Wales and the Duchess of Cornwall. If I did not extol the virtues of Poundbury sufficiently, I will remedy this by exalting what the Prince of Wales has done at Highgrove. For *Two Fat Ladies* we filmed on the Highgrove Estate, and what has been achieved there is truly marvellous. You can almost smell how wonderfully healthy and green it is. Everything is done organically, the water is filtered through withies from their own willows, the livestock gleam with the shine of good health and the cattle are a joy to any carnivore's eye. Even the arable crops have a freshness and a life to them that you do not find that much elsewhere. The gardens too are glorious, and if you are lucky enough to go when the fritillaries are in flower in the meadow garden it is just a delight to see so many varieties of fritillary growing so well.

I am a great fan of the Prince of Wales's promotion of English produce, with particular focus on unfashionable things such as mutton, though even he couldn't get that off the ground, but I remember his wonderful campaign during the CJD epidemic to persuade European chefs that British beef was still safe to buy. He invited a number of them to Highgrove and then took them on tours of various farms. I was invited to one of the dinners at Highgrove to promote this and there was huge excitement among all the chefs because they were being invited to the private home of the heir to the throne. There was, however, one curious moment when an equerry came through and said that before His Royal Highness arrived there would be a 'chance for a merchandising moment as the shop will be open'. The shop is actually very good and has some really nice and unusual things to buy, but I went up to him and I said, 'You're an equerry?' and he said 'Yes.' I continued, 'And it is your role to promote the image of your master?' to which he replied, 'Well, yes.' I said, 'Merchandising moment?' and he did have the grace to turn slightly pink. Prince Charles is sometimes his own worst enemy because the really good things that he does like the Prince of Wales Trust and Highgrove get lost in publicity that is not always positive. I remember asking the woman who was deputed to look after us, 'Tell me, is this just a perfect model estate or does it wash its face?' She said, 'Well, it does rather better than wash its face because we simply can't produce enough to meet the demand.'

One of the butchers who sold Highgrove meat was the brilliant Jesse Smith in Cirencester which is where Jennifer and I, I think, became 'gay icons', because Jennifer came into the shop saying, 'There's some lovely faggots in the window,' and I said, 'Oh, I do so like a lovely faggot,' and Jennifer agreed. I think that put the pink pound firmly on our path. It was an excellent shop and the faggots were indeed beautiful. I cooked some fillet of beef from there and not only did it taste wonderful, which is unusual for fillet as it doesn't usually taste of anything very much, but it was so well grown and so well butchered and hung that, despite being in and out of the oven like a pair of whore's drawers going up and down, as is the nature of television cookery, when it was eaten it was still absolutely perfect and tender and full of flavour.

Berkshire

I find it curious how I spend bits of my life in different counties and then don't have cause to go there again for a long time. In my late teens, just as I was leaving school, my mother bought a small farm, Lower Redstone Farm at Braywoodside, to turn the horses out on in the summer. It was about eleven acres with a small house on it, and my sister Heather was, at that time, living down the road towards Maidenhead, so I spent a lot of time in Berkshire. Indeed my mother had horses in livery with Dick Stillwell and we all hunted with the Garth and South Berkshire. Dick Stillwell at that time was Chef d'Equipe to the British Olympic team when Princess Anne, the Princess Royal, was riding for Britain, so I used to see her occasionally at the stables. We all used to ride out in Windsor Great Park. I went regularly with my mother to the racing at Newbury and continued to do so with Clive, and I also went regularly to Henley. However since my thirties I only go to Berkshire very intermittently.

Berkshire offers a great variety of countryside. The north has the fertile Vale of the White Horse, the centre consists of chalk downs, continuing the Chilterns across the Thames, comprising the highest part of the county, and the south has the heath and grasslands and woodlands. Berkshire is still rich in woodlands, 9 per cent of the total area in England, lying only behind Surrey, Hampshire and Kent. Of course Berkshire also has the Thames, and most of the rivers in the county are tributaries of it. Let us come in from the west. My mother used to have horses in training with the legendary Fred Winter, so we would go quite often to Lambourn to see them. Up here on the downs there is a great site for trainers, good gallops for the horses and it is not that far away from either Newbury or Cheltenham.

Lambourn itself has charming almshouses set round a garden and a fourteenth-century church, which has some beautiful carvings – of a bishop, a man in a fool's cap, people blowing trumpets and four hounds chasing a hare. These are probably there because the church houses tombs of the Garrard family who were lords of the manor at Lambourn. Among their duties they had charge of a pack of harriers which they kept for the King for the Royal Hunt. The church also contains the tomb of the poet Joshua Sylvester who, in between being a sycophant, wrote some really very fine poetry. He was appointed as Poet Pensioner to Prince Henry, son of James I, and when the Prince died he published a 'distillation of tears for the untimely death of an incomparable Prince'. Sucking up to James I, he wrote his counter-blast against tobacco. He followed it with 'tobacco battered and the pipes shattered about their eaves that idly idol-ise so base and barbarous a weed'. Rather more appealing were his sonnets:

> Were you the earth, dear Love, and I the skies
> My love should shine on you like to the sun,
> And look upon you with ten thousand eyes
> Till heaven wax'd blind, and till the world were done.
>
> Whereso'er I am, below, or else above you,
> Whereso'er you are, my heart shall truly love you.

Further south and heading towards Hampshire, you come to one of the towns that I have always said I would quite like to live in, which is Hungerford, where I spent an incredibly happy day speaking at their annual celebration of the granting of their charter by John of Gaunt. I had initially gone to Hungerford because of its proximity to Prosperous Farm, once the property of the agriculturalist and the inventor of the seed drill Jethro Tull. I went to the farm because of its Guernsey milk and its Prosperous cream which is to my mind the best cream I have ever tasted. You used to be able to buy it, but unfortunately, due to regulations, its present owner has given up selling milk and cream. On my sixtieth birthday for pudding we had just beautiful freshly picked strawberries and Prosperous cream and really one couldn't have asked for anything more. We also ate some of the farm's delicious cheese, but sadly this too is no longer made for public consumption. After my visit I had gone on to Hungerford to look for some lunch. The only thing that is really lacking in Hungerford is somewhere nice to eat, not anywhere grand, but somewhere to have a decent lunch. However, it has everything else including an incredibly good tapestry shop called Crown Needlework, owned by a delightful couple named Bossom. As well as being the local postman, the husband was one of the council of Hungerford.

Hungerford is owned by its citizens, and has never had a lord of the manor, which has made it very convenient for various events. It was given its charter by John of Gaunt, who had housed his army there on their way to the Isle of Wight. The citizens own the rights to pasture on the common, the fishing rights on the Kennet and the right to collect rents directly. I think there are ninety-nine houses that are old enough to be included in this particular scheme. Once a year the Tutti-men set out to collect these rents, bearing garlanded poles on the top of which are fixed oranges set with cloves. The night before there has been a beer tasting to check the suitability of the locally brewed beer for the festivities, and on the morning the regulations governing the usage of the common land are read out in the council chamber. The reason they were read out originally was, of course, because not that many people could read. It is a charming ceremony and there are very sensible regulations, such as nobody must graze on the common a cow that has recently aborted, presumably as a guard against brucellosis, a regulation governing the suitability of various animals to stand there, and very early regulations as to when you can or cannot take different fish out of the river. There used also to be a ceremony where hot pennies were thrown out to the local children, but once again Health and Safety has reined that one in.

When the Tutti-men return from their collections there is a very good lunch, all made with local produce. The year I attended we ate freshly smoked trout from the Kennet, beef that had been grazed on the common and the pudding came with Prosperous cream. At the end of the lunch the newly approved beer was poured and you were asked would you take punch and then you shouted, 'Punch,' and drank it, or in my case passed it on. After lunch newcomers to the feast were led forward to put their foot up to be shod by the local blacksmith. As he approached you with his horseshoe and his nails you would shout, 'Punch,' once more and pay a shilling towards the beer fund and you were given the horseshoe. I still travel with mine in my car. All the councillors wear a red rose cast in metal in their buttonholes in memory of John of Gaunt, whose coat of arms it was. Its neutrality also allowed Hungerford to be the place where William of Orange met with the powers that be as James II fled to France. Tony Blair's government succeeded in doing what centuries of monarchs had failed to do, which was to do away with the common rights of grazing and take them under the spectre of Defra. Hungerford had an argument with Defra because their common rights were granted by royal charter which is not, as I understand it, surmountable by Act of Parliament, and I'm happy to say they won. Hungerford has everything you could wish for in the way of shops: it has a good bookshop, an excellent silversmith and even a large Oka, that excellent chain of furniture shops owned by David Cameron's mother-in-law.

From Hungerford you turn east and you come to Newbury

with its fine racecourse. Newbury owes its fame and much of its beauty to Jack of Newbury, John Smallwood, who became a master clothier and the chief citizen of Newbury. He has been described as the most considerable clothier England has ever seen. He kept a hundred looms at work, and so sound and durable were his products that he was famous throughout the land. When he was called upon to supply two horsemen and four men armed with pikes for Henry VIII's army against the Scots, he responded by raising fifty men all well mounted and fifty footmen with bows and pikes. They were the best clothed men of all the King's troops. He marched at their head and there is an old ballad of the Newbury Archers which tells of their daring deeds. He entertained the King and Catherine of Aragon and Cardinal Wolsey and the floor, where the King sat, was covered in broadcloths instead of green rushes, some selected pieces of wool being valued at £100 each. John gave one to the King but declined the offered knighthood, shrewdly obtaining instead the right of the woollen industry to free trade with foreign lands, 'that their merchants might freely traffic with one another'. Thomas Cromwell ordered 1,000 of his Newbury Kerseys for the royal household. John endowed a fine church to the town, which has magnificent stained-glass windows with an unusual theme. They are called the Parable Windows and show the stories of the sower, the leaven and the grain of mustard seed, the tares, the widow, the Pharisee and the publican, the wise and foolish virgins and the parable of the prodigal son.

In old Newbury the Cloth Hall is a gem, resplendent with Jacobean woodwork and having grotesques' heads carved on to the beams. The upper storey overhangs the street and is supported on a pillar.

Outside the town of Newbury, towards the Greenham end, is Newbury racecourse, a course that I have always loved dearly. There was always so much pleasure going down on the train, watching the racing and coming back again. It was built in 1905 and moved to its present site in 1910, so even before all the developments that have taken place lately, it was a relatively comfortable venue when I was young. Curiously, nearby was the Greenham Common Peace Camp, which was a group of women besieging the American air base at Greenham Common. I often wonder what causes people to go and live for long periods of time in such discomfort; is it really a matter of high principle or is it just an avoidance of life? Anyway, the Americans have gone, the camp has gone and a lot of women will have many memories of their time living a hippy existence.

If you head east and slightly to the north towards the site of the first Battle of Newbury in the Civil War, you will come to the estate of Englefield. It is in a fertile part of Berkshire and has an excellent farm shop selling produce from the estate. As a Catholic, one was raised with the story of Sir Francis Englefield, who went into exile rather than abandon his faith. However if you look at it slightly more closely you will see that the Englefields were quite happy to accept Tilehurst Manor from the spoils of Reading Abbey during the Reformation and sufficiently reconciled to the Protestants to accept a knighthood from Edward VI. Nonetheless, Edward's Protestant reforms were rapid and fairly drastic and the Englefields resisted the direction that fate was taking, and Sir Francis was sent to the Tower for permitting Mass to be said in his house. His fortunes were restored with the accession of Bloody Mary, but this time he jumped the wrong way in backing Mary, being present at the trials of several of the Protestant martyrs and petitioning Bishop Gardiner to send Roger Ascham, the well-known scholar, to the stake. Mary died childless and Elizabeth ascended the throne and Sir Francis became involved in a plot to rescue Mary, Queen of Scots, and put her on the English throne. He was forced to flee and never returned. He spent the rest of his days, the next forty years, in Europe, plotting to restore the Catholic faith to the throne of England. He received 600 crowns a year from

Philip II, the arbiter of the Spanish Armada, by way of a pension. Elizabeth gave the estate to her secretary, the faithful Francis Walsingham, and when she visited he built the Long Gallery from the hillside to the house so that she would 'have to mount no step' on her visit.

After various changes following the Civil War the estate passed into the hands of the Benyon family, where it has remained ever since. I had cause to go there to open the farm shop and I was greeted by Richard Benyon who is one of the Defra ministers in the Conservative Party and the coalition government. I was able to say, when shaking hands with him while holding a large pair of shears with which I was to cut the binder twine to declare the shop open, that it was the first time in many years that I had been allowed into the vicinity of a Defra minister carrying what was, *ipso facto*, a lethal weapon!

Continue eastwards and you come to Reading, whose modern-day prosperity is owed to the Huntley and Palmers biscuit works, which at its height was so large and prosperous that the tramways within the site covered twelve miles, and the biscuits were exported all over the world. What I find delightful about Reading, however, is the fact that the earliest known vocal chorale was written in the abbey nearly 800 years ago by one of the monks who is now nameless. The original is in the British Library and you will know it, I hope, because it is the one that goes:

> Summer is a coming in
> Loudly sing cucu,
> Groweth seed and bloweth mead
> And springeth the wood anew,
> Sing cucu.

It is designed to be sung in six parts and is written in the Wessex dialect which was, historically, spoken in Berkshire. It is such a happy song and rather unusual to have been written by a medieval monastic; one thinks more of penitence and flagellation and repentance and rather dreary religious plainchant. Not a lot remains of the abbey now, other than some ruins and a magnificent gatehouse that still stands intact, but in its day it was one of the richest and most powerful abbeys in the country, thanks to its proximity to the Thames and to London. Reading Abbey was the burial place of the Conqueror's son Henry I, known as Beauclerc because of his rewriting of the laws of England. His is a tragic story because his only son, called William, drowned on the *White Ship* coming back from Normandy in the same flotilla as his father. It is said that when Henry heard the news he fell into a dead faint and never smiled again. He was succeeded only by his daughter Matilda, to whom he made all the barons of England swear fealty, the only trouble being that they did not like the thought of being ruled by a woman and so the Civil Wars of Stephen and Matilda broke out. The town will always be associated with Oscar Wilde who, after his release from Reading Gaol, where he had been serving time for his affair with Lord Alfred Douglas, wrote that brilliant poem 'The Ballad of Reading Gaol'.

Keep going east and you come to Wokingham. My brother had a factory producing packaging and very good plastic string and those straps with the buckles on the side that you see on so many tarpaulins. He actually held the patent on that design and realising that customs checks were about to be altered he started manufacturing them, which proved to be a very profitable move. Crowthorne just to the south hosts two great institutions: the first is Wellington College, which lies a few miles away and which was erected in memory of the Duke of Wellington. It remains to this day a fine English public school with a lot of its old boys going into the military. The other institution is perhaps best described by the story of Dr Minor. Sir James Murray, who was compiling the *Oxford English Dictionary*, received a great many letters helping him to track down words and phrases from all over the world. None was more valuable or showed more learning than those from a Dr W.C. Minor of Crowthorne. Dr Minor's contributions numbered several thousand and Sir James Murray determined to meet this remarkable man and he invited him to be the guest of Oxford University for a week. The reply came back stating that Dr Minor was prevented by physical reasons from accepting the invitation but he would be delighted if Sir James would visit him at Crowthorne. The great scholar travelled by train and was met by a man whom he took to be Dr Minor, but he was told, 'No, I am the Governor of the Broadmoor Lunatic Asylum.' It turned out that Dr Minor was an American of great intellect who had, in a fit of rage, killed a man in a London street and had been sent to Broadmoor. Sir James lost his nerve and returned to Oxford without meeting the author of the letters. My brother used to employ workers from Broadmoor at his factory and he said that they always worked very hard and very well and that he was delighted to employ them.

Travel on north-eastwards towards the Thames and on the outskirts of Windsor Great Park you will come to the little town of Ascot, home of the most fashionable racecourse in the world, laid out by Queen Anne. She was a great racing lady and like so many of the Stuarts had an immense passion for horses and hunting. I love the story that when she got too old and fat to sit a horse she used to follow the hunt across country, driving herself in a sporting curricle with great dash and elan, her lady-in-waiting hanging on the back like a tiger, the name for that sort of page-boy at the time. I used to go every year to Ascot and to the Royal Enclosure, and it was an occasion of great delight, meeting old friends, and there were beautiful horses and good racing. In recent years it has grown into a very large event, with the numbers permitted in the Royal Enclosure increasing enormously. Apart from the Queen coming up the course there is not an awful lot to recommend it. Like Cheltenham it has become too crowded and too impossible to see the horses and the racing, so I prefer to stay at home and watch it on television, but I have had many happy years there and a lot of fun and misbehaviour. I used to walk back to the railway station through the avenues of sweet chestnut trees skipping, mentally, from the pleasures of the day. I was once the victim of an attempted mugging in London by two Afro-Caribbean gentlemen and I put them both in hospital. When I was giving my evidence, the magistrate said, 'But why didn't you just let them grab your handbag if, as you say, it had nothing of value in it?' I replied, 'But it had my Ascot vouchers and you have no idea how difficult it is to replace those at short-term notice,' so strongly did I feel about attending the meeting.

Ascot, as I said, is on the outskirts of Windsor, which is of course dominated by Windsor Castle, built by the Conqueror and enlarged by various monarchs and one of the favourite residences of our own Queen. When I was a tourist guide I used to go there regularly with my party and find Windsor Castle almost too much, almost too wonderful; the Holbeins and the van Dycks and the Rembrandts and all the beautiful porcelain and silverware are magnificent. There is the grandeur that is St George's Chapel with the stalls of the Knights of the Garter, household names, which is the greatest honour in the land and in the gift of the monarch. The order was based on the whim of King Edward III, who did not want to see a woman who had dropped her garter shamed. The castle so overwhelmed me that I used to focus on the special bed that Edward VII had had made, which bounced on its own springs and was a levered contraption, so that he, grossly fat and still horny, could continue to have sex with his various mistresses.

My favourite visit to Windsor Castle was the autumn before last when I was invited by the Queen as part of a group of people who were deemed to have been helpful and supportive to the countryside. I was really not very well, still suffering from the after-effects of my pleurisy and still with the adhesions on the pleura giving me a lot of discomfort, but I was not going to miss that party. The Queen is splendid on all occasions but especially when she is playing hostess in her beloved home to people in whom she is really interested. What the Queen loves almost above all things is her horses, and the Windsor Castle Stud is a very fine and little known establishment. I had heard that she had just obtained some new Irish greys as coach horses and we had an interesting chat about that. The occasion was, as is everything that I have ever been connected to around the Queen, perfectly ordered and full of immensely good humour. The Sandringham apple juice was quite the nicest apple juice I have ever tasted and the canapés were all made from produce from the royal estates. If you asked about them, which of course I did, their origins were carefully explained to you. I had not seen St George's Hall since it had been rebuilt – it had been burned down if you remember in what the Queen described as an '*annus horribilis*' some years before – and as a work of rebuilding and restoration it was immaculate. It was explained to me that it was actually now the size that was originally intended when it was first built in the Middle Ages, but it had been made slightly smaller because of budgetary diktats at that time. It was a very happy evening.

William the Conqueror built the castle at Windsor because of its strategic position on the Thames, on the site of a small and little used palace that Edward the Confessor had left behind. The Thames ceases to be tidal above Kingston Lock and this mighty trading river of history has given way to the delights of 'jolly boating weather' and Jerome K. Jerome's *Three Men in a Boat*. When my brother was alive he used to book a narrow boat for two weeks and go up the Thames. I would go and meet him with some of my friends at whatever point he had chosen to stop. He would then take the car that I had driven up in and return to London, while I would continue the journey to return the boat to its original hiring. Curiously that is how I first became acquainted with Michel Roux Senior who, at that time, had not long opened the Waterside Inn at Bray. The throttle jammed on the boat I was driving and I found myself heading fairly speedily towards the jetty of the Waterside Inn in my half-ton vessel. I am afraid that when we struck there wasn't an awful lot left of the jetty. Michel came rushing out to see what had happened and after many apologies and promises of reparation and a rather good glass of Armagnac which my brother had left on board we became friendly acquaintances, and I have seen him many times since.

I love Bray. I used to come down with my parents to the Hind's Head, that well-known hotel and hostelry, which was then run by a lady called Miss William, who was a patient of my father's. It was there that I first learned about the distinction of good wine from the legendary sommelier, Theodore, and after lunch we would go for a walk round the village and go into the church. I was always much taken by the pragmatic attitude of the vicar of Bray who successfully endured the reigns of Henry VIII, Edward VI, Bloody Mary and Elizabeth. There is a song about him that goes:

> And this is law, that I'll maintain
> Until my dying day, Sir,
> That whatsoever King shall reign
> I'll still be the Vicar of Bray, Sir.

The most likely contender for this role is a man called Simon Aleyn who was vicar throughout this period. He had declared, having seen martyrs burned at Windsor, that his principle was to 'live and die the Vicar of Bray'.

In later years I had a friend who lived in the Fisheries, that wonderful enclosed area by the river at Bray Lock, which is a place that I could never afford but would very much like to live in. It was during my drinking days and Clive and I used to go and stay there and behave very badly indeed, hitting golf balls across the river, not during the hours when the lock was open, I hasten to add. We would go down to the Hind's Head and have a lot of fun. Apart from the Waterside Inn, Bray is now home to Heston Blumenthal's Fat Duck. His cookery is rather too redolent of the 'Emperor's New Clothes' for me really to want to make a return visit. It is a great pity that there isn't more of the Fat Duck and less of the nitrogen canister and chef's overworked food.

On your trip from Windsor to Bray you will have passed the meadow of Runnymede, and I hope that you will have doffed your cap to it because, of course, here was laid down the document that is known as Magna Carta. This document contains, apart from all the demands of the various barons, the unique bit that Stephen Langton was probably responsible for, which set down that no man could be tried except by a jury of his peers and that no man could be deprived of the tools of his labours. These are fundamental to the English legal system and its principle. Despite the efforts of politicians over the centuries since 1215 they are still in existence and still protect the innocent.

Berkshire has arguably one of the best educational establishments in the world in Eton, and one that I particularly admire because of its ability to place the individual scholar in whatever part of the world he will best fit. I knew a man who went there who was forever bunking off to go to the cinema. Instead of expelling him they thought about it and he became one of the leading cinema critics of his generation. Eton was, we must remember, created as a grammar school for poor scholars by that sad King, Henry VI, who has left us the school and King's College, Cambridge and King's College Chapel as his legacy. One wonders what the more belligerent and militarily successful of his relatives have left as their legacies that are half so good. Eton College is across the bridge from Windsor Castle. When Henry VI set it up, the school was designed for ten priests, four lay clerks, six choristers, twenty-five poor scholars and twenty-five men. Eton has produced many Prime Ministers, indeed we have one at the moment, and in the First World War the Roll of Honour numbers 1,157 names, more than the total number of boys who attended the school at the time. It also counted thirteen Victoria Crosses. One of the boasts of the school is that it produces boys who are cool in adversity, and possibly no remark in English history has been cooler than that of Lawrence Oates when leaving Scott of the Antarctic's tent.

Just up the road from Eton is the town of Slough. In my day Old Etonians used to refer to themselves as the products of Slough Grammar School, and they may still do so for all I know. Slough started life as the small village of Upton and really grew as a result of the First World War and the Great Depression. During the war the government used some 600 acres here for storing machinery and motor vehicles. With the coming of peace the area of unwanted stores became a by-word for one of the rubbish heaps of the Great War. A company was formed to take it all over and establish light industries on the site. Since then factories have been set up by the score and the provision of houses and schools have turned it into a sizeable town. Betjeman wrote of it:

> Come, friendly bombs, and fall on Slough
> It isn't fit for humans now.

Optomen TV made a programme called *Making Slough Happy* which I think they singularly failed to do.

Queen Victoria came by carriage from Windsor to make her first ever railway journey, taking the train to Paddington, and she declared that she was quite charmed with it. Prince Albert used to take the train fairly regularly to London and was known to send messages to the driver saying, 'Not quite so fast next time, Mr Conductor, if you please.' On Queen Victoria's first journey questions were asked in the House about the suitability of the Queen taking such a dangerous journey, but Parliament was reassured when they were told that Sir Daniel Gooch, one of the greatest designers of railway engines of the day, was the driver, that Brunel himself was in the cabin and that the Queen's favourite coachman had insisted on travelling on the footplate to look after her interests.

Buckinghamshire

What has always amused me about Buckinghamshire is that the rather manicured county with the beauty of the Chiltern Hills protecting its rural centre has historically been a hotbed of political revolt, the English Civil War and home to various powerful and radical politicians. We know that when a Member of Parliament wishes to resign he used to be asked to take the Chiltern Hundreds. Probably nowadays so many of them have had to resign that this has gone out of fashion, but I became aware of the parliamentary connections when I was really quite young.

My parents had very good friends, Joe and Molly Craig, who lived just outside High Wycombe with their three sons, Harry, Robert and Christopher, who I still see from time to time. In the period between Christmas and the New Year my father and Joe Craig used to organise a treasure hunt to raise money for the Imperial Cancer Research Fund. You would get into your cars and charge around the countryside in search of clues. When you had worked out the answer to the first clue you would go to the place it indicated and there discover the next clue, always assuming that you had got the first one right. It was enormous fun and I think it was my father and Joe Craig who set the questions. Certainly my brother always drove us and my father would be waiting to present the prizes in the large hotel at Gerrards Cross. My parents had rented a weekend cottage before the war at Gerrards Cross and so had come to know the area very well.

Let me give you an example of these clues. There would be a

quote from *Paradise Lost* and you then had to decide whether you would go to Horton where Milton was born, or to Jordans where his friend Thomas Ellwood had lived and you would then hopefully decide on Chalfont St Giles where Milton retired during the Great Plague in London. By the time Milton was installed in his pretty cottage at Chalfont St Giles he had had a fairly tortuous life. He lived through the Commonwealth with Cromwell, had been a hunted man on the Restoration, his books were burned by the common hangman and he was growing old in his loneliness. Milton came to this place and found peace. He would not have been able to see it because he was, by this time, blind, but we know he took pleasure from sitting in the garden and smelling the flowers around him as he dictated to his daughter. One does like to think that perhaps *Paradise Regained* was written because of this.

I remember one question was a quote:

> Some village Hampden here may lie
> Some Cromwell guiltless of his country's blood.

I don't know if, for the purpose of the treasure hunt, this is a deliberate misquote but if not the verse reads:

> Some village-Hampden, that with dauntless breast
> The little tyrant of his fields withstood,
> Some mute inglorious Milton here may rest,
> Some Cromwell, guiltless of his country's blood.

So did you go rushing off to look for John Hampden's residence or try to find the house where Cromwell had stayed after the Battle of Naseby and left behind the sword that brought him victory? Or did you recognise it as a quote from Gray's 'Elegy Written in a Country Churchyard' and go trotting off to Stoke Poges where it is said to have been composed? Gray was born in London and his mother fled her husband after she had borne him twelve children – rather a slow flight, one thinks – and of those children the poet was the sole male survivor on whom she lavished all her love. She was a dressmaker and had two brothers among the assistant masters at Eton which is why, at eleven years of age, Thomas was sent there. He was reserved, studious and detested games, and on leaving Eton he went on to Peterhouse at Cambridge. He then set off on a continental tour with Horace Walpole and he installed his mother and his two sisters, who were then alive, at West End at Stoke Poges where he would stay during the summer holidays when he was teaching at Cambridge. The 'Elegy', which took him seven years to write, was an imme-diate success and ran through four editions in two months and spread Gray's fame across the whole of Europe. Gray, however, was too sensitive to accept payment for the poem. His friend General Wolfe, dying on the Heights of Abraham, is reputed to have said, 'I would rather be the author of Gray's poem than take Quebec.' In 1753 his mother died and he was appointed Professor of Modern History at Cambridge. He is, appropri-ately, buried beside his mother in Stoke Poges churchyard. I love that poem, and at one time could quote the whole of it but now I can manage only about two-thirds.

Had you gone to look for John Hampden, on the other hand, you would have gone to Stoke Mandeville, which was really the place where the spark that blazed into the Civil War was lit. John Hampden owned Moat Farm and it was on this farm that ship money was opposed in 1653. Charles I had disbanded Parliament and taken away the mace and had to exist on the taxes that he, the King, was allowed to raise, without resorting to Parliament. Hampden refused to pay ship money, quite rightly, as Stoke Mandeville is a very long way from any port, which was the point of that taxation, and at the court five judges supported him but seven were against him. The decision outraged public feeling and made conflict inevitable. Stoke Mandeville is now most famous for the brilliant hospital set up for injured servicemen, and came by way of that to be the forerunner of the Paralympic Games which have now attained such importance that they run neck and neck with the ordinary Olympics. In fact they are rather more productive because many amazing inventions to help the disabled have been developed as a result.

Another fairly radical politician was Benjamin Disraeli, twice Prime Minister in the nineteenth century. The Disraelis were Portuguese Jews of good repute and a certain amount of money, and as such were ineligible to stand for the English Parliament. When Benjamin was twelve, his father overcame this problem by having his children baptised into the Church of England. Disraeli never attempted to deny his Jewishness and indeed examples of pride in his race abound in his writings. He was a successful novelist as well as Prime Minister. His novel *Vivian Grey* was published when he was only twenty-one and became an instant bestseller. Disraeli married the widow of a wealthy Tory politician, Wyndham Lewis, and thus was removed from any financial anxiety; he bought Hughenden Manor which became his country house. Disraeli was a brilliant conversationalist and a great friend of Queen Victoria, who is known to have disliked the Whig leader Gladstone intensely. Given what one reads about Gladstone, I am with Victoria all the way. Disraeli had a strange foppish extravagance about him: he wore his long black hair in ringlets and his clothes were of many hues and very un-English. His first speech in Parliament was howled down and then, when he finished, he added the defiant words, 'A time will come when you will hear me.' For all his attempted reforms, Disraeli's greatest success was the purchase, on behalf of England, of a controlling block of shares in the Suez Canal for £4 million, thus ensuring the international use of the canal for the country.

Continuing northwards you will come to Aylesbury, a town I always feel a great tenderness for because of the Aylesbury duckling. This tender and tasty duck is a cottager's duck and originally they were hung on the walls at night in little wicker baskets to keep them safe from all predators, foxes and rats in particular, and they would be let out during the day to waddle around. They average at about five pounds and have a very good flavour. The pure-bred Aylesbury duck nearly became extinct some ten years ago and the line was only saved by the efforts of a young man called Iain Dick in southern Scotland.

Aylesbury, like so many Buckinghamshire towns, contains a plethora of pubs, but probably the only one in the country that is owned by the National Trust. The King's Head, standing on the site of a medieval monastic hostelry, has been an inn since the Reformation. The lounge was obviously once the old refectory and still has magnificent leaded windows from pre-Tudor times. Two panes of glass from these windows have been built into a window at Westminster Abbey and three more are in the British Museum. Oliver Cromwell is believed to have stayed at the King's Head when the inn was occupied by Parliamentary troops during the Civil War. There are also the remains of a priest hole. The church contains an effigy of a knight in armour and chainmail, about 700 years old, lying with his head resting on his helmet and his feet on a lion. There is not much to distinguish him from all the other such tombs except that he is Robert Lee, a knight whose descendant went to America and he is the direct ancestor of Robert E. Lee who led the Southern armies against the North in the American Civil War.

I came to know Aylesbury quite well when I was working at Wotton Underwood, which you will reach by going westward from that town. Wotton House here was for 600 years the home of the Grenville family and the Grenville Chapel in the church houses centuries of that family's tombs including one Prime Minister who served from 1763 to 1765. The house, which eventually became the Dower House for the Dukes of Buckingham, is a masterpiece by Sir John Soane, and the splendid wrought-iron gates are the work of Thomas Robinson. When I was there I was working for a gentleman by the name of Grahame C. Greene who was the nephew of Graham Greene, the author, and the chief executive of Jonathan Cape, the publishing house. He lived in what had been the old brewery and I lived close by in a modern cottage standing in a courtyard of cottages. It is extraordinary to think that back in the 1960s, when so much was destroyed, the local council had been about to pull down the house when it was saved. A couple by the name of Brunner, as in Brunner Mond, as in ICI, went there to buy some statuary that had been offered for sale. They fell in love with the place, bought it and restored it.

In my day the house was still occupied by old Mrs Brunner who was wonderfully frivolous and a great raconteuse and she used to delight in taking people on tours round the house herself. The house had, in the way of the architecture of the time, two pavilions standing separately on either side of it and one of these was occupied by the late John Gielgud. He was very fond of chocolate cake and I often used to take him one when I had been baking and he would chatter away to me about this and that. At weekends there was always some handsome young man present, sitting at his feet to hear his reminiscences. That particular pavilion has now been acquired by Tony Blair who, I gather, has discovered after the event that the house is so heavily listed that he can do nothing to change it, not that it seemed to me to need much changing, but this does of course include security measures.

When I was there old Mrs Brunner, who was something of an anti, would not allow the foxes to be shot nor would she allow the hunt through the property, so the foxes had destroyed every living thing. It was quite scary at night to motor up the drive and see these red eyes blinking in the hedgerows as you went past. The foxes were so hungry they were even trying to dig up the moles. Apart from the humans, the only surviving creature was a lone peacock, whose mate had been eaten by the foxes while sitting on her eggs. He was forever standing on the roof of my cottage crying that strange sound which the Chinese describe as 'the lost souls of the dead' in order to try to find another mate.

Up above Wotton Underwood is Brill Hill, with its easily identifiable windmill. It is 600 feet above the surrounding countryside and the mill would have caught every available wind. It is a very steep hill, as I know, because once, in a thunderstorm, when I had run out of gin, I walked from Wotton Underwood to Brill to buy some. It was about four miles but fortunately I got a lift back. Close to Brill are the remains of the old castle of Boarstall, home of the Aubrey family. All that remains now is a magnificent gatehouse as the castle itself was destroyed in the Civil War.

The county town of Buckinghamshire is of course Buckingham which, with an Act of Parliament following the marriage of Catherine of Aragon to Henry VIII, was named one of the Necessitous towns of England, largely because of its prosperity from the wool trade. The wool trade is now gone, and what Buckingham has to recommend it these days is the university, set up in 1976 following the model of Harvard Business School. I had a friend who was a professor there at the time so I came to know the town quite well.

Near Buckingham is the excrescence, to my mind, on the face of the country that is Milton Keynes. Arthur Mee, writing in 1940, says this about Milton Keynes:

It lies among meadows through which wind the Ouzel and its tributary brooks, and has thatched cottages which must have looked for centuries much as they look today. Pines and larches grace the charming fourteenth-century church with a handsome tower built in a corner. The rich carving outside includes a fox, a dog, a lion and animals which seem to have escaped from a medieval Beast book. In a buttress is a graceful pinnacle niche by which is a 'scratched' sundial . . .

He continues in much the same vein. It has come a long way since then. When Milton Keynes was built it had the largest covered shopping mall in Europe. I remember spending a morning with my friend, who had a passion for bargains, looking at the prices of toothbrushes in the various chemists' shops in the mall. It was at the height of my drinking and I was desperate for a drink, but there was nowhere I could sneak off to and buy one and I remember offering to buy him all the toothbrushes he wanted if we could only go off and find a pub. Milton Keynes is most famous, perhaps, for its concrete cows, which now grace the town as some sort of indication of its rural heritage. I actually think that that is quite witty and probably about the only thing to recommend Milton Keynes.

The Dukes of Buckingham, as is the way of things, did not live at Buckingham but in the beautiful house at Stowe which is now a successful co-ed school. Stowe has been adorned in its various times by Sir John Vanbrugh, Sir John Soane, Robert Adam and Grinling Gibbons and the chapel has been redesigned by Robert Lorimer, the Scottish architect. The house was built for Sir Richard Temple, to be found being calumnied in the poetry of Pope, a soldier who lost his military command by demanding the prosecution of the ringleaders of the South Sea Bubble. Three Grenville Dukes of Buckingham lived at Stowe and the first two seemed to compete with each other to charge headlong into bankruptcy. Richard Grenville, elder son of the Marquess of Buckingham, was born in 1776, a cousin of William Pitt. He married the only child of the third Duke of Chandos and at the age of forty-six was made Duke of Buckingham and Chandos. He spent his wealth lavishly on pictures, statues, books and manuscripts, and entertained the royal family of France. He impoverished himself so badly that he had to seek seclusion abroad. He returned and in his declining years had to sell many of his treasures to keep the bailiffs at bay.

His son, the second Duke, and for many years the Marquess

of Chandos, consistently opposed free trade to gain the title of 'the farmer's friend'. The rent roll for his estate was £100,000 a year but the property was deeply encumbered and still he continued to buy land and entertain like a prince while owing his creditors over £1 million. He added to his liabilities by prodigal hospitality to Queen Victoria. Two years after the Queen's visit, the bailiffs took possession of the house, and dealers from all parts of Europe attended the forty days' sale of pictures, china, plate and furniture. The library was dispersed, the manuscripts sold and the Duke censored in *The Times* as a spendthrift. He died not long afterwards. The third Duke was an upright and honourable man who laboured to repair the ruin of his family's fortunes and to repay his debts, in both of which endeavours he was successful.

One of the places you must go to see in Buckinghamshire is Burnham Beeches which we used to go to often when I was young. The collection of beeches, many of which have lived longer than the species is supposed to, is magnificent and if you go in the spring when the bluebells are out and the tiny little acid-green leaves are just breaking through it is a joy to delight the heart. Buckinghamshire provides good hunting country and I have spent many happy days watching the Vale of Aylesbury Hunt in their yellow coats, so unique in the hunting uniforms of the country. Hunting continues to flourish within the law in the county to this day. Buckinghamshire is the centre

of attention in the press at the moment because of the new high-speed train to Birmingham and beyond. I don't really think that trains spoil landscapes but there is a lot of fuss about how it will ruin the Chiltern Hills. I will say that as the train to Birmingham, on every occasion when I have travelled on it from London, is invariably twenty minutes late, it seems to me that all that will happen will be the train will arrive on time, or on the old time. I doubt very much I shall be alive to see it reach Scotland.

Bedfordshire

I am afraid that this is going to be a rather short chapter because I know very little about Bedfordshire. It is somewhere that I have driven through on the A1 going north or south and I have been to both Woburn and Whipsnade to see their zoos. The one thing I do know is about the vicar of Kimbolton, which is, I think, technically speaking in Huntingdon. The gentleman concerned is a retired Anglican vicar who is one of the world's leading experts on pyrotechnics and who is always being called in to design firework displays. He was in fact invited to Hong Kong to help put together the firework display that took place at the handover from Britain to China. Considering that the Chinese invented fireworks, it was a very great compliment indeed. Kimbolton has the remains of an early castle but not a lot else, although Catherine of Aragon was imprisoned here in part of the new castle, as it was at the time, while her trial was taking place at Dunstable not very far away. What seems to have come down to us as a legacy in both Bedford and Dunstable are various rules for public health in medieval times. Bedford has its Black Book and Dunstable has its rules of 1221 ordering that butchers must not cast blood and filth into the street.

Henry VIII chose Dunstable Priory as the place where Archbishop Cranmer would decide the case for his divorce and at that time the town was probably at the peak of its prosperity. The closing of the priory with the Dissolution of the Monasteries rather put a kibosh on that, and thereafter it became a town of inns catering for the coaching schedule and a manufacturer of straw hats. As early as 1682 there is a report of hats being stolen from a wagon. The main purchasers of these hats were passengers staying overnight or stopping for a meal on the coaching road – and girls' schools. Villagers from miles around came bringing their plaits to sell to the hat manufacturers, some coarsely plaited and some fine, the fine ones made by splitting the straw with a special tool. The town became known for straw work in general which was predictably named Dunstable Ware.

Dunstable is very close to Whipsnade. When I was a child the London Zoo in Regent's Park was the main headquarters of the London Zoological Society, and in 1931 the society opened a remote place at Whipsnade among the Downs to give a country home and more space to some of their animals. It has now become rather greater than its London counterpart simply because there is more space for the animals to run around in enclosures, and if you go to Regent's Park there is not an awful lot to see in terms of the larger animals. Whipsnade has wolves roaming wild in a pack in a paddock, hippos in their pools, and herds of deer, something like twenty-one different types, grazing the paddock, and it is to Whipsnade that thousands of people flock every year.

An alternative attraction with wild animals is at Woburn, where in the mid-eighteenth century the fourth Duke of Bedford created a large park of about 3,000 acres and started what was really the traditional aristocrat's menagerie, something that had been fairly usual since medieval times. In the 1930s this was transformed into a zoological park and wildlife reserve where lions, giraffes, zebras and other animals roam in relative freedom. Visitors can drive through the current safari park and observe them at close quarters and have their aerials ripped off by the monkeys. While Whipsnade progresses with its zoological studies and breeding programmes and even programmes to reintroduce animals to the wild in their countries of origin,

Woburn is quite a different experience that no doubt gives a great deal of pleasure to many. It was really quite clever of the thirteenth Duke of Bedford to do this because Woburn Abbey itself is not particularly magnificent or wonderful compared with so many of the other stately homes that are open to the public, and although it has a number of good paintings such as *Jane Seymour* by Holbein, *Elizabeth I* by Gheeraerts and others by Van Dyck, Lely and Gainsborough, these alone are not enough to attract a great many visitors.

However the one name that everybody associates with Bedfordshire is that of John Bunyan, who was born at Elstow, just to the south of Bedford. Elstow itself is the site of a Norman abbey founded by William the Conqueror's niece, the Countess Judith, and throughout the Middle Ages aristocratic ladies who devoted themselves to religion came there, not necessarily to take full vows but to live in peace and serenity, occasionally being admonished by various bishops who had to remind them not to wear silver pins or their silken gowns. There is a nice story from the fourteenth century when the young nuns supported a candidate not approved by their senior nuns and the older nuns complained, 'Should the young nuns have voices? Tush! They should not have voices.' Every year the nuns held a great fair on the green near the abbey and it was Bunyan the Puritan who dubbed it 'Vanity Fair' saying, 'No erected businesses, but a thing of ancient standing; all sorts of vanity was sold there.' Indeed they probably were, with juggling games, plays, jesters and everything that one would expect of such an occasion. The soldiers of the Parliament tried to raze it in 1645 but the local people had the best of it and threw them out.

John Bunyan, like his father before him, was a tinker, a man who mends pots and pans at the door rather than what is nowadays thought of as the modern traveller. Bunyan was a wild man with no money and a tendency to drink and had difficulty making ends meet. He took a wife but she only brought him two books. It was on the green at Elstow where he declared that he heard a voice saying, 'Wilt thou leave thy sins and go to heaven, or have thy sins and go to hell?' Bunyan's life was transformed. It was, you could say, his 'road to Damascus' moment. He wrote a novel, *The Pilgrim's Progress*, which I am told is second only in stature as a religious book to the Bible, and of course he wrote hymns including 'To Be a Pilgrim'. That is a hymn that I dislike intensely and I vow that if I ever hear it played at my funeral I shall rise up from my coffin. Bunyan left Elstow and went to Bedford where he spent the rest of his life preaching, proselytising and writing. Supposedly Bunyan would go to ply his trade, mending pots and pans, at Houghton Conquest, the lovely manor built for Sir Philip Sidney's sister, and that he cast this house as 'the House Beautiful' in *The Pilgrim's Progress*. When Christian knocks on the door and meets four damsels, Prudence, Piety, Discretion and Charity, they say, 'Come thou in and be blessed by the Lord,' and he follows them in. I suspect that Bunyan probably never got beyond the kitchen door. This house was abandoned by the family, who followed James II into exile, and eventually one of the Dukes of Bedford just left it as a beautiful ruin.

Another house with tragic memories is the one at Ampthill. Ampthill Castle and Park came into the hands of Henry VIII and it was here in 1530 that he held a hunting party where Anne Boleyn gave him a present of a hunting horn and a greyhound. The following year he sent the sad Queen, Catherine of Aragon, there while the divorce case was being tried at Dunstable. She, great lady that she was, despite being poor, unhappy and unwell, had enough spirit to confront the messengers when they arrived with the papers and strike out the words 'Princess Dowager' from their draft reports. Ampthill was created a 'Royal Honour' by Henry, and Charles II on his Restoration gave the property to John Ashburnham, a member of a Sussex family. The house stands on green sand and some friends of mine who lived there when they were children used to take their friends to see what they described as 'the people's sandwiches' where the graves had slid one on top of the other.

Really that is all I know about Bedfordshire.

Hertfordshire

Caroline Lamb described Hertfordshire as 'hearty, homely Hertfordshire'. Caroline Lamb was a great sophisticate, the lover of Byron, yearned for by George III and a woman who shocked society by her behaviour on numerous occasions. If this was her view of Hertfordshire, it is therefore curious that she chose to be buried there along with her husband Lord Melbourne, Queen Victoria's favourite Prime Minister. Coming from Buckinghamshire in a south-easterly direction, we pass through Tring and Berkhamsted. Tring is most noted for the rather splendid park that the Rothschilds had laid out there with a matching house, but Berkhamsted is rather more interesting.

Originally named Beorchehamstete, it has quite grand connections. You will still find the remains of a castle there, probably built by William the Conqueror's half-brother Robert of Mortain, to whom he gave the manor. It was at one time the home of Thomas Becket when he was Chancellor of England and before he became Archbishop of Canterbury and went to his death. Henry III, who loved the place, gave it its charter as a town, King John gave it to his wife Queen Isabella and in 1216 it was taken for King Louis of France by the English barons who were rebelling against King John. There was a strange occasion when Piers Gaveston was given the castle by his lover King Edward II whose niece he subsequently married. Another French king, King John, was held prisoner there after the Battle of Poitiers.

The castle fell into disrepair in 1495 and the stones were used to build Berkhamsted Place, which Charles I inherited from his brother Prince Henry. At the time of Charles's death, rather oddly, a man called Daniel Axtell, a former grocer's apprentice, who had been converted to the Parliamentary cause, was the tenant, and it was he who made the arrangements for the King's trial in Westminster Hall, and it was he who threatened to shoot Lady Fairfax when she entered and interrupted the proceedings.

Ashlyns Park was begun by Thomas Coram, founder of the Foundling Hospital in London, as a place where he could move the children to out of London and give them somewhere to play and get fresh air and generally improve their lives. Handel used to play to people who came out at weekends as he was a great supporter of the hospital. It is recorded that 50,000 children had passed through the Foundling Hospital on the way to health and opportunity in the world. The almshouses in Berkhamsted were founded by John Sayer, who was Charles II's cook and who lies buried in the church here. Clearly cooks were quite well paid as far back as that.

Not far away is Hemel Hempstead, birthplace of Dick Turpin, the well-known highwayman. The town was famous for its paper mills, there having been a mill there since the Domesday Book. A family called Dickinson discovered a way to make paper in a continuous sheet, which made possible the editions of our daily newspapers. I used to go to Hemel Hempstead with my father when I was young because he was President of the Harveian Society, which was in memory of William Harvey, the discoverer of the circulation of the blood, who is buried here, as is another famous medical man, Sir Astley Cooper, the pupil of John Hunter. Astley Cooper was the most famous surgeon of his day, who once remarked that if a day had passed during which he had not dissected something, he would think that day lost. On one occasion he received a fee of 1,000 guineas tossed to him in a nightcap by a grateful patient. However, it was his operation on George IV that brought him a baronetcy. He also doctored horses as well as kings and used to bring animals to recover in the grounds of his nearby estate at Gadebridge. My father remarked that it was much harder to be a vet because the animals could not tell you what their symptoms were, but it was probably much more peaceful. I remember being present in the tercentennial year of Harvey when they opened the crypt in which he was interred. It sticks in my mind largely because I was quite young and we were all standing there waiting for people to make speeches when out hopped a very large toad. The society had had the crypt restored and there is a memorial now to Harvey in the church. Afterwards we went from there to Audley End to an Elizabethan dinner which I will come to when I reach Essex.

Keep heading east and you come to the city of St Albans, standing on the site of the Roman Verulamium. The town is named St Albans after the first ever English Christian martyr, St Alban, who was a Roman soldier in the reign of Diocletian. He had been born a pagan and was converted by a Christian priest. Diocletian was a major player in the persecution of Christians and Alban gave refuge to the priest in his own house and consequently was condemned to death. He was beaten with rods and then beheaded and remained only a name in the Christian chronicles until 793, when Offa founded a great Benedictine abbey as a penance, atonement for his murder of Ethelbert, and he named it after Alban. The abbey that stands there now is a Norman rebuilding of Offa's abbey with a magnificent Norman archway. It numbers among its abbots Cardinal Wolsey, who was the thirty-eighth of its forty abbots before the Reformation. Among its alumni is Matthew Paris, the thirteenth-century chronicler, not the latter-day political journalist.

Abbots Langley, a large village a few miles from St Albans is the birthplace of Nicholas Breakspear, the only Englishman ever to become Pope, which he did under the title of Adrian IV. Among the tombs in St Michael's Church are those of Nicholas Bacon, Queen Elizabeth's Keeper of the Great Seal, and his son, the rather more famous Francis Bacon. Francis died as a result of pneumonia caught while stuffing a chicken with snow in Gray's Inn Walks in London to see how long he could preserve the chicken, a very early form of refrigeration. He was brought back to lie in St Albans and his tomb is much visited by clothing historians to examine the perfect Jacobean costume that adorns his effigy. St Albans was the site of the third printing press to be set up in England following those at Westminster and Oxford. It not only printed the monastery chronicles but also an interesting book on heraldry, hunting and hawking by Dame Juliana Berners who lived in nearby Sopwell Priory.

Hertford, the county town, is not that far away and is a pleasant enough place, but not nearly as interesting as the nearby village of Hertingfordbury, which stands, pleasantly, on the banks of the River Mimram. The river flows through Panshanger Park, home for centuries of the Cowper family and latterly of the dashing Desboroughs. A hanger in this part of the world is a hanging wood coming down the side of a hill. I have always liked the allusion to the great god Pan, whose influence still lingers in country places. The church contains among its many monuments one to a distant ancestor of mine, Sir William Harrington, who is there in his shroud with his wife and their daughters. He was one of the regicides, the people who signed the death certificate for Charles I, and one of his daughters married my ancestor. There are quite a lot of legal figures in the church, one being William, first Earl Cowper, who was Lord High Chancellor and made himself unpopular by refusing the customary gifts offered to the new occupants of the Woolsack, in other words bribes. There is no monument to William but there is one to his brother Spencer, the only British judge ever to stand in the dock on trial for murder. In the relief he is shown in his judge's robe and wig.

The story goes that when he was a barrister he and three other lawyers were charged with murdering a girl by the name of Sarah Stout from Hertford. She was a young Quaker and had lost her heart to Spencer. When he was visiting Hertford for the March Assizes he went to visit the Stouts on some matter concerning a mortgage and agreed to stay the night. He was a married man but nonetheless Sarah pined for him. At about eleven o'clock at night, Spencer was sitting after supper talking to Sarah. The maid went upstairs, according to the prosecution, to warm the bed, and heard a door slam downstairs and discovered that Cowper and Sarah Stout were gone. Neither returned that night and the next morning Sarah was found dead in the river near the mill, floating on the surface. There was a crease around her neck and she was bruised around her ear. The prosecution said the girl had not drowned but had been strangled and thrown into the water, and they asserted that Cowper and two fellow barristers and a scrivener who was with them had killed her. Numerous doctors swore on oath that a drowned person would have sunk, and two sailors who had been in battles at sea were called to give similar evidence. The defence was that the woman had drowned and that the body had floated because it was held up by the stakes in the river.

The judge's summing up is highly suspect, as he addressed the jury telling them that the expert witnesses had given great cause for suspicion by their words but whether 'they or Mr Cowper are guilty or no that is for you to determine. I am sensible that I have omitted many things but I am a little faint and cannot remember any more of the evidence.' All four were acquitted and the repute is that the Tories of Hertford wished to hang a member of the famous Whig family of Cowper, while the Quakers, to absolve the community of reproach, had done all they could to clear the girl's name. The whole case caused a great furore and one of the relatives demanded the right of ordeal by battle to re-try the issue. In the absence of modern forensic techniques, we shall never know more about it, and Cowper went on to obtain high honour in his profession.

The lovely house at Epcombs near to Hertingfordbury, also

on the River Mimram, is supposed to have been a place where Jane Austen stayed and based the Bennet family upon the inhabitants. It is from here that the New River was formed using the waters mostly of the Lea but also of the Mimram and other surrounding rivers. It was canalised and used to supply water for the East End of London. The flinty ground in Hertfordshire is known for producing particularly clear and fresh water. The Lea is a river that is overlooked nowadays because it has become so polluted over the intervening centuries, but Izaak Walton used to go and fish it with great enthusiasm. It is interesting to note that more recently it was full of American sentinel crayfish which had replaced the native British crayfish, until the Polish immigrants came at the turn of the millennium. Not being ones to leave behind anything that was good to eat, they completely cleared the river of crayfish. They also, I believe, cleared it of most of its carp and quite a lot of its swans and, quite frankly, well done to them!

Nearby is the town of Ware, which was once so prominent that Hertford was known as Hertford-by-Ware. Its prosperity was associated with the malting industry, which left it with a number of cone-shaped cowls from the many kilns used to heat and sprout the grain. It is mentioned in William Cowper's poem 'The Diverting History of John Gilpin' where he should have dined at Edmonton but carried on to Ware because his horse bolted. It is, however, most famous for the Great Bed of Ware, now standing in the Victoria and Albert Museum. In Elizabethan times ordinary people started to move about the countryside more and it was unusual, in any walk of life, ever to sleep alone. If you were a well-to-do married couple you would share a bed and when the husband was away the wife would probably share it with one of her maids or ladies-in-waiting. In ordinary houses children all slept together, usually divided by sex but not always. An extra form of heating, I suppose, as much as for reasons of space and the cost of beds. Of course, if you stayed in an inn you had to pay through the teeth in order to get a room just for yourself and your wife or servant. The Great Bed of Ware was so famous it is even mentioned in Shakespeare.

Hatfield to the south-west contains two great houses of the Cecil family. Hatfield House itself was built by Robert Cecil when he had been persuaded, for want of a better word, by James I to move out of Theobalds, the house he had inherited, and in exchange was given Hatfield. Robert never lived in it because he died when it was barely finished and lies in Hatfield Church. The site was originally a palace for the Bishops of Ely and Cardinal Morton, Treasurer to Henry VII and the inventor of 'Morton's Fork', whereby no one was to be exempt from taxation. He would visit your house and if you were living high on the 'hock' he would say, 'Well, obviously you are doing very well and the King would appreciate a gift.' If you were living in some penury he would say, 'Obviously you are terribly thrifty and are saving all your money and therefore perhaps you would like to give some of it to the King.' Hertfordshire was historically a great place for the making of bricks, the local clay being very suitable, and when Cecil started to rebuild the house he built it in brick. All three of Henry VIII's children seem to have spent quite a lot of their child-hood here, and it was here that Elizabeth received an invitation to go to court to acknowledge Lady Jane Grey as Queen. She refused, saying she was ill, but a few days afterwards she was well enough to go to town and proclaim her sister Mary Queen, riding at her side into the city. When Mary died in 1558 it was to Hatfield that a cavalcade came, riding down to find Elizabeth, sitting under an oak tree, and acclaimed her Queen.

This magnificent house is built in the shape of an 'E' in honour of Elizabeth and cost about £40,000 in the money of the day. Like all the Cecil houses it is outstanding and has some interest-ing possessions. There is the Rainbow Portrait of Queen Elizabeth, a letter in Mary, Queen of Scots' handwriting, Lord Burghley's diary recording the defeat of the Spanish Armada and

Queen Elizabeth had left behind one of her hats and a pair of yellow silk stockings. The estate is 15,000 acres in size with the River Lea washing its northern end and is seven miles around. The Marquess of Salisbury, who was Prime Minister, lies at rest in the church here, as does Lord Melbourne with his wife Lady Caroline Lamb. I find it difficult to believe that if she had known Hatfield House she should have described it as 'homely'.

The other great Cecil house is Theobalds, a little to the south-east over on the Essex border. It was built by Lord Burghley, Elizabeth I's trusted adviser, and inherited by his son, Robert Cecil. Not long after his accession, James I fell in love with the house and Robert Cecil gave it up. Various members of the Cromwell family lie in the church but the most curious story connected with Theobalds was the end of the life of Richard Cromwell. Following the death of his father he stepped down from his office as Protector, and the question remains, did he jump or was he pushed? Cromwell went into exile and wandered about on the Continent for twenty years. He came back a widower and took the name of Clarke and lived, with his friend Mrs Pengelly, at Cheshunt, near the former royal residence. He paid Mrs Pengelly ten shillings a week for his board and lodgings. There were also added extras, for we find among the accounts charges for tobacco, brandy, pipes and a loan of £2 with an entry 'when you had your feast'. There was a further charge of six pence 'for repairing your britches', twenty shillings for a new hat and an entry for £3.18s.0d, 'money you were pleased to give Tommy on his entrance at the Temple and a guinea to buy him his law books'. He also left behind in the care of Mrs Pengelly his little shagreen green trunk which he had had with him on all his travels. It seems rather sad that the man who was, albeit briefly and not very successfully, Lord Protector of England, should have spent his days in what was, to all intents and purposes, a lodging house.

I spent quite a lot of my early childhood, before I went to

boarding school at the age of ten and a half, in the area around Bishop's Stortford. My childhood friend Diana (Dippy) Parker lived with her parents at Much Hadham and then at Brent Pelham and finally at Hatfield Broad Oak. They were the happy, innocent days of childhood where we played all sorts of games in the fields and in the barns and I remember happy days out with the Puckeridge Hunt. It was extremely rural countryside and it was the first time I realised that there was such a thing as an outside loo when we visited Dippy's old nanny and her husband at their cottage and I asked if I could use the facilities. I remember, possibly with hindsight, some rather sinister pigs in a field that followed us along the hedge line. Some years later I read that the Hosein brothers had murdered Mrs Muriel McKay, who had been kidnapped by mistake as they thought she was Rupert Murdoch's wife, and had murdered her and fed her to the pigs. I always thought that they were probably the same pigs. The A1, formerly the Great North Road, which runs through the county, leads you out at the top into Cambridgeshire but I am going to go eastwards into Essex.

Essex

Oh, I do like Essex. I can think of almost no county that is so independent and proud of itself in the face of bad press, being the butt of jokes and in close proximity to London. Essex retains its individuality and it would seem that it was always thus. Just sitting here I can immediately think of half a dozen names from Roman times of Essex people who stood up to be counted. Let us start with the greatest Celtic leader of them all, Caractacus, an Essex boy who took on the fight against the Romans. Against every eventuality he kept fighting them and fighting them, uniting the tribes, right across Britain, against the might of the Roman war machine. The martial discipline of the Romans was as incomprehensible to the Celts as the Martini-Henry rifle and the Gatling gun would be to tribespeople in later centuries. Again and again they hurled themselves against it until, as Chesterton so evocatively put it, 'They were carried home on their clansmen's wicker shields.' Eventually Caractacus was captured and he and his wife and children were taken in chains to Rome. Expecting to die, as was the way with captives in Roman triumphs, he made a splendid speech recorded by Tacitus for posterity, and I quote:

> If to the nobility of my birth I visited the virtues of moderation, Rome would have beheld me, not in captivity, but as a royal visitor and friend. I had arms, men and horses, I had wealth, can you wonder I was unwilling to lose them. I stood at bay for years; had I acted otherwise where on your

part would have been the glory of conquest and on my part the honour of brave resistance? I am now in your power. If you are bent on vengeance, execute your purpose; the scene will soon be over and the name of Caractacus will sink into oblivion. Preserve my life and I shall be, to a far off posterity, a moment of Roman clemency.

Claudius removed his chains and Caractacus and his family lived in captivity in Rome until, broken-hearted, he died.

Think of the Houses of Parliament and next to them stands a statue of an Essex girl in her chariot. She is Boudicca, who was insulted by the Roman general Aulus Plautius who seized her lands and assaulted her daughters. She raised the Iceni in fury against him, burning Roman Colchester and Roman London. You can still see the traces of the fire if you look at the old remains of the Roman London wall. She very nearly succeeded in hurling the invaders from our shores. If Boudicca was the original Essex girl – given the Celt's fashion statements she undoubtedly had big hair and bling, so why not white shoes as well, and she was undoubtedly in a strop – then surely the Essex geezer personified is Old King Cole. You will remember the nursery rhyme that says:

> Old King Cole was a merry old soul,
> And a merry old soul was he
> He called for his pipe and he called for his bowl
> And he called for his fiddlers three.

I do like the thought that Old King Cole was actually the father of St Helena, the mother of the Emperor Constantine. It was she who went out and allegedly discovered the True Cross. I will come to the other two characters that are in my mind at the moment when I reach Colchester, but for now we are still on the Hertfordshire border.

Audley End stands on the edge of Saffron Walden, with its

great park extending as far as the Cambridge Road and with the River Cam running through its grounds. It is one of the most magnificent houses in England and certainly the most magnificent in Essex. It was built on the site of an abbey given by Henry VIII to Lord Chancellor Sir Thomas Audley, and it was his grandson Thomas Howard, the Lord Treasurer, who built the splendid house there. James I, viewing it before it was finished, apparently said to Thomas Howard, 'It is too much for a King, but it might do very well for a Lord Treasurer.' The palace is said to have cost £200,000 in their money and, in fact, what we see today is only a third of the original house, as John Vanbrugh removed three sides of the quadrangle to leave it in its current state. It still remains a great Jacobean house. On the day of our visit to William Harvey's grave, you may remember that I said we ended the day at Audley End for an Elizabethan banquet; how my father must have enjoyed planning it, for he was the gourmet in the family. We had swan and a whole sturgeon and all sorts of Elizabethan delicacies, and everybody had to dress in Elizabethan clothing or you weren't allowed in.

Saffron Walden is so named because its main industry in medieval times was growing the saffron crocus. Saffron remains the most expensive of all the spices, indeed probably the most expensive of all ingredients. It is basically the dried stamens of the autumn crocus which had to be picked by hand from their place in the heart of the crocus flower and then carefully dried. It was the crocus that took Marco Polo to China, exporting it from Italy, and it is saffron that gives us that wonderful clear yellow that so distinguishes Chinese robes and hangings. There is a story that the plant was smuggled into this country in the staff of a 'palmer', in other words a pilgrim, coming back from Italy, but I think this is unlikely because it would be difficult to grow crocus in any quantities in that manner. To this day, if you go to the Tourist Information Centre in the council offices in Saffron Walden, you will be able to buy saffron crocus plants, although the industry has long since finished. Saffron was one of the joys of medieval cooks because of the brilliant colour that it would give the otherwise lacklustre dishes.

Not far south of Saffron Walden is the village of Great Dunmow, which was always a cause of delight to me because every four years, in a leap year, the Parish Council of Dunmow awards the Dunmow Flitch, a flitch being a side of bacon usually cut from the fat end. This was given to the couple who were deemed not to have quarrelled in the previous year. Whether or not the inhabitants of Dunmow were particularly belligerent I really don't know, but I do love the thought of this reward for peaceful behaviour among the village's married couples.

Essex was always a heavily forested county and at one point the Essex forest ran from Epping as far as Colchester near the coast on the Colne estuary. Clearly most of it has gone now but Epping Forest still remains as a pleasant place for walkers, and a handy spot to dump dead bodies. Essex is very much a county of two halves: the rural north, which is still surprisingly wooded and farmed, much as it must have been for centuries; and the industrial south which, with its frontage on to the Thames and the docks that accompany such a position, is also much as it must have been for centuries. It is to the industrial south that we owe the image of Essex so beloved of television at the moment, 'shaggin' 'em in Dagenham' as the song goes, *The Only Way Is Essex* and other such programmes and the wonderful vulgarity of the Essex girl. I first went to south Essex as early as I can remember because, in those days, the big passenger liners coming in from the Far East used to put in at Tilbury Docks, twenty-four miles in from the mouth of the Thames, and we would go down to meet my grandmother off the ship. She would come over every two or three years on a Cunard liner from Singapore. In those days the docks were proper working docks, which the trade unions hadn't succeeded in killing quite as effectively as they did in the 1960s, and there was great excitement about going down into dockland. There was also something slightly darkly disreputable, fathered by thoughts of Dickens really, although Dickens never wrote about the Essex docks.

It was the Ford Motor Works that were created in Dagenham in the 1930s that gave the area its reputation. I suspect, however, that the original 'Belle of Barking Creek', if you like, was the abbess who in the late twelfth century levied a tax on all ships putting in to her jetty and started a tradition of shipping unloading further up the Thames from London. When I was a young barrister in the late 1960s and early 1970s this part of Essex was still very much the preserve of docklands and East End gangs. I can remember the wife of one docker who I was representing in a matrimonial case being incensed because she could not understand why the extra luxuries that her husband had been wont to bring home, items that had fallen off the back of a cargo ship, could not be written into the maintenance order for herself and her children. 'But,' she wailed, 'we would have beef every week and whisky and all those things. Are you saying that we cannot build this into the order?' I had great difficulty in explaining that actually these were illegal perks and no, we could not. One firm of solicitors who used to instruct me handled more murder cases than any other in the British Isles, this at a time when the East End of London was torn apart by violent gang warfare. We all know about the Krays, but they were certainly not the only gangsters working the East End and the River Thames.

Traditionally there had been a lot of poverty and poor housing in this area and as such it had attracted the great reformers. Elizabeth Fry, the wife of a rich Norfolk banker, came to minister to prisoners and their families. The conditions in English prisons in her day were unbelievably squalid and harsh and a very far cry from the television sets and the cells that we have now; not that I am saying that prison is a pleasant place but it is an awful lot better than it was. Also to this part of London came Dr Barnardo, who was so horrified to discover children sleeping in the streets, homeless and unwanted, and fighting for their livelihoods with knives and teeth and boots, that he started by renting rooms to accommodate them in the Thameside villages and then opened his first home. He had a tough time of it, regularly beaten up by the street victims who didn't want his help and suspected him of ulterior motives, and hassled by the police who just thought he was an interfering busybody. There is, however, no doubt that the Barnardo's Homes helped tens of thousands of poor children to achieve a reasonable life. Also from this area came Joseph Lister, the discoverer of sepsis and the man who brought to light the importance of hygiene in hospitals and operating theatres. He would have had plenty of scope to develop his research in Thameside Essex.

When I was a barrister my senior clerk in chambers, one Barry Madden, was from Romford so I got a lot of work in Essex at that time in my career, going to the crown courts at Woodford and Chelmsford. Most often I went to Chelmsford on all sorts of cases and I loved going there. I remember that they had two judges sitting permanently, one of them probably one of the most unpleasant judges I have ever had to appear in front of, who hated women at the bar and only started being civil to me after he discovered that I was a Roman Catholic. The other judge was Francis Peter who had been at Downside with my brother, and was a charming and delightful man, one of the best judges I have ever encountered. I used to pray on the train on the journey there that I would be in his court rather than the other.

These visits to Chelmsford took me to one of the strangest places I have ever been in my life: Wapping Railway Washing Plant. I leapt on to the train at the last minute, at the same platform as usual, and was slightly daunted when all the lights went off and there appeared to be nobody else on the train, composed of individual carriages in those days. After a while we drew into this huge industrial unit which was clearly a washing shed as it had numerous industrial shower heads. I got out of the train and had to walk the whole length of the platform, hoping that the water wouldn't be turned on until I got to the other end. Happily it wasn't and the workers all roared with laughter but were terribly nice and called me a taxi and I arrived at court not too late.

Essex has a large expanse of coastline. It is cut off from London by the Thames at the bottom and then you work up the coast past Shoeburyness, where there was a school of gunnery and there always seemed to be red flags flying because they were having firing practice. Carry on and you come to the mouth of the Crouch with the area so beloved of sailors known as Burnham-on-Crouch. Keep going north and you come to the Blackwater Estuary and the Isle of Mersea. What always amazes me about the Blackwater Estuary is that in an area so close to London and at the edge of one of the most populated counties in England, you should find this wonderful wilderness of marshland inhabited by wading and migrating birds. Here, as in the east Kent marshes, is the home of the Essex wildfowlers. In earlier times, given its proximity to the London markets, it was a huge commercial wildfowling site with geese and ducks being sent in large quantities to be sold in London. Historically there were so many punt-guns in use in this part of the coast that a friend of mine, who was a keen wildfowler, said that he was surprised any bird actually managed to land on the estuary and survive to take off. It isn't like that today of course; wildfowling is a hobby and you have to be slightly mad to do it. You have to know the flight patterns of the birds and you are very dependent on the weather; the worse it is, the better the chances of getting something, so you slog through the mud and the rain or the sleet or the snow, because remember the wildfowling season ends in February. You trudge all the way out there and if you do manage to shoot something you then have to carry it all the way back again, but wildfowlers love it and I can see the attraction. I will talk a bit more about wildfowling later.

Continue to the far end of the Isle of Mersea and at the next estuary, if you turn inland, you will come to the town of Colchester, which was the capital of Roman Britain. After Boudicca's rebellion, the Romans turned Colchester into a large walled garrison town, and much of what was Roman Colchester can be seen in the modern layout of the town, and especially in the museum, which contains some wonderful artefacts. There is a delightful relief of a Roman centurion, Marcus Favonius, complete with his vine staff of office, the plaque set up by two of his freemen. There is also a cavalry officer called Longinus riding over a fallen foe and the famous Colchester vase, which shows scenes of gladiators fighting and attacking a wild beast. Another scene is of a hound pursuing a hare and two deer. The Romans imported the brown hare into England for the purposes of coursing, which was one of their favourite sports. Here we have it in the first century. Until the hunt ban, Essex was an area keen on coursing; that is, naturally, coursing under National Coursing Club rules rather than poaching, which is all you will find nowadays.

The great treasure of Colchester is the oyster, and the city is one of the best places to eat native British oysters. It is said that the Emperor Nero could identify the source of any oyster he tasted, and his oyster of choice came from Colchester. A few years ago I spoke at the Colchester Oyster Festival, which is a proper festival held when the beds are open in September/October time, and the main delight was plate after plate, as many as you could eat, of these lovely crisp, nutty little oysters. With a native oyster you actually have to bite it and they are quite different from the Portuguese oysters which are the most commonplace. I heard that one man had eaten six and a half dozen, that is seventy-eight oysters. Just as I was about to make my speech I noticed one woman had left early, so I referred to the man who had eaten all the oysters and mused whether that was his wife going home early to prepare, since oysters are known to be a great aphrodisiac.

I am a member of the Worshipful Company of Butchers by the efforts of a dear friend of mine called Colin Taylor, who is proud to describe himself as an Essex boy, and it was really he and his wife Jean who made me realise the vitality and independence of the Essex character. Essex is London's seaside. Compared with the rather faded respectability of Broadstairs and Margate, there is nothing refined or genteel about Clacton or Southend-on-Sea (pronounced as Saarrfend). They are still visited by large numbers of Londoners who for some reason or another cannot afford to troop out to the Costa del Sol and they are a joy of 'kiss me quick' hats and seaside rock and candyfloss and clockwork golf and amusement arcades, including 'Peter Pan's Kingdom' in one case. They are what they are and they are very Essex.

Essex will surprise you. You will be given instructions to turn down a certain road to go and visit some friend who you know lives on a farm. The only road available to you seems to be marked as a cul-de-sac and goes through a housing estate. Then you come out the other side of the housing estate and the cul-de-sac is seven miles long and almost immediately you are into the country. Although Essex is fairly flat it is still proper countryside, properly farmed. Part of that agricultural heritage is to be found at Tiptree, which is a well-known centre for jam

making, and although they no longer grow all their own fruit because they are far too big an organisation, that is how they started. Certainly twenty years ago there were orchards of various suitable fruits all around the factory. Nearby was that extraordinary building known as Layer Marney Tower, part of a grand design by the King's Chancellor in the reign of Henry VIII. It stands in total solitary magnificence because the rest of the house was never built around it, the Chancellor having fallen on hard times; in fact I believe he lost his head.

So, leaving Essex behind us, let us move on to Suffolk.

Suffolk

As somebody who had lost my heart to the loom of the South Downs and the hills and hangers of Hertfordshire long before I ever saw the flat lands of East Anglia, I used to assume that people who lived there yearned for hills and only lived there 'a faith demure', but I was wrong. Some years ago I took a friend of mine, whose family had lived in the flat lands for a great many centuries, down to Aldeburgh, and as we got into that county she said, 'Isn't it wonderful. Now you can put your head up and see the sky, and see what everybody's doing and all that lovely open air and freedom of space.' I said, 'Wouldn't you rather have hills?' to which she replied, 'Good Lord no. They'd just get in the way.' When you consider that the two greatest landscape painters in English art history, Constable and Gainsborough, both came from Suffolk, you have to realise that Suffolk is not only extremely beautiful but has something about the light that makes it special. Suffolk is constantly at war with the sea, which eats away large chunks of it, not in the dramatic way of the Yorkshire coast, just inexorably as the North Sea beats against its shores. Surprisingly for a county with so much sea coast, it really has only the ports of Felixstowe and Lowestoft to take its goods in and out of the country. Historically the area was a great producer of wool and, as in other wool counties, there is a plethora of beautiful churches offering up the sins of the wool master to God. Since the decline of the wool trade, only remnants of market towns remain where the wool clip would have been sold to keen would-be buyers.

Both Constable and Gainsborough came from the south of the county by the Essex border. Constable was born at East Bergholt, where he lived much of his life until fame took him to London, and Flatford Mill, which he painted regularly, is but two miles from his place of birth, although Dedham Mill, another favourite subject, is actually over the Essex border. Go a little round the border to the north-west and you will come to Sudbury, which is where Gainsborough was born. East Bergholt is just a little rural village but Sudbury is somewhat grander. One of my favourite epitaphs is there, to a rich man called Thomas Carter, who died in 1706.

> Traveller I would relate a wondrous thing. On the day on which Thomas Carter breathed his last at Sudbury a camel passed through the eye of a needle. If thou hast wealth go and do likewise. Farewell.

This obviously refers to the biblical quotation about it being easier for a camel to get through the eye of a needle than for a rich man to get into the kingdom of heaven. This refers not to an actual needle but to a gate in the wall of Jerusalem.

Also in Sudbury is the head of Simon of Sudbury, who was Archbishop of Canterbury, born during the early part of the fourteenth century when Edward III was establishing a colony of Flemish at Sudbury to teach woollen manufacture to the locals. Simon had crowned Richard II and was made Lord Chancellor, but afterwards became a hated figure by applying the poll tax to the whole nation in a graduated form. Mrs Thatcher should perhaps have learned from Simon of Sudbury. The crown jewels were in pawn, the King was steeped in debt and every available source of taxation was exhausted, hence the imposition of the poll tax. This led to the Wat Tyler rebellion; while Richard was meeting the rebels at Mile End, part of the mob broke into the Tower, crying out for the Primate and calling him a spoiler and a traitor. He was dragged out of the Tower where he was killed with eight blows of an axe, which was what it took to remove his head. This was carried round the city on a pole and then brought back to Sudbury. The rest of his body was buried in Canterbury.

While you are in the area you might like to go and visit Long Melford for the pleasure of seeing the most magnificent church in what is not really a very big place. More wool money?

Go north and you will come to the cathedral town of Bury St Edmunds. Does any other town in England have a name that states quite specifically why it is there, in this case the burial place of St Edmund the martyr? St Edmund was a Saxon king who went out to fight the Danes and was taken prisoner at Hexne. The Danes said that they would spare his life if he would give up his Christian faith, or so the story goes as recounted by Abbot Fleury; he refused and was shot to death with arrows. His body was brought to the abbey where it was buried. The place was turned into a shrine for pilgrimage, an extremely valuable asset at any time until the Reformation, which does rather make me doubt the whole story and suspect, cynic that I am, that Abbot Fleury was merely looking for a nice little earner for his abbey. There is a magnificent medieval gateway to the old abbey which still graces the town.

The crown court at Bury St Edmunds, a marvellous venue, was the site of the trial of William Corder for the murder of Maria Marten, which led to the very popular Victorian melodrama of *Maria Marten; or the Murder in the Red Barn*. The story went that William proposed to the beauty of the village of Polstead and arranged to meet her in his mother's red barn from where he would take her to Ipswich and marry her. During the day Corder was seen to go to the barn with a pick on his shoulder. Maria duly appeared dressed as a boy to avoid detection and was never seen alive again. Corder went to her parents and declared that the marriage had taken place and that Maria had gone to stay with friends at some distance so that the wedding should not be discovered. He then pleaded ill health and left Polstead with money obtained by a trick from the Manningtree Bank. A card later arrived bearing an Isle of Wight address but a London postmark, telling Maria's parents that the girl was happy in her new life. Maria's stepmother dreamed repeatedly of the red barn, and the year after Maria's departure the building was searched and her body was found beneath the floor. Corder was traced to a house in Brentford where he had married somebody else and the trial was a complete sensation, so much so that *The Times* gave a quarter of its whole space to it. The court was so crowded that solicitors fainted in the crush.

I once had to give evidence as a witness in the Bury St Edmunds court and I have to tell you that the witness box, which is high above the court and almost level with the splendour of the judge's bench, would have been a frightening place if you had been the sort of witness who had to be cross-examined. My evidence was not quite so exciting: it involved the ex-husband of my client who had followed her to her place of residence, and, intending to snatch the child of the union, had murdered her lover with whom she was now living. My evidence only concerned whether or not he could have obtained her address which would have made it murder, or had simply followed her in a fit of rage, which made it merely manslaughter.

Head towards the coast from Bury St Edmunds and you will come to Framlingham. One of the very first poems I ever learned went:

> 'Twas early last September night at Framlingham-on-Sea,
> 'Twere fair day come tomorrow and the time were after tea,
> I met a painted caravan a down a dusty lane,
> A pharaoh and his wagon going jolt and creak and strain.

A pharaoh is an old word for gypsy because gypsy is a foreshortening of the word Egyptian. I remember that I had always had it in my head to go and visit Framlingham and so one day I did.

Rather to my surprise it wasn't actually on the sea, being instead quite a way inland, but it was well worth the visit. Framlingham was the seat of the Dukes of Norfolk of the Mowbray line, many of whom are buried in the church, which is very fine and has a fifteenth-century embattled tower and a roof of Spanish chestnut with rich fan vaulting. This is picked out in golden stars and a spiral band painted red, white, black and gold around it. There is a magnificent alabaster tomb to the first Earl of Surrey, Sir Henry Howard, of whom more later, who lies with his wife and their sons and daughters. The Howards, who did have an indirect claim to the throne, were regularly beheaded by the Tudors: Philip, Earl of Surrey, the eldest son of the third Duke, was beheaded by Henry VIII, as was the fourth Duke by his daughter Elizabeth. Here you will also find the tomb of Henry Fitzroy, Duke of Richmond and Somerset, who married one of the Howards. He was the illegitimate son of Henry VIII who had apparently intended to make him King, an indication of this being that he had given him precedence when he was six over all the English nobility, but he died young and by then Henry had a legitimate son by Jane Seymour. The third Duke had a narrow escape; he was due to be beheaded by Henry VIII and was awaiting his execution in the Tower, when Henry VIII died and he was finally set free by Mary Tudor. The Howards have always been staunch Catholics.

Even better than the tombs in the church are the remains of the castle of Framlingham, which stand on top of the mound that the Saxon kings of East Anglia had fortified and was built by Roger Le Bigod at the time of Richard I. When you reach the top of the mound and cross the moat the walls are over forty feet high and in some places are eight feet thick and enclose an area of more than an acre. Their foundations descend thirty feet below ground. It has thirteen towers, four of immense strength built of solid masonry.

Henry Howard, a saint and martyr in the Catholic Church,

did not escape the wrath of the King. He was brought up as a companion to the Duke of Richmond at the court of Henry VIII and accompanied him abroad and stayed on at the French court. Henry was an arrogant, hot-tempered and impetuous man, reckless in his speech, which is what eventually led to his death, and he was really devoid of any sort of balance. Two years after he was made a Knight of the Garter he used to go around breaking the windows of the citizens with a catapult just for amusement. It was when he was imprisoned for his various misdemeanours that he started writing the poetry for which he is perhaps best known. Henry, so incensed by the probable appointment of Edward Seymour to be the young Edward VI's guardian after Henry VIII's death, set out to magnify his own claim to the throne and sought to quarter the royal arms with his own on the family shield. To a king as nervous about the succession as Henry VIII, bearing in mind that it was Henry's father who took the throne by battle at the end of the long and horrendous Wars of the Roses, Surrey had truly overstepped the mark. At the age of thirty-six he was sent to the block. He and his friend and mentor Sir Thomas Wyatt, who was imprisoned in the Tower for a time for allegedly being Anne Boleyn's lover, really established the use of blank verse and are taken to be the creators of the English sonnet. All that from just one little poem that I did for an early elocution exam!

If the coastline of Essex is jolly and slightly vulgar and all about having a good time, the coastline of Suffolk was always much more refined and now has become, you might say, slightly pretentious. On reflection this last remark is maybe unjustified because it is based entirely on my opinion of the town of Aldeburgh. In the sixteenth century Aldeburgh was a port specialising in shipbuilding, and indeed Sir Francis Drake's two vessels in which he circumnavigated the world, the *Greyhound* and the *Pelican*, later renamed the *Golden Hind*, were built at Aldeburgh. Incidentally the name Aldeburgh means Ald Burgh or Old Fort. However, in the 1940s Sir Peter Pears and Sir Benjamin Britten decided that they would set up a music festival there to be a showcase for their own musical talents. I met them when I was young and didn't much like either of them. They used to come to my parents' house in Circus Road because their great friend Florence, who was terribly nice, lived in the next street to us and taught my sister Heather singing. I've never been a fan of their music, which smacked too much to me of 'Emperor's New Clothes', but then I'm not gifted with musical talent or appreciation so perhaps I am doing them a disservice. It may be that I am simply too unsophisticated to appreciate it. The music festival takes place at Snape, which is an extension of Aldeburgh. The Maltings at Snape do have a very nice restaurant and the town is reputed to have a very good fish and chip shop, but there are several and it was clearly not the one I found. A couple of years ago I was sent some pictures of the procession that marks the start of the festival and I have to say that the best thing seemed to me to be the group of Tibetan monks in their robes, complete with their horns, which they sounded as they went along the seafront. I expect they came from the nearby monastery of Tibetan Buddhists.

Aldeburgh, like most of the beaches up this coast, has a splendid shingle beach, but for some reason – and to my mind this goes along with the pretentious notion – there now stands on it a sculpture of an iron scallop shell by Maggi Hambling, who erected it in memory of Benjamin Britten and Peter Pears. I am afraid that I am with those residents who regularly petition to have it removed. Quite apart from anything else I cannot see the relevance of a scallop shell. This was never a pilgrim destination, I don't think that either Britten or Pears had any particular relevance to scallops and this is not a coast, as far as I am aware, that is noted for its harvest of scallops.

Keep going up the coast and you come to Dunwich, much of which did not survive the depredations of the sea and now lies buried under the waves. They do say that at high tide you can hear the bell in the church tower ringing from far below the ocean. Continue north and you come to Southwold. Southwold has something of a reputation for the English Edwardian School of Art, largely laid at the door of Philip Wilson Steer, who came and painted the remarkable beach huts which now change hands for the price of a small house in an industrial area. It is an attractive town with a remarkable church with a fantastically decorated roof. It also boasts an amber shop, which largely sells amber and jet taken from the eastern coastline of England. I own a very pleasant amber brooch in the shape of a beetle which I bought there when I was attending the Southwold Literary Festival.

On the Suffolk/Norfolk border you will find the town of Eye, where my nanny came from. She was a splendid old girl who had a wart on her chin from which hairs sprouted. When my mother tried to persuade her to have it looked at or to remove the hairs she said, 'Nonsense, they keep the babies quiet,' as they were fascinated by the hairs. I can remember the burr of her Suffolk vowels and years and years later when I was called to the bar and it was reported in the William Hickey column, she wrote to me from Eye. My only visit to Eye was to attend the local magistrates' court. I can remember it because I had to take a train, I suppose it was to Ipswich, then hire a car and drive to Eye. It was pouring with rain, and all I recollect is field upon field of wet cabbages. I couldn't find the magistrates' court so I stopped and asked the way of two locals and explained that I was a barrister looking for the court. They mused about the fact that I had come all the way from London.

I recall the case quite clearly for a peculiar reason. I was sent from London to represent somebody who was likely to lose their driving licence and their only plea to mitigate such a penalty was that they had to take a forty-mile round trip every week to buy goat's milk for their son who was severely dairy allergic. Never underestimate the cunning of local police. When I arrived at the court, which only sat on special occasions, there was one other case in court that day. This was a local woman from Eye who was charged with allowing her goats to stray on to the highway. She was protesting loudly that her goats had been wandering along the roadside verges for nigh on thirty years so why was she being prosecuted now. It may not have been obvious to her but it was very obvious to me that the magistrates would realise only too well that goat's milk was readily available in the village. There was a tea break between the two cases and I remember they got a little primus stove out from under the clerk's bench and started brewing up and I only redeemed myself from the smear of being a London barrister by talking about Edith Ancliffe, my one-time nanny, and was told, 'Oh yes, we remember her. It was her brother who jumped off the bridge to celebrate VE Day.' 'Was he all right?' I asked. 'Oh yes,' they replied, 'it wasn't a very high bridge, he was just celebrating.' Regardless of Edith Ancliffe, I lost my case.

Travel along the Norfolk border going westwards and you will come to the town of Brandon, which is the home of the oldest known English commercial industry, that of flint knapping. It is a pleasant place on the banks of the Little Ouse but just a couple of miles outside the town are the pits of Grime's Graves, 5,000 years old and with pits going down as deep as eighty feet. You can see the flint workings and even the remains of the antlers that were used as picks for digging out the flints underground. One interesting fact I remember reading was that there was extensive evidence of trepanning among the skeletons of the old flint workers, and these had been done in Neolithic times with amazing precision. The medical journal I was reading could not explain whether these were done as a result of accidents in the mines or because of some form of religious ritual. In the 1960s and 1970s people who took a lot of hallucinogenic drugs used to have themselves trepanned because they thought it would let more light into the brain and they would be even more receptive to the drugs. Neolithic people would also have had access to hallucinogens in the form of magic mushrooms. In any event, this rather dangerous operation, which would have had to be done with a flint instrument, was clearly successful because there had been bone growth around the site and the people to whom it had been done had lived for many years afterwards. As late as the 1940s, flints were still quarried on Ling Heath Common near the graves, and I am told that if you went round the back of the pub you would find flint knappers at work making flints for the old flintlock guns still being used in the Congo and Malaya and other remote parts of the world.

The area west of Brandon on the Cambridgeshire border was home during the Second World War to the great bomber bases of Lakenheath and Mildenhall, which continued as American air bases long after the war was over. Further to the south-west but still in Suffolk, you come to the racing town of Newmarket. It was the Stuart kings, all the Stuarts being brilliant horsemen, who established Newmarket as the home of racing and it was Charles II who opened what is now the National Stud there. Go up to Newmarket Heath any morning and you will see strings of racehorses from the different racing establishments in the town, upward of fifty, being trained. It is a beautiful sight on a fine morning and a wonderful thing to see. There is a Munnings picture of King George V's trainer, George Lambton, watching his string on Newmarket Heath, and in the picture I remember that there was a little boy on a pony sitting beside his father and another little boy beside me saying to me, 'Do you know who that is?' I said, 'Yes, it's your daddy,' and he said, 'Oh, I was rather hoping you might think it was me.'

The Jockey Club, the powerhouse that governs English racing, has its headquarters at Newmarket and the sales ring at Tattersalls is probably where the most valuable horse-flesh in the world is sold. I once did a cookery demonstration in the sales ring and it was a wonderful venue and great fun because up on the board behind me were the prices, which nowadays would be electronically changed, being set in pounds, dollars, yen and all sorts of other currencies. I used to go to the sales at Tattersalls with my mother and she would occasionally buy mares to be sent back to Australia. I remember how exciting it was then when the prices were merely in thousands. At Newmarket racecourse there used to be a special stand that was known as the Iron Stand into which divorced men would go, because they were not socially acceptable, to separate them from their friends who were deemed more respectable in the enclosure.

So let us now cross over the border into Norfolk.

Norfolk

Norfolk is a county that over the years has provided me with more pure unadulterated joy than any other county in the British Isles. Let's start at Great Yarmouth, down at the bottom coastal corner abutting Suffolk. Yarmouth has perhaps slightly lost its way, historically; now it is a place for pleasure with lights and flowerbeds and everything that people want when they go to the seaside, but once upon a time it was one of the greatest fishing ports in the country. Daniel Defoe called the quay the 'finest in England, if not in Europe'. Three rivers, the Bure, the Yare and the Waveney, flow into the North Sea at Yarmouth, through a channel made in the 1560s by a Dutch engineer. The old channel had become so blocked that it was a hindrance to trade. The Romans called the town Garriannonum, and the ruins of the old castle, known as Burgh Castle, straddle the border with Suffolk. A long spit of sandbank runs out as a tongue on the northern side and it is this that has come to provide the natural harbour over the centuries.

Yarmouth owed its wealth to the herring. In its heyday it had an immense trade in herrings, with thousand of Scottish fisher girls, many from Musselburgh where I live, following the herring down the east coast of England all summer coming, finally, to Yarmouth in the autumn to work virtually round the clock. The twist in the sandbank meant that the drifters that fished the herring could come into the harbour, twenty acres in size, which could gather 1,000 brigs and other little vessels, barrel steamers, salt steamers, pickle steamers, as well as the drifters themselves, in its shelter. When the shoals were running the drifters worked every hour they could to provide the raw material for the herring industry, 500 million fish in a good season. The drifters would beat across the tide, paying out from eighty to a hundred nets, cabled together like railway carriages and stretching for miles. Making and mending the nets was a great business in itself. Once brought into harbour, the herrings were swung on to shore in great baskets, sold by auction and hurried off to the pickling enclosure on the sand dunes. The fisher wives would pack them into barrels after having gutted, beheaded and even filleted them. The barrels were filled with pickle and the lids put on them by coopers and then they were dispatched to the Continent. Latterly, they were frozen hard for foreign export.

Standing as it does on a sand drift, Yarmouth has little space for wide streets, and so what remains of the living quarters for the fishermen and the visiting herring girls have grown up into little alleyways called rows where you can almost touch the sides as you walk through them. So jumbled are the houses that many of their walls are whitewashed to reflect the light. In the sixteenth century there used to be a special cart device for traversing these alleys with the wheels set under the body of the cart rather than at the sides as usual. I would love to have seen Yarmouth at the height of its herring days but I dare say the smell was pretty overpowering.

The glorious days of the 'silver darlings', and the herring fleet that helped feed the empire are gone and very few fishing boats now work out of Yarmouth harbour. However, we are still left with the memory of those days in the form of the Yarmouth bloater. This is a herring that is smoked with its innards still inside; it has a very individual taste and one that is, perhaps, too unusual for the bland world in which we now live, though I have to say that I'm very fond of bloaters. A year or so ago, Hugh Fearnley-Whittingstall tried to reintroduce the bloater, but I think met with little success. They are almost impossible to buy unless of course you go to Yarmouth. The other great product from the herring that went all over the world was the red herring. We all know the phrase about the red herring, and these were herrings that were salted and then had to be soaked in many changes of water before they were edible. They went out of favour in England quite early on but were still much sought after in Africa and the West Indies. The advantage of a herring that is so salted that it becomes rigid is that its chances of deterioration are fairly small. The Africans would boil them up with sweet potatoes in a sort of fishy stew which is not bad and really appealed to their tastes.

The gales in this part of the country can get quite forceful with very stormy days, and it was George Manby, probably as a result of the drifters fleeing before the storm to harbour, who invented the rocket that could throw a line to a floundering ship and bring it to shore more safely and more quickly. It is an invention that, over the years, has saved thousands of lives. In this year of Charles Dickens's anniversary, when everybody is reading his works, you will be reminded of Yarmouth in the story of *David Copperfield*, who came to the town on top of Ham's broad shoulders. As he approached the beach he saw a boat turned upside down with a chimney on the keel. This was Peggotty's hut where she lived and it was a magical place for him. Dickens gives a wonderful description in the book of a storm off Yarmouth with the sweeping gust of rain coming up like showers of steel and the sailors huddled into sheltered corners peering out to sea. He describes how the waves roared up the beach, the thundering billows dashing themselves to pieces as if they would scoop up the very foundations of the town.

Buried in the church at Yarmouth is Oliver Cromwell's granddaughter, Bridget Bendish, who was very much his favourite and used to sit on his knee during council meetings. He vowed that he would rather trust her with any of his secrets than any of his councillors. She was a great patron of the poor and would work on her husband's farm dressed in the meanest of clothes, eat and drink whatever was put before her and afterwards fall into a profound sleep. She would then rise with new vigour and ride her chaise to a neighbouring town with all the smartness of someone who expected to be the first person in Europe. She was obviously a remarkable woman and she would drive her one-horse chaise up to fairs, as a grazier of cattle, singing psalms as she went across the open heath.

Head inland from Yarmouth and you will come to the county town of Norwich, which is a pleasant place with a cathedral and old buildings, but that is not what Norfolk is about for me. However, I would mention that during the game season the butchers' shops sell a lot of game, including the more unusual birds such as snipe or even woodcock. You can buy, and this I used to find an excellent purchase, bags of what is known as 'broken game', which are the birds that have perhaps been too over-shot to be sold as a whole bird with a bit of rabbit thrown in and various other items, which make the most perfect base for a game pie or even a game casserole.

Between Norwich and Yarmouth is the area known as the Broads, which was basically a gift, possibly unwanted, from the monks of Ely to the inhabitants of Norfolk, when they cut a channel to link the Great Ouse and the Little Ouse. The Broads, mainly in Norfolk but some of them spill over into Suffolk, are a network of seven rivers and sixty-three lakes or broads covering a total area of 117 square miles of which over 77 square miles is navigable. Most of them are completely open to navigation but some have restrictions in place in autumn and winter. Until the 1960s the Broads were considered to be a natural feature, and it was only when Dr Joyce Lambert proved that they were artificial that the flooding of medieval peat excavations was discovered. It was the Romans who first extracted peat from the area, while local monasteries exercised their right to cut peat on an extensive scale, selling the fuel to Norwich and Yarmouth; the cathedral at Ely used to get through 320,000 tonnes of peat a year.

With rising sea levels the pits flooded, and dykes and wind

pumps failed to prevent the ingress of water; the result was the reed beds, marshes and wet woodland that you see today. Various schemes throughout history were set up to try to drain the Broads again, to maintain the channels or put in locks, but none of these was commercially successful. However, as early as the 1870s the Broads became popular as an area for boating holidays, helped by being within easy reach of London. Small yachts were first available for hire in 1878, Blake's, still in business today, started an agency in 1908 and Hoseasons, set up by a man called Hoseason from Orkney, began operations after the Second World War. At the height of their popularity in the 1980s there were some 2,400 cruisers for hire, but that has now dropped back to about 1,700. There are no locks on the Broads and they provide very safe sailing in the sense that you cannot get swept out to sea. They are fairly shallow too, the majority being less than thirteen feet deep, so if you do capsize you can right yourself quite easily.

What I loved to see when I used to go on the Broads were the old Norfolk wherries, the former cargo boats of the area that had been restored and were still in use. We used to base ourselves at Horning, which has been referred to as the Venice of the Broads and was a charming place with a nice pub and a pleasant church near the remains of St Benet's Abbey, founded by King Canute. The abbey was heavily fortified and held out for a long time against the Normans until, so the story goes, a monk betrayed them into the hands of the enemy on condition that he would be made abbot. The Normans kept their pact and made him abbot and then they hanged him.

The coast to the north of here is where I have spent many happy days. The north Norfolk coastland is a world of wild birds and sandy beaches and fields. The samphire grows copiously along this coast, one of the few places in England where it does grow, and the little houses by the side of the road used to advertise fresh picked samphire or pickled samphire which you could buy and take home with you. Directly north on the coast you come first to Cromer, famous for its crabs, which are supposed to be one of the best eating crabs anywhere in the world. Certainly they are quite delicious and I have eaten more than my fair share of them. My paternal grandfather, whom I never knew, died in Cromer. He was a doctor and his lungs never recovered from going in to save the injured in a house that had been bombed by a Zeppelin in the First World War. He got dust in his lungs which thereafter always gave him trouble. One February he was so full of coughing and wheezing that my grandmother said, 'You know, you love Cromer, why don't you go to Cromer and get better, it's so bracing.' So off he went but Cromer in February proved to be a little too bracing and he died.

Along the coast to the west you come to Sheringham and Cley Next The Sea. If you stand on the bridge of the windmill at Cley and look out on the River Glaven and the marshes around with their innumerable creeks and wild birds but not a lot else, it is extraordinary to reflect that this was once the third largest port in England. It traded with continental Europe and the Netherlands and shipped out huge amounts of grain. There is nothing there now really apart from the windmill, a few houses and the pub. I learned to sail from Blakeney, a little bit further west. The coast has become very silted up, and the number of times one spent hours on end marooned on the mud flats waiting for the tide to come back, because you had misjudged it, was a very good lesson in both patience and navigation. My parents had a friend who lived at Blakeney, Air Chief Marshal Sir David Brackley, the man who invented the dive bombing principle for the air force, and it is said that he worked it out watching the terns diving off Blakeney Point. Blakeney Point is a great long beach where you can walk for miles and watch the terns and other wild birds. Blakeney was also the name of a famous horse that won the Derby, bred by Sir Arthur Budgett, who was a friend of my mother's; in fact he had two Derby winners, the other called Morston. Morston Pit, as it is known, is further west still.

I spent many happy hours at Morston Pit, for when the tide is in the sea bass come up the channels and you can fish for them. I used to go with my friend Christine Coleman and her husband who is a Norfolk boy. They had a boat, just a little boat for fishing, and we would go fishing off the point when the tide was full. When the tide was out Douglas would dig samphire and dig for cockles – there are particularly good cockles on this coastline – and Christine and I would go and swim in the channels with the seals. There are a lot of native seals on this part of the coast, and when the tide goes out the channels are still quite deep enough to swim in and be swept down with the flow of the water. There is no danger of being swept out to sea because you would run aground before you ever made the turn. The sun made the channels always warm enough to swim in because the water was so shallow. The seals lay about on the sandbank and sometimes they would deign to come and swim with you. At the end of the day, tired like children, we would go back to Douglas's mother's house and have freshly caught sea bass with samphire and either a starter or sauce of Stiffkey blue cockles, as they are known in this part of the world, depending on how many Douglas had managed to dig up. It was a sort of happy reinvention of childhood.

Next along the coast is the town of Wells-Next-The-Sea which was the venue for my one and only expedition into the world of wildfowling. Without the BBC and *Clarissa and the Countryman* it would never have come about, because really I was not of an age or an ability to start wildfowling, not to mention that the previous December, in 1999, the year Jennifer died, I myself nearly died. I had had an umbilical hernia that the National Health Service failed to stitch up properly and it ripped out when I was visiting Spain. Be ill in Spain, it is considerably better. I had only just had the staples removed when we went to film at Wells with the wild-fowlers. I was a bit apprehensive about the whole experience. The pink-foot geese that adorn that coast roost out on the sandbanks quite far offshore and you have to be *in situ* to wait for them when the dawn comes up. We set off in the dark and had to walk something like three miles across pretty rough ground and I was really rather anxious for my scar, but I was inspired by this little ten-year-old boy. He was the son of one of the wildfowlers who lighted my footsteps every inch of the way with his pencil torch light and I didn't feel I could let him down by not going on, although the urge was strong on several occasions to say go on without me. Wildfowling was in his blood; his great-grandfather had once been one of the keepers at Sandringham and had been one of the pallbearers, all keepers, for the late King George V. The King was an immensely keen and very good shot. I remember when we finally arrived saying to this little boy, 'It's a beautiful morning,' and, true wildfowler to his fingertips, he said, 'We need more wind.'

Wildfowlers only really thrive in very bad weather but it was a beautiful morning with a Michelangelo sky and 30,000 pink-foot geese flying over our heads. After the war a combination of over-shooting and the Siberian gulags had pretty well decimated the pink-foot population. The pink-foot nest in Siberia, and with the influx of the political prisoners to the gulags, the goose eggs were about the only accessible food for them, and so there were huge depredations on the breeding populations of pink-foots. It was the wildfowlers themselves and not any other organisation, so don't let anyone tell you otherwise, who restored this area, keeping careful watch on would-be poachers and only allowing people who were members of the wildfowling community, properly licensed and trained, to go out on the marsh. Gradually the geese came back and now have returned in huge numbers. The noise can be absolutely deafening and it is a wonderful sight as they fly above your head. Because it was such a fine day they were flying very high, so although we fired off our guns for the benefit of the television cameras, there really was scant hope of bagging any that day. However, it was something I would never have experienced had it not been for that programme. I survived the day and have a wonderful memory of it.

If you go to Wells-Next-The-Sea you can sit in the car park and watch the geese fly overhead, as they go inland every day to feed on the sugar beet fields. What happens is that the local beet farmers leave the tops of the beets in the fields after the harvest. The geese come in and feed on them and leave a generous donation of manure behind so that everybody bene-fits. Once you go slightly inland a large area is devoted to growing sugar beet and the landscape is littered with the towers of sugar beet factories. Due to EC quotas, the amount we are allowed to grow has dropped back a bit, as so much of it is cultivated in Poland and other new EC member countries. Where the farmers grow wheat instead, the geese are perhaps not so welcome. There is, incidentally, a very good café in Wells where you gratefully go to have your fry-up after you've spent the morning out on the marshes.

Before you round the corner into the Wash you come to Burnham Thorpe, the birthplace of England's most famous sailor, Admiral Lord Nelson. Nelson was a Norfolk boy and must have learned to sail off this treacherous, but interesting, coast. Then you proceed south to the town of King's Lynn, somewhat silted up now but in the Middle Ages an enormously prosperous fishing port. I once spent several hours in King's Lynn because I had been bidden to speak to the Sandringham Women's Institute and their president the Queen, of whom I am a huge admirer. I was so over-excited that I had left the house where I had been staying in Leicestershire the previous night at some ridiculously early hour, though I wasn't due to speak until half past two. So I filled in the time by looking around King's Lynn, which is an elegant town with some splen-did old houses and interesting churches. When I was at school we used to think it was terribly funny that King John had lost

A stained-glass image of a wool merchant holding the Church of St Peter and St Paul, Northleach, Gloucestershire. The town was an important centre for the Cotswold wool trade, and it was the wealth, and perhaps sins, of the local wool merchants that transformed the church in the fifteenth century.

A champion Shire horse at the Great Eccleston Agricultural Show, Lancashire. Held in July since the mid-nineteenth century, this event has one of the largest Shire horse entries in England and is a showcase for every aspect of rural endeavour.

A miniature from a manuscript by John Arderne, who spent twenty-one years practising medicine in Newark during the fourteenth century. His humane approach to his patients and his insistence on such things as aseptic surgery were centuries ahead of their time.

The Abbots Bromley Horn Dance, Staffordshire. This English folk dance dates back to the Middle Ages, and is held annually on Wakes Monday in early September. It is a great display of male virility.

Gypsies and travellers wash and groom their horses in the River Eden in preparation for the Appleby Horse Fair, Cumbria. This is unique in Europe and has existed under the protection of a charter granted by James II since 1685.

William Cecil, Lord High Treasurer to Queen Elizabeth I, riding a mule in his garden; his 'old bones ached' so much he could no longer promenade as had been his custom. He built and mostly designed Burghley, in Lincolnshire, one of the largest and grandest houses of the Elizabethan age.

The Dunmow Flitch – a side of bacon – is awarded to a married couple who in 'twelvemonth and a day' have 'not wisht themselves unmarried again'. The Flitch Trials are held in Dunmow, Essex, every four years, and are thought to date back to the 1100s.

A family of hop pickers in Kent, 1935. Hop picking was often done by families from the East End of London who welcomed the chance to get out of the city for a few weeks.

Exeter Cathedral's thirteenth-century misericords
are some of the earliest known; here an elephant is
set between a Crusader and a monk.

High Force at
Forest-in-Teesdale,
County Durham,
drops twenty-one
metres and is one of
the most spectacular
waterfalls in England.

My favourite poster published in 1908 by Great Northern Railway. Skegness, in Lincolnshire, is a popular holiday resort and was also the site of Butlins' first holiday camp, opened in 1936.

The sundial at St Breward Church on Bodmin Moor, Cornwall. I discovered only recently that a direct ancestor was vicar here for over thirty years in the sixteenth century, and I found his name, Thomas Bathe, on the list of former rectors there.

William Walker, the diver whose heroic work between 1906 and 1912 saved Winchester Cathedral by shoring up its decaying foundations.

The ancient tradition of well dressing is celebrated during May in Tissington, Derbyshire.

Erasmus Darwin, ladies' man and a founding member of the Lunar Society, and grandfather of Charles Darwin. His house in Cathedral Close, Lichfield, Staffordshire, is well worth a visit.

The magnificent tomb of Richard Beauchamp, Earl of Warwick, in the Beauchamp Chapel, St Mary's Church, Warwick.

Hannah Glasse, to my mind one of the greatest of English cooks, was raised in Hexham, Northumberland. She wrote her first book, *The Art of Cookery Made Plain and Easy*, in 1746.

Proper agricultural shows have traditionally been held every year in many counties all over England and still remain hugely popular. A prize-winning South Devon bull (below), and a dairy maid with her charge at a show in 1913.

Hunting continues to flourish, within the law, to this day.

his clothes in the Wash. In fact, what he had lost by underestimating the tide was his entire baggage train, including quite a lot of his jewels and valuable possessions. However, before he went he pawned some of his treasure to the Mayor of King's Lynn, including a magnificent cup dating to about 1150 with precious stones and jewels and a jewelled and valuable sword. He never went back to redeem them because he died a week or so later at Newark. It is said that the late Queen Mother, when she was Queen, endeavoured to obtain these treasures from the town but was told that she could only have them if she paid compound interest on the original loan which, after a period of eight centuries, made this really rather impractical. I must say that I had the most lovely day and left in a little golden bubble, in fact in my case probably a large golden bubble.

King's Lynn was the east coast headquarters of the Hanseatic League, and two of its warehouses still remain which were in use from the thirteenth to the eighteenth centuries. This league was one of the big trading companies of the Middle Ages and was based in the North German states and consequently was very handy for dealing with the Continent. Among those born in King's Lynn was Captain Vancouver, who set sail at the age of thirteen as a midshipman with Captain Cook and eventually was responsible for discovering Vancouver Island. He spent the end of his days in Richmond upon Thames on what is now the Star and Garter Hill and he said that this was the most beautiful view in the world, which is curious as many deem that to be Vancouver Island.

The estate at Sandringham was bought by Edward VII, then Prince of Wales, on his marriage to Princess Alexandra of Denmark. It enabled him to have a home away from his mother Queen Victoria; he also wanted a place where he could pursue the country sports that he loved. In the chapel at Sandringham there is a rather sad brass plaque that reads:

Peace, perfect peace, forever with the Lord.
In loving memory of my beloved
Husband from his broken-hearted wife, Alexandra.

Given how badly Edward VII treated her with his endless mistresses and misbehaviour it is a tribute to probably one of the noblest consorts ever. When Edward was dying, she invited Mrs Keppel, his last long-term mistress I suppose, to attend his deathbed, which I think showed a Christian charity beyond all understanding. The estate at Sandringham is the English country home of the House of Windsor and is owned by them privately. When the unpleasant Edward VIII abdicated, he insisted that George V buy it from him rather than passing it over as part of his birthright, and that was the reason why the monarch was given tax breaks by a government who were grateful to him for taking up the crown that Edward had relinquished.

Norfolk is the home of the Agricultural Revolution of the eighteenth century and the large estates that still make up quite a lot of its countryside are a tribute to that. Holkham Hall is the seat of Lord Leicester, one of the fathers of the Agricultural Revolution, set in the countryside by the marshes and the sea. The park is nine miles round with 1,000 acres of trees, all grown on the sandy barren flat on which Thomas Coke, the first Earl, built his fine house. Thomas William Coke, known as Coke of Norfolk, the first Earl's great-nephew and a descendant of Lord Chief Justice Sir Edward Coke, lived for eighty-eight years and in that time brought about many dramatic changes. He was the leading agriculturalist of his age, and changed the poor rye-growing country that supported a few meagre sheep into a rich corn-growing land abounding with flocks and herds. He said that when he first saw Holkham there were two rabbits fighting over one blade of grass and he decided that things had to change. For years he represented the seat of Norfolk in Parliament and was proud of being a commoner. George IV said to him one day that if he carried out a certain task, 'I'll knight you,' and Coke used to declare that had the threat been carried out he would have struck the sword from the King's hand. At the end of his days he accepted an earldom to please his family and possibly Queen Victoria. He married quite young to his cousin Jane Dutton, who died, and he remained a widower until late in life.

He was riding out and met one of the daughters of his neighbour, the fourth Earl of Albemarle, Lady Anne Keppel, on her own. 'Anne, my dear,' he said, 'how would you like to be mistress of Holkham?' She told him she would like nothing better and he said, 'I will send my nephew to court you.' Anne drew herself up and said she would never be mistress of Holkham on those terms, so he married her himself. At the time he was nearly seventy-seven and he became the father of a son and then three more sons and a daughter. Probably his greatest contribution to agriculture was the development of selective and improved stock breeding. It is said that at the time of the Agricultural Revolution the size of a sheep was that of a small Labrador dog, but not by the time Coke had finished.

The church at Holkham is the only one anywhere dedicated to St Withburga, daughter of a king of East Anglia and sister of St Elthelreda of Romsey. She was born at Holkham and moved to East Dereham where she founded a small convent of nuns. She was very old when she died among the band of nuns she had brought together and was laid to rest in the churchyard in East Dereham, her coffin later being moved to Ely where her sister had been abbess. Not far away is another great estate, Houghton Hall. The house is the biggest in Norfolk and was built by the first Prime Minister, Sir Robert Walpole. The Walpoles had lived at Houghton since the time of King Stephen and Matilda in the twelfth century. It is a magnificent house and now one of the two estates of the Marquess of Cholmondelely. The previous Marquess, Hugh, had a passion for white animals and so there is a very fine herd of white deer that graces the park and looks like something out of a medieval psalter as they roam through the trees. When we shot *Clarissa and the Countryman* there, we filmed the feeding of the deer: the keeper stood in the middle of the park and gave a haunting call and the deer appeared from all directions, making their way through the trees like something out of a fantastical magic dream.

The final estate I would mention is that of Kimberley, which was historically the home of the Wodehouse family, the Earls of Kimberley. It was visited by Queen Elizabeth, and in one of the chests there was found the golden bodice of one of her dresses that she had worn during her progress through England. No doubt while staying there she enjoyed the coursing, for this part of Norfolk is a great coursing area. The first coursing club ever set up was at Swaffham, not far away, and the Kimberley Coursing Club was founded by a breakaway group from that one. The property is in the hands of one of the great doyennes of coursing, a woman called Mary Birkbeck, whom I came to know over the years and greatly admire. She is eccentric, feisty, and the only person in the coursing world who wore even worse hats than I did. When we were attempting to test the law after the ban, one of the two prosecutions was brought against Mary and the Kimberley Coursing Club by the RSPCA. I never quite know how they get away with spending money on things that don't seem to be part of their original charter. I was not at that meeting but the two people who were prosecuted, Mary and a wonderful man by the name of Les Anderson, were both of advancing years and there was a marvellous picture in one of the newspapers of them walking away from the court with their respective zimmer frames and the ironic caption beneath: 'Criminals!'

When the ban came in, Alun Michael, the minister concerned, had said that his reason for taking particularly prohibitive steps within it against coursing was to stop the illegal poaching that takes place all over the country wherever there are hares. But that particular form of poaching was completely illegal under the law anyway, so there was no need to change it. The interesting thing is that while there have been two prosecutions under the ban, the police do almost nothing to dissuade the poachers who either come out from the East End of London or are travelling folk who trespass on people's land, usually at night, and whose main interest is to bet as to how quickly a dog can kill the hare. This is nothing like coursing under National Coursing Club rules, which were first laid down by Queen Elizabeth I. I have spent many happy days coursing in this part of the world and for *Clarissa and the Countryman* we even filmed the deerhounds coursing at Holkham, which they used to do to maintain the sporting instincts of the breed. It was wonderful to see these huge hounds, some of which were winners at Crufts and other such shows, having a lovely time. As deerhounds are also sight hounds, and as the hare is not their natural quarry, the hare would usually whip through a hedge, leaving the deerhounds to stand looking rather bewildered and then bounce back to their owners to be patted and given some treat.

One last place of interest is Thetford, down towards the Essex border, which was the birthplace of Thomas Paine, the revolutionary writer, who spent his days living in the White Hart in Lewes. But I am mentioning Thetford for another reason and that is because it was the last great working rabbit warren in England. It covered an area of a square mile and produced thousands of rabbits for the table. It was a remainder from medieval times, and it always seems to me ridiculous that we now have so many rabbits in this country – every landslide on the railway or the roads is caused by rabbits and they under-dig buildings – and yet all the rabbit we eat is imported from the Continent or from China, and heaven knows what they do with it in China. We even import the glue that gilders use, a particularly fine glue made from rabbit bones, because of the activities of the animal liberationists, for want of a dirtier word, who have stopped the rabbit trade in this country. There was a time when Spitalfields market sold 1,000 rabbits a week, a beam of rabbits, and the fur trade in London had a leftover of something like 100,000 rabbit scuts at the end of its trading year. This was the bit they kept to count the rabbits that had gone through their hands. Five rabbits eat as much as one sheep, but in this world turned upside down we don't even eat the rabbits.

I want to leave you with a rather ridiculous story that I really like about the old Duke of Norfolk, Bernard, a remarkable man who was senior steward at the Jockey Club, and a very good one, for many years. The story goes that a corrupt bookmaker or owner sent Norfolk a box of expensive cigars and a case of rather good port, presumably to win favour on some particular appeal. These were returned to him by the Duke, who was a man of great propriety, with a terse note saying, 'I never drink nor smoke – Norfolk'!

Anyway, we must now leave the lovely county of Norfolk and I am going to move into Cambridgeshire.

Cambridgeshire

The long thin county of Cambridgeshire is really about three things: Cambridge University in the south, the wonderful cathedral and the Isle of Ely in the north, and in between the strange, slightly sinister Fens. The story of Cambridgeshire is the story of the Fens, the attempts to channel the rivers that turned it into a flooded marshland and to reach the rich alluvial soil that is so important to the county in terms of vegetable and crop growing. Man has changed the landscape here since Roman times. Wisbech used to be at the mouth of an estuary 2,000 years ago and now it lies ten miles from the coast. The waters of the Great Ouse and the Nene made their way to the sea at Wisbech but now the Great Ouse runs into the sea at King's Lynn, having joined the Little Ouse, once a separate and much narrower river. The whole landscape is criss-crossed by dykes. If you don't know your way and you get lost in the dark it is quite easy to be unable to get from north to south because of the dykes, and a lot of the roads run along the top of the dykes, which is slightly unnerving if you are driving in the dark and your car lights aren't that efficient.

This happened to me once when I had been speaking in Ely Cathedral and I was trying to get back to the very nice hotel where I was staying outside Ely, on one of the rivers. I actually got quite spooked driving around, completely lost, with no houses or buildings in sight and occasionally just the light of what would turn out to be a caravan or a barn. I was reluctant to stop and ask the way, although it wasn't that late, simply because the area is inhabited by migrant workers from central Europe who, I suspected, would not speak English and who I found rather threatening. There has always been a reputation for threatening behaviour in the Fens. When I was young I remember hearing about 'Fen tigers', who were the wild men who lived in the Fens, and even in my youth they used to stage what were known as 'man fights'. The two contestants would have their hands tied behind their backs and would fight brutally, sometimes even to the death, using their feet and their heads and their bodies as they could. That evening, praying for some sort of guidance, I came over a slight rise and there, lit up above me, was the loom of Ely Cathedral with its spotlights. It really was like a revelation from God; I suddenly realised that I had gone all the way round the outside of Ely, but now I knew where I was heading.

Until Norman times even Ely was part of these un-crossable marshes. If you didn't know the way you got lost and that was it. When I was young we all knew the story of Hereward the Wake, the last Saxon to hold out against the Norman invasion, and of how he took to the marshes in that part of the world. The Normans were unable to find him or find a way through and he would break out from time to time and raid them. It was a world full of eel fishers and wildfowlers living in small villages on whatever bit of land was above the water level. Fishermen and eels were such an important part of the whole economy of the area that they were known as 'Fen men's gold' and taxes were paid in eels. The Abbey of Ely paid 10,000 eels a year to one of its sister abbeys for the import of stone from that particular abbey towards building the cathedral, which means that this magnificent edifice was paid for by little slippery eels; in fact not necessarily so little, because there are records of eels of huge size being taken out of the waterways, having lived for forty – and in some cases it has been suggested even a hundred – years in the rivers. Today there are one or two hardy souls who still fish for eels in the old traditional way, moving about the rivers in fairly flat-bottomed punts using the wicker eel traps that are like a sort of long conical basket.

The trouble with government agencies is that they always rush in without actually doing their homework properly, which I think is a feature of government, and so in restoring the sluice gates on the various rivers they replaced them with metal structures that the elvers could not slip through on their journey up the river. As a result the eel population was greatly diminished. Almost at the very last minute, the agency recognised this fact, and is now making sure that there are at least holes through which the elvers can slither, so hopefully the eels will be restored to the Fens. Eels, once so much part of the national diet, have gone out of vogue nowadays, and we are most likely to eat them in a Chinese restaurant in London. I love eel and I think that this is a great pity. Eel skin is a wonderful, durable, soft, supple leather and was used to make shoes for the Fen dwellers, being, as you would imagine, fairly waterproof. Back in the early 1990s there was a fashion for eel-skin wallets and purses. Unfortunately this did not take off because it was discovered that eel skin has some natural static that wiped the magnetic field off credit cards, so the products were dropped rather hastily.

Ely Cathedral is always referred to as 'the ship of the Fens' and you can see why. If you drive towards it from any angle of the countryside you will see it from miles and miles away, whether it is lit up or in daytime, and its bells can be heard for eight miles across what once was marsh, where nothing but reeds and sedge held back the seas, but is today green fields, orchards and vegetable cultivation. The Normans laid siege to the abbey but the Abbot of Ely resisted for two long years from 1069 until 1071 when the abbot promised obedience if the Normans would spare the city and the church. In the seventh century St Etheldreda was given the Isle of Ely as a marriage settlement. Etheldreda was orphaned and widowed within a few years and was then persuaded to marry Egfrith, who became King of Northumbria in 670, but before long she obtained leave to retire from court to live a holy life. She used her wealth to found a monastery here. Her grave, long since lost to us, lies somewhere by the church that she built. Her name was somewhat corrupted into Audrey and an annual fair has been held in Ely for about 800 years known as St Audrey's Fair. Here you could buy gewgaws, laces and toys and it was from that event that the word tawdry has come into our language.

Construction of the cathedral, as we know it, began at the end of the eleventh century. To my mind it is one of the most beautiful cathedrals, if not the most beautiful cathedral, in the whole of the British Isles. Ely is shaped like a large cross and you can even see it on a clear day from Peterborough, some thirty-five miles away. The floor of the cathedral covers an area of 46,000 square feet with a length from east to west of 537 feet. The nave is 248 feet long and is half as high again. The turrets on the western tower climbed 215 feet above the street. The building must have been an influence on the great Christopher Wren because his uncle was bishop there for nearly thirty years. The great tower has nearly a hundred Norman arches inside but the western transept, known as St Catherine's Chapel, has nearly twice as many. The eight oaks that form the eight corners of the octagon were searched for throughout England but were found not that far away at Chicksands in Bedfordshire. They were sixty-three feet long and free from any fault and formed a vital part of this structure.

Two of the chapels built in 1488 are remarkable for being built of chalk. There is a hard, local chalk in this part of the world called clunch and one of them, the Lady Chapel, is the most richly carved and best preserved of all the chalk buildings in England. You will already have read of my appreciation of misericords and, although a lot of the ones at Ely have been replaced, the old ones, about fifty-nine in all, are a lovely collection. There is one of a bear in a tree, a woman with two demons, a huntsman with a dog and a hare, another huntsman with a horn and hounds, a deer and a horse, an old man and his wife grinding corn in a hand-mill, plus various biblical scenes. The

Chapter House and the Lady Chapel are magnificent; in fact, all in all, you should go and see it for yourselves. It is interesting that, due to the presence in the cathedral of various tombs of the Cromwell family, who were local to the area, the cathedral did not suffer as much at the hands of Cromwell's Puritans as many others in the country.

I remember being taught at school that it was the Cavalier landowners returning from exile in Holland who were responsible for the draining of the Fens, but in fact it had begun rather earlier, for both Elizabeth and James I passed laws governing the draining of this area on a large scale. Charles I called in the Dutch engineer, Cornelius Vermuyden, who was promised 93,000 acres as a reward, and a company of gentlemen adventurers was formed by the Earl of Bedford to finance the scheme. Charles, who had fostered the scheme, was to get 12,000 acres. The Civil War intervened, however, bringing the work to a standstill, but Cromwell took it up again. Vermuyden, who had been sitting it out in Fen Drayton in a house that can still be seen with a Dutch inscription over it, restarted his work. New channels were cut and windmills were brought in to raise the water from level to level. In more modern times this has been performed by steam pump but, perhaps, in this greener age, we might go back to windmills. Both Telford and Rennie were called in to help mitigate the effect of the tidal bore and at that point the engineering works on the shore of the Wash cost £200,000.

As I said, the other great institution is Cambridge University. Cambridge probably owes its existence to the fact that it stands on the highest ground on the chalk hills at the other end of the county. It was originally known as Grantabrycge and in the Domesday Book had become Grantebrige. The Normans possibly changed the name to Cantebrigge, and it didn't actually become Cambridge until as late as Shakespeare's time. Today the town mostly supplies the wants of the university, but it was probably the importance of it as a trading post that caused the university to grow there. Monastic bodies were keen to build up the educational movement, and at its inception Cambridge benefited from the migration of many Oxford students who were leaving that university because of the trouble between 'town and gown'. By 1221 it was already an important educational centre in its own right. The collegiate system started at about this time, when the Bishop of Ely of the day, Hugh de Balsham, founded Peterhouse College. Many books have been written about Cambridge and its university and I certainly do not intend here to compete with any of them, but I would just like to mention one or two colleges because I am fond of them. My brother was at Cambridge and I can remember going down with my parents to watch him play rugby when I was really quite young, as my brother was thirteen years older than me. I have never been anywhere colder on this earth; I have to say that when the wind blows straight off the Urals across the Fens, Cambridge is very cold indeed.

One of the colleges I like and which shows that women were involved in education from a very early age is Clare Hall, named after its foundress Lady Elizabeth de Clare. I have, however, always found it curious that until not terribly long before I was born, the university colleges of Oxford and Cambridge did not admit women. Heaven forfend! They would nonetheless allow a woman to pay for the setting up of one such establishment. My brother was at Caius College, pronounced 'keys', or to give it its correct name Gonville and Caius, which was founded in about 1348. Gonville was a Norfolk rector who died two years after its foundation and John Caius was a Norwich physician who re-founded the college some 200 years later. It was the Alma Mater of William Harvey, whom we have mentioned earlier. Cambridge has suffered less from latter-day development than its fellow University of Oxford, and when you go to Cambridge it is much easier to see the colleges standing in their own surroundings. One of the great glories of Cambridge is, of course, King's College, with its magnificent chapel. It was started by Henry VI, that unhappy king, but the build, disrupted by the Civil War was not completed until 1544 during the reign of Henry VII. The university continues to grow, with new colleges set up in more recent years. Churchill College was founded in 1960 to focus on the study of science because Churchill had expressed a concern that there were not enough scientists in the country, a concern that is still being expressed as far as I can see. And Lucy Cavendish College was set up for graduate women in an interesting, fairly modern building with a wonderful use of pale wood in its dining hall and its public rooms.

The Fitzwilliam Museum houses the art collection of the seventh Viscount Fitzwilliam, who willed it to the university together with £100,000 to provide a good, substantial, convenient museum, repository or other building for it. The museum was finally completed in 1875, although it continues to be a work in progress. The Italian pictures include almost all the famous painters, Titian, Tintoretto and Veronese among them. The Dutch and Flemish collection boasts a Pieter Brueghel the Younger as well as Rubens, van Dycks and Rembrandts. There are some wonderful medieval illustrated manuscripts here and the English collection has a rare portrait of Queen Mary I by Hans Eworth, plus a fabulous collection of miniatures by all the greats from Nicholas Hilliard to Isaac Oliver to Samuel Cooper.

All around the town of Cambridge now, outside the immediate town, there is a lot of new development because Cambridge has, in this computerised age, become one of the great centres for some of the best brains in high technology in the country. It is a highly paid field and has brought a great deal of wealth to the area.

The other town worth mentioning is Wisbech, where King John heard the news that his jewels had been lost in the Wash. This is the town that gave us the man who really was responsible for the abolition of slavery, Thomas Clarkson, whose father had been headmaster of the grammar school. Clarkson had made friends early on with Granville Sharp, the man who forced the court decision that 'slaves cannot breathe in England . . . They touch our country and their shackles fall,' as William Cowper put it, and with William Wilberforce, whose name is the one we all know in connection with the suppression of the slave trade. It was Clarkson who visited all the various ports that received slave ships and calculated that rarely fewer than fifty and often more than eighty of every hundred Negroes died on their voyage into slavery. The intervention of the Tsar of Russia, who was glad to be a patron of the Anti-slavery Society, was a curious thing really, when you consider that serfs in pre-revolutionary Russia were little better than slaves. Clarkson lived to see the reforms passed when he was seventy-three years old and he lived for another thirteen years thereafter.

Cambridge has some great houses, such as Anglesey Abbey and Wimpole Hall, greatly enlarged by the Earl of Hardwicke, but really I think I will leave you to find out the rest for yourself and move on to another county.

Leicestershire

For many years now Leicestershire, a county that I visit quite frequently, has meant two things to me: hunting and food. And as of a week ago, as I am writing, it now also means the Midland Border Terrier Club, of which I am proud to be the Patron, following in the footsteps of, among others, Patrick, Earl of Lichfield. Their headquarters is based at Melton Mowbray, which suits me very well because Melton Mowbray is one of the places I associate with food. I became friends with Jan McCourt of Northfield Farm at Cold Overton, just off the road between Oakham and Melton Mowbray, some twenty-odd years ago when we were both marching in the army of Henrietta Green, trying to promote the interests of small British producers of real food.

You may have seen Jan and myself on the *Great British Food Revival*, where I was supporting his breeding of a rare-breed pig, the British Lop, which the breed chairman described as 'rarer than the giant panda'. As Jennifer and I had been successful in removing the Gloucester Old Spot not only from the endangered list but even from the rare-breed list since we filmed it some fifteen years ago, I thought I would turn my attention to the British Lop. There are only three breeding herds in Cornwall and Jan has the largest herd outside the county, and to my mind it is an even better eating pig than the Gloucester Old Spot. In any event, over the years I have gone regularly to Northfield Farm, not only because he is my friend but because he is one of two people in the British Isles from whom I will buy pork on a regular basis, the other being Peter Gott at Sillfield Farm in Cumbria. Jan also sells rare-breed beef at the farm shop from various rare-breed cattle he has on the farm, my favourite being the shorthorn, which I think is some of the best beef around.

As a result of this connection, a few years ago now I was introduced to Matthew O'Callaghan and his campaign to register the Melton Mowbray Pork Pie as specific to Melton Mowbray and its environs (in EU-speak 'Protected Geographical Indication'). If you had told me before that date that one of my heroes would be a vegetarian Labour councillor in the Midlands, I would have told you to put more water with it. However, Matthew is a fine man and when I said to him, 'We will remember that the Melton Mowbray Pork Pie was invented for hunting, won't we, Matthew,' he responded, 'We most certainly will, Clarissa.' We had our picture taken holding up Melton Mowbray Pork Pies and of course the pastry is shortened with lard so I said to him, 'Well, just be careful you don't lick your fingers!' As a result of Matthew's enthusiasm, not only is the pork pie registered so that it has to be made in Leicestershire and in the immediate surrounding counties, but Stilton cheese is also registered to the county.

As you'd expect, Stilton was originally made at Stilton in Cambridgeshire, but the marriage of the young woman who had the recipe into a Melton Mowbray family moved its base of manufacture to Melton Mowbray. It was popularised by a publican who used to sell it to the people who had come up for the hunting. In Georgian days the shires, which were based around Leicestershire, were where all the young bucks of the day used to come to their hunting boxes because the hunting in Leicestershire was supposed to be the finest in the country. The cheese was also sold to stagecoach passengers travelling to London and to other places in the eastern shires, and with the development of the railways it became one of the most popular cheeses throughout England and indeed the wider United

Kingdom. The other native cheese of the county, Red Leicester, is now no longer made in Leicestershire, because the name was bought by a big cheese manufacturer based in Shropshire, so that the Red Leicester you buy in supermarkets has nothing to do with the county. There is, however, one farm making proper Red Leicester cheese under the name Sparkenhoe, and if you see this buy it, because it is quite different from the commercial Red Leicester and is utterly delicious.

I first came across it at the original Melton Mowbray Food Festival which, in the first two years, was held in the cattle market in Melton Mowbray and was to my mind without doubt the best food festival in the country. Under the aegis of Matthew O'Callaghan again, it combined all that was good in the East Midlands, so that you had Sparkenhoe and Stilton cheeses, Melton Mowbray Pork Pies, farmers like Jan selling local meat and even a stall selling bison that was raised in the area. All this was combined with stalls selling produce from the Asian communities, in particular in Leicester, and the West Indian community, and it was just everything that a good food festival should be.

I am afraid I might have offended James Martin, the television chef, who was also demonstrating at the festival. He was provided with six bodyguards, and so he went everywhere with six large men in yellow jackets while I myself, number three on the Animal Liberation Front death list, had nothing by way of protection but my friend Isobel who was helping me with the boxes and my Stanley knife with which I opened the boxes. I was demonstrating after James Martin, and as I was about to go into the hall I saw an early eighteenth-century re-enactment group, with musket, fife and drum. I said to them, 'Come on, lads, you're coming in with me,' and so in we went from the back of the hall, the group with their muskets, playing their fifes, beating their drums and trailing their pikes, and everyone turned round to look. I said, 'You see, I too can have a body-guard,' and everybody cheered. But James Martin, who was still backstage, looked slightly upset so I would like, publicly, to apologise to him. I was not, at that time, a great fan of his, but after I saw a programme he made about trying to improve the food in the hospital in Scarborough following the death of his grandmother, which I thought was so brilliant, I would now like to make amends for my behaviour.

Unfortunately after a couple of years it became too expensive to continue with the festival in the cattle market because government funding reduces for every year that a food festival has been going, and so it was moved to the local agricultural college, where it became just another food festival in a muddy field, perfectly good, but not the exceptional event it had been in its early years.

It was in the festival's second year at the cattle market that I first learned of a fruit called the chequer from which the word 'exchequer' apparently comes. It is a smallish berry with a most delicious flavour, much loved in the Middle Ages. So if you are looking for rare trees to put in your garden, consider the chequer. I don't know where you would find them, but no doubt if you are good at your internet you'll track them down. Melton now also hosts a Pie Festival, but it is not something with which I have become involved.

There are also a number of small breweries around the county and one of them produces a beer called Paint the Town Pink. This is in memory of an occasion when a group of young bucks who had been dining at the Melton Hunt Club got hold of several cans of scarlet paint and proceeded to do that very thing and paint the town pink. Pink is how you describe the bright scarlet colour of a hunting coat, because the best ones were made by Mr Pink, the tailor, in London. Incidentally, it was while speaking at a Melton Hunt Club dinner that Oscar Wilde uttered his memorable words – the unspeakable in pursuit of the inedible – only not quite as they have been taken up. What he actually said was, 'They say of us that we are the pursuit of the uneatable by the unspeakable,' which does put a slightly different aspect on it. I could never quite understand why an Anglo-Irishman, however inclined to green carnations, should at that time in history have been anti-hunting, and quite clearly I was right. Talking about hunt coats takes me across to the other side of the county, to Market Harborough.

Market Harborough, which is a charming old town at the centre of the county, played a large part in the Civil War, and in fact had Rupert of the Rhine held his entrenched position here and not ridden out to confront the New Model Army, the outcome of the Battle of Naseby might have been very different. It is interesting, because not very far away in the same county is Market Bosworth, outside which the Battle of Bosworth Field took place, the deciding factor in the Wars of the Roses. This was where Richard III lost the battle to the first Tudor king, Henry VII, and was dragged from the battlefield and his corpse thrown into the market square and left there for people to come and identify. A group of trees on a hillock just outside the town has always been referred to as King Dick's or Richard's Camp, and it is believed that that is where Richard III addressed his troops on the eve of battle. It you go to Market Bosworth you will see the battlefield laid out before you, although of course historians can never agree on anything so there was a great deal of them asking where Richard's camp was and the various positioning of troops, but it is fascinating nonetheless.

Cromwell's headquarters before the Battle of Naseby were at Market Harborough and he returned there victorious while Charles I fled first to Leicester, where he found a town full of wounded prisoners, and then he moved on to London. Cromwell wrote trenchantly to Parliament:

Sir, this is none other than the hand of God and to him alone belongs the glory wherein none are to share with him.

Your General served you in all faithfulness and honour . . . Honest men served you faithfully in this action. Sir, they are trusty; I beseech you in the name of God not to discourage them . . . He that ventures his life for the liberty of his country, I wish he trust God for the liberty of his conscience and you for the liberty he fights for.

Parliament of course didn't listen and we ended up with a dictatorship.

Market Harborough is home to one of the leading hunt tailors in the country in the form of a business called Frank Hall. He himself has long since gone to chase foxes in the sky, but when I went there the shop was being run by Mr Ripley, his one-time apprentice and now successor. One aspect of one of the *Clarissa and the Countryman* programmes was to show all the jobs required to put someone on a horse, whether it be the saddles, bits, bridles, whips, boots, hunting clothes, livery men, blacksmiths or seed merchants, so one of the clips we filmed was at Frank Hall's and I am now the proud possessor of this beautiful hunt coat. I hasten to add that the licence fee-payer did not purchase my outfit. In the fitting room at Frank Hall's there was a series of photographs taken of the late King, the Queen's father, out hunting, a smile on his face, whereas he always looks very serious and solemn. I suspect they were taken when he was still Duke of York, and not only was he smiling but I've never seen a picture of him looking quite so happy. I found it very moving. It was fascinating to go upstairs to the sewing room and see the tailors sewing, sitting cross-legged, on these ledges, just like the bronzes you see of tailors, or the pictures in Beatrix Potter's tale of the mouse who was the Tailor of Gloucester.

You normally have quite a number of fittings for a garment like this, which is made out of Melton cloth; this is very thick, although not as thick as it once was. Johnny Scott had an old one that would literally have stood up on its own and water ran straight off it. Anyway, I had one fitting for my coat, and when I went for the second fitting, apart from a slight alteration to the upper arms where my years of being a cook and lifting heavy pans had built up my biceps, it fitted perfectly. Then one day some time later I was sitting at a show and this woman came up to me and said, 'How's your hunt coat?' I said, 'Do you know, it's the most extraordinary thing but I only really had one fitting,' and she replied, 'I know, I had the other thirty.' Apart from her upper arms, she was the same size as me, and so Mr Ripley had persuaded her to come in and take fittings for my coat.

The grammar school in Market Bosworth, which was originally founded in Tudor times, was refurbished in 1601 by a man called Sir Wolstan Dixie, who had inherited his fortune from a Lord Mayor of London in Queen Elizabeth's day. Samuel Johnson came to the school as a poor usher and taught the boys grammar. It was not a happy period in his life and afterwards he wrote of it that it was as unvaried as a cuckoo's note and he did not know whether it was more disagreeable for him to teach the boys or for them to learn. He also acted as a sort of private chaplain to another Sir Wolstan Dixie and it was the humiliation he suffered at the hands of this man as much as the boredom and tedium of the school that made him leave it after a few months and go off and start his literary career.

Oddly enough the Luddites got their name from an inhabitant of the village of Anstey just outside Leicester. Ned Ludd was the village simpleton – I suppose these days he would be described as having learning difficulties – and after listening to the complaints that were being voiced about the newly invented Arkwright stocking frames and other such mechanical means of producing stockings and other garments, he went off and smashed two stocking frames. It was a time when much of the industry in Leicestershire depended on weaving. The lengthy duration of the Napoleonic War had pushed up the national debt from £240 million to £860 million and so the situation, much as it is at the moment, brought a particularly heavy burden of taxation on the working classes with the loss of jobs and industry. Anyway, Ned

Ludd's action caused the workers to riot. The lace workers in nearby Nottingham joined in and the rest, as they say, is history. The militia was brought in, mills were burned down and there was heavy damage to the woollen and cotton industries. If you go to Leicester and visit the museum you can see an example of the old stocking frame, which is sometimes set in motion when they are having displays, and you can understand how it would be seen to take work away from the masses.

Leicester, the county town, started life as a Roman city. There are the remains of a fine forum and very splendid artefacts have been found. The Earls of Leicester are best known, of course, in the form of Simon de Montfort. The town was the heart of an industry making boots and shoes to be exported all over the world, and in its heyday there was no article of clothing from head to foot that was not manufactured in Leicester. Cardinal Wolsey is buried in the city, never having managed to return to his see at York, and his grave is now in the middle of a public park. Leicester used to be a splendid municipality, with 2,000 acres of land on which it produced stock and raised 8,000 chickens supplying 6,000 eggs a week to the hospitals and other institutions in the town. It was one of the first cities to adopt electricity in 1901 and used to sell millions of units a year at very cheap rates to its residents. However, sadly Leicester isn't like that any more.

I had one of the most frightening adventures of my life there. I turned off the ring road because there had been a car crash and I wanted to avoid being stuck in traffic, and soon found myself lost. I couldn't tell you where I was but it was not terribly far from the city centre. As we know, Leicester has a very high Asian Muslim population and I found myself in an area where all the men were wearing Islamic clothing and all the women were wearing burkas and walking slightly behind them. None of the men would talk to me when I tried to find out where I was and how to get out of there because I was an English female and they don't talk to females they don't know, while if the women could speak English they weren't about to show it by having a word with me. Eventually I had to stop at a newsagent's and the only way I could discover my location was to buy a map of the city. Somebody, very reluctantly, pointed to where I was and then I had to work out the rest for myself. I am not a particular admirer of Islam or indeed, I should add, almost any other religion, but I have many good acquaintances and even some friends among the Muslim community, yet here I was in the heart of a city in the middle of my own country a complete outcast and pariah. If multiculturalism works, which I have always been rather dubious of, surely it must be multicultural and not monocultural. I just wanted to relate this to you because I think you ought to be aware of such things.

However, everything has an upside and one of the results of this is that Leicester has a very good selection of Asian restaurants where you can eat excellent curry. The city also has a thriving market attended by farmers from the local countryside and quite a number from the Asian community too, who sell not only herbs and spices and Asian vegetables but also delicious ready-made goods. So thinking back to the East End of London of my childhood, I can only hope that in generations to come there will be a merging of the cultures and not the exclusion zone that is the ghetto.

You will also find Lutterworth in Leicestershire. Lutterworth saw the demise of the first of the great religious reformers, one John Wycliffe, who was born near Richmond in Yorkshire and studied at Balliol. At a time when the Catholic Church was in chaos with corruption, two competing Popes in Rome and Avignon and avariciously seeking to acquire power and property, Wycliffe enjoyed the protection of John of Gaunt as he preached against the machinations on the Continent. His clerical enemies in England appealed to the Pope and a Bull arrived ordering that Wycliffe be arrested and sent to Rome. This was, of course, exactly the type of papal encroachment that every-body was resenting. Edward III had died and Richard II, a ten-year-old boy, had just come to the throne. The King's Council were asking Wycliffe whether they might prohibit treasure being sent out of the country at the demand of the Pope and Oxford University refused to admit the right of the Pope to send them a Bull, much less to imprison one of their members, so they declined to send Wycliffe anywhere.

Wycliffe began to write his views on freedom of speech and unfortunately, whether or not it was under his influence, the Peasants' Revolt, led by Wat Tyler, broke out, making more people think that Wycliffe was dangerous. He then denounced the central Roman Catholic doctrine of transubstantiation and this could not be ignored. Wycliffe and his supporters, known as Lollards, were expelled from Oxford or silenced. Wycliffe then retired to his rectory at Lutterworth, where he died of natural causes. Thirteen years later the Bishop of London, Richard Fleming, carried out his instructions from the Church by digging up Wycliffe's body, burning it and casting the ashes into the waters of the River Swift. Probably in Wycliffe's day the River Swift was a clean and fast-flowing river, whereas today I think the ashes would get caught up on the old supermarket shopping trolleys and other such items that adorn it.

Also in Leicestershire is Loughborough, the 'city of bells', which has wonderful collections of bells in its various churches and was responsible for casting the largest bell ever made in England for St Paul's Cathedral. It used to be marvellous to hear the bells ringing on a Sunday and I hope that it still is. Abutting Leicestershire to the east is the county of Rutland.

RUTLAND
Rutland is a triumph and a lesson to us all. In the early 1970s central government decided that the time was right to reorgan-ise the county boundaries. As a result of this, on 1 April 1974 the

county of Rutland ceased to exist. Apparently all this nonsense about it being the smallest county in England was just a waste of administrative effort and so the county was made part of Leicestershire. The people of Rutland wouldn't stand for it; they could have given Gandhi lessons. They continued to pay their rates but they continued to write their cheques to Rutland County Council, and continued to use the term Rutland on their envelopes and letter headings and everywhere else. In the end so great was their stubbornness that the government gave in and, following a review in 1977, Rutland once more took on county status.

It is a small county, its capital being the town of Oakham with, at its centre, its fine old public school. Oakham still supports a weekly market where local produce is sold, and is a pleasant town with all the right sort of shops and bookshops and I am always happy to visit it. I suppose you could say that the crowning glory of Rutland is Belvoir Castle, and certainly the kennels of the Belvoir Hunt are very splendidly set out. Belvoir, the home of the Dukes of Rutland, stands high on a spur overlooking the Lincolnshire Wolds. Those of you who have seen the film *Little Lord Fauntleroy* will recognise it instantly. It is a magnificent pile with timbered woodlands and the Vale of Belvoir beyond. The original castle was built by Robert de Todeni, who carried the Conqueror's standard at Hastings. It was shattered in the Wars of the Roses and in the Civil War it withstood a siege by Cromwell who then razed it to the ground. On the Restoration of the Monarchy it was rebuilt on the same foundations but now looks like a house rather than a castle. It contains many fine treasures including a silver punch bowl so large that Violet, Duchess of Rutland, had her four children painted sitting in it. It is one of the sites of the CLA Game Fair so that one goes there every three years. I remember seeing these wonderful pictures in the Belvoir Hunt tent of a ladies' point-to-point, some time between the wars, where they were all riding side-saddle and all had removed their skirts and were shockingly clad in only breeches and boots to get over the point-to-point fences and were looking out on the vista of Belvoir Castle.

I am now going to move on to Lincolnshire.

Lincolnshire

Lincolnshire is the second largest county in England and, just as its larger northern neighbour Yorkshire is divided into three administrative counties, formerly known as ridings, so Lincolnshire is divided into parts. These are the Parts of Holland in the south and the Parts of Kesteven and the Parts of Lindsey, each with its own county council. Holland means hollow land and, although mentioned in the Domesday Book, there is not much early history about it because for much of the time it was largely under water. Kesteven is from a Celtic word meaning Coed or wood, and was clearly a richly wooded territory with a royal forest within its boundaries from Norman times until the thirteenth century. Lindsey, which means the Island of Lindissi, was the area around Lincoln named Lindum Colonia by the Romans; it enjoyed the status of a kingdom. It was never an important kingdom, although, from its size alone, it must have played a significant part in recorded history. Lincolnshire occupies approximately 1.7 million acres, of which 270,000 are in Holland, 470,000 in Kesteven and 960,000 in Lindsey. Historically the largest centres of population were Lincoln, Scunthorpe, Grimsby, Cleethorpes, Louth, Grantham, Stamford and Boston. The rest of the county, which is largely agricultural, was divided into parishes. They say that England below the Wash could be largely self-supporting in food, and much of this could easily be supplied by Lincolnshire, which produces crops of wheat, sugar beet and potatoes and, rather interestingly, quite large supplies of vegetables. Thanks to Lincolnshire, England is the second largest grower of coriander in the world, the largest being India. The county exports a lot of vegetable produce to China, especially baby sweetcorn in the hundreds of thousands of tonnes.

As we are coming in from Rutland, let us start at the town that stands immediately on the borders, which is Stamford. Stamford is just off the A1, the Great North Road, at the junction of Lincolnshire, Northamptonshire and Rutland, and through it flows the River Welland, which leaves the hills to make its way across the Fens. The name means stone-paved ford and this was obviously before the bridge was built across the Welland. The word stone is particularly relevant because not only was there a stone quarry at Stamford, but also there were about half a dozen well-known ones in the immediate area. Stamford is a beautiful town and the George, once a celebrated coaching inn, still remains an excellent hotel with a very good restaurant. Funnily enough, the day I first filmed with Patricia Llewellyn on Sophie Grigson's *Eat your Greens*, I was too tired to make my way back to London and had a little celebration by booking in at the George. Having paid for my room, I had completely run out of money, apart from what I needed for petrol, and I remember I went to bed without any dinner. Much of the fine building in Stamford dates from the Middle Ages with some excellent fifteenth-century glass in the Church of St John's. I particularly like the inscription on the memorial of an innkeeper named Pepper which reads thus:

> Though hot my name, yet mild my nature
> I bore good will to every creature,
> I served fine ale and sold it too
> And unto each, I gave his due.

The Church of St Martin, though due to boundary specifications it is officially in Huntingdon, contains the Burghley chapel, with monuments of the Cecil family whose home is close by. William Cecil, first Lord Burghley, has a magnificent marble and alabaster tomb, as befits the greatest man of Elizabethan England. It is richly carved and painted and he is shown in his armour wearing the gorgeous scarlet mantle of the Order of the Garter, his noble head on a pillow of gold brocade, his wand of office in his hand and a lion at his feet. His mother and father have a memorial close by. Burghley was very much one of Elizabeth's new men; his grand-father was a publican and his father owed his elevation to fighting bravely at the Battle of Bosworth for the winning side. This helped him to obtain a place in the royal household and also to get his son a place at court when he had finished his education.

A short way from the church is the gate of Burghley Park which is still the home of the Marquesses of Exeter. Given that the Elizabethan Age was an age of building – no longer the castles of more dangerous years, but now magnificent houses – Burghley nonetheless takes your breath away. I have always loved the fact that William Cecil used to ride up and down from London, where he was the First Minister, on an ass. For some reason which I have never really discovered he had some physical problem that prevented him from riding a horse. There is an enchanting picture at Burghley of William Cecil in his robes riding this animal and looking entirely happy about it. He also instituted a scheme whereby travellers riding past Burghley were allowed to stop and be offered hospitality, presumably each to their own peer group. I used to think that this was the most charming custom until I remembered that the Elizabethan era was the height of the sort of 'big brother' mentality that meant that everybody was watched and reported on to the Spymaster General, Sir Francis Walsingham. What better way to gain information than to eavesdrop on travellers going up and down the Great North Road? The house is now held in a trust as the last Marquess of Exeter only had daughters. One particularly nice thing to go and see is the figurehead on the last Marquess's Rolls-Royce. He was an Olympic runner and a well-known athlete, and eventually, due to the depredations of his sport, Burghley had to have a hip replacement but it didn't take. The procedure had to be done a second time so he had the metal ball from the first hip operation mounted as a figurehead on his Rolls-Royce.

Head out of Stamford on the Spalding road and you will find yourself in the heart of the Lincolnshire Fens, miles and miles of flat country divided again by more great canals where the water has been channelled. Spalding is the heart of the bulb growing area of Lincolnshire, the last of the towns on the River Welland before it flows into the Wash, and is typical of the more splendid of the Fenland towns. I used to think that Holland on the notice boards as you went into Spalding referred to the country, but of course I now realise that it refers to the ancient division. If you visit at the right time of year you will see rows and rows of flowers, mostly tulips, flowering in waves of colour. Daffodils, tulips, narcissi and hyacinths are grown for their bulbs so they are allowed to flower and the goodness goes back into the bulbs which are then lifted and sold for flowering the following year. Not all of them are sold as bulbs, however, and as many as 25,000 tonnes of the blooms can go by rail to different parts of the country each year. The abbey here was founded by Thorold Buckenhale, who was possibly the brother of Lady Godiva of naked riding fame. Ivo Taillebois, who was the Conqueror's nephew and carried his standard at the Battle of Hastings, married Thorold's niece and heiress and he lived at Spalding Castle. There is nothing left of the castle today but you can still see bits of the priory.

I have been to Spalding quite often as the guest of the wonderful former master butcher called George Adams, who inherited a large number of butcher's shops but sold them and, foreseeing the way the market was going, became one of the largest pig breeders in northern Europe. He kept just one shop here in Spalding so that he could have decent hams and haslet and pork pies for his own table. He and his wife Joan lived at Pinchbeck Hall, one of the finer buildings at the edge of Spalding in Pinchbeck, where I stayed with them and, later, after his death, with their son Mark. It was the village of Pinchbeck that gave its name to the metal that is used for making jewellery, especially in Victorian times, and looks something like gold.

On the outskirts of Spalding is the Romany Museum run by a splendid man called Gordon Boswell, who has a collection of caravans from all the different periods of gypsy building. His oldest one, which dates back to the last quarter of the eighteenth century, is known as a stone breaker because it was so big and heavy that it would break stones as it went along the road. It was, however, so perfectly balanced that it could be pulled by just two horses. Showing it to me, Gordon said, 'If you consider the quality of the residence of the average labouring man at this time in history, and you compare it with this, which would you rather live in?' And there was absolutely no contest. It was incredibly comfortable and well-fitted and cosy. He told me that he was born in a rod tent on the sands at Southport in February, and I said, 'Yes and I know why your parents were there.' He said, 'Don't be ridiculous, you can't possibly know.' I said, 'They were there for the Waterloo Cup,' which was the Blue Riband of hare coursing events, always held in the third week in February. After that we became very good friends.

Go down to the furthest eastern corner on the border with Cambridgeshire and you come to Sutton Bridge. Here the land has been reclaimed from the marshes of the Wash and the town, now a small port, lies on the River Nene. In the nineteenth century it became quite important because of the construction of the long embanked road over the treacherous Cross Keys Wash. In 1831 a wooden bridge made by Rennie and Telford was thrown across the river to give access to the road. It was replaced twenty years later by a swing bridge designed by Robert Stephenson, and finally in 1897 by the present hydraulic swing bridge. The river near the bridge is deep enough to float a warship at high tide, but the town's attempts to become a major shipbuilding harbour failed when the dock collapsed as a result of faulty construction shortly after being opened.

My reason for going to Sutton Bridge, in case you're wondering about all of this, was that nearby there is an estate, also called Sutton Bridge, that was bought between the wars by the Ministry of Defence to provide for wounded veterans who wished to have smallholdings. Originally there were about 400 of these. The estate was bought from St Bartholomew's Hospital so there has never been a major landowner in the area. In the beginning the veterans slightly ran riot, poaching everywhere, even in Sandringham, and the estate was never out of the papers for all the wrong reasons until, finally, quite a brave land agent said to them, 'Why do you go off poaching when you could have such a good shoot yourselves?' And they replied, 'Who, us, where?' Anyway, all those years later I came across them at the Purdey Awards, where the estate had won an award for being kept so beautifully for shooting and with entirely wild pheasants. The remaining forty smallholders by this time worked so hard planting game crops and improving the environment that two years earlier there had been so many wild pheasants that the villagers were complaining that they were invading their gardens. These are not the sort of pheasants that have been put out as poults for shooting; these are born and bred in the wild.

So Johnny Scott and I decided that we would go and film there. The people who hold the shoot and the smallholdings now are the most brilliant shots. After the Second World War the Americans had left large quantities of ammunition lying about because towards the end of the war all of Lincolnshire had American troops bivouacked there getting ready for D-Day. The young local lads used to amuse themselves by picking up the ammunition and making handguns, mostly from wood, which they would then use to fire these bullets. One shudders to think what might have been, but they all had their hands intact, none of them had come to grief, and they had grown up to be superb shots. The little wild fen pheasants that we went out to shoot were incredibly fit; they shoot off the fen like a rocket and go straight up, then the second Exocet kicks in and up they go still further until they are flying higher than the pylons. They are incredibly difficult to shoot, and there was very little point, other than playing to the cameras, of me putting up my gun. Even Johnny, normally the most beautiful of shots, shot considerably fewer than he would usually have done. We had a really happy day and I went home with a couple of brace of these little pheasants and they were quite delicious, with a much nicer flavour than that of birds hand-reared for shooting.

I am often amused by your urban television chef who has never shot and who has got hold of old game books which say that a pheasant takes twenty minutes to cook. One of these little wild pheasants takes exactly that, as they are much smaller and they really don't take long to cook at all. Your modern pheasant, however, frequently imported at some stage from America, is a much bigger bird, and if you cooked it for twenty minutes you'd have a semi-raw pheasant. I do not include Jamie Oliver in this particular category since he, of course, shoots and so knows what the weight of a pheasant is.

Retrace your steps westwards then turn north and slightly inland from the line of the Wash and you will come to probably one of the most famous names in Lincolnshire, which is that of Boston, with its unique Boston Stump, as the tower of the church is called. This can be seen not only from the sea but from miles around the countryside. The name is a derivation of St Botolph's town. He was a protagonist of Benedictine monasticism who came from Iken in Suffolk; not only does his reputation live on in Lincolnshire but also there are traces of him to be found in Denmark and Norway. Boston is something of a place of pilgrimage for both Americans and Australians. Everybody knows the name of Boston, Massachusetts, and of course it was from Lincolnshire that the Pilgrim Fathers first set out on their voyage. They took with them many dishes that remain in the American repertoire but not in ours, such as clam chowder, made with flour and water biscuits, and cobblers which are either sweet or savoury pies topped not with pastry but with rounds of scone dough, which are hardly found in England at all but which are still very popular in America. Probably the Pilgrim Fathers ate their first turkey over here because turkeys were raised in this part of the world as early as the reign of Henry VIII.

In Norman and medieval times Boston was a major commercial port, one of the largest in England, trading wool between Europe, Flanders and the Rhineland. Foreign merchants opened business houses here, not only buying English wool but also selling goods of their own in exchange. Boston's trade in the early Middle Ages was reckoned to be second only to London's and, possibly, by the end of the thirteenth century, second to none. The church with its unusual tower was built in the fourteenth century. On a clear day from the top of the stump there is an amazing panorama, taking in the towers of Lincoln Cathedral thirty miles away and Tattershall Castle, and Hunstanton across the stretch of the Wash. The tower was finished in 1520; its foundations are thirty-six feet deep and are said to have been begun in the early fourteenth century. Although Boston is no longer a large commercial port it does still have a very good market in the old Market Place. The Australian connection was established by Matthew Flinders, a local boy, who set sail from here to Australia and was, among other things, the discoverer of the island of Tasmania.

Continue to follow the coastline north and you will come to Skegness, Skeggy to the natives, which is famous really for two things: that wonderful poster of the fisherman in his waders and sou'wester dancing on the golden sands, which was an old railway poster for Skegness as a holiday resort; and second for being the site of the first Billy Butlin's Holiday Camp. At its height Butlin's, despite its North Sea coastline and chilling east wind, was the focal point of many people's holidays. Butlin's Redcoats were renowned for the entertainment they provided, and many famous names in show business began their careers as Butlin's

Redcoats. I owe my original television debut on Sophie Grigson's *Eat Your Greens* and my fame and fortune to Chapel St Leonards, which is really just an extension of Skegness, because it was here that my friend Stefan was growing cardoons at my behest and I was being filmed coming out of the tent among the cardoons beside the sea. Stefan had the last remaining field in that part of Lincolnshire, so when you peered over the hedge you saw the Friar Tuck Fish and Chip Shop, the Maid Marian Bingo Hall and everything else that epitomises that type of English seaside resort, so it made a great setting for the programme and, of course, the sandy soil was brilliant for growing cardoons.

Head inland north-westwards from Chapel St Leonards and you will come to Louth. This is a charming town which somebody once said had grown old gracefully, with winding streets and nice buildings but, more importantly, it is the home of Lincolnshire chine. The Lincolnshire Curly Coated pig, extinct some time in the early twentieth century, was a huge pig historically raised for tallow, as it carried an enormous amount of fat. That does rather explain why, with the advent of electricity, it went out of fashion, but its neck was so thick that it was impossible to split the pig down the middle in the ordinary way and so the cuts were made on either side of the neck. The neck was removed in one piece, brined and stuffed with parsley and other spices, then allowed to go cold and served as Lincolnshire chine, which is delicious. When I was filming for the *Great British Food Revival* and talking about pigs, we went to Louth and watched the making of chine, a dish that was saved by the intervention of one man called Eric Phelps who was the main producer of chine in Lincolnshire. He was a butcher and he took on MAFF, who had said that a European diktat regarding the butchery prevented the making of chine. They do this quite often, the agricultural agencies; it is known as guilding, I believe. So Eric got the original diktat translated and it said no such thing at all, so he fought the battle and won. It was quite funny, because one scene in the programme was me going out into the streets of Louth with a plate of chine, the BBC thinking that nobody would know what it was, and saying, 'Do you know what this is?' and everybody replied, 'Yes, it's chine and I would love a bit.'

When you continue north up the coast you come to the mighty River Humber, but I am going to go straight across the middle and head for the county town of Lincoln with its magnificent cathedral. The Romans built the first town at Lincoln to guard the crossing of several roads, the most important of which was Ermine Street, and Lincoln grew from there. The whole town is dominated by the cathedral which stands on a hill above it. John Evelyn, when he visited in the seventeenth century, described the town as 'windy and steep' and it is much the same today. Lincoln Cathedral is the third largest in the country after St Paul's and York Minster, and while it may not have the elegant beauty of Ely or the spire of Salisbury, the sheer massiveness of it makes it incredibly imposing and gives a sense of its importance. It is a noble, triple-towered cathedral and is often, because of its position, slightly veiled in mist, but it dominates the vista from a long way around. Most people with even a slight knowledge of English history know about the massacre of the Jews at York in 1190, but there was a similar incident in Lincoln too. It was, indeed, in Lincoln that the little boy Hugh, St Hugh to us now, was supposed to have been murdered by the Jewish community and cannibalised. This particularly nasty story is even found in Chaucer in 'The Prioress's Tale' and the cathedral contains the shrine of St Hugh which was a major shrine during its heyday.

Due to its size and importance as a diocese, Lincoln has had a number of important bishops. Cardinal Wolsey for instance was Bishop of Lincoln, but one lesser known incumbent and one of my great heroes was a man called Robert Grosseteste. The name literally translated means big balls or big testes and this made very evident to his colleagues that he was of peasant Saxon stock. His parents are supposed to have been smallholders or agricultural labourers or even possibly merely freemen, and very little is known about his early education. His memorial in the cathedral says that he was educated in Paris but there is no evidence for that. In any event, however, he is now acknowledged as the father of modern theological thinking. He was a highly successful bishop and, although he started off supporting the thoughts of Thomas Becket as to the rights of the Church, he eventually came round to recognise that the depredations that Rome was trying to levy on the English faithful were just too high. He was between seventy and eighty years old when he died, still Bishop of Lincoln, and he was noted, among other things, for the excellence of his manners. There is a story told of a Norman baron who was amazed upon dining with him that the bishop rebuked a page who served the larger fish to the bishop and told him to exchange it. By order of precedence the page might have been right, but the baron was of course his guest. The baron's reaction was slightly patronising and insulting, but still the bishop's behaviour showed that he had come a long way from his humble origins.

Lincoln was one of the great financial centres of England in the Middle Ages, being a staple town, one where wool was sold, weighed and then shipped out from Boston, but it was also a cloth town famous for its Lincoln green, as worn by Robin Hood and his Merry Men, and for its fine scarlet cloth. It suffered heavily during the wars of Stephen and Matilda and indeed is believed to be the town in the old nursery rhyme, 'The Lion and the Unicorn were fighting for the crown', the Lion being Matilda and the Unicorn the coat of arms of Stephen of Blois. Lincoln is also the site of one of the very early Parliaments in the reign of Edward II, when he wanted supplies for the war with Scotland, because the Pope had declared that Scotland was a sovereign country. The Mayor of Lincoln has the right to have a sword carried in front of him in procession, a right granted to him by Richard II. The town suffered again during the Civil War between the Royalists and the Parliamentarians.

I am now moving north-west from Lincoln, which I do recommend you go and see for yourselves, on to a town that should not be missed if you are passing through Lincolnshire. This is Gainsborough, worth a visit most especially because of Gainsborough Old Hall, which I will come to in a minute. Apart from that there is little left to commemorate Gainsborough's rather remarkable history. It was here that King Alfred married Ealswitha, daughter of the chief of the Gaini, the local tribe, and also here that Sweyn Forkbeard, King of the Danes, came up the River Trent with his son Canute and overran the countryside. Sweyn died the following year and the big tumulus, at what is still described as the Danish Camp, was believed to have housed his body, which was subsequently embalmed and sent to Denmark for burial. If you read George Eliot's *The Mill on the Floss*, the town that she calls St Ogg's is in fact Gainsborough, home to her mill, which has long since been pulled down, but she gives a vivid description of the river and the town:

A wide plain, where the broadening Floss hurries on between its green banks to the sea, and the loving tide, rushing to meet it, checks its passage with an impetuous embrace. On this mighty tide the black ships – laden with the fresh-scented fir-planks, with rounded sacks of oil-bearing seed, or with the dark glitter of coal – are borne along to the town of St Ogg's, which shows its aged, fluted red roofs and the broad gables of its wharves between the low wooded hill and the river brink, tingeing the water with a soft purple hue.

The Old Hall is the perfect example – and one of very few remaining – of a medieval baronial hall. It was the home of the powerful de Burgh family who, unfortunately for them, backed the Yorkist cause in the Wars of the Roses and so lost out. Over the years the hall had a chequered career. It has been a linen factory, a theatre, a machine workshop and even an auction house. However, the good efforts of the Bacon family, who owned the site, maintained it and kept it sound, although it was really Sir Hickman Bacon, a remarkable eccentric, who preserved it for posterity. He set up the Friends of Gainsborough Old Hall and sold the hall to them for £1, thereby making it a legal transaction. To this day the Friends are headed up by Sir Nicholas Bacon, the Bacons being the senior baronets in England, and it is managed in rather lacklustre fashion by English Heritage.

Having been to the Old Hall with a friend of mine, who is a member of the Bacon family and who lives nearby, I fell in love with it and desperately wanted to film there when we were making *Two Fat Ladies*, but we were told that on no account would they allow a cooking programme to be shot there. However, thanks to the good offices of Sir Nicholas and the Friends, I was finally allowed to film my BBC4 programme there, *The King's Cookbook*, which is based on the oldest English language cookery book, written by Richard II's cooks, *The Forme of Cury*. I even got to light a fire in one of the two huge brick fireplaces. For me it was a quite delightful and very exciting experience. The hall still has its original medieval lavatories, now no longer in use, which used to drain straight into the River Trent, but the river has now moved so this would not be feasible these days.

We were aided and abetted in this Optomen production by the very good re-enactment group that is based at the hall, known as Lord de Burgh's men, in memory of the original builder of the hall. The group gave me one of their badges of membership which is a brooch in the form of an armoured fist. I am always rather wary of re-enactment groups, because so many of them don't quite get it right, but you couldn't say that about Lord de Burgh's men. Everything about them, including their cookery – they cooked various dishes for the feast for us – was excellent. They made their clothes themselves from the proper cloth and they even have a band of archers. I remember shooting at a target with one of these archers and he was so knowledgeable that I asked, 'How do you know so much about it?' He said, 'Oh, I expect I was there,' meaning at the Battle of Crécy, and he may very well have been right.

English Heritage on the other hand were not only reluctant to allow us to film longer hours, although we were presumably paying their wages, but insisted on keeping the hall open, with the result that every so often my cookery would be interrupted by a tour of people who would come through and stand there gawping and generally preventing us from getting on with the job.

You can leave Lincolnshire through the town of Grantham, birthplace of Mrs Thatcher, whose father had a grocer's shop in the town, which might be of interest to you if you happen to be a Thatcherite. I am now going to move into Nottinghamshire.

Nottinghamshire

Nottinghamshire is one of the smallest counties, covering only half a million acres. It is a county of much variety, and since the Middle Ages has been enormously prosperous because of the presence of coal. The rich coal seams run between Nottingham, which is fairly far south in the county, and Worksop in the north, and the area mined, before the closure of the pits, was in excess of twenty-five miles from south to north. These seams led not so much to the mining of coal but to extensive industrial development. In Elizabethan times the county invented the stocking frame and a pair of stockings was actually made for Queen Elizabeth I. Since then the area remained the centre of the stocking trade for a long time and manufacture spread from hosiery into clothing as well. For much of its history the main industry in Nottingham was lace and some of the best lace in the country was manufactured here. You will remember perhaps in the BBC's *Lark Rise to Candleford* the terrible impact that the invention of machines for lace making had on the inhabitants of Lark Rise. Nottingham also had extensive leather and printing industries and for quite a large part of its history was a huge producer of cigarettes. In fact until the Puritans under Oliver Cromwell put an end to this, at one point it was growing its own tobacco. In more recent times it saw the birth of the Raleigh bicycle which was made in the city.

Standing as it does in the heart of the Midlands, the county has seen quite a lot of fighting and bloodshed, but none probably more bloodthirsty than the little known battle at East Stoke in 1487 where Lambert Simnel, the son of an Oxford joiner, was set up by one Richard Symonds, a priest, to pose as the younger of the two little Princes in the Tower, the Earl of Warwick. Symonds, it is believed, hoped that if the ruse succeeded, Lambert would make him Archbishop of Canterbury. Simnel was crowned in Dublin and marched into England with an army of Irishmen and 1,500 German mercenaries and went to York. Led by the Earl of Lincoln and Viscount Lovell, he marched south and forded the Trent at Fiskerton towards East Stoke on their way to take Newark. At East Stoke they were met by the King's army marching out from Nottingham and for three hours they stubbornly fought in one of the most terrible conflicts known until then, which ended in the rout of the Yorkists and the shattering of their hopes for ever. The site of the battle was known thereafter as Dead Man's Field and the track running down to the river is still called the Red Gutter. The Earl of Lincoln, who had serious claims to the Plantagenet crown, died in the battle. Henry VII sent Lambert Simnel back to Piel Island to work as a scullion in the castle kitchens there for the remainder of his days. The only mystery is what happened to Lord Lovell, Richard III's right-hand man. Rumour said that he escaped to Minster Lovell in Oxfordshire and died in hiding.

Nottinghamshire's favourite son, however, at least in the folk memories of the English, was of course Robin Hood, the outlaw of Sherwood Forest. Nobody is really sure who Robin Hood was; some legends have him as a returning Crusader whose estates had been stolen by King John while he was absent fighting with Richard Coeur de Lion in the Holy Land; some stories say he was the Earl of Loxley, some that he was a fugitive Nottinghamshire miner; but the man, fictional or not, who is supposed to have robbed the rich to give the money to the poor has until the present day been the subject of dozens of books, plays and films. Almost invariably the stories say that his arch-enemy and the person upon whom he wreaked the most havoc was the Sheriff of Nottingham.

Perhaps in this day and age when the bankers have been robbing the poor to make themselves richer, Robin Hood's popularity will soar in the country's memory.

Nothing now remains of the original Nottingham Castle which was destroyed during the Civil War, except the site and the caves that are dug into the rocks at the foot of the castle escarpment and were possibly used in the Middle Ages to store hay and grain and other necessities for the castle. In later years they were actually lived in by local people. There must have been a certain amount of poverty and homelessness as shown by the fact that General Booth, founder of the Salvation Army, was born in and started his work in Nottingham. The building that now stands on the site is very new and houses a museum full of interesting local artefacts. I remember going there with my dear goddaughter Sara, who at that time was only three years old, and who was dragged screaming and yelling away from an exhibition of medieval glass of amazing vulgarity because she loved it so much that she wanted to stay and look at it. I am glad to say that her taste has improved since then.

Richard III left Nottingham Castle for Bosworth Field and a day that was to bring in the Tudor dynasty. And it was at Nottingham that Charles I raised his standard on Standard Hill overlooking the castle grounds. I have never really been quite sure why he chose Nottingham, as it was a town and a shire that held out strongly for the Parliament. The notable Colonel Hutchinson refused the Duke of Newcastle's offer to hand over the castle for a sum of £10,000 and a requirement to join the Royalists' side. His answer was that if the Duke wanted the castle he must wade to it through blood. When the war was over, Parliament gave the garrison £1,000, a lot of money, but the castle was dismantled and mostly demolished. The first Duke of Newcastle cleared away the ruins and he and his son transformed the walls into a ducal palace. Part of the Duke's statue on horseback is cut from a single block of stone and is still positioned over the doorway. The Industrial Revolution and the introduction of stocking looms on a much larger scale led to rioting and the castle was burned by the mob and remained a blackened shell for over forty years until it was restored.

Twentieth-century Nottingham has seen a lot of architecture of the civic pride type. The facings for the new Council House are from stone that was marked down for St Paul's by Christopher Wren but never used. There is a fine modern campus university which owes a great deal to the influence of Sir Jesse Boot, the founder of the chain of chemist's shops of that name. He began his career behind the counter of his parents' herbalist shop and went on to fame and fortune. Following the Great War Sir Jesse, who by this time was very rich but with chronic rheumatoid arthritis and his body failing him daily, dreamed that he would build this University College which opened in 1928. The city also has a very fine Peace Memorial, raised to commemorate the end of the First World War.

The impressive Natural History Museum was once Wollaton Hall, the home of the Willoughby family, the most remarkable of whom to my mind was Sir Hugh Willoughby, who was born in the early sixteenth century and won distinction as a soldier. Willoughby was made admiral of three little ships sent to seek an eastern route to Asia along the north of Europe. They left in May 1553 but the vessels were driven apart. Richard Chancellor, who was the Pilot General, found his way into the White Sea and travelled across country to Moscow where he made plans for the setting up of the Muscovy Company, of which one of my ancestors was a founding member. Willoughby sailed on with two ships to Nova Zembla, the first Englishman to penetrate so far into the Arctic, a wild and inhospitable coast where Lapland joins Russia with neither food nor clothing for an Arctic winter that nobody had anticipated. Nothing was heard of them for almost two years and they were presumed lost, but in Willoughby's diary we learn that they spent months at the end of 1553 seeing if they could find any people, but reported no signs of any habitation. The last entry tells us that they were alive in January 1554, having survived one Arctic winter, but when they were finally all found in the spring of 1555 by some Russian fishermen, they had frozen to death.

Unsurprisingly, the industrial prosperity of Nottinghamshire led to the building of many great houses. Near Worksop there is an area known as the Dukeries on account of the number of Dukes who lived there, the main ones being the Duke of Portland at Welbeck Abbey, the Duke of Newcastle at Clumber Park, the Duke of Kingston at Thoresby Hall and the Duke of Norfolk at Worksop Manor. Welbeck is perhaps the most amazing and unusual of these houses. It did indeed start life as an abbey founded in the middle of the twelfth century by a man called Thomas de Cuckney and remained so until the Dissolution of the Monasteries. After various trials and tribulations it was bought by Bess of Hardwick, who left it to her son Sir Charles Cavendish, whose son was made Duke of Newcastle for services to Charles I. It was he who built the old and very magnificent riding school at the abbey.

What is particularly remarkable about Welbeck is its underground aspect. The ceremonial entrance to the abbey is through the Iron Gates of Lady Bolsover Drive. Once it was a mile and a half tunnel under the lake, lighted artificially by skylights in the roof, and was wide enough for a horse and cart or today a modern motor car. It is only part of the huge system of underground tunnels and rooms dug out by order of the fifth Duke of Portland whose family seat it then was, who employed thousands of men and spent huge sums of money on these undertakings. He was a recluse, to put it politely, and extremely eccentric. Nowadays, well who knows, with that much money I was going to say he would probably be in the care of social services, but maybe not. One of the underground chambers is 160 feet long and 63 feet wide and is the biggest room in England without pillars. It was sometimes used as a ballroom and contains paintings of members of the Cavendish family with whom the Bentincks claimed a connection by marriage. The Duke also built another riding school 400 feet long and 106 feet wide with a roof in three divisions supported by fifty pillars, arched and lavishly decorated with a frieze. Welbeck has magnificent gardens that are well worth the visit and it is rather sad to think that the reclusive Duke who built the underground rooms would probably never have seen the gardens.

Nearby are Thoresby Park, built in 1683 by the Earl of Kingston, the most richly wooded of all the nearby ducal estates, and Clumber Park. Clumber is eleven miles round and is perhaps most remembered for the development of the sporting Clumber spaniel. The Clumber is the largest and heaviest of all the spaniel family, with a stocky frame and a very thick bramble-resistant coat and was originally developed to work either singly or in small packs, driving pheasants from heavy cover. You don't see many of them nowadays, other than occasionally at some of the game fairs around the country, but really they have fallen out of favour, partly due to inbreeding; they produce an enormous amount of drool and have problems with breathing because of their size as well as problems with hip dysplasia. Modern shooting and shooting estates have moved on rather, and there is not the same need for this particular breed or the position it occupied in the sporting world. Their puppies are enchanting and if you see a good one it is a beautiful dog indeed. They were much favoured by Edward VII and George V, both of whom were keen shots.

Another dilettante inhabitant of Nottinghamshire was the poet Lord Byron, who inherited Newstead Abbey, which fell into the hands of the family after the Dissolution of the Monasteries by Henry VIII, granted to Sir John Byron of Colwick in payment of a sum of £800. The Byrons sided with the Royalist cause in the Civil War and Sir John Byron's grandson, who eventually inherited Newstead, also called Sir John Byron, died in penury in Paris. Because he had no children, upon his death his brother Richard inherited it. There was obviously bad blood in the family as the great uncle of Lord Byron the famous poet, killed his cousin in a duel and was found guilty of manslaughter but acquitted on payment of a fee. He retired to Newstead where he allowed the place to fall into dilapidation, cutting down the timber and killing the deer. He ill-treated his wife, bullied his tenants and died in the only room left in the house that was weatherproof. The property passed to his great-nephew, a boy of ten living in Aberdeen, who was of course George Gordon Noel Byron. His mother, the widow of 'Mad Jack' Byron, another scoundrel who spent her fortune and bullied her badly, moved with her son to Newstead. Byron wrote of it:

Through thy battlements, Newstead, the hollow winds whistle,
Thou, the hall of my fathers, art gone to decay;
In thy once smiling garden the hemlock and thistle
Have choked up the rose which late bloomed in the way.

Not perhaps his greatest work. He and his mother were too poor to live in the abbey which they let and lived at Southwell nearby. After leaving Cambridge, Byron came back to Newstead, to which he became very attached and vowed never to leave. However blood will out and he was so heavily in debt that in 1814 he sold it to a school friend from Harrow, a Colonel Wildman, for £100,000, and Byron never saw the house again. Wildman spent a quarter of a million pounds on the restoration of the property but, with the abolition of the slave trade to the West Indies, his income plummeted, and on his death it was sold to a man called William Frederick Webb. A story about Webb, who was an excellent swimmer, recounts that when returning from Africa he was horrified that the captain of the ship would not stop to pick up two lascar seamen who had fallen overboard.

The captain said, 'We don't stop the ship for lascars.' Webb replied, 'Then perhaps the captain will stop for a white passenger,' and leapt into the sea. The house is now divided into private flats but there are the Byron rooms which contain a number of Byron relics: Byron's boxing gloves, a lock of his hair, his fencing sticks, two helmets he wore in Greece and various other items, including artefacts from the Greek government who were well aware that Byron died fighting for the liberty of Greece. There is also a striking monument to Byron's Newfoundland dog Boatswain which Byron said:

> possessed beauty without vanity,
> Strength without insolence,
> Courage without ferocity
> And all the virtues of man without his vices.

In his will Byron directed that he should be buried in the vault below the monument, near his beloved dog, but in fact he is buried at the church in Hucknall.

The bit of Nottinghamshire that I most like is Newark, not just because of the ruins of the castle, which show that it must have been one of the strongest in England, but because I used to come here with my father to see the memorial to John Arderne. According to my father, John Arderne was the first real English doctor. We don't know where he was born but, during the first outbreak of the Black Death, we know, from his writings, that between 1349 and 1370 he lived in Newark. There is no doubt that he was a medical genius. He went to London at the height of his reputation and his patients included the Black Prince, whom he accompanied to France and to the Battle of Crecy, Henry of Lancaster, and other such well-known warriors, famous preachers and rich merchants. At a time when the Church really controlled medicine, he obviously knew the works of Hippocrates and Galen, but what particularly appealed to my father was that he was known as a brilliant operating surgeon, remarkable in an age when the Church banned the study of anatomy and only the University of Syracuse taught it at all. In a period when there were no anaesthetics, Arderne insisted that the patient should be rendered unconscious before an operation with the proviso: 'If you must cut do so boldly, loss of blood is less and the shock minimised.' Five hundred years before Pasteur and Lister he recommended the necessity of aseptic surgery saying, 'Keep wounds clean, they should heal without suppuration but where this does occur assist the process by washing that the wound may heal from the bottom upwards otherwise do not dress too frequently.' He was an amazing man whose teaching seems then to have been lost without trace until many hundreds of years later.

Derbyshire

Derbyshire is a county that has almost everything going for it – good rivers, good fishing, wealth engendered by its mining both of coal and other minerals, some of the finest houses in England as well as the glories of the Peak District and Dovedale and its surroundings – but to me it really means two of my heroines. I don't have many heroes or heroines in my life, but Derbyshire has produced two women, both by the name of Cavendish, both of whom married into that family and both of whom brought it glory and enhancement. The first of these was Bess of Hardwick, the daughter of an ordinary farmer, John Hardwick. I suppose one of the main benefits in her life was that one of her close friends was William Cecil, who was to go on to become Elizabeth's First Minister and the most powerful man in Elizabethan England and who, therefore, enabled the marriage of Bess to three husbands, one of whom was the Cavendish in question. Bess had been told by a fortune-teller in her youth – and remember that Elizabeth was very keen on fortune-telling and John Dee and his associates – that she was born to build, and that when she stopped building she would die. She took this very much to heart. She married four times, each one to better advantage.

Her first husband was Robert Barlow, the fourteen-year-old heir to a neighbouring estate, who died not that long after the marriage, leaving her with certain land holdings in Derbyshire. She then married Sir William Cavendish. The Cavendish family had acquired a lot of benefits from the Dissolution of the Monasteries and by this marriage she had eight children, two of whom died in infancy. Two of her sons were the ancestors of the Dukes of Devonshire and the Dukes of Newcastle. When Sir William died she then married another landowner called Sir William St Loe, who had also benefited from the sale of properties on the Dissolution of the Monasteries and held quite extensive property down in the West Country, which she persuaded him to sell and to buy the Chatsworth Estate. After being widowed for the third time, some years later she married George Talbot, Earl of Shrewsbury, who was considerably older than she was and already had a number of children by his previous marriage. George Talbot, as it was subsequently proved, was a vacillating man at a time when Queen Elizabeth needed all the friends she could get. In any event here we have Bess with various properties, the ones she has inherited from her husbands, and she is a very rich woman so she built Chatsworth, which is still with us today although in a slightly added-to form from her day.

However, the most magnificent house in the county, as far as I am concerned, is Hardwick Hall. There is a local rhyme that goes, 'Hardwick Hall all glass and no wall'. This was the period in history when glass was being manufactured for the likes of Bess and William Cecil, who were building new-style houses that no longer needed to be castles. They were a statement that such wars as the Wars of the Roses were not going to recur which, of course, proved to be untrue. So the first thing that hits you when you go to Hardwick Hall is this amazing expanse of glass. It is built with wonderful roofs with Bess's initials carved in stone to stand against the skyline. Indoors, the painted plasterwork in the Great Hall on the first floor is wonderfully colourful and attractive, but the most impressive feature is of course the glass. Her building and decorative skills were clearly passed on to her descendants because one of her sons added to and embellished Chatsworth until it was nearer what we know today. The other took the property at Bolsover and did much the same there. George Talbot had inherited the manor at Wingfield, and it was while Bess was there that they were given the custody of Mary, Queen of Scots, who began her imprisonment in 1569 at Wingfield and returned again in 1584. It was during her stay here that Anthony Babington, who managed to visit her frequently disguised as a gypsy, organised the Babington Plot, which was the final straw that broke the camel's back and took Mary to Fotheringhay. George, like so many men of his generation, fell for the Queen, and was probably involved in various plots, but it was his marriage to Bess that saved him from losing his head.

By the mores of her time Bess wasn't terribly well educated, but she was an accomplished needlewoman, as was Mary, Queen of Scots, and the collection that remains, the Oxburgh Hangings, contains magnificent hangings and embroideries and so forth worked by her. The pieces she stitched are truly sumptuous and there is no doubt that the bed hangings at Hardwick Hall, which are black velvet beautifully embroidered with silk flowers, were wrought both by the captive Queen and by Bess of Hardwick.

Bess did indeed stop building one winter when there was a bitter frost and the builders were unable to work because the mortar froze as soon as they mixed it. Bess went out, no doubt to chivvy them, and caught pneumonia and died. Bess had aimed truly high, and on a visit from the Countess of Lennox had succeeded in marrying one of her daughters to Charles Stuart, Earl of Lennox, who had a claim to the throne. Their only daughter Arabella was famously confined to Sir Thomas Perry's house after her controversial marriage to William Seymour. She escaped in a bid to reach France to reunite with him, but was captured by the King's men at Calais and died of starvation in the Tower of London after refusing to eat. Curiously, Bess would have been pleased because one of Arabella's descendants is our own Queen, Elizabeth II.

My other Derbyshire heroine has also lived in Chatsworth and she is Deborah, Duchess of Devonshire, the present Dowager, and a woman who is greatly admired. She was born one of the Mitford sisters and we all know the extraordinary sequences of their upbringing through the writings of her sister and especially in the book *Love in a Cold Climate*. In the days before I came to understand bloodhounds and their uses historically, and not just as a chaser of runaway serfs but also as tufters in stag hunting, the only place I really felt comfortable seeing bloodhounds was at the show at Chatsworth, because there is that wonderful bit in *Love in a Cold Climate* where the children are the live bait and run in front of the bloodhounds and are chased by them and I thought that the Duchess must really understand them. There are numerous reasons to admire the Duchess, including her amazing dress sense. I know two elderly nuns who think that she is wonderful but are particularly mesmerised by what she is wearing whenever she appears on television. I must say, however, that when I was filming *One Man and his Dog* at Chatsworth and she came up to present the prizes she was wearing a sort of ice-cream pink and white candy-striped outfit, almost like a deckchair, which on anybody else would have looked slightly strange to put it mildly, but on her looked the epitome of haute couture.

My main reason, however, for admiring her is for everything she has done to fight the cause for farm shops and farmers' markets. When she first opened the shop at Chatsworth, and in those days a farm shop was really something quite unheard of and the best you would get was eggs at the farm gate or home-made jams, all she was allowed to sell in the way of meat were frozen legs of lamb. She fought the local council every inch of the way and today the farm shop at Chatsworth has amazing butchery counters selling all sorts of meat from the Chatsworth Estate. She battled for all of us who love country produce and want to see successful diversification within the farming community and last year, 2011, the Countryside Alliance gave her a Lifetime Achievement Award for setting off the local food movement. Never has an award been better given. She is also very sound on the vital question of hunting. I remember when, at the beginning of all this brouhaha, she and her late husband Andrew appeared in one of the newspapers in front of Chatsworth House saying that they would gladly go to prison for the sake of hunting. I think that her husband's ancestor would have been very proud of her indeed.

Derbyshire, despite its mining heritage, contains some of the most beautiful scenery in England such as Dovedale, where my friend Christine used to drag me on walks. I should say that I have never been a great one for walking for the sake of it; however the Dales are quite stunning and I have to admit that I probably wouldn't have climbed some of the peaks that I did if my gin and tonic hadn't been concealed in the knapsack that Christine was carrying so that if I wanted a drink and didn't want to start shaking I would have to keep up. The climbs were something I am glad to have done in my time. Derbyshire has two main rock formations: the limestone, which is full of caves and therefore provides adventure for those people who are fascinated by exploring caves and underground rivers; and the gritstone, which is perfect for people who like going upwards and the Roaches escarpment provides excellent pillars for the rock climbers to ascend.

In the days when spa treatments were supplied by natural resources, rather than those dreadful smelly indoor spas that the young go to, the hot springs of Buxton and the waters of Ashbourne were a great draw to people who wanted to improve their health. Abutting the River Wye, Buxton is the highest town in England, 1,000 feet above the surrounding area, and the spring produces hot water at a constant 82°F regardless of the time of year. We know that the Romans with their passion for hot baths certainly came to Buxton, because they built roads here from some of their military stations around about. The spring is known for its healing properties and, in the Middle Ages, despite its remoteness, pilgrims flocked to the well at the foot of the cliff and the walls of the old well Chapel of St Anne were hung with sticks and crutches that people had been able to discard after bathing in the waters. Henry VIII had the relics removed and the well and chapel were locked up and sealed, but by Elizabethan times the waters were again much sought after. Mary, Queen of Scots was brought here for the benefit of her health and she scratched on the window with a ring: 'Buxton whose fame thy milk warm waters tell, whom I perhaps shall see no more, farewell'. Buxton is set on two levels, the higher and the lower, where its fine old Pump Room is situated and the waters are drunk from the flowing source. The splendid Crescent that was built by the fifth Duke of Devonshire in about 1780 was designed by John Carr of York in the Doric style and is said to have cost £120,000.

Water is a constant feature in Derbyshire and if you go to Tissington you are at the centre of the Derbyshire tradition of well dressing. I like to think that perhaps I can trace the custom back to my friend the great god Pidd again since it is a very old tradition indeed. The Victorians spent a lot of time inventing or recreating after a fashion what they thought were old medieval festivals but the interesting thing here is that the wells are dressed in celebration of Ascension Thursday which was a Catholic feast from before the Reformation and therefore an unlikely choice for a Victorian festival. The six wells of Tissington have never failed. They protected the villages from having to go elsewhere to fetch water and so isolated them from possible infection of the plague at the time of the Black Death and again from the terrible drought that occurred in the seventeenth century. The wells are by the road that makes a circular tour of the village: Hands Well, taking its name from the folk who once lived here, the Hall Well under a stone canopy opposite the Jacobean Tissington Hall, the Town Well, the Yew Tree Well, the Children's Well and the Coffin Well, named for the shape of its trough in a cottage garden. The decorations are made with flowers, moss and leaves all pressed into wet clay and they are put in position in time to be judged. A church procession goes round blessing the wells and singing hymns.

The FitzHerbert family who live in Tissington Hall have

done so for more than 400 years and its very splendid gates are supposed to be the work of Robert Bakewell, the famous Derbyshire craftsman. One of the more famous of the FitzHerberts is Alleyne FitzHerbert, found as 'Little Fitzherbert' in a letter written by Thomas Gray in 1771. At twenty-four he was appointed British Minister in Brussels, and at thirty he acted as a peace-maker between France, Spain and the Netherlands. He was then sent as Ambassador to Russia where he accompanied Catherine the Great on her tour of the Crimea, warmed by her gift of a fur pelisse, cap and muff for the sledge journey, where huge bonfires were lit across the route and horses waited in relays. He became Chief Secretary of Ireland, an Ambassador to The Hague and influenced important treaties with Russia, Denmark and Sweden. It is interesting that such a useful man came from a small village in Derbyshire.

Another town with historic hot springs is Matlock. The Romans had lead mines there and once again they must have enjoyed the pleasures of the hot springs. In 1698 a bath was built over a warm spring with a few small rooms for visitors. Today Matlock abounds in hotels and has startling ascents; it had a cable car that went up the steep gradient for nearly a mile and was one of the steepest of all such tramways in the world. The town has attractive riverside gardens and at one time had a great many mills. The hot springs are now remembered in the Hydro. It was John Smedley, a hosiery manufacturer, who having recovered from a breakdown visited the spa and sought to practise the water cure on others. He made his first experiments on his own workforce at Lea Mills nearby and this started the great Smedley Hydro. John Smedley made a fortune out of his air and water cures, probably a greater one than he ever made out of his stocking business. Riber Castle was built for John Smedley so that you could catch the breezes from 850 feet above sea level. There is a wonderful view of the Derwent valley, the main river of Derbyshire, from Matlock town. The church contains a set of six paper garlands, and these were carried in the funeral processions of maidens who had died too soon to marry. You find them in other places throughout Derbyshire and they come into Shakespeare in *Hamlet* when the priest protests against Ophelia's wearing these 'crants' because she had committed suicide.

People also went to Bakewell for the waters but Bakewell is far more famous and far more endearing to me as the birthplace of the Bakewell pudding, which is actually more of a tart than a pudding. I was always told that a publican in Bakewell who was hosting a political dinner was rather harassed and told his kitchen maid to pour some frangipane mixture into a pie dish that had already been baked and cook it again. She, misunderstanding him, poured it on to an already made jam tart and cooked it. When he saw what she had done it was too late to do anything else and so he said to the diners, 'Look what I have invented especially for you,' and that was the birth of the Bakewell pudding. Whether this is a true story or not I don't know, but it is one that I am very attached to. If you go to Bakewell you will find numerous shops offering you Bakewell tart or Bakewell pudding.

Derby, in the south of the county, is the county town, and is best known for the fact that it was where Bonnie Prince Charlie turned back from his expedition to take the English crown. He might have succeeded if he'd kept going, as George II was packing to flee to Hanover and the Bank of England was paying out its creditors in sixpences, but for reasons that we shall never really understand, Charlie decided to return to Scotland, and from that moment he had lost all hope of anything but the bloody massacre at Culloden. Derby is also known for Crown Derby Porcelain which, at its height, was one of the most successful of the porcelain factories in the United Kingdom.

The town is the resting place of an extremely unusual man, Henry Cavendish, born in Nice in 1731, a grandson of the second Duke of Devonshire. He left Cambridge without having obtained a degree and inherited a fortune of over £1 million in the money of the day. He was a strange, shy, nervous man who stammered badly and couldn't tolerate the presence of women. He would apparently leave written instructions as to his meals which always consisted of a leg of mutton for dinner. If he had guests, and he would only dine with his fellow scientists if he couldn't avoid it, he had two legs of mutton. He had a laboratory in his drawing room, a forge next door and an observatory above. It was he who first weighed carbon dioxide and experimented with hydrogen, which he found was the lightest of the gases. He revealed that carbon dioxide prevents combustion and is incapable of sustaining life and that if you fired an electric spark into a vessel containing hydrogen and oxygen what you got was liquid. He virtually laid down the foundations of chemistry as we have come to know it and to build on his work. Finally he went home to die in his native Derbyshire.

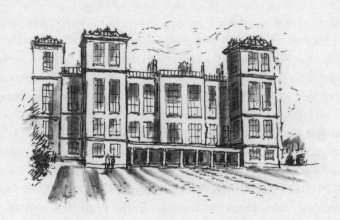

Staffordshire

Staffordshire is a county that I really admire. I have yet to meet anybody from Staffordshire that I didn't instinctively like and although now, sadly, the five towns that were the fortune of Staffordshire and now make up Stoke-on-Trent have lost their way, Staffordshire in the eighteenth century must have been an amazing place to live with the great minds of Josiah Wedgwood, Erasmus Darwin and the Lunar Men coming up with the ideas that made so much that was positive in the Industrial Revolution. Staffordshire is Mercia, which obviously extended over a wider area, but it was the base of Ethelfleda, the 'Lady of the Mercians', King Alfred's warrior daughter, who defeated both the Danes and the Welsh and carried on her father's belief in a united England. It was really she who made it possible for her nephew Athelstan to become King of all Britain. Before her, King Penda of Mercia was one of the last remaining pagans, but his sons converted to Christianity and brought missionaries to Staffordshire. These included St Chad, the founder of the See of Lichfield. Both Lichfield and Stafford were built and fortified by Ethelfleda.

Stafford itself gave us Izaak Walton, who was born and baptised here, and there is a stone bust of him on a wall in the nave of the main church. He was born in 1593 and went to London as a young apprentice, but he never forgot Stafford and was glad to come back when, after the Battle of Marston Moor, his Royalist sympathies were doomed. His must have been interesting dinner parties because he was a great friend of John Donne who was a vicar of St Dunstan's Church on Fleet Street, close to Walton's ironmonger's shop. Thanks to him he was friendly with Ben Jonson, John Milton, Samuel Pepys and John Evelyn, and probably also through him met and married his wife who was the great-grandniece of Archbishop Cranmer. Izaak Walton was in his sixtieth year when he published his best known work, *The Compleat Angler*, still an authority on early fishing and a delightful read about his own expeditions. The book traces the journey made by the old fisherman Piscator and his younger companion Venator. Walton finished his days at Shallowford, fishing the River Meece, and I came across his property by accident when out on a pootle with my friend Christine. The farm has a strange name, Halfhead, and is a brick and timber building that has been burned down twice but rebuilt. He left it to his native town of Stafford, stipulating that the rent should be used to apprentice two poor boys and provide a marriage portion for a servant girl and to buy coal for the needy.

When I went there, and I like to think that I might have had a hand in saving it, it was about to be sold. Izaak Walton wouldn't really have recognised it because in order to get to the river you had to cross a major railway line which thundered past not far from the house. There was a fishing museum upstairs that had opened in 1924 and contained, among other things, the head of a thirty-pound pike, a terrifying creature to behold you would have thought. Walton wrote a charming little verse on the contentment of his life at Shallowford:

> Here, give my weary spirits rest,
> And raise my low-pitched thoughts above
> Earth, or what poor mortals love:
> Thus, free from lawsuits and the noise
> Of princes' courts, I would rejoice;
> Or, with my Bryan and a book,
> Loiter long days near Shawford Brook

There sit by him, and eat my meat,
There see the sun both rise and set,
There bid good morning to next day;
There meditate my time away,
And angle on; and beg to have
A quiet passage to a welcome grave.

The curator told me that the council was about to close the house and museum with a view to selling it off. I was writing for *Country Life* at the time so I wrote a piece about it which caused an uproar and I am led to believe that as a result the place was saved.

We all know about Staffordshire's connection with potteries, but Wolverhampton, to the south of Stafford, which is the capital of the Black Country and the biggest town in Staffordshire outside Stoke-on-Trent, was the centre of an immense iron industry. The Romans worked iron just outside Staffordshire and at its height tens of thousands of acres and a multitude of workers in nearly 200 trades provided it with a thriving industry. Curiously a number of streets in the town are named 'Folds', such as Blossom's Fold, Mitre Fold, Farmers Fold and Pountney Fold and so forth. This is a reminder of the fact that situated where it is in the centre of the Midlands, Wolverhampton was a huge market for the sale of wool. The dialect of the Black Country is particular to itself and I remember going to an evening of Black Country humour, oh, back in my twenties, where I found it almost incomprehensible. The best bit of the evening, I thought, was the plateful of the local Black Country dish of faggots and mushy peas. That was my first taste of a faggot and since then I've always loved them. I think what I have particularly liked about Staffordshire is how the different areas have kept their identity and this was so well recorded by Arnold Bennett. Wolverhampton today is a very different kettle of fish and has a large Muslim population, mostly first or second generation, but one does hope that when they become absorbed into England they will somehow maintain the quality of this independent county.

Another example of that independence is to be found at Abbots Bromley and its Horn Dance. Abbots Bromley lies in the heart of the Needwood Forest, once the hunting grounds of John of Gaunt, covering an area of twenty-five miles and governed by the Forestry Laws, which were incredibly severe. The festival is supposed to celebrate the villagers' privileges of taking dead wood from the forest and grazing pigs in it at certain times of the year. Also the right to gather wood by hook or by crook, which allowed you to pull branches down from trees with a billhook and a crook rather than just gather them from the forest floor. The dance is made up of twelve people: Robin Hood on a hobby horse, Maid Marian, a jester, a boy with a bow and arrow, two musicians and six men wearing ancient stags' horns. I suspect that it is a pre-Christian ritual and that the figure we now identify as Robin Hood in his Lincoln green was in fact Herne the Hunter, a pagan figure associated with stag hunting and woodlands, and that the dance of the stags rutting and shaking their horns at one another was part of a wider fertility dance. In any event it still continues to this day and is a delightful link with our historic past.

Nearby is Bagot's Bromley, the pre-Domesday Book home of the Bagots. I always liked the story of Lord Bagot riding a rather second-rate horse through his park which was dominated by magnificent trees, and a friend asking him why he did not sell the £30,000 worth of oak that he would never miss, to which Bagot replied, 'The Bagots are not timber merchants.' At one time there was a tree called Bagot's walking stick, which was incredibly old, seventy feet high and still throwing out live shoots, but although that has now gone there are still wonderful trees to be found in the park, including a large number of Spanish chestnuts of great age. When I was young there were in all nearly 20,000 trees, amounting to some half a million cubic feet of timber. I think that is one of the great delights of Staffordshire, that for all its heavily industrialised past, it is still quite easy to get out into really splendid countryside.

Another example of this is the area known as Cannock Chase, again twenty-five square miles of moorland with valleys, streams and hills, and also a hunting ground for various medieval kings. The most moving thing in Cannock Chase is the German war cemetery, for those who died in the UK during both World Wars. These were the mariners or pilots or aircrew or, in some cases, even infantry who have been gathered together from all over the country and from prisoner-of-war camps such as on the Isle of Man and buried in these beautiful, peaceful surroundings. There is a chapel where people can go and meditate and think about war and its consequences. The memorial itself is in the form of a shrouded figure being absorbed into the earth. There is no feeling here of nationality or jingoism or anything like that, but just a quiet and attractive place for those whose remains lie here. It is horrifying, as it always is in war cemeteries, to discover quite how young many of the dead were and I think it is a great thing resulting from a German and British agreement. It also has a rather good little café that serves, to my delight, that other great Staffordshire delicacy, the North Staffordshire Oatcake.

I have a theory that this oatcake is an invention of the returning Crusaders. In the hills round Leek you will find what were known as Saracen villages because the Lord of Leek was supposed to have brought back with him Saracen falconers – rather like bringing back Nazi stormtroopers really if you think about it – who settled there. The inhabitants of these villages, while not small and dark and eastern, nonetheless did not have the long-boned Viking features of the other settlers in the area, and cooked their food differently too, using dried fruit and herbs in a way not found elsewhere. I like to think that they brought back with them their own particular flatbread, which evolved into the Staffordshire oatcake that is so very different from any other form of oatcake. It is more like a sort of flat pancake made with ground oats and water and salt and hung up to dry. It does excellently when wrapped round ham or smoked salmon or anything you like, really, and served with some sort of sauce or just eaten dry. You can actually buy them in the railway station at Stafford, which is a nice continuum of national dishes seldom found in other English railway stations.

Apart from iron and copper, and of course pottery, Staffordshire had many other industries. During the Great War, Burton-on-Trent had a huge industry making machine guns, and it was also once the centre of a clothing industry. However, the one product that the town is best known for is beer. In the thirteenth century the Abbot of Burton was using water from the wells here for brewing and it is this clear water that dictated that Burton was to be a brewing town. In the eighteenth century Burton beer became world famous, finding customers overseas such as Peter the Great and the Empress Catherine of Russia, and in Danzig it was drunk to celebrate the departure of Napoleon Bonaparte. William Bass founded a business producing 2,000 barrels of beer a year and the brewery covered 750 acres of works and sent out hundreds of thousands of barrels in total. The scale of the business meant that Burton was able to develop the ancillary industries for brewing such as the coopers, machinery manufacturers and maltsters. In the late nineteenth century, twenty breweries employed 6,000 people and produced 2 million barrels a year. The town had more level crossings than anywhere in the world because of the trains going back and forth from the various breweries.

What must have been wonderful in the last quarter of the eighteenth century was the Lunar Society of Lichfield, who were a collection of manufacturers, professional men and entrepreneurs who met by the light of the full moon in one another's houses, hence their name. Possibly their senior partner, for want of a better expression, was Erasmus Darwin, the grandfather of Charles Darwin, the pioneer of evolution. Erasmus's house in the Cathedral Close is well worth a visit. He was a rather fat doctor, an inventor and an educationalist, particularly keen that women should be educated. He clearly loved women and had fourteen children by different wives and mistresses. You may well come to the same conclusion as I did that the idea of evolution really came from Erasmus, a much more attractive character than Charles, when you hear that at one point he put an escutcheon on the outside of the carriage he used to go and visit his patients, with a picture of a shell on it and a motto underneath that read: 'Everything from shells'. This was regarded as such a revolutionary idea that the Bishop of Lichfield told him to remove it or he would be thrown out of the town.

Another member of the Lunar Society was Matthew Boulton, the flamboyant head of the 'first great manufactury' at Soho just outside Birmingham, set up with his partner James Watt of steam engine fame. Joseph Priestley, the preacher who stuttered badly but whose pen was wonderful, was also a member, and he was the man who isolated oxygen and became the first visionary leader of 'Rational Dissent'. Probably the greatest member of them all was Josiah Wedgwood the potter; he and Erasmus were fathers-in-law to each other's children. Also of their number was the Scot James Keir, the clock-maker John Whitehurst who dreamed of time beyond hours and minutes, and various doctors such as William Withering, who brought digitalis into mainstream medicine, and assorted philosophers.

Ten of these members became Fellows of the Royal Society, but what is most surprising is that very few of them had university educations. Most of them were nonconformists or free thinkers and they were therefore all placed outside the establishment, a great advantage when they talked of inventions and reforms and riots and love and laughing gas. It was an age when science was favoured because it was considered gentlemanly and cultured, but in the Lunar Society you found a group of people who put science to use in practical matters, especially as regards industry and the inventions and creations that made the world of eighteenth-century Britain great and prosperous. For example Christopher Smart, writing in 1760, says:

> For matter is the dust of the earth, every atom of which is the life.
> For motion is the quality of life direct, and that which hath not motion is resistance.
> For the earth which is an intelligence hath a voice and a propensity to speak in all her parts.

This may not seem so radical a series of thoughts to us today but believe me they were in the mid-eighteenth century.

Interestingly, missing from this group was Samuel Johnson. Revered beyond his abilities, he was an inhabitant of Lichfield and his house has been open as a museum for many years. Johnson's father had been a bookseller in Lichfield and on my visits to Lichfield it was always a good place to buy books, but sadly not any more. It was said of Johnson that when he talked, nobody else got a word in edgeways, which was always rather my impression of him. Johnson and Erasmus Darwin would have disagreed violently on the education of women, since you will remember that it was Samuel Johnson who said: 'Sir, a woman's preaching is like a dog's walking on his hind legs. It is not done well; but you are surprised to find it done at all.' It says a lot about the regard or lack of it in which he was held that he was not allowed to join the Lunar Society. Should you wish to read more about them I can recommend to you a book by Jenny Uglow called *The Lunar Men: The Friends who Made the Future 1730–1810*.

Stoke-on-Trent has absorbed all the five towns of Arnold Bennett's novel *Anna of the Five Towns*, Burslem, Longton, Hanley and Tunstall, which are now all part and parcel of the greater conglomerate of Stoke-on-Trent, with a single Lord Mayor to direct their destinies. At its height, and well into the twentieth century, the area had hundreds of potteries, the huge firing ovens first developed by Josiah Wedgwood, with their curious chimneys being as much a feature of the landscape as the oast houses of Kent. Names such as Wedgwood, Spode, Copeland, Minton and other well-known local craftsmen thrived and flourished. Originally and consistently what Stoke produced was slipware made with the local clay which, when it was dug, was left to mature for two or three years before being turned into earthenware pottery. At a time when the holds of the East India vessels couldn't contain enough porcelain coming in from China in the blue and white patterns we have come to know – it was brought back as ballast – and the great factories of Meissen and Sèvres were producing much sought-after porcelain of their own, what Stoke was producing, until Josiah Wedgwood came along, was everyday pottery; it was used throughout the country but it wasn't terribly unusual or attractive.

All that began to change with Josiah Wedgwood and the fine white biscuit ware that he developed, which was dipped into a finish glaze and subjected to a final firing. The perfection of this earthenware was Josiah Wedgwood's greatest achievement, but what he will really be remembered for was his untiring experiments in producing new forms, new colours and new designs and for employing English artists to decorate the pieces. It was, however, Josiah Spode who produced the bone ash porcelain for which the town became so famous. It must have been a very smelly place in its heyday, with all the piles of bones lying around waiting to be burned, and the heat from all the kilns and furnaces.

As the industry grew James Brindley, another member of the Lunar Society, was involved in building the canals, most especially the Great Junction Canal, which linked the Mersey, the Trent and the Severn, thus enabling the Stoke potteries to ship their wares all over the country and consequently be transported abroad, especially to the Americas. Decorating the various pieces for the factories was mostly piecework done at home by various artists and this led to a surprising classlessness about Stoke-on-Trent. If you had talent you moved up the social scale, earned more money and you were encouraged to do more and perhaps even develop your own designs. As late as my youth people were still hand-painting pottery at home in Stoke-on-Trent and I have a friend, Monica Ford, who was recruited just after the war from one of the City of London art colleges to be trained as a pottery designer. The firms focused on designing not only for the home trade but also for overseas trade, and researchers were sent out to America and Canada and other such places to discover the tastes of different areas, those of the northern states of America, for instance, being quite dissimilar to those of the southern states. The ware was manufactured specifically for particular markets and sold incredibly well.

Today Stoke-on-Trent is a lost town really, with very few potteries still at work, Emma Bridgewater possibly being the most notable. All the business has been moved to China and the Far East, leaving unemployment and poverty in its wake and letting a whole generation of talent go to waste. Now one hears that, with the rise of the Chinese economy and a shortage of available cheap labour as people grow wealthier, the big companies are talking of moving back to the United Kingdom. One does wonder, however, how they will find the talent and the workers necessary to reintroduce the potteries to England. The idea that began with Mrs Thatcher that we should become a country of service industries rather than of productive industries has left whole generations with very little to do and it will be interesting to see how things develop.

Another reason why I love Staffordshire is that the motorcycle and sidecar that was our trademark on *Two Fat Ladies* was later purchased by a remarkable man called John Pointer, who lived at

Wetley Rocks outside Stoke. He went from being the son of a smallholder who drove a lorry for De Mulders, to being the owner of the largest rendering plant in Europe, putting water back into the Trent and electricity into the National Grid. He was a good friend and sadly he has died now but his sons carry on the family business. One of them drove me in my sidecar in the Lord Mayor's procession a couple of years ago, which was for me, a London child, one of the most memorable days of my life.

I could go on about Staffordshire for much longer without saying anything of great note, but I will mention an excellent hunt in the moors in the north of the county, the Staffordshire Moorland. When hunting was legal, Prince Charles used to go out with it, and now it hunts within the law most satisfactorily. There is also a good racecourse at Uttoxeter which fits in very neatly with Walsall as I shall explain. I came to Walsall for the first time with my friend Christine, because there is a flour mill there and Christine wanted some flour for the bread-making machine she had bought for her husband. We saw a sign that said 'Leather Shop' and we went in to discover that Walsall is the centre of English saddlery and bridlery and everything connected with the horse furniture industry, as well as carriage driving accessories. When we were making *Clarissa and the Countryman* Johnny and I filmed there, and it was wonderful to see these industries that had been carried on since certainly the

eighteenth century, if not earlier, and that were still thriving. Interestingly, the shop we went into sold, under their own label, a lot of the products that they were manufacturing for the smart London shops such as Smythson's and Asprey's, so it was a very good place to buy your diaries or address books at a third of the price you would have paid in London.

So we will leave Staffordshire sadly behind us and move into Cheshire.

Cheshire

Cheshire is a county in which I have spent a lot of time, certainly in the last twenty-five years and before that at various times, and it is one where I have enjoyed myself enormously in all sorts of adventures. The first time I went to Cheshire was with some friends, all of us eighteen-year-old girls straight out of convent school on our first expedition let loose on our own, determined to have a wonderful time before we went on to university or whatever else we had decided to do with our lives.

We hired a cabin cruiser on the Chester/Llangollen Canal and I remember that there was a plaque in this little boat saying that it was one of the small boats that had been across to Dunkirk in 1940 to help ferry the stranded army to the larger boats that would bring them home to England. This really made us feel even more adventurous. I can still recall the huge sense of freedom and the thrill of knowing that we would be able to stop at pubs and go in and have a drink and there would be boys, although it was all very innocent. My friend Carrots, who was very keen on playing the oboe and had written her first symphony at the age of fifteen, used to get up and play her oboe first thing in the morning. We were so angry with her that we hid her reeds and she spent a lot of the trip trying to manufacture reeds out of the bulrushes that grew along the bank, without very much success. As her daughter Lucy is now at the Royal College of Music playing the oboe and the cor anglais, I feel rather guilty that somehow I prevented Carrots from having a similar career herself. We cooked rather simply on a gas cooker

– I don't remember if it had an oven and if it did I don't think we used it – and we bought supplies in canal-side shops.

One day, as it was getting dusk, we moored our boat under the loom of Beeston Castle and determined that we would climb into it, and so we scrambled up a very steep slope which had discouraged centuries of would-be invaders, mainly the Welsh I would imagine in that part of the world. We managed to get in by climbing over a gate and felt that we were terribly daring. Beeston Castle, now owned by English Heritage, used to be owned by the Tollemache family. This was an extremely wealthy family and when they got fed up with their original castle they simply moved to the hill a mile away at Peckforton and built another one. It always seemed a pragmatic move to me not to try to keep altering the one you are living in, which was very large and massive, but simply to build something rather more comfortable.

The old Earl of Dysart and his wife, Wenefryde, were great friends of my grandmother. The Earl looked like a tramp but he was, among other things, the possessor of a million-pound note, and there are some wonderful stories about him. On one occasion the milkman at Ham House in London, which they owned, was busy chatting up the cook and she said to him, "'oo's 'olding your 'orse?' The milkman looked across to the animal and said, 'Oh, there was some old boy bumbling around outside who looked as if he was homeless and living rough so I said I'd give him sixpence if he held the horse,' and she said, 'Lawks! That's 'is Lordship.' The milkman rushed back to his horse, full of apologies and pulling his cap, and Lord Dysart said, 'Oh, that's all right but where's my sixpence?' On another occasion a bank clerk dashed up to his manager and said, 'Excuse me, sir, there's an old tramp outside who wants to show his friend his million-pound note.' The manager replied, 'Oh, that will be the Earl of Dysart. Just take him down to the vault and show it to him, will you?' After the old boy died, Wenefryde rang up my grandmother from the Ritz Hotel and said, 'Come over, it's the anniversary of Owain's death so I've taken a suite and invited people round for champagne.' When my grandmother got there she said, 'Is this where you spent your honeymoon?' 'Good Lord, no!' said Wenefryde. 'He was far too mean to take anything but the smallest of rooms for the one night we stayed here and I always promised myself that one day I would come back and do it in style.'

I have over the years spent quite a lot of time following the Cheshire hounds, more latterly car following, in the company of their legendary huntsman Johnny O'Shea, who hunted the pack for twenty-five years. He said that the five o'clock fox – while the light lasts there is always a four o'clock or five o'clock fox to entertain those who haven't gone home because of the weather or idleness – went through the grounds of the new castle. We sat there and waited, and sure enough the fox came through followed by the hounds and then the hunt. I don't remember if the hounds ever got the five o'clock fox, but it always gave them a good blow for their efforts. Guy Ross-Lowe and Lavinia, Dowager Marchioness of Cholmondley, set up a coursing syndicate in order to give Johnny O'Shea something to occupy his time when he had to leave hunting because of his hips, and it was Johnny Scott who brought me into it about a year after it was created. So, while coursing was still within the law we had several dogs, and at a few periods did really rather well in our efforts to win prizes.

Twenty-five years ago my friends Guy and Carolyn Ross-Lowe opened a pub in what had been the old school on the Cholmondeley Estate opposite Cholmondeley Castle. Guy had been Johnny Scott's best friend since the age of five when they went to dame school together, so I had known him for a great many years. His wife Carolyn was the sister of a woman who had a flat next door to Books for Cooks when I was working there. It is a curious fact of life that my favourite pub in England is one that I never went to when I was drinking alcohol, so I have never drunk anything there but ginger beer, but I have had enormous fun within its portals and have stayed there regularly on my trips up and down from Scotland. Carolyn always used to say, 'Well, you know you can come and stay with us,' and I would reply, 'Yes, but I like staying in the pub.' The lodgings are situated in what was the schoolmaster's house so they are separate from the pub.

Carolyn cooked beautifully and Guy was a great raconteur and a splendid mine host. Sadly Guy died and the old adage was then proved, that it really doesn't do to try to do business with the great estates that have survived so long because the estate, which had a very good deal in the first place, but in my opinion did not do enough to help Carolyn in the difficult times following Guy's death. Eventually Carolyn gave up the pub. I hope that the extremely nice couple who currently run it have a better deal with the estate. The pub has now had a lot of money spent on it so it is not the same and has something of the flavour of an urban wine bar about it, but business seems to be good and I still stay there on my travels and I hope it is all a great success. It does boast, among other things, the best fried bread in the country, which I once put in my ten best things to eat for *Country Life*. The fried bread is made by Shirley Collins, the stalwart of the pub, the 'Ma Larkins of Cheshire', who looks after the rooms and cooks the very good breakfasts.

Cholmondeley Castle, which stands on the site of the old castle, is an early nineteenth-century house and is really the Cholmondeleys' secondary estate, the main one being over in Norfolk at Houghton, where the current Marquess and his wife and their twin sons spend most of their time, leaving Cholmondeley Castle as the residence of Lavinia, Dowager Marchioness. Her late husband, Hugh, was everything you could ask for in a country estate owner. He knew every tenant and every property on both estates, but was mildly eccentric. He collected, among other things, antique porcelain and lead

soldiers, and he had a fine collection. I have been to Cholmondeley
Castle for dinner on a couple of occasions and it is a splendid
example of nineteenth-century wealth. They have some very
good pictures including a pleasing Sickert of Hugh's mother
Sybil. The gardens, which are beautiful, are open to the public
at certain times of the year and there is an attractive park with
two lakes in it. Ginger McCain, the trainer of Red Rum, moved
his training establishment from basically the sands of Southport
to Cholmondeley Park and this is now run by his son Donald. I
remember taking an elderly nun of my acquaintance there, who
was mad for the racehorse Amberley House, winner of the
Grand National.

The lush pasture of Cheshire meant that it has, historically,
been a dairy county, producing milk and cheese for the surrounding conurbations, with Manchester and Liverpool not far away.
Until quite recently the dairy industry has been suffering badly
at the hands of the big milk companies, which have been importing cheaper milk from Poland, surprisingly, and, even more
surprisingly, from Austria, and of course the supermarkets'
determination to keep milk prices ridiculously low has not
helped the industry at all. However, recently salvation, such as it
is, has come in an unlikely form from the Starbucks coffee chain,
which like so many American corporations does its best to buy
local, or at least in the country in which it is based. It has started
buying its milk in England and the increasing popularity of the
latte, a drink I've never really been able to understand, has been
of enormous benefit to the industry. Think how much milk
there is in a glass of latte.

Equally important in the county is the cheese industry.
Cheshire is the oldest known cheese in England. It is believed
that the Romans ate a cheese that was almost identical to the
one we now eat. A vein of salt runs down the west coast of
England through Lancashire, Cheshire and into Somerset and all
along that path cheese is produced. This is because the salt could

be used in preserving the cheese and so led to the development of the whole cheese industry. If you find a town name ending in 'wich' in Cheshire and the surrounding counties, it means salt; it refers to the fact that there has been a salt industry in the area. Salt production in Cheshire has been carried on since Roman times and salt is an extremely valuable mineral that we can't live without. In Tsarist Russia you used to have the choice of going to the salt mines or living on a salt-free diet for six months and the result was exactly the same: you died. In fact you might have survived the salt mines but you would not survive the salt-free diet. It was so important in Roman times that the word 'salary', which referred to the income of a Roman soldier, actually came from the word 'salt'. I was somewhat mystified over the last two bad winters to hear that the government was importing salt from Spain to clear the roads when there must be enough salt in Cheshire to clear every motorway in the country in perpetuity. Originally the salt used to come out in streams in Cheshire, and in the springs in the fields, and this was collected in big lead pans and stored in large basins, then heated to drive off the water to leave the deposit of salt. Latterly, it has been mined. During the *Restoration* programme I stood up for the Lymm Salt Works, which didn't actually win, but as a result of the programme they obtained Lottery funding and now they not only have a museum but are once again producing salt, although not in any great quantity.

Nantwich holds an annual Cheese Fair, which is the largest in the world. I have judged there and it is an amazing sight with all sorts of different categories, including some that are, perforce, quite horrible. You have everything from locally made cheeses to imported plastic cheese from China and other remote places where you would not expect there to be any cheese production at all. Apart from the big cheese producers in Cheshire and Shropshire, there are a number of very good artisan producers in this area. Mrs Kirkham's and Mrs Appleby's are two that spring to mind, both of which won at Nantwich in the artisan cheese category. Real Cheshire cheese is quite unlike the crumbly plastic stuff you buy in the shops and has a really rich and interesting flavour. I love to think of the Romans, lolling on their couches, eating Cheshire cheese. As we know, cheese on toast was given to us by the Welsh and the Welsh marauders would have come through the Cheshire Gap, or the Welsh Gap as they call it in Cheshire, presumably seizing not just the leaner hill sheep and the fatter valley sheep as in the old nursery rhyme, but also truckles of cheese as well.

Cheshire is very much divided into a play of two halves. Southern Cheshire is farming, dairy farming in particular, old money and families that have been established there for centuries, while the northern half, which goes up to the Mersey, is much more industrialised. It was always said that people were living above their means in Cheshire as opposed to above their shops in Manchester. Historically, when you had made your pile and wanted to move to somewhere more salubrious, you bought property in Cheshire. The same remains true today, but it is fascinating because the north seems to be home to a lot of footballers and their wives. Michael Owen, the England footballer, has built himself a training stables there which is extremely lavish, and the area around Carden Park sports two extremely expensive restaurants. The town of Knutsford used to have a Rolls-Royce garage and saleroom, and there are not many of those around the country, but it has now given way to a Porsche saleroom; there I gather they may sell more Cayennes, which is the Porsche four wheeled drive, than anywhere else in the country. Knutsford, in a previous existence, was famous for being the site of Mrs Gaskell's novel *Cranford*, which was done very well on television a few years ago. Mrs Gaskell had come to Knutsford at about a year old as Elizabeth Cleghorn Stevenson, a motherless child, and she grew up there until she married William Gaskell, a famous Unitarian minister. The Gaskells had four daughters and a son who died shortly before his first birthday, after which Mrs Gaskell sought solace in writing.

Cheshire has had many industries, Macclesfield for instance being at one time the home of a thriving silk weaving industry. But it was another, that of making soap, specifically Sunlight Soap, that brought wealth to William Lever. Like all good philanthropists he devised what he saw as a New Jerusalem at Port Sunlight. William Lever's claim to fame was that it was he who first thought of making a piece of soap an attractive object, an item that you would want to buy for reasons other than washing. His soap had a convenient shape, an attractive colour and a pleasant scent. Before that soap was a rough commodity that the grocer would cut from a large bar to your order. Mr Lever progressed to be Lord Leverhulme and he set up the Lady Lever Art Gallery in his New Jerusalem, with a fine collection of British art at a time when everybody was buying foreign art, so to speak. It is a dignified building of its day, covering an area as big as Westminster Abbey, which contains not just pictures and sculptures but also furniture, tapestry, china, glass, textiles and even suits of armour. The gallery is well worth a visit and houses paintings by Romney, Gainsborough, Ramsay, Constable and many more. It was a subsequent Lord Leverhulme who bought the Altcar Estate from the Earl of Sefton, who had no children and was dying, in order to preserve not only the best grey partridge shooting in the country but also the running of the Waterloo Cup.

The canal where I went boating in my youth is part of a great conglomeration of canals that covers the Midlands, thanks to the industries of the eighteenth and nineteenth centuries linking all the different rivers, among them the Mersey, which forms the northern border of Cheshire. Ellesmere Port was one of the ports for the Manchester Ship Canal and a major gateway for iron ore, and if you drive past the town at night it is lit up like something out of a science fiction movie. The embankment that separates the ship canal from the Mersey is massive, being 140 feet wide at the base and 70 feet wide at the top; the canal itself is 120 feet wide here. The Shropshire Union Canal joins the Manchester Ship Canal to link the north-west of England with the Midlands. From here all ore was transferred to be carried to foundries in Staffordshire and the Black Country and on to barges going to the River Severn and to Bristol. Others would remain in the Mersey and discharge cargoes of grain and more latterly petroleum and other fuels.

You might ask yourself why I should have been going past Ellesmere Port in the dark. The answer is that the town contains a greyhound lapping track where we would go to exercise the dogs when it wasn't the coursing season. It has, I believe, been somewhat dolled up, but it used to be a venue of fairly rough and ready humour with the hare regularly breaking down between races, more to encourage people to go to the bar and spend money than through any electrical malfunction, I suspect. I always remember Lavinia, Lady Cholmondeley's request for a gin and tonic being met with a bewildered stare, and when the staff eventually managed to find some gin and she asked if there was any ice, they nearly had a nervous breakdown. I did, however, get served one of the best bacon butties I have eaten there, with a very nice woman saying in her Cheshire accent that she suspected that I wanted bacon fat rather than butter to lubricate my bacon butty. And I recall a man in a wheelchair asking me if I had tried the curry sauce with chips and I said that no, I hadn't. 'Probably wise,' he said, 'it was the last thing I ate before I ended up in this wheelchair.' I'm still not quite sure whether or not he was joking.

Chester itself goes back long before the time of the canals. It was called Deva by the Romans after the River Dee that runs through it, and once the Romans had gone the locals called it Chester, which referred to the fact that it had been a huge Roman camp, *castra* being the Latin for encampment. It was an important town both before and after the Norman Conquest and the Earl of Chester was a mighty lord indeed, keeping watch over the Welsh Marches and the gate to Wales. The Welsh were a ferocious enemy until subdued by Edward I, and there were various regulations that placed curfews on Welshmen staying in the town after dark. Chester has a number of the charming black and white buildings that are to be found all over the county and its most remarkable architectural feature is its Rows, which are covered walkways on the first floor, with shops behind where you can do your shopping under shelter. It was probably the first town in England, and perhaps anywhere, to have a raised pavement the whole length of its streets. Chester is a walled city and the red sandstone walls were most likely built by the Romans and later rebuilt and extended by Ethelfleda, Alfred's daughter.

The River Dee is to this day a salmon river and Handbridge was the quarter occupied by the fishermen who used to net salmon to sell in the local markets. Above the bridge is the Salmon Leap where salmon leapt to reach their spawning grounds further up the river. The salmon will jump up to six feet provided there are places they can recover for their next leap. In the days when the Dee was full of salmon it must have been a pleasant occupation to stand on the bridge and watch them on their journey.

Chester's cathedral is unique in that it was set up by Henry VIII, following the Reformation, on the site of the old abbey, which had been built by Hugh Lupus, the first Norman Earl of Chester, in 1092. It was an abbey for Benedictine monks and produced among other famous churchmen Anselm, Archbishop of Canterbury. He retired to the monastery and died there as a monk in 1109. The Earls of Chester have gone, but continuing the tradition of powerful landowners in the country, Cheshire contains the seat, at Eaton Hall, of the country's largest landowner, the Duke of Westminster. The old stable block maintains all the magnificence one would expect, but the main house was demolished and its replacement now resembles a kind of Mediterranean hotel more than a stately home. I remember visiting and among all the magnificent pictures there was Dürer's *The Hare* and I said to Anne, Duchess of Westminster, 'How charming that you should have a facsimile when you have so many great paintings.' She was rather miffed and said, 'No, no, that's the original.' I said, 'Oh, I thought the original was in Germany,' and she replied, 'No, we lend it to them occasionally!'

The Wirral, which is a rather smart area of Cheshire, again on the Mersey boundary, is a great place for wildfowlers. I remember Johnny Scott and I were speaking at the Wirral Wildfowlers' Dinner in 2001 when we heard that the foot and mouth outbreak had been declared. More recently I met a young man – we were doing something on the radio together – and he said that he was sorry that he hadn't been at the Wildfowlers' Dinner, which his father had organised. He explained that this was because he had been in Antarctica on an expedition and he wanted me to know that his mother had sent him a copy of the *Two Fat Ladies* cookery book and that they had toasted the day in question by making my Danish Prune and Apple Cake from that very book. The recipe fitted the bill exactly as the only ingredients they had had available to make a cake with were prunes and apples!

Lancashire

So let us take a 'ferry across the Mersey', as the song of my youth from Gerry and the Pacemakers used to say, and go to Liverpool. The city has come a long way from its origins as a fishing village on the Mersey which, in 1207, was given a charter by King John; the cause of its success has been shipping, especially the trade with the West Indies and the Americas. It was, in the seventeenth century and into the eighteenth, the centre of the slave trade, a three-way trade that sent the output of the Lancashire cotton mills and all sorts of shoddy (fibre or cloth made from woollen refuse) to Africa to exchange with the tribal chiefs for slaves and then took the slaves to the West Indies and brought back rum, tobacco and spices. It was the main outlet for the other industries in the whole of northern England, as well as the cotton trade. Liverpool, understandably in these politically correct times, is deeply ashamed of its slave trade, but there are bas reliefs and other memorials to attest to its major role in the prosperity of the city. Liverpool was also the centre of the transatlantic passenger trade and the Cunard Building, which is now being sold to an insurance company, is a memory of quite how profitable that trade was.

The city suffered badly from bombing during the Second World War and a lot of its most important buildings are no more. However, still towering over everything is the Royal Liver Building, topped by its familiar Liver Birds, much loved by inhabitants and visitors alike. The docks were obviously the target of the German bombers, but the Canada and Albert

Docks still stand, although nowadays they have been developed into other industries and uses. At their height the docks were some seven miles in length, with nearly forty miles of quays and 650 acres of water space. They had the latest developments in dock gates, swing bridges and container handling apparatus and during the war had radar facilities. Today Liverpool is really a shadow of its former self, with huge unemployment and very little, comparatively, in the way of shipping. The city has not really found any profitable alternative, and like a faded empire that refuses to admit it has terrible problems, both financially and socially, carries on bravely and tries to present a good face to the world.

Liverpool has two cathedrals, the Anglican cathedral and, more exceptionally, the Roman Catholic cathedral. I once had a friend, a barrister, who played rugby for Waterloo, and was incredibly handsome; he was a Catholic and on dining nights in hall used to sing 'In My Liverpool Home', which contains the line: 'If you want a cathedral, we've got one to spare.' The Anglican cathedral is very large, 619 feet in length and contains, most interestingly I think, a monument to the Liverpool Member of Parliament who was killed by Stephenson's Rocket, the first known railway casualty, an unfortunate man by the name of William Huskisson. The Anglican cathedral, curiously, was designed by the Catholic Giles Gilbert Scott.

Liverpool has a large Catholic population because of its proximity to Ireland and the immigration of large numbers of Irish who had come over to work and to help build the docks and who have settled there. It was suggested that there should be a Roman Catholic cathedral sited at Everton, for which Edward Pugin submitted a design in 1853, but very little was actually built. Then in the 1930s Edwin Lutyens was commissioned to design a cathedral to contrast with Gilbert Scott's. In the event only the crypt was built and this is now contained in the present structure because the war brought a halt to the building. In 1960

Cardinal Heenan, the Roman Catholic Cardinal Archbishop of Westminster, promoted a competition to design a completely new church and the designer Frederick Gibberd was selected. Construction took five years and the building was eventually consecrated in 1967. It is a splendid building of light and colour and has an unusual structure. Cardinal Heenan's brief made it very clear that he wanted a building where people would be associated closely with the liturgy, and it is designed so that, cleverly, 2,000 people can be within eighty feet of the celebrant of the Mass. The superb modern stained glass is designed by both John Piper and Patrick Reyntiens and is something of a masterpiece. Lutyen's crypt is closed by the famous Rolling Gate which symbolises the stone that closed Christ's tomb.

Liverpool is the home of the Royal Liverpool Philharmonic Orchestra and has always had a distinguished history for music in modern times; however, today Liverpool is best known for pop music. The Cavern, in Mathew Street, now best remembered for its launching of the Beatles, saw many other famous pop stars go through its portals in the 1960s. Like all such venues it was, when I was there, smoky, dark and cramped, but it had great acoustics. Apart from the ferry across the Mersey, there are now two tunnels under it, the most recent of which, with typical 'scouser' wit, is nicknamed the Mousehole. Lancashire is a county of wit – at one time comics supported three good theatres in Liverpool. I don't know what it is in the Lancashire soul but they are genuinely witty, funny people and some of our greatest comedians have come from there to prove it. The humour is not just peculiar to Liverpool, although they would have it so, but is an attribute that extends right across Lancashire until it becomes, on the other side of the Pennines, the grittier, dourer wit of Yorkshire.

Nearby is the famous racecourse at Aintree, the site of the world-famous steeplechasing race, the Grand National. When I was young the National was a much more testing course, although heaven knows it is testing enough now and really is quite dangerous to ride. Aintree belonged to a woman called Mrs Topham who had thought of selling off the site for a housing estate, but was dissuaded by a splendid man named Ivan Straker not to do so and to keep the whole thing going. The course was redesigned and today attracts huge numbers of Liverpudlians and other people from further afield. When I was young it was very much 'county' and you went wearing your tweeds, but nowadays it is full of rather drunk young women wearing clothes more suitable for a cocktail party, with strappy heeled shoes and sleeveless tops, and I can only assume that it is the quantity of alcohol they have consumed that stops them from freezing to death. They are there with their escorts and clearly have a lovely time. I have been to Aintree only once in recent years, although I used to go regularly with my mother and I suspect that in future I shall always watch my Grand National and the Aintree meeting on television. The Grand National, as you may remember, was set up to entertain the crowds who had gathered to watch the Waterloo Cup further up on the Altcar Estate near Southport, which was held on the Tuesday, Wednesday and Thursday, and then people could all migrate to Liverpool and enjoy the steeplechasing on Saturday.

Southport is further up the coast. The whole coast north of Liverpool up to Blackpool and beyond was very much the holiday coast for workers from Liverpool. Southport has a long promenade and wonderful sunsets and a lot of hotels built to handle this trade which are slightly grander than the boarding houses of Blackpool to the north. The Waterloo Cup was started in 1836 when the owner of the Waterloo Hotel in Scarisbrick persuaded the Earl of Sefton, a great sporting man, to set up a sixty-four dog stake at a course on his estate at Altcar. This was the Blue Riband of coursing and had always remained so until the event was stopped by the hunting ban.

Coursing under National Coursing Club rules is not to be

confused with the illegal poaching that the newspapers always used to describe as coursing. Under the rules the hare is given a law, or lead, of one hundred yards or so and then the dogs are slipped. Greyhounds are sight hounds so when the hare goes out of their line of vision they stop. There are a number of soughs in the bank at Altcar, which are special tunnels the hares can go into and either stay or run through the bushes at the end or go through the nominators' car park where the greyhounds would not follow. At the height of its popularity eleven trains an hour would carry spectators to the Altcar Estate where the trains would stop at a specially constructed station and tens of thousands of people would enjoy their day, whether in the cheap seats on the bank or on the more expensive side of the nominators' car park. I have spent many happy years going to the Waterloo Cup, although our syndicate never had a dog that got into the second round. The coursing was held over three days and was run on two separate parts of the estate. Day one was designed to test the speed of the dogs, day two was to test their stamina and the third day was just to decide the final. We would go and stay in various hotels in Southport – they must be missing business – and generally have a lovely time.

The public footpath ran along the edge of the course and on day one the antis would turn up in force and be escorted through by the police at lunchtime, when a break was taken. They would usually be wearing masks of some sort and shouting abuse at the people assembled for the event, 'Paedophiles' being their favourite. In the evening they would stalk the streets of Southport hurling further abuse and it really wasn't safe to go off the main road if you looked as if you were the sort of person who might be involved in the sport. I know of a couple of occasions when two elderly ladies were beaten up quite badly and on another one an eleven-year-old boy was virtually kidnapped and threatened. I remember being outside the Scarisbrick Hotel when the antis were being particularly unruly, and an Irishman saying to the police officer, 'Why don't you stop them? If we behaved like that you would arrest us all.' The policeman said, 'Well, they know where we live,' to which the Irishman said, 'Why don't you just go away and leave us to deal with them?' The policeman replied, 'Oh, we can't do that, they're exercising their right to protest.' The Irishman retorted, 'In 1916 you shot my grandfather for exercising his right to protest.'

The Earl of Sefton and subsequently Lord Leverhulme who bought the estate from him made sure that their tenants grew crops in the areas surrounding the coursing ground that would attract and keep hares and that they kept cattle away because hares will not go near fields where there are cattle. The gamekeepers were forever having running battles with the poachers who tried to get on to the estate. The area was also one of the best grey partridge shoots in the country and provided a green space that separated Southport from Liverpool. Today it is a sad place with very few hares, most of them poached out, and as I said I am sure that the hoteliers of Southport badly miss us in February, which is one of the empty months for hotels and restaurants anyway.

In February Altcar is one of the coldest places on earth. As you spent two and a half days on the trot outside, despite being wrapped up as warmly as you could in everything that you could possibly wear, I don't think I have ever been so cold in my life. At the last Waterloo Cup to date I went over to the bank to escape the journalists who were running around trying to interview anyone they recognised, and I came across a man in ripped jeans and trainers with thin socks and a very thin fleece and I said, 'God, you must be cold.' He replied, 'Well, if I'd asked for outdoor clothes they would have smelled a rat.' I said, 'What can you mean?' It turned out that he was on the run from the local open prison because he did not want to miss what could have been the last Waterloo Cup. I found him a spare woolly hat and the ambulance people gave him a foil blanket and somebody else offered him some socks and he settled down to enjoy his day.

I must say that I miss the ribald humour of the Lancastrians who flocked to the bank. There was Vinny Faall, who resigned from his job as a dog catcher with the RSPCA because of its campaign against hunting on which they had spent £5 million, although I'm sceptical whether it is even within the remit of its charter. It was money that Vinny said would have been better spent spaying every feral cat in the country. I will always remember the year when he leapt down the bank and led a group that marched in silence towards the antis. They made an impressive array and the antis recoiled, the police clutched their batons tighter and as they reached the road by the antis they all burst out whistling 'Always Look on the Bright Side of Life' and marched right round and back to the bank again. It was a great day.

The Waterloo Cup was a very different meeting to normal coursing meetings because it was a big public meeting attended by large crowds. Usually coursing meetings are run on a much smaller and more private scale around the country with fewer dogs.

Not far off is Ormskirk, whose parish church contains the Derby Chapel, the resting place of the Stanley family, Earls of Derby, whose home was nearby at Knowsley. The first Earl of Derby was the third husband of Margaret Beaufort, mother of Henry VII, and played a decisive role in the Battle of Bosworth, which saw the succession of the Tudor dynasty. I can't really quite understand why Richard III ever thought that the Earl would support any other side than his stepson's, but anyway he came into the battle at the decisive moment and turned it. I really like the fact that above the gateway at Knowsley is carved the words 'Bring good news and knock loudly', and also the fact that Edward Lear was once tutor to the Stanley children and wrote many of his nonsense rhymes while he was living there.

The Stanleys have had a hand in the shaping of England since they moved from Cheshire to Lancashire in the fourteenth century and acquired Knowsley by marriage. They have provided Prime Ministers and Ambassadors and a Secretary of State for War in the reign of George V, which is all the more remarkable when you consider that they were a Catholic recusant family. There have been warriors in their history too, one of whom, the youngest son of the first Earl, was a hero of Flodden Field immortalised by Walter Scott: 'Charge, Chester, Charge! On, Stanley, on!' These were the last words spoken by Scott's hero Marmion. And of course the family title has been immortalised in the main race of our sporting calendar, the Epsom Derby.

Knowsley is the last place where I ever filmed with Jennifer Paterson. They have a safari park which is the descendant of the menagerie that the Stanleys had opened in earlier times, being one of those families who were keen on breeding rare and exotic animals. Jennifer loved what she described as circus animals. When she was a child she had always had an ambition to be the lady in the pink tutu standing on the back of a Rodenbach, the focus of all the lights. We had a lovely day but we had difficulty getting her away from the elephants. 'Just another cabbage,' she said, 'just another cabbage.' Finally I had to remind her that the lions and tigers were not pussycats that she could stroke through the bars. The lions at Knowsley breed so successfully that they send these beasts to zoos all over England and the Continent. While we were there a young lioness out in the paddock dropped her cub and I asked the keeper, 'Why is she out here?' 'Oh,' he said, 'they breed at will. Nobody worries about it.' It was as if they were in the wild.

For whatever reason Liverpool has never developed much in the way of a food tradition, which may be because historically Irish food has always been fairly primitive and poorly cooked or it may be because of poverty, but Liverpool's only notable dish is lobscouse, which is a sort of thin watery stew of meat thickened with ship's biscuits. Matters improve when you travel to the other great Lancashire conurbation of Manchester. On the northern outskirts of Manchester is Bury, the home of a very good black pudding. I remember being on Paul O'Grady's chat show and talking to him in the make-up room where he was vaunting the merits of Bury Black Pudding, the most famous of Lancastrian pudding producers. Also on the outskirts of Manchester, this time to the west, is Eccles, the home of the Eccles cake, a delicious concoction of larded pastry stuffed with raisins. Once you get into Manchester itself you realise that the love affair with food continues. If you have not yet picked up that I infinitely prefer Manchester to Liverpool, I expect you will soon.

Manchester is a creation of common sense and commerce. It is a city of ideas, of a refusal to give up when times change, and two great ideas came out of Manchester. One was free trade and the other was transport, which were interdependent. It was Manchester that started the first canal and the first railway. Manchester's wealth is founded on the cotton and wool trade, and as far back as the thirteenth century Manchester was already making cloth. By the sixteenth century people were talking favourably of Manchester's cottons and woollens and in the eighteenth century the factory system began.

Even when I was young, Manchester Grammar, now an independent school, was regarded as one of the finest schools in the country, public or private. Manchester education owes a very great deal to a man named Humphrey Chetham, a man so rich from textiles and banking that when he received a call from court to go and be knighted he preferred to pay a fine for disobeying the summons, and went on with his work in Manchester raising money to rebuild the Church of St Paul, which was then a school for educating poor boys. Humphrey Chetham died without achieving this but left a plan for his executors who carried it out. I was reminded of him very recently when I spoke at a dinner for the World Presidents' Organisation, which is a charitable institution that helps the children of the poor to get on in the world, to learn trades and skills that will enable them to find employment. The people attending were all heads of large retail or trading companies and virtually all of them had started life selling off a barrow or had otherwise worked their way up from the bottom of their particular trade. They were a great bunch and represented a great deal of money, all from Lancashire and much of it from Manchester. One had no doubt at all that they were spending a lot of it very generously for their cause and were, therefore, very reminiscent of the aims of Humphrey Chetham.

Mancunians don't take anything lying down, and a perfect example of this is the Manchester Ship Canal, which turned the inland city into an important port. Manchester had two small openings to the sea, one the River Irwell with its locks and the other the Bridgewater Canal, but these could carry only barges and the city of Liverpool charged high fees for transferring goods from ships to barges. A party of businessmen met in 1882 and set up the first Ship Canal Committee. It took three years and £350,000 to get the necessary bill through Parliament to allow its construction, but when its chief proponent Daniel Adamson returned from London with his bill, about 30,000 people joined in a triumphal civic procession in his honour. Much ingenuity was spent finding a way not to interrupt the rivers, railways and canals already built by crossing their lines with a new waterway; as Manchester is sixty feet above sea level, this necessitated the installation of many locks. It was a laborious task with the locks having to be made before they could cut the bed of the canal. However, after six years of hard work, the canal was opened in 1894 and enabled ships to load and unload without having to go through the tariffs imposed by Liverpool.

Most importantly to me, Manchester has an enthusiasm for ethnic food. Most of you will have heard of the famous Curry Mile, which is literally a mile of different Indian and Pakistani restaurants, most of which serve interesting and unusual dishes side by side with the old favourites. It is the only place in the country where I have ever come across curried goat's feet, and very good they were too. I can't help smiling every time I go to the Curry Mile and see the statue of Oliver Cromwell looking down it. Cromwell was a great one for commerce, whatever else, and it was he who reintroduced the Jews into England during the period of his rule in order to improve and increase commerce and banking within the country, the Jews having been thrown out in the time of Edward I. Cromwell's statue originally stood in front of Manchester's magnificent Town Hall, which the dignitaries wanted Queen Victoria to open, but they were told that she would not come to open a building that had a statue in front of it of the man who had chopped her ancestor's head off. So the statue was moved. At the time its new position was in a very ordinary area but now it has changed out of all recognition and I don't think that Cromwell would have minded. Manchester also has a very good Chinese quarter with excellent restaurants serving authentic Chinese food side by side with the usual chop suey and chow mein, and at one point it had an excellent Armenian quarter too. This had probably the only collection of Armenian restaurants in the country presided over by the Armenian food writer Arto Der Haroutunian. Armenian food is incredibly delicious and it is always a great regret to me that the Armenian quarter has now died out.

I once stayed in a house in Manchester that showed me that the city had not always been peaceful. The house, which was possibly late eighteenth century, had been the home of mill owners who had installed a metal door at the top of the staircase that you could pull shut, rather like a drawbridge, to stop rioters, should they have broken into the house, from killing the family. I always thought that it was rather naïve as the rioters could easily have burned down the house around them. Manchester is one of the few cities that I am well acquainted with. It has trams, and all that teaches me about trams is that I don't want them in Edinburgh where I live, or indeed anywhere else. One is forever getting stuck in the tram lines and they are a very great help to getting lost in what is something of a conglomeration of a city. Manchester has excellent art galleries, a very fine library and it is a great patron of the arts.

A little to the north-west of Manchester is the town of Bolton, which goes back to the twelfth century as a town associated with the spinning of wool and the making of woollens. Two hundred years later Flemish weavers flocked to the area, introducing clogs which came to be worn throughout the mill areas of Lancashire well into my lifetime. Bolton seems to have produced more than its fair share of contributors to the prosperity of the county. It is there that Richard Arkwright kept his barber's shop while he was working on his invention of the power loom, which would revolutionise the cotton industry. Another Bolton man is Samuel Crompton, who speeded up the production of textiles enormously with his spinning mule, and the town was also the birthplace of Lord Leverhulme whom we have already met. Samuel Crompton, whose statue stands in the middle of Bolton, started his life as a child of a poor family paying a few shillings' rent a week, living in a tenemented great house that had fallen into disrepair. He played the organ and the fiddle and struggled in poverty until his great invention made possible the most delicate muslins and yarns of unrivalled fineness. His birthplace was saved by Lord Leverhulme and is now a museum and it still retains its attic, six feet square, where Crompton pursued his experiments and developed his invention. The house is known as Hall i' th' Wood, and is a building of Tudor origin which must have been lovely in its heyday.

Head back towards the coast through all the towns whose names are associated with the cotton industry and the Industrial Revolution, through Blackburn that gave us James Hargreaves and the spinning jenny that enabled spinners to keep pace with the looms fitted with John Kay's flying shuttle, and you come to what was the great holiday resort of Blackpool. The Blackpool

Tower has restaurants and winter gardens and shops all under one roof and used to have a zoo too. When other holiday resorts are sadly contemplating the end of their season, Blackpool bursts gaily into the thousands of lights that constitute the Blackpool Illuminations that can be seen however you approach the town, adorning the tower which measures 518 feet to the top of the flagstaff. A lift will take you to the top of the tower, above which is the crow's nest, 480 feet above the sea. It stands in an area of 600 square yards and 6 million bricks were used in its construction; the tower itself took over 2,500 tonnes of iron and steel. Its enormous ballroom can accommodate 6,000 and is the largest dancing venue in England, which has now been brought back to delight us in the revival of ballroom dancing that is BBC's most popular show, *Strictly Come Dancing*.

At the beginning of the nineteenth century Blackpool was simply the site of a peaty pond called the Black Pool, although it was fashionable with some for sea bathing, and had a coach service set up for ferrying folk from Manchester in 1781. Its only house was Fox Hall, the home of a Royalist who kept a chained fox as the emblem of his house. Blackpool prides itself on keeping up to date and has I think the most terrifying Big Dipper I have ever seen anywhere, the screams of its riders being audible from quite far away. Blackpool is wonderfully, wonderfully vulgar and I say that in admiration. You go there and you can buy 'kiss me quick' hats and sticks of rock and all the traditional paraphernalia of the British seaside. Yet despite the passion the British have acquired for rushing off to ruin the Costa del Sol and such places, the resort has managed to hold its own. Its atmosphere and amenities are a far cry from the boarding house days of its origins, but fewer people go on the beach and gone are the knotted handkerchiefs and the rolled-up trouser legs, and the town is full of happy, if over-merry, people there for stag and hen weekends and to celebrate the wealth of the pink pound. It really should be very proud of its continued popularity.

It is interesting that only eight miles from Blackpool, inland from the Fylde peninsula, you will come to Eccleston, which hosts the Great Eccleston Show. I remember going there some two years ago now, having been tracked down to a pavilion in the grounds of Holker Hall during their flower show by a formidable woman called Sheila, who persuaded me to go to the Great Eccleston Show. When I got there I discovered, to my surprise, that not only was it a perfect rural show but it was also the show that had the largest catchment of heavy horses, carthorses if you like, anywhere in the British Isles. Lancashire is very easily in touch with its rural roots.

The county town of Lancashire, for all the rich conurbations within the area, remains the city of Lancaster. The town is closely associated with John of Gaunt, who was Duke of Lancaster and who rebuilt the castle when it had fallen into disrepair as a stronghold against Scots marauders. Lancaster's castle has massive strength and was later fortified to resist the Armada, a turret called John of Gaunt's chair being raised to serve as a beacon tower should the Armada come that way. The dungeons of Lancaster Castle are fairly formidable, with oubliettes for people who were thrown into solitary confinement never expecting to be removed from it. The well near the stone steps to the dungeons was where the Lancashire witches, all ten of them, were dragged to their deaths on the gallows, having been chained to the walls there. The castle dungeons were also used for the containment of lunatics; Mental Health Orders were quite different back then. The Crown Court used to be in the Great Hall of the castle, and may still be, and the Lancashire Assizes have been held there since 1176 until shortly after the Second World War. It has been said that more people have been sentenced to death there than anywhere else in England. It has seen many well-known defendants including the Quakers George Fox and Margaret Fell. You will also find there the old black branding iron that burned the letter M for malefactor on to a man's hand, a practice that continued until 1811. This iron, with its restraining clamp, is supposed to be the only one left in England.

Afterwards, the castle had a long history as an army garrison, and I remember a friend of mine, who grew up there for part of her childhood when her father was a serving officer, telling me that it was on pain of terrible punishment that children were instructed never, never, never to walk across the parade ground. Our present Queen carries the title the Duke of Lancaster, and when you give the loyal toast in Lancashire you toast not the Queen but the Duke of Lancaster. Apparently she has always had the ambition to retire to either the Lune or the Ribble valley, I can't remember which, and raise horses.

To me, one of the most interesting things about Lancaster is that it was the home and the site of the first restaurant of a brilliant chef named Paul Heathcote who was the man who turned black pudding from a local peasant dish into a foodstuff of fine dining and gourmet meals. He is a brilliant chef and it was really he who started the movement to establish decent restaurants in the north of England away from the south. His first book, written in co-operation with the lovely Matthew Fort, was entitled *Rhubarb and Black Pudding*, and I was happy to have him as one of my customers when I was a bookseller. He has now cut back on his empire but still retains his restaurant at Preston. I met him recently at a dinner that was held in the Northcote Manor Hotel near Clitheroe. Clitheroe stands on the division of the border with Yorkshire and the Northcote is an excellent country house hotel with very good food. It holds a food festival every year.

Clitheroe stands in the Trough of Bowland (pronounced without the 'w'), and is now a peaceful place, but at times had a fairly hard past. There used to be a fortification called the Castle on the Crag which was the home of generations of robber barons who would ride out and raid anybody travelling across from Lancashire into Yorkshire. It is the smallest Norman castle in England and the De Lacy family who lived there ruled over the town and the surrounding countryside until the last of them was hanged for treason. From Clitheroe you can see Pendle Hill which was made famous in the seventeenth century for the Pendle witches. These were a group of women, probably no more than would-be feminists, who dabbled a little in herbalism and some of the darker arts, particularly at the time when James I had started the furore against witches, always one of his great phobias, which had carried on into the Puritan years. The ten women, varying across the social divide, were dragged in chains to Lancaster and tried on virtually non-existent evidence and then hanged. Today it is an attractive spot to visit.

Warwickshire

Warwickshire is a county in which I have spent a lot of time pootling about. My best friend from school, Christine Coleman, has lived there for some forty years and during that period we have gone out and about and visited all sorts of fine homes and countryside and I have grown very fond of the county. Christine lives in Birmingham or one of its suburbs so we might as well start there. When she first moved to live in the district from Sussex, Birmingham had magnificent galleries and libraries and public buildings from the Victorian age, but it was scruffy to put it mildly. It is the second largest city in the United Kingdom and home to a lot of industrial creations and this is curious in that not so long ago it was really quite small. The area on which Birmingham now stands was the estate in Dickens's *Bleak House* which was then owned by the Jennings family whom Dickens renamed Jarndyce. A court case in Chancery over the ownership of the estate had whittled away the whole of it in legal fees, which is what Dickens took as his story. The estate was bought by the future city fathers of Birmingham, who then enlarged their town to become the city it is today.

Historically the town was known for the manufacture of weaponry and it is for that reason that during the Civil War Prince Rupert and his troopers set fire to the town as punishment for making and supplying swords to the Parliamentary forces. The metalworking quarter of Birmingham still exists, now punctuated by an extensive canal network with cafés lining its banks. You can go on boat trips around the area but in Victorian times these were working canals. The metal industry that was once so successful has been transferred into what is known as the Jewellery Quarter, and while much of the making of cheaper jewellery has been transferred to China and the Far East, this remains an area where good stuff is created.

Birmingham has an armoury because, apart from the swords and sharp-edged weaponry that it used to produce it also manufactured guns, although today this industry has gone, with the exception of the business of Ridley which produces fine quality rifles for the luxury market, superbly engraved and sculpted in some cases. Some guns are made for the American luxury market, big bore guns, two, three or four bore, and some of them even have women's legs sculpted in such a way that the legs point towards the hole that is the barrel. These are not designed to be used but rather to be displayed and shown off among the rich cognoscenti of the United States and, in some cases, rich Arabs. The business had expanded quite considerably after the partition of India when the chief executive realised that there were an awful lot of beautifully made rifles and sporting guns sitting around the homes of the now rather broke maharajas, so he sent people out to buy them and bring them back and the guns were then restored and sold into the English market. Their main designer when we were filming *Clarissa and the Countryman* there had moved across from the jewellery sector to work on engraving guns because he found it offered more opportunity for creativity. I took my little sixteen-bore gun to him, and he engraved a woodcock's head and a woodcock flying away, designed by the famous sculptor Simon Gudgeon, on to the plate at the bottom of the stock.

When I first went to Birmingham University, which I was told was a red-brick university, I expected it to be singularly uninteresting, rather along the lines of, say, the University of East Anglia, and just modern buildings, but in fact it stands on a splendid site in Edgbaston. It is red-brick but it is late Georgian red-brick. It has a magnificent clock tower which stands 320 feet high and can be seen for miles around; it is a memorial to the first Chancellor of the university, one Joseph Chamberlain, who raised more than half a million pounds towards the cost of building the university.

The Bullring, which was Birmingham's market area, was one of the scruffy places I mentioned, although it had a variety of stalls covering quite a large area, including one that sold fresh oysters, served singly. I remember going there with my godson who had discovered oysters at the age of twelve in Brittany and had become devoted to them. This was only his second tasting of oysters so we went and bought some and ate them and he said, very solemnly, that they weren't as good as the ones in Brittany. Of course Birmingham being almost in the very centre of England, he was perfectly right. The whole area has now been tidied up enormously and large sums of money spent on its restoration.

Birmingham is once again a very fine city with entertaining modern sculpture added to the great Victorian galleries. If you wish to see the best collection of pre-Raphaelite paintings in the country you should go to the Birmingham Museum and Art Gallery, where they have a large collection by various pre-Raphaelites but most especially by Ford Madox Brown, who was closely linked to the pre-Raphaelites, including his very emotive picture, *The Last of England*, in which a couple look scared and rather forlorn sitting in a boat pulling away towards their destination. The gallery also has a particularly revolting painting which used to delight small children entitled *Little Baa Lambs*, which is about as sick and chocolate boxy as you could hope to find. There are also some marvellous Rossetti paintings. Outside on the steps is a sculpture of a naked woman in a fountain and this is known, with typical Birmingham wit, as the 'Floozy in the Jacuzzi'. And there is a statue of a man sitting on the steps of the library building with his papers, also in bronze, blowing haphazardly on the steps around him. These are two of the nicest pieces of modern civic sculpture that I have seen.

Birmingham is particularly noted for, if not the invention of, the development of Balti cooking, which is now very popular around the country. Balti food – the word comes from northern India and simply means a bucket – is served in individual handled dishes and eaten with naan bread and it is the particular combination of spices from that part of northern India that makes it so unique. What was also eye-openingly startling was in the area of Sparkbrook where you would order what was known as a 'table naan', which was literally the size of the table on which you were eating. You could either pour your Balti dish on to part of it and then break the naan around it and use it to mop up and eat the main dish in the normal manner, or sit around the table and eat communally out of the different dishes in the centre of the table. You were not expected to use knives and forks. My friend Camellia Panjabi, with whom I first went to this area when we were recording a programme for radio called *Curious Cooks*, told me that it was the movement of the Punjabi farming community from the rural areas into the city of Delhi that led to the development of Moghul cookery, as it was incorrectly called, and that they would always use tandoor ovens to bake their bread. They then adapted their ancient tandoor oven for cooking chicken and meat as well. At any event it is a lively area full of families, mostly from the Asian community, but from the local Warwickshire community too, going out to eat in the restaurants, and is about as different from Leicester, which I have already described, as you could possibly find.

While we were shooting the programme on the Waterloo Cup for *Clarissa and the Countryman*, we filmed in a Balti restaurant in Sparkbrook with one of the local Pakistani families, who trained their extremely successful coursing dogs by walking them. Coursing is the largest sport in Pakistan, readily attracting crowds of over 35,000. The four boys would get up early and walk the dogs four times around the circumference of the local park which constituted a mile each circuit. On the days when the dogs were being trained to the lure they would train them in the park really early before anyone else was about. They couldn't have been more helpful or hospitable and we had a great time.

The city is liberally scattered with parks. I think there are thirty-two parks, twenty-seven recreation grounds and nineteen small open spaces, including the 524 acres of the Lickey Hills Country Park. From the top of Beacon Hill in the park you are supposed to be able to see ten counties on a fine day. The community at Bournville on the outskirts of the city was created by the Cadbury family to house their workers in pleasant country surroundings. John Cadbury started his chocolate-making business with a pestle and mortar in a Birmingham warehouse more than 150 years ago. He was followed by his sons, George and Richard, who set up the village and used to send flowers from the gardens at Bournville to the Manchester market to prove that without doubt it was both a factory and a garden. It is said that Richard and George starved themselves and went without their morning papers to put together the money for this venture but they lost thousands of pounds before they succeeded. It was truly philanthropy at its finest.

One of the parks surrounding Birmingham is Sutton Park at Sutton Coldfield, which is one of the largest parks in Europe, covering 2,400 acres of wild and wooded country, of moorland and lakes with Gravel Ridge running through it. This is all that remains of the ancient Icknield Street, the Roman road, one of the most important in England. John Vesey, who became Bishop Vesey, attained the grant of all this land from the King, Henry VIII, and he then bequeathed it to the town for ever. It was a hunting park that the King would enjoy visiting and the bishop's name lives on not only in the memory of those who enjoy Sutton Park, but also in the local Bishop Vesey School and various other places named after him. There is no doubt that Shakespeare, who was born thirty-six years after the park was opened, knew it, because in *Henry IV Part I* Sir John Falstaff explains to Bardolph:

> Get thee before to Coventry; fill me a bottle of sack; our
> soldiers shall
> March through; we'll to Sutton-Co'Fil' tonight.

We know that Shakespeare had kinsmen who lived at Sutton and it is believed that he set scenes in *A Midsummer Night's Dream* in some of the woodland in the park. I have spent many happy hours walking there and swimming in the lakes. There used to be an open-air swimming pool where we went with Christine's children but, sadly, this was closed down by the local council.

I have visited many fine houses in Warwickshire on our various pootles and possibly the one that I enjoyed most was Baddesley Clinton, the home of the Catholic recusant family Ferrers for many centuries. The house is a fine courtyarded Tudor building with a 500-year-old front door, and is surrounded by a moat, probably from Norman times. It has a number of priest holes, one of which is actually below the level of the moat, and some of the most famous names among the Catholic Jesuit priests who were persecuted by Elizabeth were known to have visited and said Mass and hidden there. The grounds have fine topiary.

Old yew trees seem to be fairly common throughout Warwickshire and perhaps the best of the topiaried yews are to be found at Compton Wynyates, another great house that I have had pleasure in visiting. This was the Warwickshire home of the Marquess of Northampton, whose family had lived on the estate since before Magna Carta. If you visit, the dining room is full of pictures of them: Henry, who entertained Queen Elizabeth; James, who fought at Edgehill, and William whom Cromwell referred to as 'that sober young man and ungodly Cavalier'. The yews in the garden are much older than the house; in fact they are probably older than the first brick of the present house which was laid in Tudor times. There is a large group of clipped yews in strange forms over which supernatural creatures creep, one of them in the shape of a little old man in a top hat. Roundhead troopers were barracked here during the Civil War and so the chapel with its fragments of broken stained glass is bare and forbidding as a result of their exercising their puritanical rights. The second Earl of Northampton, Cromwell's Cavalier, fought at Edgehill in Warwickshire. Unfortunately just a year later he took to battle at Hopton Heath and it is documented that, charging too far ahead of his supporting troops Northampton was surrounded, refused to yield and was killed. His body was exchanged for the cannon that he had captured and he is buried here. It seems to me rather a waste of a man's efforts to exchange his dead body for the gun he had taken all the trouble to capture, but what is it they say, 'The Cavaliers – wrong but romantic'.

The county town of Warwickshire was Coventry, a much older town than Birmingham, standing slap bang in the middle of England, which was part and parcel of its prosperity. We all know the story of Lady Godiva, the wife of the Earl of Mercia, a Saxon woman married to a Norman who, in protest against the level of taxation that was being imposed upon the citizens, rode naked through the town. The citizens of Coventry were so supportive of her that, with the exception of Peeping Tom, whose name will for ever be immortalised in history, they did not look upon her nakedness. Coventry is also famous for the burning of its eleven martyrs in the city centre, the majority by Mary Tudor, eleven men and women who went to the stake for their faith, including a mother whose only crime was that she taught her little ones to say the Lord's Prayer and the Ten Commandments in their mother tongue.

Coventry, whose industry improved enormously with the

coming of cycles and the motor cycle and the motor car, of whose production it was at one point the centre, was horrendously bombed during the Second World War. If you look at pictures of the town before the war it was very much a medieval city centre with wonderful old buildings and fine tapestries more than 400 years old, until the German bombers came over and gave us a particular taste of the firestorm of bombing. The cathedral was completely destroyed and the new cathedral built next to the ruins of the old walls is a triumph of modern architectural creation. Probably one of the most moving things in it is the Crucifix made from nails burned and twisted by the fire of its predecessor.

However, enter Warwickshire from any direction and the sign will always say 'Shakespeare's County', and it was in Stratford-upon-Avon that William Shakespeare, our most famous playwright and probably the most famous in the world, was born and where he then came home to die. Stratford has made a thriving industry out of Shakespeare, as has the Royal Shakespeare Company with its new theatre, and tourists come from all over the world to see Shakespeare's house, his wife Anne Hathaway's cottage, Shakespeare's grave, and to attend plays in the theatre. The Shakespeares were a Stratford family for many generations before William. His father was a glover and William himself was apprenticed to be a glover but evidently found better things to do with his hands. Shakespeare's legacy is to be found in the surrounding countryside, for Henley-in-Arden was very much the rural area in his plays. Sir John Falstaff, his great merry hero, and the countryside surrounding Stratford recur throughout his plays in one form or another. His house continued in the family until almost in living memory, when it was passed over to the Shakespeare Birthplace Trust. Shakespeare lies under a fairly plain tomb with words that have possibly protected it throughout the centuries:

Good friend for Jesu's sake forbear,
To dig the dust enclosed here,
Blessed be the man who spares these stones,
And cursed be he who moves my bones.

This is not, perhaps, the finest piece of English ever written by the Bard of Avon but it gets the message across.

Stratford is full of half-timbered houses and I always remember Dame Edna Everage doing a skit in which she visited Stratford-upon-Avon where she saw a Morris Traveller, rather like the one on the cover of this book, and she said, 'Look, they even have half-timbered cars.' That is, I would say, a perfect description of a Morris Traveller and, despite its appearance on the book jacket, please don't think it is a car I have ever liked or driven. I prefer something rather more dashing myself.

Moving on from Stratford we come to Warwick itself, which used to be the county town of the area, with its magnificent castle. However, when I arrive in Warwick, the first thing that springs to mind is Guy Warwick. If we believe the stories, Guy Warwick was the son of a steward to the Earl of Warwick at the time of Athelstan and fell in love with his master's daughter Felice. He was considered unworthy of her and undertook various heroic labours in order to win her, going to Constantinople to fight the Saracens and then returning to slay the dragon that was devastating northern England. His valour won him his bride but his adventures continued, for there was more fighting in the Holy Land, and after that the Danish giant Colbrand to encounter at home, with, allegedly, the war between England and the Danes dependent upon the result. Guy killed Colbrand in a single contest, but in his remorse he retired to Guys Cliffe, hewed out a cave which we can see there, and passed the rest of his days in rigorous seclusion, only communicating with Felice again on his deathbed by sending a ring to summon her to him. My sympathies have always been with Felice for having to pass her days, presumably, in isolation.

What particularly appeals to me is Guy's porridge pot, which is a huge cauldron holding 120 gallons. I expect he needed all that porridge for his endeavours. There is also what is supposed to be the rib of the Dun cow that he ate at one sitting, which unsurprisingly is so large that it proved to be the rib of a whale, and also his walking shaft which turned out to be the shaft of a lance made six centuries after Athelstan.

One of my pilgrimages in Warwick is to the Beauchamp Chapel of St Mary's, where probably one of the most formidable men of late medieval English history, Richard Beauchamp, a renowned alchemist and scientist, is buried. He lived through the reigns of Henry IV, Henry V and into the reign of Henry VI, then an infant, on whose behalf he governed France, and was appointed Master of the Horse. The magnificent Beauchamp tomb is over 200 years old, and when the floor of the chapel fell in it is reported that Beauchamp was seen as fresh and perfect as the moment he died and then crumbled into dust. He lies dressed in armour and wearing the garter. His head rests on his helmet and at his feet are a griffon and a bear. The tomb has thirty-two canopied niches with figures of all the Beauchamps and was made in London by a Dutch goldsmith with the help of a barber-surgeon who was engaged to correct the smallest detail of anatomy. Seeing it close to, it is beautifully done, every buckle, every strap and hinge perfect. The inscription tells us that he was one of the most worshipful knights of the day, and his effigy is looking up at the Madonna enthroned in the rood in red and gold as the Queen of Heaven. Also on the rood is a gallery of angels playing musical instruments and singing and dancing to them, painted on the finest glass in the middle of the fifteenth century. The music is printed on a scroll and is a genuine old version of 'While shepherds watched their flocks by night'.

Warwick Castle itself is a fine example of a medieval castle that has been inhabited through its history by great families.

Among these was Warwick the Kingmaker who, during the Wars of the Roses, was responsible for deciding who should sit on the throne. Wherever he cast his benevolent eye that person was king until, in the words of the nursery rhyme where he is represented as Humpty Dumpty, 'he had a great fall and all the king's horses and all the king's men couldn't put Humpty together again'. Warwick, which is now used for many events, such as jousting and falconry, houses many treasures, including Cromwell's helmet, Queen Anne's travelling trunk and Marie Antoinette's clock. Perhaps it was most famous for the Warwick vase, which was found in the bed of a lake in Tivoli, but sadly that is no longer in the castle and visitors have to make do with a reproduction. The original, believed to have been made by the master sculptor of all time, Lysippus, in white marble sumptuously carved, is now in the Burrell Collection in Glasgow.

Ilmington is worth a mention because it was the home of Sir Thomas Overbury, whose story really led to the independence of the British judiciary. Overbury was a friend of Robert Carr, the royal favourite and catamite of James I, preceding the Duke of Buckingham, and became Lord Rochester and Earl of Somerset. Carr was ill-educated but had wonderful legs and he fell in love with Frances Howard, the wife of the Earl of Essex. On his friend's behalf Overbury wrote her burning letters and passionate poems which Carr sent as his own. Overbury started the intrigue but when he found that a divorce and remarriage to Carr were intended he took fright and denounced the pair in unmeasured terms. Carr persuaded James to send Overbury to the Tower where he was poisoned. Once this was discovered, Carr and Frances Howard were accused and James endeavoured to put heavy pressure on the Chief Justice of the King's Bench, Lord Coke, to throw out the charges against them.

It wouldn't be right to leave Warwickshire without mentioning Kenilworth with its castle, now in ruins, that was built by Robert Dudley, Earl of Leicester, who was Elizabeth's favourite and aspired to be her husband. We are told that Elizabeth came to visit and was entertained for nineteen days, which must have involved the most horrendous costs. Shakespeare as a boy is supposed to have attended this festival with his school fellows and was amazed by the fireworks as well as the plays and masques that were put on for the occasion.

Cumbria

In the far north-west is the area that is now known as Cumbria, a conglomerate of former counties that when I was young consisted of North Lancashire, Westmorland and Cumberland, and extends right up to the Scottish border. The sea coast is mostly taken up with the vast expanse that is Morecambe Bay. This is an extremely dangerous area, where the tide comes in faster than a galloping horse and which, over the centuries, has seen the deaths and near deaths of hundreds. The Quaker George Fox found his faith when he was crossing the bay and the tide turned; he had underestimated its speed and it looked as if he and his entire party were going to be drowned. He prayed for deliverance and at that moment the wind changed and held back the tide long enough for them to get to safety. Traditionally there was a guide who would take you across the sands by the shortest route and, while the post still exists, nowadays, with the presence of the railway and the road, the guide's main job is taking parties of walking tourists across simply for the sheer pleasure of it. You will remember that not so long ago some Chinese cocklers were trapped by the tide and drowned. If you don't know it, the bay is no safer today than it ever was. It is however moving: an area of about 200 acres on the Grange-over-Sands side has silted up and a farmer there has acquired all this extra land for grazing his salt-marsh sheep. Conversely, the bay has eaten away a similar amount at its northern end.

Cumbrian salt-marsh lamb is delicious. For centuries the beasts at Holker were sent to local markets and sold as ordinary lamb although they are grazing on fields that flood twice a day with the incoming tide, eating all the succulents and marsh herbs that survive the tides. Only when Lord Cavendish of Holker Hall realised that the French had been selling their salt-marsh lamb at a premium did the lamb start to be sold as a delicacy. It does have a very distinctive and delicious flavour but, of course, it is not of interest to the supermarkets because there isn't that much of it and you can't eat lamb all year round. I do, however, remember when one of the major supermarket chains wanted farmers to inject their sheep with hormones so that they could have lamb throughout the year. What they thought these sheep were going to feed on is an unknown quantity.

Two other delicious specialities come from the district. One is the Morecambe Bay cockle which, given the nature of the area and tides, is both particularly delicious and particularly dangerous to harvest. The other is the Morecambe Bay shrimp, which is the native brown shrimp and quite different in flavour and considerably more delicious than the smaller pink shrimp. Here I would like to pay tribute to a man called Les Salisbury who, when Young's decided that it was too expensive, difficult and dangerous to continue to catch brown shrimps and moved its packaging plant elsewhere and potted only pink shrimps, stepped in and saved the brown shrimp fishing industry in the bay. Historically most of the shrimp fishermen came from a village called Flookburgh. The flook in local parlance is a type of flat fish found in the bay and is not eaten as much as the other flat fish we know – plaice, sole and brill – but when properly treated is still very good eating.

The idea of potting fish, meat and game under a layer of butter or oil is as old as time, but is followed with great enthusiasm still on this part of the coastline. The freshly caught brown shrimps are cooked in sea water, often while the vehicles that trawled them, which used to be horse-drawn, are still out on the bay, and when they are brought back to land they are topped and tailed, usually by fisherwomen from Flookburgh, although nowadays some are done by machine. Then the shrimps are mixed with butter and nutmeg and a touch of cayenne and put into pots and a layer of melted butter poured over the top. This will preserve them for quite a long time as long as they are kept at a cool temperature. The theory is that you upend the tub on to a piece of hot toast, the butter will melt in the heat of the toast and you will then eat the shrimps. I, however, have always found that if you put them on a warm surface like the top of an oven or some such, to start the process, it is rather more successful. I once had a consultancy for Robin Birley and I remember explaining to his chef Alexis, who was French, that this was how you were supposed to eat potted shrimps. He was delighted because he said that he could never understand why the English enjoyed them because his kitchens were turning them out on to cold toast, not hot, and so the butter wouldn't melt.

For most of its history Flookburgh was the seaside holiday home of the Dukes of Devonshire, and it was only about a hundred years ago that the Holker Estate was given to a second son as his portion by a doting father. It was a Duke of Devonshire who built the railway round the edge of Morecambe Bay, something that the architect said could never be done, and this completely transformed what was really a very remote area into somewhere accessible.

The town of Grange-over-Sands which used to be the setting-off point for the guided route across the sands overnight, became almost a holiday resort. Today Grange-over-Sands has the reputation of being the home of 'grey sex', and if you go and stay in its various hotels, some of which are extremely nice, you will notice that the holidaying population is mostly my age and upwards. Grange is an agreeable town of realistic proportions and has proper shops. The one that always used to entertain me was called Popplethwaites, which boasted the fact that it was a hardware store and funeral director. I always thought that I would like to die in Grange so that I could be buried by Popplethwaites. It is also the home of an excellent butcher called Stuart Higginson, a Yorkshireman of Viking proportions, who while in Australia met and married a local Cumbrian girl and came back to set up his shop here. One of Stuart's great attributes is that he makes, to my mind, the best black pudding in the country; it follows his mother's recipe and she still oversees its production. You can also buy it in the excellent farm shop in the Tebay services on the M6.

Further along the coastline is Barrow-in-Furness. The Industrial Revolution brought the railway here, much to the disgust of Wordsworth who thought it was threatening his Lake District home. Walney Island and Roa Island were at one time occupied by a vast iron ore works and steelworks and there were acres of docks where immense cranes towered over the engineering sheds. By the railway station sits an old locomotive with a proper dome over its shining oiler which is known affectionately as Old Coppernob and it ran for over fifty years. I once reversed my car into the town hall here and the car still bears the dent, although I didn't do the town hall any harm I'm happy to say. In front of the building is a statue of Lord Frederick Cavendish, who was murdered by Irish freedom fighters in Phoenix Park in Dublin. The iron works and shipbuilding works at Barrow are now in decline and really the town now has rather a dismal air. Piel Island out in the bay guards the narrow channel into the harbour, and Piel Castle was built on it about 700 years ago by the Abbot of Furness as a protection against the raiding Scots. Much of the castle has now fallen into the sea but it was there in 1487 that the Earl of Lincoln with his German mercenaries and Irish soldiers landed to attempt to put Lambert Simnel on the throne.

I used to spend quite a lot of time in this part of the world when I had a consultancy at Holker Hall for Lord and Lady Cavendish to set up their shop, delicatessen and café at the hall. If you go to Holker the house is interesting, but what you really want to see are the magnificent gardens. The Cavendishes are incredibly keen on gardening and every year they have a big flower show, usually a week to ten days after Chelsea, and many of the contributors at Chelsea go on to Holker and save plants to display there. It is highly regarded as a place to win. Over the years the Cavendishes have built various specific gardens for the festival, including some using pillars of local slate because the slate quarries at Burlington produce excellent variegated-coloured slate.

Another thing I delighted in doing was going to the races at Cartmel. This is one of the smallest racecourses in the country but you have a really enjoyable day's racing there. You can see most of the action and the catering produces delicious local food instead of the rather nasty industrial food that you get at most meetings. It was at Cartmel that Christianity first came to this region when King Ida of Northumbria converted with all its Britons. The Cartmel post office, which runs an excellent store and delicatessen, is responsible for the best commercial sticky toffee pudding that you can buy, which is made on the premises there. Now you can buy it in other parts of the country too and I do recommend it to you. Sticky toffee pudding is local to this bit of Cumbria and I remember there was a great brouhaha back in the 1980s when the hoteliers around the Lakes all vied to say that they had invented it. Lord Cavendish's mother gave me a seventeenth-century recipe for the dish which is one of the many things in this area to have their source in the West Indian slave trade.

Whitehaven, further north along the coast, was the main slave port with the West Indies before the development of the deep harbour at Liverpool, and every returning sailor would bring back a few West Indian spices or a nutmeg as his perks, which didn't take up much room and sold at a good profit. Sailors also used to bring back dates which are one of the main ingredients of sticky toffee pudding, while West Indian sugar was of course a great asset to making the toffee sauce. It was at this point in the late seventeenth century that sugar began to be imported in quantity to England and the British Isles as a whole. This probably led to the advancement of dentistry and the deterioration of teeth. In the late seventeenth century one of the Lord Mayors of London came from Whitehaven and at his mayoral banquet he served what was known as Cumbrian Red Spiced Beef. I am always looking out for the authentic recipe but it was probably something like jerk with West Indian spices. I am quite certain that it was this West Indian trade that led to the curing and spicing of various products in this region, which was also particularly noted for the production of macon. Macon is hand-cured mutton, which local curer and smoker Richard Woodall was still making as late as the 1990s, but which didn't sell terribly well because it is not to the modern taste. I love this part of west Cumbria with its high fells looking over the bay and I actually prefer it to the Lake District itself.

At Coniston, where you go to climb the fells or look across the lake and see the Old Man of Coniston, as this mountain is called, you will also find the former home of John Ruskin. The house, Brantwood, is open to the public and contains all Ruskin's books and drawings and reproductions of many of his paintings. It was from here that he would go out to deliver his famous Oxford lectures and compose his monthly letters to the workmen of England who, I am sure, were delighted to receive them. It is as a social reformer that he is best remembered and he was buried in a pall made at Ruskin's Linen and Lace Industry at Keswick, which he had set up in his efforts to reform working conditions. He could have been buried in Westminster Abbey but he preferred to spend his eternity sleeping by Coniston Water. Coniston Water is five miles long and half a mile wide and it is here that, in 1967, Donald Campbell died in a terrible accident while attempting to break his own world water speed record on the lake.

Near Kendal there are a splendid couple of houses: Levens Hall, an Elizabethan building that is supposed to be the most haunted house in England, which has very lovely gardens and an excellent farm shop; and Sizergh Castle, the home of the Strickland family, which is an old pele tower but with Elizabethan additions. This was where they used to have the famous horse trials and hound show where they had an amazing singing competition in the evening where all they seemed to sing was 'John Peel'. John Peel was of course a Cumbrian and the other great Cumbrian huntsman was Joe Bowman, whose song was called 'Joe Bowman's Hounds'. John Peel you may remember was dug up by the antis back in the 1970s and they scattered his bones. He hunted a bobbery pack, i.e. a mixed pack of assorted dogs, and the original song was not 'in his coat so gay' but 'in his coat so grey' because the coat he wore was a farmer's coat of grey like a Hodden cloth.

It was Wordsworth who made the Lake District famous and brought the Victorian tourists flooding to it. He was born in Cockermouth and schooled in Lancashire and returned to the Lake District to make his home in a cottage at Grasmere, where he wrote nearly all his poems. His last resting place is in the village churchyard. He had a great love affair with the Lake District and if you go and see the daffodils at Bassenthwaite in the spring you will think of his poem:

> I wander'd lonely as a cloud
> That floats on high o'er vales and hills,
> When all at once I saw a crowd,
> A host of golden daffodils,
> Beside the lake, beneath the trees
> Fluttering and dancing in the breeze.

Perhaps rather less well known are some of his other Lakeland poems. In one he pictures nature as a little lady and he writes:

> 'She shall be sportive as the fawn
> That wild with glee across the lawn
> Or up the mountain springs;
> And hers shall be the breathing balm,
> And hers the silence and the calm
> Of mute insensate things.

'The floating clouds their state shall lend
To her; for her the willow bend;
Nor shall she fail to see
E'en in the motions of the storm
Grace that shall mould the maiden's form
By silent sympathy.'

Grasmere, where Wordsworth came to live at the age of twenty-nine with his sister Dorothy at Dove Cottage, is the home of that excellent product Grasmere Gingerbread. This is more a kind of biscuit than a cake and I suspect goes back to an old medieval recipe when that was how they used ginger most effectively. There is a traditional Scottish biscuit called Parlie which was made for the Scottish Parliament more than 300 years ago which is similar but not so strong and pungent in nature. The recipe for Grasmere Gingerbread is a closely guarded secret and you buy it in these little silvery tins and it keeps for an incredibly long time. It is the perfect snack to stick in your pocket when you are going off to climb a fell.

The Lake District is made up of a number of lakes, the chief one being Windermere, the largest lake in England at over ten miles long and nearly a mile broad. Windermere is now a great tourist attraction with tours around the lake and many boats, both powered and sailing, dotting its surface. In comparison, Ullswater is seven miles long and three and a half miles square, Bassenthwaite is four miles long and Derwentwater nearby is three miles long. There are numbers of other smaller lakes, the most spectacularly desolate of which is probably Wastwater, which abuts Scafell Pike, the highest mountain in England; Scafell Pike rises to 3,200-odd feet and is more than 300 feet above Wasdale, where the bed of Wastwater is below sea level.

The Lake District is now a National Park and, bearing in mind what I have said previously about National Parks, I feel very much the same about the Lake District. Rather curiously, I suppose, it is part and parcel of the English character that where the park stops so do the tourists. I once went camping with my friend Christine and we crossed the boundary of the National Park on Ullswater and found a camping site in a field some four miles further on and there wasn't a sign of anything resembling a tourist. I remember it well because the old lady who owned the farm told us that she had only moved once in her life and that was from one side of Ullswater to the other by boat following her marriage. She had lived in this little Lakeland farm ever since. We had a lovely time and, although conditions were rather primitive and the lambs who had just been taken away from their mothers kept us awake by their continual baaing, it was Lakeland as Wordsworth probably knew it rather than what it has now become.

Christine and I took the steamer that goes down the lake and we walked back along the lakeside shore. I had been told that this was flat and level, but it turned out to be amazingly rocky and uneven, and there was a constant stream of people walking round the lake which rather detracted from the charms of its isolation. However, it was something I was pleased to have done, although the next day I couldn't walk because I had been wearing the wrong footwear. So I asked Christine what we should do as there was too much traffic on the roads to drive around and we decided we would go to Buttermere and take a boat out. There was nobody at Buttermere and it was blissfully peaceful. It was the day of the Fell Race which was probably why it was so quiet because everybody was watching the race. Every so often you would see these lean figures, almost emaciated, pure sinew and muscle, toiling up the crag and across the top as we sat contented and cool on a rather hot day dabbling our fingers in the water and having the occasional swim. Buttermere is the home of the Buttermere char, which is quite an oily fish that keeps well. This unique fish is a member of the same family as the Arctic char, which is a salt water fish, but was trapped in the lake at Buttermere during one of the Ice Ages that so sculpted the area and it has adapted to live there. They live at great depth in the lake, which is one of the deepest lakes in the whole of England, and are quite difficult to catch, but in Victorian times potted char was made for the tourists and sold in specially made pots decorated with a picture of the char on the lid. These pots are now seriously collected by kitchenalia enthusiasts. I have never tasted potted char which is very seldom made nowadays.

In Buttermere lived the daughter of the innkeeper of the Fish Inn, one Mary Robinson, who was beguiled by a passing con man who was considerably older than her; she was just a slip of a girl and he was forty-four. His name was John Hatfield. He was born of ordinary parents but he presented himself as having a connection to the Duke of Rutland. He had in fact married the daughter of Lord Robert Manners, who gave him a wedding present of £1,500, a lot of money in those days. He squandered this and deserted his wife and children and she is reputed to have died of grief. Hatfield then proceeded to go around the country claiming links with the Duke of Rutland, and on several occasions was bailed from prison, where he had been sent for debt or fraud, by various clergymen who believed his story. He went to prison in Scarborough for seven years but managed to con a lady from Devonshire into paying his debts. He married her and they went to live at Tiverton in Devon, but he later abandoned her. He next appeared in Keswick in some style with a carriage and horses, pretending to be a Member of Parliament and a brother of Lord Hopetoun. Under the name of Hope he married Mary of Buttermere but was arrested and tried for forgery and hanged the year after his marriage. Her legend lives on in Buttermere and she was very well portrayed by Melvyn Bragg, who is a local lad, in his novel *The Maid of Buttermere*.

The hills of the Lake District are the home of the various fell packs, one of the best known of which is the Eskdale and

Ennerdale, and the sort of country they hunt in around there is almost terrifying in its height and inaccessibility. The hounds are obviously hunted on foot and the terriers that traditionally run with the hounds have much longer legs. The Lakeland Terriers and the Patterdale all need every inch of their legs in order to get up to the top of these massive crags. Fell hunts have a tradition of not being much pestered by antis who wouldn't have the breath to get up there. For *Clarissa and the Countryman* we filmed with one of the fell hunts and certainly I wouldn't have the breath to get up there either.

Our camping, which I mentioned earlier, nearly ended in tears because Christine had volunteered to bring the food, and our ideas of what was suitable camping food were rather different, but we were saved by Henrietta Green's *Food Lovers' Guide* which referred us to the smoker at Brougham. The magnificent ruin of Brougham Castle makes you understand why Eleanor of Aquitaine was imprisoned by her husband Henry II after she had poisoned Rosamund de Clifford, his mistress. Rosamund was not just any silly little fly-by-night girl but the daughter of a huge and powerful Norman family. Brougham was the home of one branch of the Clifford family and stood, in its day, as one of the Marcher castles on the Scottish border, since in the thirteenth century the western Marches came down as far as Cockermouth and Penrith. It is more often known as the Windsor of the North and certainly the castle is massive in size. In the chancel of the chapel there is the grave of Udard de Bron, a Norman Crusader and rebel, whose sword can still be seen at Brougham Hall, taken from the coffin where it had lain with him for 700 years. Udard's skeleton was in perfect condition, his legs crossed and his arms still round his sword, his teeth clean and white, and lying beside him was a fragment of an enamelled glass vessel supposed to have been brought back by him from the Holy Land.

The story of the bravery of the Lady Clifford at the time of the Wars of the Roses is worth recounting: her husband had been killed at the Battle of Ferrybridge, and the Yorkists who were on the opposing side had gained the crown. Lord Clifford might have been dead but he left two sons behind and the Yorkists often came to Brougham to demand that the boys be handed over. Lady Clifford said that the boys had vanished and she thought the servants had killed them. As the Yorkists had nothing to gain by killing her, they went away and the Clifford estate passed to other people. Eight years later there was a rumour at court that Lord Clifford's heir was still alive hiding in Yorkshire. A search was instigated but Lady Clifford received a warning from a friend at court, possibly Margaret Rivers, the mother of the Queen, Elizabeth Woodville, and when Yorkshire was searched, no trace of the young man was found.

Fifteen years later the Lancastrians regained the throne after the Battle of Bosworth and Lady Clifford announced that her son lived. He was summoned to appear before the House of Lords and his title and estates were restored to him. He was unable to read and write, he walked like a commoner and his hands resembled those of a working man, but he was indeed Henry Clifford. He had been seven years old when he was sent away from home and he had lived in a cottage wearing rags and sleeping on straw. The woman in the cottage had once been his nurse and she was very kind to him; it was her husband who taught him the work of a peasant shepherd. He went to Bolton Abbey where he learned to read at the age of thirty, and he was such a loyal subject to his king and so beloved by his tenants that he is always referred to as 'the Shepherd Lord'. Like Wordsworth before me I love this story; it has all the elements of second-rate historical fiction but it is in fact completely true.

Luck be mine, not only did I find out about this massive castle and the Shepherd Lord, but the smoker was exceptionally good and sold, among other things, smoked Buttermere char, which I had never eaten before and found delicious. It reminded me of a similar char I ate in Sweden which was also another trapped member of the char family and which was smoked over juniper berries. So the tinned chicken in white sauce was confined to heaven knows where and Christine and I had a lovely holiday.

The Derwent, the main river of Cumbria, flows through Cockermouth. I don't really know Cockermouth, having only been there once for a book signing, but Jennifer knew it well and used to go and visit at a nearby house called the Phipps, which gave rise to a recipe of hers in the first *Two Fat Ladies* cookery book which was called Beanz meanz Phipps. Cockermouth, you will remember, was severely flooded just a few years ago and I was talking recently to the owner of the bookshop who said that they had lost everything in the floods, as had so much of the lower town.

If you go eastwards across Cumbria you will come to what has been described as the most historic town in the region, Appleby. It actually existed before the Domesday Book and claims to be the smallest county town and certainly the smallest size of town; its population was 12,000 in 1388, whereas nowadays it is somewhere around the 2,000 mark. Once a year at the Bank Holiday at the end of May it comes alive when it hosts the centuries-old Appleby Horse Fair. I first heard of this when I was arguing a case in the Court of Appeal about the progeny of Kuaiking, a racehorse, and whether my client had endeavoured to mitigate his loss. After we had gone through the market sales and private sales and so forth, Lord Denning, with his wicked smile and his Hampshire accent which got broader the more wicked he was being, said, 'And tell me, Miss Dickson Wright, did you enjoy the Appleby Horse Fair?' I didn't really know what the Appleby Horse Fair was in those days but I smiled knowingly and said, 'No, how silly of us,' and he laughed and so I set out to find out about it.

It is probably the largest horse fair and one of the few remaining in the country and Romany gypsies from all over the British Isles come to it to buy and sell horses. There are trotting races with the skeleton gypsy driving carts they have and I believe, although I don't know, that if you go after closing time it is a great centre for cock-fighting. When I was in Lincolnshire you may remember that I visited the Romany Museum run by Gordon Boswell and I remember him saying that he and his wife would harness up and drive one of their elderly gypsy caravans and set off from Lincolnshire to Appleby and it would take them three days or more each way and that it was their annual holiday. You will always see a splendid array of gypsy caravans on the roads round Appleby at the time of the fair. Should you find yourself in the vicinity at that time it is well worth a visit, but make sure that your wallet is carefully hidden.

I have forgotten to mention Muncaster down south on the River Esk, just inland from Ravenglass on the west coast. Muncaster Castle is a fine building in the most beautiful setting and it is particularly famous for its rhododendrons, which have been planted across the valley facing the castle itself in the Pennington racing colours. It has been the home of the Pennington family for virtually 800 years and you can see here the 'Luck of Muncaster'. The story goes that Henry VI, after he had fled at the Battle of Hexham, was found wandering near Muncaster Fell, broken and defeated, and was led to Sir John Pennington who took him in under his hospitable roof and cared for him. The King gave his host a small shallow green glass bowl, decorated with gold and enamel, measuring six inches across, with a prayer that his family might prosper so long as the glass remained unbroken. There is a picture in what was supposed to be the King's bedroom of him kneeling before an altar with the bowl in his hands. Another painting, on a wood panel, shows him holding the 'Luck'.

I should also have remembered to mention Endmoor, just off the M6 down near Kendal, the home of the Kendal Mint Cake, that singularly unpleasant mint-flavoured cake so beloved by Arctic explorers and mountaineers simply for its energy-giving properties. It is virtually all sugar and is very good for keeping up the spirits. Of a very different nature is the produce from my friend Peter Gott at Sillfield Farm near Endmoor, from whom I acquire my Christmas ham every year. He breeds not only rare-breed pigs but also has a large herd of wild boar. Every now and again the antis will go and release them which is a particularly stupid and irresponsible thing to do because the only place for the boar to go would be downhill on to the M6 motorway. Fortunately they are quite happy where they are and just mill about waiting for their morning feed and don't go far out of their enclosure. The wild boar is an extremely dangerous animal and not one that should be roaming round the Cumbrian countryside.

Cumbria is also the home of that very early, I suspect, form of wrestling, rather on a par with Greek or Roman wrestling. You will see it at the local shows if you are fortunate enough to go to them, where young and not so young men with their knickers outside their underwear, because they wear shorts over a full set of long johns, grapple for holds and attempt to throw each other. It is a remarkable sight and one you should try to see in your lifetime.

If you head up the M6, eventually you will come within sight of the Scottish Borders at Carlisle, whose local red sandstone walls give it a surprisingly modern look. Carlisle has been somewhat battered by Scottish invaders over the centuries and it was here that Bonnie Prince Charlie marched through with his army of 4,000 to conquer England and then returned, defeated, listlessly riding a horse. You can see the chair that he rested in that night at the museum, but after he had passed through, King George's men came to batter down the city walls with eighteen-pounder guns and to pack 300 of the garrison the Prince had left behind into the cathedral and ninety-six more into the castle dungeons.

The city appears to have grown up around a Roman camp on the opposite bank of the Eden from which Hadrian had started to build his wall, and it remained a Marcher castle throughout its history until the Act of Union. Mary, Queen of Scots was first imprisoned here after her defeat at Langside, and was no doubt already hatching many of her plots.

Carlisle has a fine cathedral, with possibly the second best cathedral window in the British Isles, only the one at York being finer. The cathedral is a massive building of red sandstone and grey stones with a very short nave and, in all its glory, a choir. It was quite badly knocked about by Cromwell's troopers during the Civil War. St Cuthbert's Church in the town has an eighteenth-century pulpit which used to be lowered into place in time for the sermon by ropes attached under the floor and worked by a handle turned in the vestry. When the sermon was over, the handle would be turned again and the pulpit returned to its original place. It must have been fascinating for small boys forced to attend the dreary sermons.

North of Carlisle, Scotland lies beyond the Solway Firth, which is a fairly impressive and dangerous stretch of water full of quicksands. I was once trapped in a Cumbrian quicksand and only saved by the quick intelligence of my friend and hostess who told me to roll. As I roll quite well I managed to escape from it. I remember when we were filming *Clarissa and the Countryman* we put a six-foot stick into one of the quicksands and it was swallowed up in less than a couple of minutes. Quicksands usually form where fresh water and salt water mix and affect the flocculation of the particles of the soil. We also filmed haaf-netting on the river. This is a most curious form of fishing dating back to Viking times where you stand with a net that has a central pole and then two sideways pieces, between which the net is attached. The woodwork is made of cedar so that it floats very easily and you stand in the current of the river. It is rather like wildfowling in that you need to know what routes the salmon will take up the river and then they will swim into your net and you flip it over and wade to shore with your prey.

I thought it would be rather boring but actually it's quite fascinating. You stand up to your oxters in the river so that you are down at that level and when the salmon comes towards you it is rather like seeing a torpedo approaching you and is quite unnerving. The netters catch other fish too. I caught the only round fish of the day, a grey mullet of about four pounds in weight, and Johnny caught a couple of good-sized flounders. We stood in a line with several other netters so the salmon wouldn't go through the middle and then as the tide comes in, the person who is furthest out moves in and takes up position nearer the shore. It is an extremely interesting way of fishing and not one that is going to depredate salmon stocks all that heavily, I suspect.

Retrace your steps to Hadrian's Wall, built to keep out the marauding Scots by the great Emperor, turn sharp left and head across the Vallum Militarium, the military road, towards Northumberland.

Northumberland

This county, the most northerly on the east, is one I've always thought that I would quite like to live in, with a lot of wide open spaces, high moors, beautiful coastline and the sort of light that makes you understand why Holy Island produced all those thousands of saints. It is just generally a good place. What is particularly wonderful about it to me is Hadrian's Wall and the Vallum Militarium, which is the road that runs alongside the wall to the north of the A69. I was always taught that Hadrian's Wall was built to keep the Scots out, which of course it was. Hadrian spent a lot of his fairly short reign constructing walls all around the borders of the empire as it was at that date. Long before I ever saw Hadrian's Wall, I was fascinated by its significance, and the thought of Roman troops (I assumed they were from Italy, but I have now discovered that many of the men stationed on the wall were from Africa, having been transported to the northernmost part of the empire) having to hold the line against the marauding Picts from the north coming out of the heather painted blue and clutching their poisoned spears. I used to drive along the military road very early on a summer's morn, and with the roof of my convertible down I really felt quite like a Roman centurion in his chariot. All you would see was camp lights glittering in the wall now and again and this long straight road rising before you.

When you approach from Cumbria you come to Haltwhistle, which boasts that it is the most central town in the British Isles. The name means junction of streams by the hill and it is where

309

the Haltwhistle Burn joins the South Tyne, a beautiful spot with the remains of an earthwork rising above the small, partly industrial town. The church, dating from 1200, is remarkable in that it has no tower and is nearly hidden by houses in the main street which makes it very difficult to find. Just outside Haltwhistle is your first really good sighting of Hadrian's Wall, a little to the north of the A69. The Romans called this road Stanegate and there is a well-graded embankment with a deep cutting above what would have been the wall.

The Stanegate Fort seems to have been one of the early forts to be erected before the wall was built; nearby are the remains of a quarry from which the stone was taken to build the wall and a remarkable group of sentry camps thought to have been built to house and protect the men constructing the wall. At Chesters the military way crosses the stream to the north burn of the Hallam and just below it are the remains of a large Roman water mill which was excavated in the early twentieth century. The two big mill stones are now at the museum at Chesters. On Hadrian's Wall close by is the Cawfields mile castle with sides eight feet thick and a massive masonry gateway; the side entrance for the gate still has the opening bolt. This is the first mile castle ever to have been excavated, as early as 1847, and it was probably the reason why Collingwood Bruce came to write his famous, and certainly the first, handbook on the wall in 1863. Seventeen forts were built along the wall, all of which were small towns with the garrison and various hangers-on; quite a lot of them have been excavated in the last century, but there are still more to go. Between the Roman wall and the Carlisle to Newcastle road there are two standing stones which are called the Mare and Foal and are probably the remains of an old stone circle.

A little to the north is Bellingham with its sinister story of the 'long pack'. About 300 years ago a retired Indian Army colonel called Ridley occupied Lee Hall, having acquired a fortune in India. One winter's afternoon when the family were in London a pedlar called at the house and begged a night's lodging. Alice the maidservant refused to let him stay but she did allow him to leave a long pack which he said he could carry no further and would come back to collect the next day. After he had gone the maid examined it, and to her horror she saw it move, so she went out to fetch help and called for the ploughboy Edward, who fired the gun he used for scaring the crows into the pack. The pack moved horribly and a great groan issued from it and a wide finger of blood gradually spread across the floor. Edward had killed a robber. The servants realised that he was part of a plan for a raid on the house. They gathered together as much help as they could and finally had twenty-five armed men on guard. Nothing happened until, at one o'clock in the morning, Edward finally blew a silver wind-call he had found on the body and at once the cry was answered and the sound of galloping horses was heard. When the horsemen entered the courtyard they were met by a volley from the defenders and they fled, leaving seven dead and dying behind them. The defenders dared not venture out and when daybreak came they saw that all the bodies had vanished. Significantly, members of several respectable local families were never seen again. As for the man who had been shot in the long pack, he was never identified and is buried in a nearby churchyard.

Travel eastward along the line of the wall and you come to the town of Hexham with its beautiful priory. The first church in Hexham was built with stones brought from the Roman Corstopitum, now called Corbridge, further east. Everywhere you look in this part of Northumberland there are legacies of the Romans, and in the church here there is a doorway that has been cut from a Roman altar stone and has the words Apollo, Apollo Matona inscribed upon it. There is also an inscription where the name of the Emperor Geta has been erased. He was the son of the Emperor Severus and was murdered in York in 211 by his brother Caracalla. It was

Caracalla who ordered the erasure. You will also find a nine-foot monument that shows a Roman soldier riding down an enemy and the translation of the inscription reads 'to the gods of the shades Flavinus of the Cavalry Regiment of Petriana, Standard Bearer of the White Troop, twenty-five years of age and seven years service is buried here.'

Christianity came to Northumberland early but officially in 625, when King Edwin married Aethelburg of Kent and was accompanied north with St Paulinus, assistant to St Augustine. St Wilfrid came in 665 from Lindisfarne, Holy Island, to build the church at Hexham, which he dedicated to St Andrew. In 681 it became a cathedral until 821 when, due to the depredations of the Danish invasions, the see was merged with that of Lindisfarne. In 871 the Danes destroyed the original church, and it was not until 1113 that the canons were sent there from the diocese of York; twenty-five years later it became an Augustinian priory and remained so until the Dissolution of the Monasteries. It is a superb building with magnificent acoustics and well worth a visit. There are several Roman altars in the church and something like fifty Roman and Saxon stones built into the inner wall of the nave.

The fine stone bridge over the Tyne, after the junction of the two Tynes, affords the best view of the town. The Battle of Hexham took place here in 1464 when the Lancastrian cause was finally shattered. Henry VI's favourite, the Duke of Somerset, was taken prisoner and beheaded in the market place, and Queen Margaret and her infant son hid in the woods nearby and finally managed to escape to Scotland. Hexham was also home to Isaac Allgood, the father of Hannah Glasse, to my mind one of the greatest of English cooks, who was writing her first book, *The Art of Cookery made Plain and Easy*, in 1746. I made a programme for the BBC on her life and was horrified to discover that the archive of her letters – which is on loan, as I subsequently discovered, to Hexham County

Council – was unavailable for consultation until the following October, apparently because of building work. I managed to get in touch with Mrs Allgood, the widow of Isaac Allgood's descendant, and she said very firmly that I was to tell the county council that if I wasn't given access then they should be returned to her because they were only on loan.

I cannot understand why Hexham doesn't make more of this daughter. She was born in London, illegitimate, but was raised, from the age of eight until she was sixteen, by her father and his wife with their children in Hexham. When she was sixteen she ran away to London where she had an unhappy marriage and spent a lot of her later life in debtors' prison as a result of her husband's gambling debts, but she, at one point, was highly successful and made an enormous amount of money from her cookery book. I don't know why – and I'm saying this in the hope that someone will see this and pick up on it – Hexham doesn't have a Hannah Glasse cookery festival, as places with no connection to anybody culinary seem to be having food festivals, to promote Northumbrian food and Hannah Glasse's brilliant cooking. She was the first person, incidentally, ever to give a recipe for curry in the English language in an English cookery book.

The word 'cor', as in Corbridge, means crow, and it is amazing just how much there is about crows in this part of the world, presumably from all the historic killing that occurred, which led to a proliferation of the crow count along the site of Hadrian's Wall. The first person to excavate was King John, who visited the ruins in 1202 and went poking around looking for treasure. Fortunately he left the second-century hoard of 160 gold coins which were found in the twentieth century. One of the best finds in this part of the world is the Corbridge Lion, a masterpiece of Romano/Celtic sculpture about two feet six inches long; it is a lion standing on the back of an unresisting stag and was a site for a water pipe. Hadrian's Wall is full of Roman finds and excavations, the two best being at Brocolitia and Vindolanda, where the finds were feted by archaeologists as the most important ever. These are a series of postcard-sized pieces of flat wood which when read comprise letters and notes written from the Romans on the wall to people down south and their replies. They had been set fire to when the wall was evacuated and considered of no importance, and a lot of these little cards were found still quite intact in the middle of what had obviously been a bonfire. They contain, for instance, notes from the Governor's wife to her sister in Kent saying, 'Please send me a barrel of apples because we simply don't get good apples up here,' and there is a note in reply from the same sister saying she wished she was with her for her birthday and was sending her some chickens. They give fascinating insights into all the minutiae of life that made up the day-to-day world of the Romans who lived at the edge of the empire.

Brocolitia lies at Carrawburgh beside the Vallum Militarium. The ramparts here are well marked and in places lofty, and the vast gateway is easily traced. The fort is about forty to fifty yards long and 120 yards across and covers about three and a half acres. The inscription from above the gateway, now in the museum at Chesters, mentions the Governor Sextus Julius Severus who is known to have been in Britain about AD 130; the fort is supposed to have been built in his time to fill the long undefended gap between Chesters and Housesteads. The first garrisons here were Aquitanians and Goederneans and they were followed by the third and fourth centuries of Batavians. The name Longilius Commindos, a Roman subaltern, and that of his wife Aelia are found engraved in what was thought to be a cold Roman bath, and when the stones were lifted there was an amazing hoard of votive offerings and temple furniture. There were carved stones, altar jars, incense burners, pearls, brooches and no fewer than 13,487 coins, four of gold, 184 of silver and the rest of bronze. Many more were known to have been stolen by weekend visitors. There was also a carving of three water nymphs holding jars and pouring out a stream. When excavations went deeper a shrine to Mithras, the soldier's god, complete with a ritual harp and the bones of pigs, lambs and goats, was found.

At the eastern end of the wall, around Wallsend as it is now known, part of Newcastle-upon-Tyne, there was originally a colliery. When Tsar Nicholas I was shown the pit in 1814 he shrank back from it and declared it was the mouth of hell and that none but a madman would enter. Wallsend was also the home of the Swan Hunter shipyard, to whose employees who lost their lives in the First World War the large white Memorial Hall in the town is dedicated; it features bronzed figures standing in an arched recess. At the entrance to the public library is a white marble figure of Britannia holding a trident, which belonged to the *Mauretania*, probably the most famous ship to have been built here. It broke many Atlantic records and travelled 2 million miles before finally being sent to the breaker's yard.

Robert Stephenson, the father of railways, was born nearby in 1803. His father mended clocks and shoes and made clothes for Robert when he went to school in Newcastle at the age of twelve, riding there on a donkey. Poor health forced Robert to take a situation in Colombia working as an engineer in gold and silver mines but, hearing that a prominent Newcastle factory was facing collapse, he came back and sorted out the tangle of affairs that had caused the degeneration. As a result he then felt able to ask his father for the financial assistance needed to perfect the *Rocket* before its historic trial.

Newcastle was occupied in Roman times and a fort was discovered guarding the bridge over the Tyne. Newcastle rather surprisingly, or perhaps not, is interspersed with Roman remains. Every so often, even in the middle of the city, you will come to the remains of part of Hadrian's Wall or the fort the Romans called Condercum which covered five and a half acres and lay astride the wall. Bits of it remain at the foot of the road called Denhill Park. Henry II built the new castle to defend the town against the Scots. About 150 acres in size, it was provided with strong walls two miles round. The town's real prosperity came with the development of the coal mines, which are among the earliest in the British Isles and certainly the first from which coal was exported. There were various industries attached to the garrisons. Shipbuilding started up and a galley was built on the Tyne for Edward I. Charles II granted Charles Lennox, Duke of Richmond, a shilling a ton on all coal leaving from the Tyne for use in England and the Richmond shilling continued until the twentieth century, although much diminished by the growth of the railways. The walls of Newcastle were set in the reign of Henry VIII to be of a strength and magnificence far surpassing all the walls of the cities of England, but in 1644 the Scots laid siege to the city and after three months the mayor, Sir John Marley, surrendered to the Scots. Thereafter the castle fell into decay and there was a military occupation there until 1819 and the last prisoner in the dungeons was released in 1828.

Newcastle has its fine new conference centre situated on the Tyne and I remember standing on the opposite bank to protest against the proposed hunting legislation when the Labour Party were having a conference there. We hung broken chairs over the side of the river railing with labels saying 'unsafe seats', talking about the targeting of such seats against mostly Labour MPs in the next election. Tony Blair came in by helicopter and we all booed as if in a pantomime and he waved merrily to us and minced into the building.

Heading up the coast the holiday area for Newcastle, as Blackpool is to Liverpool perhaps, is Whitley Bay. Though in no way as famous or as large as Blackpool, it has a lot of shops and nightclubs and amusement arcades and all that the English hold dear in a holiday resort. The Dove Marine Laboratory has a large aquarium, now part of Newcastle University, because Cullercoats next door, when it stopped being a thriving coal port, became well known for fishing and it was of particular value to trawlers working the North Sea fishing grounds. These days all this has moved on but it remains a holiday resort.

It was a little to the north, at Ashington, near South Shields, that I first really discovered about sea coal. We were filming for *Clarissa and the Countryman* and Johnny, whose daughter Rosie had been born in Ashington Hospital, knew about the habit of sea, coaling along the coast. The original sea coal used to have fallen from exposed cliff seams into the sea where it was then gathered by men with horses and carts and shovels, but now it is mostly residue from the power station at Ashington. Of course if you put coal into sea water it washes off all the dust and you get very good clean coal that burns slowly with a clear flame. On the way to collect coal we stopped to eat the Ashington Dip, which is a rather delicious bap with ready-made sage and onion stuffing, over which is poured the juices collected from roasting a pork joint and topped with a few scraps of cold pork. Best eaten standing up and very good it is too.

If you head up the coast through the pleasant fishing villages, now mostly sailing marinas and holiday resorts, you will come to Alnmouth, which John Wesley, in 1748, described as 'a small seaport town famous for all kinds of wickedness'. He didn't specify what type of wickedness and certainly there is no sign of it today. In the 1770s the place was bombarded by John Paul Jones, a notorious pirate, but now it is unspoiled, with fine sands and a golf course. A little inland, also on the Aln, lies the mighty castle of Alnwick with its surrounding town, all part and parcel of the vast domain of the House of Percy. It was always said until quite late into our history that 'the north knows no prince but a Percy' and the original Percy who first built the castle was one of the Conqueror's magnates. You can't miss the castle with its imposing keep and ring of grey stone towers over which appear leaning figures. You will discover as you get closer that these, are actually carved. It is still the home of the Percy family to this day.

By the mid-eighteenth century, little was left of the original Norman castle and medieval additions, and it was then that the first Duke of Northumberland transformed it into a vast palace to the designs of Robert Adam and James Payne and local architect Vincent Shepherd. Shepherd spent almost all his professional life in the service of the Duke. It was at this point that the carved figures were put on the battlements. They were made by a man called James Johnson of Stamfordham over a period of twenty years to represent warriors repelling an attack. The castle was again reconstructed in the nineteenth century by Anthony Salvin, an authority on medieval military architecture, for the fourth Duke. The ceiling of the great hall is painted with scenes of Chevy Chase, the battle where the Percys were defeated by the Scots under the command of the Earl of Arran, and it is curious to think that when Elizabeth, daughter of the Duke of Northumberland, married the fourteenth Duke of Hamilton, these two families who had been the main participants in this battle were joining ranks together almost 600 years later. The great hall itself is decorated in the Italian Renaissance style and is full of treasures. The Hotspur Tower is the only survivor of the four original town gates built 500 years ago by the son of Henry Hotspur, the redoubtable Earl, who was slain at the Battle of Shrewsbury.

If you go up the coast further you will come to Craster, the birthplace of the kipper. The smokehouse at Craster is still there, despite all the efforts of the EC to do away with the kipper. It boasts that in 1861 herring was first smoked in the way that the Scots smoke salmon, in other words, cold smoked. Before that, as we have seen, the kipper had been either salted or bloated. The tiny harbour of the fishing village was built by the Craster family in 1906 in memory of one of their number who died on active service in Tibet. There was a Roman fort here called Corchester from which the name of the village is derived. It claims, but then so does Maxton in Roxburghshire, to be the birthplace of Duns Scotus in 1265, a scholastic theologian doctor and Franciscan. Among other things, he instigated the Scotus system, which was much reviled by humanists and it was the sixteenth-century reformers who coined the term 'dunce', as a play on the name.

Also at Craster, and well worth a visit while you are buying your kippers, is Dunstanburgh Castle, the biggest ruin in the county. It stands on the ridge on a crest of basalt rock running straight out to sea for a hundred feet and the contours of the site demanded a curtain wall. This encloses an extent of about ten acres, formerly defended with flanking towers on every assailable side. It was built by Thomas, Earl of Lancaster, one of Edward II's most disloyal subjects but presumably another of his catamites. It has a big inner ward where the flocks and goods of his tenants could retreat when threatened by the fairly constant assaults of the Scots. In 1322 Thomas was intercepted at Boroughbridge and executed at Pontefract for treason. During the Wars of the Roses the castle held out for the House of Lancaster and continued to be a defensive asset until Tudor times when it fell into decay. The interior was so free of buildings that by the death of Elizabeth I it produced in one year 240 Winchester bushels of corn and several loads of hay. It was much loved by Turner as a place to come and paint and three of his paintings are in the museum at Dunstanburgh Castle.

At the south-eastern end of the castle is the Egyncleugh Tower which faces on to the seaward side. The tower gets its name from the egyncleugh or rumbling churn, a narrow, rocky inlet below, into which the sea rushes during stormy weather, sending up great columns of spray. The constable's quarters were moved into the tower at the time of John of Gaunt, when the great gatehouse was converted into a keep. Another name for the tower is Queen Margaret's Tower, as she is said to have been lowered from the tower during a siege and, braving the raging sea in the deep gulley below, to have reached a ship waiting in the adjoining Queen Margaret's Cove. Dunstanburgh was turned into a fortified harbour during one of the periods when Berwick-upon-Tweed, further north, was lost to the English. It is small and difficult to access, but Henry VIII's fleets docked here in 1514. The Dunstanburgh Diamonds was a name given to pieces of spar that were found in the cliff and converted into jewellery.

Heading north we come into the land of the saints. So strong and clear is the light north of Craster that you can see why the area was home to and encouraged and produced so many saints. Seahouses, which boasts that it was the place where battered fried fish and chips were first brought together for public consumption, faces the Farne Islands. These are bare and desolate rocks, about thirty in total and at least four of them, the Elbow, the Fang, Islestone Shad and Glororum Shad, are actually never above water. They are, however, unique as the cradle of Christianity. They are also a bird sanctuary. They belong to the National Trust, and the Farne Island Association looks after the few ancient buildings and maintains four bird-watchers on the Inner Farne and groundsmen during the spring and summer.

The Inner Farne is the largest island, an area of sixteen acres or so, and eleven of the other islands that make up the Inner Group are bare rock. On the north and west are cliffs of seventy to eighty feet high and in the north-west corner is a deep fissure called the Churn where the storm-swept water rises up in a shaft reaching heights of ninety feet in the northern gales. The most conspicuous feature of the island is the lighthouse, which is no longer manned but works automatically. Before the lighthouse was built, a fire used to be lit on top of the grey stone pele tower built by Comas Castell, Prior of Durham, in about 1540. After the Dissolution of the Monasteries the tower was retained by the crown as a fort for coastal defence and it now falls under the government. The stone-lined cistern beneath the tower is called St Cuthbert's Well, but a more impressive memorial to the saint is the chapel built on the site of his oratory 600 years ago. It is forty feet long and was restored with old materials in the middle of the nineteenth century. The monuments include one to Grace Darling and there are also the traces of another chapel and of the walls that enclosed the tiny settlement that was established by the Durham monastery in 1255.

The first recorded saint, and possible visitor, to the Farne Islands is St Aidan, who withdrew from the neighbouring Holy Island and came here for prayer and meditation. From his cell he saw the burning of Bamburgh by the pagan Penda of Mercia and legend tells how his prayers changed the wind and turned the flames on the attackers. St Aidan died at Bamburgh in 651 and twenty-five years later St Cuthbert of Lindisfarne came to the islands. At this point the Farne Islands seem to have been the last refuge of what were referred to as the 'pygmy flint people', the earliest Northumbrians, of whom traces have been discovered. Here, with his own hands, St Cuthbert excavated a circular enclosure and built a windowless dwelling with walls of earth and stone, half living room and half oratory, with an opening in the roof for a view of the sky and the sound of the sea and presumably for the smoke, cut off from the view of every object but heaven. Ten years later St Cuthbert's solitude was broken by a royal visit imploring him to accept the bishopric of Lindisfarne. King Eegrith landed with a prelate, a crowd of notables and a reverend from Holy Island, and on their knees begged Cuthbert to leave. After two years at Lindisfarne he resigned the bishopric and again sought solitude on the Inner Farne. Though ill he refused any companionship, but after a storm lasting five days the Abbot of Lindisfarne couldn't resist making a visit from Holy Island and found Cuthbert lying in a hut with an ulcerated foot and unable to move. In 687, only three months after his return, Cuthbert died.

The Farne Islands are the only breeding place on the east coast of Britain for the grey seal, the rarer of the two British species, protected under Act of Parliament nowadays, and also of the St Cuthbert's duck, which is the eider duck, Northumberland being the most southerly nesting place of this particular bird; its favourite islands are the Farnes. The eider is noted for the quality of its feathers in making eiderdown quilts, and one likes to think that St Cuthbert might at least have kept warm. It was here that, in 1810, Robert Darling, Grace Darling's grandfather, was appointed keeper. The remains of the tower where he kept his light have been taken down and a house has been erected for two birdwatchers to stay for nearly three and a half months every year. It was from the Longstone Rock in the Farne Islands that William Darling and his daughter Grace made their famous rescue early one morning in September 1838, after the steamer *Forfarshire* from Hull had been wrecked on the big Harcar Rock. Grace Darling died four years later, a girl of twenty-six, and she is buried in the churchyard at Bamburgh.

To come to Bamburgh is to understand the terror that a Saxon peasant must have felt at the sight of the raw power that emits from Bamburgh more than from any other castle I know, even those on the Welsh coast. King Ida, according to the *Anglo-Saxon Chronicle*, began his reign in 547, and it was he who built the first Bamburgh Castle, which was originally surrounded by a hedge and afterwards by a wall. His grandson Aethelfrith 'the Destroyer' – don't you just love that name? – gave the settlement to his wife Bebba, and it was then named Bebbanburgh in her honour. In the middle of the seventh century Penda, King of Mercia, set fire to the outworks but, as we've heard, the prayers of St Aidan allowed it to continue its existence, and it was the centre of a kingdom extending as far south as the Humber and a bulwark of the Christian faith in a land that remained largely pagan. The town was sacked by the Danes in 993 and remained desolate until the time of the Conqueror, who is thought to have built a very strong wooden castle here as a fortress for the Governors of Northumberland. In 1095 Robert Mowbray, Earl of Northumberland, was besieged by William Rufus, who set up a wooden structure called Malvoisin to cut off the castle from any outside help. Mowbray managed to escape and was eventually captured at the priory at Tynemouth. He was forced to surrender Bamburgh, which was being held in his absence by his young wife and his steward, who had the wonderful name of Arkly Moreal.

Bamburgh was rebuilt in stone in the Norman period to resist the Scots. It was visited by King John and by Henry III. Edward II's favourite catamite Piers Gaviston was shut up here and so was David Bruce after his capture at Neville's Cross in the middle of the fourteenth century. During the Wars of the Roses the castle was besieged twice and was so badly battered by cannon fire that it became a ruin. A trust was set up in the eighteenth century to restore the castle and it helped the poor of the village with a free surgery and dispensary; a windmill was erected to grind corn for the poor and a tower was turned into a granary. A light was kept burning in the keep every night and a system of signals established with Holy Island to warn passing ships. Horsemen patrolled the coast on stormy days and shipwrecked mariners were accommodated in the castle. The castle was bought and splendidly restored at the end of the nineteenth century by the first Lord Armstrong of Cragside. It is still lived in by the Armstrong family and is regularly open for inspection; it is well worth a visit. The terrace gives a wonderful view over the village to the Cheviot Hills. The massive keep of Bamburgh Castle is still early

Norman, though internally it was altered in the eighteenth century, no doubt to the delight of the occupants. In what was probably once part of the walled gardens of the castle there is a herb garden where you can buy good plants. I happily bought a very nice quince tree from them and a lot of herbs which are still flourishing ten years on. The beach at Bamburgh is splendid and great for exercising horses and you will frequently see it in television dramas.

Keep going up the coast and you will come to Holy Island, as it is now called, which is the historic Lindisfarne. It has been known as Holy Island since the eleventh century because of the number of saints who lived and were buried there. St Aidan came from Iona at the invitation of King Oswald and established the first monastery at Lindisfarne, consisting of only a collection of huts and an oratory within a defensive enclosure. From here the monks set out to preach Christianity, first to the neighbouring villages and later to more distant places in the south of England. St Aidan was, as most of the people who seem to have come from Lindisfarne, an aesthetic evangelist entirely indifferent to his dignity as Bishop of Lindisfarne and yet intimate with kings and nobles. By his humility and devotion he influenced all who came in touch with him, and his astonishing achievements were the result of the popular veneration in which he was held.

The story goes that on the night Aidan died, the young Cuthbert was tending his sheep on the hillside. He saw stars falling, and later when he heard the news of Aidan's death, he realised that the stars had indeed been angels descending to carry the saint to heaven. He then put his sheep in the fold and turned his steps towards the monastery at Melrose to begin his life of Christianity. It was Cuthbert who wrote that charming description of our stay in this world as being like a bird that flies through the brightly lit great hall of a king and then disappears on the other side into the darkness again. Cuthbert died on the Farne Islands but was buried at Lindisfarne. Eleven years after his death in 698 the monks dug up the body and, finding that it was not decayed, they clothed it in new robes and a new wooden coffin adorned with suitable carvings.

Shortly after Cuthbert's death the Lindisfarne Gospels were produced. These are a masterpiece of seventh-century art illuminated by Eadfrith, a monk, who became Bishop of Lindisfarne; they are now in the British Library. Eleven years after Cuthbert's death they were carried off with Cuthbert's body and fell into the sea, but were recovered at low tide and were taken to Durham. An Anglo-Saxon translation was added by a priest named Aldred in 950. The Venerable Bede also spent time on Lindisfarne; in 793 the priory was sacked by the Vikings and most of the monks were killed. Surprisingly, the priory survived for nearly another hundred years, but when the Vikings came again it was destroyed.

The most northerly town in England and the only county at one point north of the Tweed is Berwick-upon-Tweed, which is further north than a lot of places in Scotland and was once independent of both. Officially styled the County of the Borough and Town of Berwick-upon-Tweed, it had to be specially mentioned in Acts of Parliament until as late as 1746. Its position at the mouth of the Tweed made it a focal point between England and Scotland as well as a suitable market and port for both countries. Between 1147 and 1482 when it finally became attached to England, it was a scene of constant strife, changing hands thirteen times. For a long time afterwards the Mayor of Berwick-upon-Tweed had to sign declarations of war and peace treaties separately, and there is a belief that Berwick-upon-Tweed is still at war with Russia as a result of not signing the Treaty of Paris at the end of the Crimean War in 1856. Whether this is true or not, it is a rather nice thought.

In 1174 William the Lion, King of Scotland, stood in chains at Berwick before Henry II and surrendered the town to the

English as part of his ransom. Richard I sold it to the Scots in return for money for his Crusade, but not long afterwards it was razed to the ground by King John. It was here in 1291 that Edward I turned down the claim of Robert the Bruce and nominated John Balliol to the throne of Scotland, but within a year Balliol had rebelled and Edward massacred the townspeople of Berwick in revenge, destroying the Red Hall, the headquarters of the Flemish traders, and re-populating the town with English traders. The town was then recaptured by William Wallace in 1297, but was soon relieved, and after Wallace's execution in London in 1305, one of his arms was set up on the bridge at Berwick as an awful warning to the rebels. In 1306 the Countess of Buchan was imprisoned here for her part in crowning Robert the Bruce at Scone, and for years she was publicly exhibited in an open cage in the castle. In 1328, in an attempt at peace, Edward III's sister, Joanna, married Robert the Bruce's son David, later David II of Scotland. He was her toy boy because she was all of seven while he was only four, and the following year he was to succeed to the throne of Scotland and be crowned at Scone.

In 1333, after the Scots had recaptured Berwick, Edward III marched north and took revenge. The English Army were posted on Halidon Hill, two miles north-west of the town, their position being rendered secure by the marshy ground before them. The Scots, led by Regent Archibald Douglas, advanced to attack and the pike men floundered in the morass and were reduced to a mere fragment by the English archers before they could reach the enemy ranks. They were then slaughtered by the English men-at-arms. The carnage at Halidon Hill brought respite to Berwick but not for long. Again and again at various times throughout the fourteenth and fifteenth centuries it was to suffer at the hands of the besiegers, and the long story of bitter strife was not ended until 1482, when the key town was finally surrendered to the English crown. In 1603 its gates were opened to James VI as he was on his way south to ascend the English throne as James I and the two countries were united. Berwick ceased to be a challenge to either country.

The Tweed at this point is spanned by three bridges, and the walls and fortification of Berwick are well worth a visit, as is the town itself, which is a delightful place both historically and socially. Its castle is a ruin, the best surviving part being the White Wall, which was built as a spur or outwork to guard a steep flight of steps lately called the bricky-necks, the remains of which can still be seen ascending to the water tower on the river bank. One of the great and fairly unique features of the wall is the enormous bank of earth behind it. The King's Mount and various other mounts all aimed to give a greater range to gunnery from within the castle walls. When you travel north on the train to Edinburgh you get a splendid view of the different bridges and the walls of Berwick-upon-Tweed if you are sitting on the right side of the train. The River Tweed can be a dangerous river on account of its extremely strong currents. There is a rhyme that says, 'Tweed to the Till though I run still so it can kill'. It is an excellent fishing river with some of the most expensive salmon fishing in the British Isles.

The Tweed and the Cheviot Hills form the barrier between England and Scotland. I have hunted the Cheviots on a quad bike on both sides of what is known as the Scottish Fence under the mastership of Michael Hedley, whose father, on his death this year at the age of ninety-six, had been the longest serving Master ever in any hunt in the United Kingdom. The Cheviots are the first landmark for ships coming in from the Baltic. They have magnificent views and wild country in which you can get lost in the twinkling of an eye. You can be going along thinking that everyone is around you and you look again and they have all vanished into a cleft. It must have been impossible in the days of the English-Scots wars to defend any marching column successfully.

If you go to Chillingham Park, which lies amid the Cheviots, you can see a herd of Chillingham cattle which are the early form of White Park cattle. They have been at Chillingham for over 200 years, since a member of the Massereene and Ferrard family married a Hamilton and a breeding herd was established from Hamilton Palace. From the shape of their skulls it is known that they are descended from the original British wild ox, and in fact it is advisable to treat them with great respect because they can be extremely dangerous, as generations of Scots raiders who endeavoured to steal them would have found out to their cost. Two well-known artists, Thomas Bewick and Edwin Landseer, had to retreat in a hurry up a tree when endeavouring to sketch the cattle, and the fifth Earl of Tankerville had his pony gored out from under him. If you wonder why I have not said much about the west of Northumberland north of Hadrian's Wall, it is because it is a very wild moorland with little habitation.

Herefordshire

Herefordshire will not be a particularly long chapter, not because I don't love it, but it is amazing how all the fury of its early years battling with the Welsh invading from the Welsh Marches and carrying off the fatter valley sheep has now melded into a county that is peaceful, rural, not heavily populated and just very lush and pleasant and indicative of everything that is good about Britain. They used to say of Herefordshire that it was famed for its six Ws: wool, water, wood, wheat, wine and women. Up in the north of the county is Leintwardine, where to my mind the holiest man in the kingdom lives, a retired Anglican vicar so beloved by the village that on his eightieth birthday the whole village threw a party for him and set the church bells ringing to celebrate. Leintwardine is famous for its squirrel feast. The remarkable publican Flossie, who has recently gone to pull pints in heaven, used to host this after a procession through the streets of Leintwardine to the pub to eat squirrel stew. The squirrels in question are of course grey ones; quite apart from the fact that red squirrels are so rare, there is no meat on them. I have historical American books and even quite modern ones that are full of squirrel recipes; squirrels make perfectly good eating although they are rather fiddly and difficult to skin. You need to do it as you once used to do with a veal calf and make a notch in the skin and put a hosepipe underneath it, an air hose, and just blow it off. Leintwardine may be a rural Herefordshire village now, but it stands on the site of the Roman city of Bravonium and on a hill two miles south was the Roman camp of Brandon, surrounded by ramparts on a ditch from which

Roman earthworks ran parallel with Watling Street, which passed below the foundations of Leintwardine church.

The church contains a monument to an interesting man, Sir Banastre Tarleton. Joining the army after leaving Oxford where he had studied law, he went as a volunteer under Cornwallis to fight for Britain in the American War of Independence. He performed very valorously at the British victories at Charleston and Camden and his reputation for courage was not dented when he had to surrender his sword at the fall of Yorktown. He fought in Portugal and Ireland and was made a baronet and served in Parliament for Liverpool. At the height of his fame he sat for Sir Joshua Reynolds and became friendly with the Prince Regent's mistress Perdita, who helped him write his book on the American war. This was perhaps a mistake all round; it revealed him as a popinjay and a braggart and except for some valuable details, the book is almost unreadable. It led the reader to infer that the writer had been inadequately supported by Cornwallis, apart from which the United States might have remained a British colony. His writings shattered his military fame and he was reduced to pecuniary distress. Rather more delightful in the history of Leintwardine church is the latest addition, which is a set of misericords carved in memory of Flossie the landlady of the pub and hostess of the squirrel feast, showing her with her barrels and surrounded by the old-fashionedness and charm of her working life. Leintwardine has an annual coracle regatta, as it is one of the few places where coracles are still made.

It is curious that the description of Herefordshire should contain wool and wine, as I always think of it as a county of cattle and cider and perry. The Hereford cattle, with its familiar white face and dark red coat, is instantly recognisable to even the basest townie and is a delicious eating piece of beef; the wing rib that I had last New Year came from a Hereford and my butcher Colin Peat of Haddington had hung it for about six weeks. It was, to my mind, the best piece of beef I had ever eaten, and that is saying a lot. Leominster, with its feeling of ancient prosperity and its beautiful black and white merchants' houses, is to me very typical of the county; and about a mile away from town across the sixteenth-century bridge is Eaton Hall, the home of the Hakluyts, a name that has appeared in the county roll since the thirteenth century. One of the Hakluyts fought at Agincourt but Richard Hakluyt, who was an English seaman, wrote a fascinating book called *Divers Voyages*. I know about the Hakluyts because I had an ancestor who was Richard Hakluyt's hydrographer on many of his voyages around the world. Colwall by the Malvern Hills, with its mysterious block called the Colwall Stone, was the childhood home, at Hope End on Oyster Hill, of Elizabeth Barrett Browning, and I think she describes the county very well in her poems. She writes:

> Dimple close with hill and valley,
> Dappled very close with shade

It was a fall from her pony here that turned her into an invalid and a prisoner of her father. She was taken to London for medical reasons and wrote, I think very sadly, in one of her letters: 'Beautiful, beautiful hills they are! And yet, not for all the whole world's beauty would I stand in the sunshine and the shadow of them any more. It would be a mockery, like the taking back of a broken flower to its stalk.'

One of her hills would have been the Herefordshire Beacon, a gaunt hillside, 1,114 feet high, its bare top ridged against the skyline, the remains of a prehistoric camp so steep, so secure behind its ditches and mounds that it must have been impregnable. History and tradition put King Caractacus here to make one of his last stands against the Romans. The main river of Herefordshire is the Wye and the valley of the Wye is amazingly beautiful. At Bredwardine, with its six-arched bridge, you can see the peaceful river, quite different in its country surroundings to the furore of the traffic and tourists that is Ross-on-Wye, or indeed Hay-on-Wye just over the border in Powys, with its bookshops and its large book festival. The county town of the shire is Hereford itself which has a beautiful medieval bridge across the Wye and a fine cathedral. Little is left of the castle which was a huge, strong fortress and very important in the fight against the would-be invading Welsh. It was here that Simon de Montfort brought Prince Edward, later Edward I, as a captive after his defeat at Lewes.

The cathedral grew up around the shrine of St Ethelbert, who was beheaded in 794 in the reign of King Offa, the man who built Offa's Dyke. Apparently Ethelbert was the would-be love of King Offa's daughter, and Offa's wife wanted her husband to kill him, but he refused so she tricked him and had him killed by her own guards. However, what he did to acquire sainthood is not very obvious from any of the stories about him. The cathedral has the largest chained library in the world, although oddly there is another very large one at the other end of the street in the Church of All Saints, where David Garrick, the actor, was baptised. A fine medieval church, in the eighteenth century it was left an abso-lutely priceless collection of 300 chained books by a William Brewster; in the middle of the nineteenth century this was saved in the nick of time from being illicitly sold to America for just £100 by one of the churchwardens.

In the cathedral library, and indeed the one at All Saints, are books that were being read 1,000 years ago. The books are locked and chained as they have been for centuries, which enabled people to come and read them *in situ* without being allowed to take them away and perhaps steal them. The cathedral library was the oldest to have three rows of shelving and the reader sits on a seat fitted to the floor with a sloping desk in front of him. Interestingly, Sir Philip Sidney's tutor, Canon Thornton, who was librarian at the cathedral, was the Vice-Chancellor of Oxford when Thomas Bodley furnished the Bodleian Library and he copied the shelves from Hereford. The cathedral library houses an 800-year-old Limoges enamelled reliquary which is an object of great beauty. It is presumably a reliquary of St Thomas Becket as the enamelled scenes show his martyrdom before the altar at Canterbury. The cathedral contains a very rare Norman chair, too, sat in by King Stephen, of Stephen and Matilda fame, who was grandson of the Conqueror. It is a very simple chair with a back and two arms but it is in surprisingly good condition given its age. The cathedral also boasts a very beautiful Norman font. There is much to delight in Hereford Cathedral, and indeed in Hereford itself, and I suggest that you go and see it for yourself.

That I think says it all about Herefordshire; it is a place of delight, rural, historical and a pleasure to visit, with good butchers, good pubs and really somewhere you have to experience for yourself. It is also very good hunting country; there are the Golden Valley, the Radnors and many other hunts. In fact, when the Hunt Declaration signatures were taken, Herefordshire had the highest of all counts of those standing up to declare that they were prepared to go to prison for hunting. Go there and enjoy it, eat the beautiful beef, taste the cider and perry that come out of the Bulmers orchards and eat the soft fruit that is prevalent as a crop throughout the county.

Then move seamlessly north into that other Marcher county where all the bloodshed has gone and, calm at last, 'all passion spent', as the poet said, you will find yourself in Shropshire.

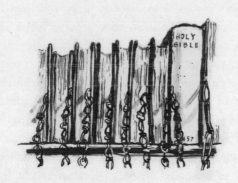

Shropshire

Shropshire has its own poet in A.E. Housman and his work 'The Shropshire Lad', and it is well summed up by the words he wrote:

> Clunton and Clunbury,
> Clungunford and Clun,
> Are the quietest places under the sun.

Certainly Clun, lying as it does by Offa's great dyke, which he built to defend the kingdom from Wales, is very quiet and peaceful now, but around it there are five ancient camps with ramparts twenty-five feet high, enclosing twelve acres with a well in the middle, said to have been the camp of Caractacus, whose last battle was not far away at Bucknell. The last stand of the Britons against the Romans took place in this part of the Marches. And if you travel up the line of the Marches there is a string of castles, not the mighty castles of Edward I's bully-boy attitude to Wales, but solid defensive castles protecting against Welsh invasion. The first of these that you come to is Ludlow.

There is something magical about Ludlow. It stands on a hill rising 200 feet above the wooded valley, with the river acting as a moat around it, and if you go to the castle grounds at early dusk there is a real feeling that the Ludlow of the Middle Ages is still there and if you only blink hard enough you will see it. Ludlow was A.E. Housman's home; he loved it and he wished his memory to be linked with it. I'm fond of his lines:

Oh, come you home of Sunday
When Ludlow's streets are still
And Ludlow bells are calling
To farm and lane and mill.
Or come you home of Monday
When Ludlow market hums
And Ludlow chimes are playing
'The conquering hero comes'.

The castles run in a line from Chepstow to Chester but I think that Ludlow is probably my favourite; the young Prince Arthur, Henry VIII's older brother, brought his young bride Catherine of Aragon here and there is still a Queen's Walk around the castle walls. The Duke of York, the younger of the two little Princes in the Tower, was born here, and it was from here that the Princes were taken to London where they met their deaths. John Milton gave his first showing of the masque *Comus* in the Great Hall at Ludlow Castle. The castle may be a ruin, but it has more feeling of inhabitants about it than any castle I have been to that is still lived in.

Ludlow has now set itself up as a food town and has a large food festival and a number of Michelin-starred restaurants, but it wasn't always so. When I went to Ludlow twenty-odd years ago with my friend Christine for a week's pootle based on the town, the only places to eat were the Chinese takeaway and an Indian restaurant, and not a very good one at that, a fish and chip shop and various pubs. Ludlow now owes its present reputation to one man, Shaun Hill, of whom I have always been an enormous fan. I am invariably asked in any question and answer session what I am going to have for my last meal and, on one occasion, when speaking in Wales, I was asked the rider, 'And who is going to cook it for you?' I answered without a moment's hesitation, 'Shaun Hill,' and the friends I was staying with then whipped me off to the Walnut Tree at Abergavenny, where he is now cooking, as a special treat. I told him that I had said this and he said, 'You'll just have to keep coming back and rehearsing the menu, Clarissa.'

What I love about Shaun's cooking is that the flavours are exquisite and that, although he is a chef, he does not indulge in all this chef's nonsense of stacking and piling and drizzling and ending up with nothing that tastes of anything. When he left Gidleigh Park in Devon he moved to Ludlow and opened a twenty-two-seater restaurant called the Merchant House in the town, and I was fortunate enough to eat there. It was everything you would want a restaurant to be: it was comfortable without being over the top, and he didn't turn the tables round so that you could sit comfortably over your meal. Then gradually more and more chefs came to Ludlow simply to pick up the shortfall of people who couldn't get in to Shaun Hill's or people who had perhaps stayed for a few extra nights and wanted somewhere else to eat. So Shaun Hill has left behind a legacy of restaurants. And the fish and chip shop is still very good.

Ludlow also has two excellent butchers by the names of Wall and Francis. Wall is particularly good for rare-breed meats, his pork pies and his cured bacon, and Francis is particularly good for game in season. My friend Douglas, Christine's husband, who will go many miles off his travel route in order to call in at a first-rate butcher, is a regular visitor to Ludlow, and he told me a lovely story about how he had gone first to Wall and they were selling their pheasants at £1.99 each, dressed, and so he had gone across to Francis and they were selling their dressed pheasants at 99p each. He had asked about this and Francis said, 'Oh, well, you know even Ludlow can have its price wars.'

Not far away from Ludlow is Cleobury Mortimer which I suppose you could say was the home of Piers Plowman, because William Langland was born here in 1332 and there is a charming Victorian memorial to him in the church. After Chaucer, William Langland was perhaps the most important

336

contributor to fourteenth-century literature. We know very little about Langland apart from the poem itself, but we do know that he was reputedly the son of Stacy de Rokayle, an associate and follower of the de Spenser family, and an unknown peasant mother. He was educated at Malvern by the monks and became a deacon but never a priest, and married and lived in London until he died at about sixty years of age. Although the poem was published during Langland's lifetime, there were three slightly differing versions of it, as is so often the way. While the great Professor Skeat accepted that Langland was the poet and author of all three, other would-be pundits saw many hands and minds at work and, rather as with Shakespeare, were not prepared to accept that one man could have written all his works. It is a fairly radical poem for all its dreaminess, seeing the ills in court and Church, the cruelty of the nobles, the rascality of the lawyers and the sufferings of the serfs, but he also exposes the laziness of some of the poor and the discontent of peasants where industry might improve their condition. He was a disciple of John Wycliffe and had enormous influence on the movement that led to the outpouring of the Peasants' Revolt in 1381. Langland would not have approved of that, for he was touched with the truth of his faith and he idealises the suffering peasant as the embodiment of Our Lord himself.

Running from Cleobury Mortimer to Bewdley in Worcestershire is the Wyre Forest, once a hunting forest; it is the wild cherry of the Wyre Forest that yielded the first cultivated stocks of the fruit for England, and in springtime the valleys are still wonderful with their pink and white blossoms.

Go nor-nor-west, passing the remote Brown Clee Hill, connected by the Devil's Causeway with the Roman Watling Street, and you will come to Bridgnorth. Bridgnorth is really two towns built on a sandstone cliff, the upper town with the castle and the lower town with the River Severn flowing peaceably through. There is a distance of about 200 feet from the low to the high and you used to have to climb up stone steps cut sheer through the rock, but thank heavens somebody built a funicular railway. I remember meeting my friend Christine there on my birthday because her husband sent me the first baby broad beans in a Thermos flask with a knob of butter contained in the lid, and I sat happily by the side of the Severn and ate them and felt that this was a true celebration of my birthday, having gone down to the river on the funicular railway. The castle has a curious ruined tower leaning over the park and while the Leaning Tower of Pisa is five degrees out of true, Bridgnorth Tower is fifteen degrees, and so startling that you think it is bound to fall down, but it has stood for 800 years and is still perfectly safe. It is thirty feet high and as broad as it is high and is all that is left of the castle built in the first year of the twelfth century by a Norman rebel baron.

Bridgnorth is on the Staffordshire side of the county and reminds you that Staffordshire was the hotbed of the Industrial Revolution in so many ways. If you go a little further north you will come to Coalbrookdale and Ironbridge, both symbols of that revolution. Coalbrookdale had large and flourishing iron works, which seems slightly hard to credit when you are there. The woods around have been cut down to feed the furnaces and yet there are still ancient timbered cottages wedged between houses and shops. The church was built in 1851 by Abraham Darby of Coalbrookdale, who was the master iron maker, and at Ironbridge you will see what is supposed to have been the first iron bridge ever built, erected by his father Abraham Darby in 1779. The bridge is 196 feet long with one span of 100 feet and two smaller ones, the total weight of iron being about 380 tonnes. Coalbrookdale works were extremely innovative and influential and the bridge was as big a wonder in its day as the iron boat George Wilkinson launched not far away at Broseley. Ironbridge itself is well worth a visit as the whole area has been set out as a monument to the ironworking of the area and of the Industrial Revolution as a whole.

Head west–north-west and you will come to the town of Shrewsbury, where the Severn, the longest river in the British Isles, forms a loop around the town providing it with a moat. It is almost an island, and consequently has a number of very fine bridges. Shrewsbury has been the site of a renowned boys' school since the sixteenth century, which numbers among its old boys Sir Philip Sidney and Charles Darwin. Philip Sidney was the man who, when dying in the European wars, was offered a drink of water and immediately told his helper to offer it to the dying soldier who lay next to him. This was always held out to me at school as the perfect example of Christian charity, which I suppose it was. Shrewsbury has a wonderful array of black and white houses, some of them very old. When Arthur Mee visited it in the 1930s he found the fishmonger selling salmon out of the Severn in the house where Henry Tudor had stayed on his way to Bosworth Field. The town has some ridiculously narrow lanes which are known locally as shuts and have wonderful names such as Grope Lane, Shoplatch, Dogpole and Pride Hill. The school has moved across the river to Kingsland, and the new school has a modern and stately look, modern if you happen to be a Victorian I think; the statue of Charles Darwin in front of the original school building looks at the Welsh Bridge, which he used to cross each morning. Darwin's father was a doctor in Shrewsbury and there is a painting of him in the Natural History Gallery in the town. There is also a portrait of Clive of India, who was a Shropshire lad from further north in the county and who was elected Member of Parliament for Shrewsbury in 1760 on his triumphant return as the first Governor of Bengal. He was still a Member of Parliament when his impeachment came, but more of Clive when we get to his birthplace. Shrewsbury has a very good independent bookshop and it has been my pleasure to do book signings for them on two occasions.

To the north-west of the county is Oswestry, a very old town, which has been destroyed so many times in the battles with the Welsh that there are not a lot of ancient monuments left. It was here that St Oswald, the Christian King of Northumbria, was slain in battle by the Mercian King Penda and, because he was a Christian, Penda, a man noted for the cruelty of his actions, crucified him to a tree. There is a well bearing his name that is supposed to have been, according to legend, where part of the saint's body fell and water gushed from the spot. It is ironic – curious, perhaps – that Oswestry was the birthplace of the war poet Wilfred Owen. He went to the First World War at the age of twenty-one in 1914 and he survived, although he was wounded, until he was killed in 1918 the week before the Armistice. He is perhaps the greatest war poet of the First World War and to me his finest poem is 'The Parable of the Old Man and the Young', where he describes Abraham taking Isaac to sacrifice him to his God and the voice of an angel says:

> Behold,
> A ram caught in a thicket by its horns;
> Offer the Ram of Pride instead of him.

> But the old man would not so, but slew his son,
> And half the seed of Europe, one by one.

In the north of the county is Market Drayton, which holds an annual fair. It is a nice old tradition that there is a court held on the spot to settle all differences arising out of the fair. The disputants appear before it, as we are told, with dusty feet; in other words without formality. Robert Clive – Clive of India – was educated here and you can still see his old desk with his initials cut into it. As a schoolboy Clive was something of a thug, he and his gang levying protection money on shopkeepers in return for not breaking their windows, and he was something of a daredevil too, climbing the church tower while the townspeople watched the small figure lower himself from the top to sit astride a gargoyle. Clive was born at nearby Moreton Say where his family had lived for 300 years. His father, an impoverished squire, sent him as a teenager to India to be a writer for the East India Company. He was not a great success and he attempted to take his own life, but he missed twice, either because the pistol misfired or because he literally missed, and so he is supposed to have said, 'I'm reserved for something.'

Rather fortunately for Clive, hostilities broke out when the French attacked Madras, and but for Clive it might have been France that ran the Indian Empire. Clive obtained a commission and it became clear that he was a military genius. He relieved the besieged Trichinopoly. He obtained permission to lead an expedition against Arcot and with only 500 men he drove out the garrison and entered a city of 100,000 people and prepared to defend his gain. With a low and lightly built wall, a choked ditch, crumbling towers, a shortage of food and depleted forces, he sustained a seven-week siege by 10,000 men and put them to flight after a battle of some eighteen hours. This established his prestige in the British Army and the whole course of history was altered. His health had suffered and after his marriage he returned to England to enter Parliament, but was sent back to India a couple of years later as Governor.

One of his first tasks was to avenge the tragedy of the Black Hole of Calcutta. Clive took Calcutta, but the East India Company decided to make terms with the Nawab of Bengal, Siraj Ud Daulah, much to Clive's disgust. He planned to overthrow him and replace him with a figurehead and obtained the assistance of a wealthy Hindu banker who, late in the negotiations, demanded £300,000 for his part. Without batting an eyelid Clive prepared two agreements, one of which admitted the claim and one of which omitted it, and at the relevant moment he produced the second one that repudiated the first.

He installed his figurehead Mir Jafar and accepted from him £300,000 and land rents worth £30,000 a year. When he stood before the Parliamentary Commission accused of extortion he exclaimed, 'At this moment I stand astonished at my own moderation.' He was raised to the peerage and sent back to India to reform the civil and military services. On his return to England, impeachment proceedings were once again attempted against him, but the House of Commons found that he had rendered 'great and meritorious service to his country'. He had indeed, he had given them the Indian Empire, but he died a few years later at his own hand as he had intended to do all those years before.

Up near Whitchurch on the Cheshire border is Hodnet, the one-time home of Richard Heber, a man of great pragmatism. He was a collector of books and he always attempted to have three copies of most books, one to use, one to lend and one in reserve. He actually left behind three libraries. His brother was vicar of the church in Hodnet. I mention Hodnet because I attended a lovely occasion there. I was asked to open the new Infants' School at Hodnet School and the RAF wanted to land me on the school playing field by helicopter, but there is a thriving motorbike and sidecar club in Hodnet and they were determined that due to *Two Fat Ladies* I should ride in procession through the village in the sidecar of a motorbike. Anyway, they reached a compromise and I was led in procession in the sidecar through Hodnet on to the playing field where I got into the helicopter which then rose above the school and flew round a few times before lowering me back on to the playing field. After that I went in and carried out my official duty opening the Infants' School and generally spent a delightful day. In my kitchen I have a very nice serving dish, decorated by the children with two fish and an inscription saying 'From the pupils of Hodnet School', and I recall that happy day every time I use it.

I often make my way into Cheshire through the town of

Whitchurch, of which I am really quite fond. It is one of those towns that has everything useful, chemists, banks, hardware stores, a tapestry shop and an independent bookshop, and it has without doubt the best Tourist Information Centre that it has ever been my privilege to go to. On occasion when I have forgotten to book somewhere to stay for the Game Fair, or some other place where accommodation is almost impossible to find at short notice, they have rolled up their sleeves and found me somewhere not only nearby but also extremely pleasant.

I also go to Whitchurch to pay tribute to John Talbot, the first Earl of Shrewsbury, who is buried here. He is the Shrewsbury of Shakespeare's *Henry VI, Part I*, and when he died in France in 1453, still a warrior at the age of seventy, he asked the soldiers of his bodyguard to bury his heart in the church porch at Whitchurch so that, as they had fought and stridden over his body while he lived, should they and his children for ever pass over it and guard it in death. There is an old photograph of his

skull on which you can quite clearly see the mark of the battle axe that brought about his death. He lies in the Church of St Alkmund, his effigy in battle armour with the Order of the Garter over it. I don't know who St Alkmund was, but there are several churches in Shropshire dedicated to him. John Talbot was important in the wars against Owain Glyndwr and he was twice Governor of Ireland where he was so violent that contemporaries said of him that not since the time of Herod was anyone so wicked in evil deeds. He fought in the French wars against Joan of Arc and when, due entirely to his rashness, he was defeated at Patay and taken prisoner, he had to pay an immense ransom. Joan was captured about the same time and I suppose they might have been exchanged for each other except that Talbot was totally convinced that she was a witch and an emissary of Satan.

Now we will travel over the border into Worcestershire.

Worcestershire

This will probably be another short chapter because I don't know much about Worcestershire, which always seems to me a county that the world slightly forgot. The Malvern Hills lead us into Worcestershire but they are not of a huge height. The Worcestershire Beacon is slightly shorter than the Empire State Building in New York, and if you headed due east you would cross no higher land until you met the Ural Mountains on the far side of Russia, which is why parts of Worcestershire can be really very cold in winter. It is said that on a clear day you can see twelve counties from the top of Bredon Hill. Worcestershire is visited by both the Severn and the Avon rivers and its other main river is the Teme.

My main reason, historically, for going to Evesham was to buy asparagus, since the Vale of Evesham is a great asparagus-producing area, as well as growing many other soft fruits and vegetables. Evesham is on the bank of the Avon and we are told that the site was picked by Eoves, a swineherd from whom the town has taken its name. He is supposed to have seen a vision of the Madonna on the river bank and hastened to Worcester to tell his story to Egwin, the bishop. Egwin decided to found a monastery here. He resigned his bishopric and when he died in 717 he was the first Abbot of Evesham. The abbey became a place of pilgrimage, probably because of Eoves's vision, and was a great money earner, as it is today; you only have to think of Lourdes or Fatima to realise that to this day religious visions and the like remain a great source of income to the inhabitants of such a place. Lucky are they that have visions and relics. As is the norm with sites of pilgrimage, Evesham still maintains a number of old inns and what are now hotels dating back, in some cases, as with the Crown, to the age of Chaucer.

I also come to Evesham to think of the memory of Simon de Montfort, whom I first knew of when I was visiting my friends in Sussex as a child just outside Lewes. Simon was a great reformer. He and his army were advancing along the Severn with his hostage, King Henry III, and he was received at the abbey, and dined there; at the King's request they heard Mass while his troops were camped in the town. Simon was attempting to join his son at Kenilworth but Prince Edward, later Edward I, one of the great battle leaders of our time, gathered his forces and, by the most astonishing forced march, managed to position himself to defend the roads through which Simon must pass. Edward had already beaten and destroyed de Montfort's son Simon's army at Kenilworth. Simon found himself completely trapped, the loop of the river behind him and Edward's army in front, and when he saw Prince Edward's army he is reputed to have said, 'May God have mercy on our souls for our bodies are theirs.' The fighting lasted only three hours and many of Simon's men were killed in the streets by the people of Evesham. Simon's son, Henry, fell in front of him and his chief supporters around him. His horse was killed under him and he fought desperately on foot until finally, stabbed from behind, he fell down exclaiming, 'God be thanked,' and died. It always amazes me how rapidly people moved around the county in those days on the really quite poor roads. On this occasion Prince Edward is reported to have marched his troops an average of forty miles a day.

Move north-west and you come to Worcester itself, first inhabited in the seventh century on a bank above the Severn floods. I suspect it has always been dominated by the cathedral, much as it is today. At its height in the Middle Ages, Worcester had become the fifth city in the land and the centre of a diocese that covered the greater part of the neighbouring counties. Worcester suffered in the Civil War because it held for the King and the city walls and many of its houses were destroyed by Cromwell's troops in 1651. Most of the good houses in the town date from the post-Reformation period. The cathedral became a place of pilgrimage because it contained the tomb of Bishop Wulstan. He and another sainted Saxon bishop, St Oswald, lie here as, rather curiously, does King John. King John loved Worcester and visited it at least eleven times that we know of and his will is preserved in the chapter house here; in it he ordained that he should be buried at Worcester, and he lies between the shrines of the two Saxon saints, thereby fulfilling a prophecy, reputed to be by Merlin, that he should be placed among the saints. His very fine effigy is in Purbeck marble; also buried here is Prince Arthur, the elder brother of Henry VIII. Worcester was the home of the Worcester Porcelain Company whose works were on the south side of the cathedral. It was largely because of them that the Birmingham–Worcester Canal was built.

Worcester is also the home of the condiment Worcestershire sauce. The story goes that the landlord of the local inn, Mr Perrins and his friend Mr Lea, a chemist, attempted to make the sauce and that it tasted rather unpleasant, so they left the barrels standing for some time in the cellars of their premises. On tasting them again several years later they discovered that they had a winner on their hands. Rather curiously my friend Audrey D'Aragona, who ran the Roman Cookery School, once followed the recipe of the Roman cookery writer and gourmet Apicius for his *liquinum*, which was Roman fish sauce, and what she got, following the recipe meticulously, was Worcestershire sauce. I love the thought of the Romans lounging on their dining couches with their togas and their sandals and their socks pouring Worcestershire sauce over all their larks' tongues and peacocks' brains and so forth.

I once attended the anniversary of the Worcester Women's Institute, which was the first WI meeting I had ever spoken at. I was expecting perhaps 150 to 200 people at the most. Imagine my surprise when I said to Madam President, 'And how many are we today?' and she replied, 'Well, only the 900 we could actually fit into the hall.' It was there that, looking at them, I remarked, 'What I see before me is raw power.' Bear in mind that it was the Women's Institute that saved marmalade for us, and also that it was the Women's Institute at their conference in Wembley who were the first people to slow-handclap Tony Blair when he was Prime Minister. I remember that as I was slightly late because I had got lost and the antis who had been there waiting to pillory me and picket the building had been shooed away by the formidable ladies of the Women's Institute. The county obviously has quite a strong presence of antis because I heard that they were protesting and picketing a restaurant in the shire that had been serving a pâté made with squirrel and *pâté de foie gras*, not because of the *pâté de foie gras*, which they might have some reason to object to (although not to my mind), but were protesting because of the use of squirrel. God help us all!

One of the other places that I know in the county is Droitwich, whose name ends in 'wich', indicating a source of salt. The salt springs are supposed to be ten times saltier than the sea and were described as the most potent in Europe, and the Romans came here both to bathe in the springs and to take away the salt, which was of course an extremely valuable asset. The town still has medicinal baths where you can bathe in the incredible salty water and which are supposed to have remarkable healing properties.

To the north of the county is Kidderminster which, apart from being famous for the manufacture of carpets, was also the home of Rowland Hill, the father of the Penny Post. Hill used to recount how his mother dreaded the postman's knock as there was no money in the house to pay the postage on the letter. Consequently, after many years as a schoolmaster and after inventing a water wheel and a printing press and engaging in reform and in the colonisation of South Australia, he threw himself into the business of cheapening the postal rates. Charges had been high, services had been limited and irregular, and huge districts had never seen a postman. This took him many years and the opposition from the Post Office was exactly what you might imagine. However, he succeeded in the end and the Penny Post was instituted. Looking at the rising price of postal charges, one rather wishes that he might come back to us again.

This, I am sorry to say, is all that I know about Worcestershire, which is something that I must remedy in the years remaining to me, but we will now move out of the county.

Northamptonshire

Northamptonshire is another area of the country that sadly I don't know enough about. From my childhood education I know that it was and has been for a long time the centre of the shoe trade in England, based in Northampton itself. This is not as prosperous as it once was due to the import of shoes from abroad, and therefore it was perhaps fitting that when we were making *Clarissa and the Countryman* I should go to one of the finest boot makers in the country, Horace Batten of Raventhorpe, in order to have my hunting boots made. Because of my broken instep I cannot bend to get into an ordinary boot and so he devised something in the manner of the old field boot with laces across the instep, except that when you look at the boot it is not obvious. They are a beautiful pair of boots and I polish them lovingly even if I don't wear them any longer.

My only other visit, as an adult, to Northamptonshire, was to Althorp, the home of the Spencer family, where I went to speak at the Althorp Book Festival. This was something of a strange instance because until two days beforehand I thought that I had accepted an invitation to go to the Aldeburgh Book Festival. Whether this was a misprint or whether it was before I had my cataracts done I'm not quite sure, but when I said to my friend and agent Heather Holden-Brown, 'It'll be nice to be by the seaside,' she said, 'What on earth are you talking about, Clarissa? Althorp is nowhere near the sea.' So, duly informed, I set off for Althorp instead. I've never been a huge fan of the poor, sad, late Princess Diana, and I was slightly apprehensive about going to

Althorp, but much to my surprise I found that I really liked Charles Spencer, that he was a good man with sound principles on things that mattered to me and that he had a passion that I also share for Prince Rupert of the Rhine, about whom he had written a really good book.

The Spencers owed their estate, their house and indeed their fortune to sheep. The estate was first bought in the early sixteenth-century by John Spencer, a sheep farmer of Wormleighton in Warwickshire, who created a park of 300 acres. The Spencer estates have totalled 20,000 acres, although I don't know where they stand now, all under sheep. The house was begun in 1573 and inside the eighteenth-century façade that you see is a Tudor house. What I love when you go in through the front hall of Althorp is that it is adorned with hunting scenes and pictures of huntsmen and hounds and of a huntsman watering his horse. Northamptonshire has always been very good hunting country. There is a seventeenth-century falconry called the Standings because it was a hawking stand where ladies could watch the sport and it was here that Charles I was playing bowls when the news came that a party of horse had arrived at nearby Holdenby with Cornet Joyce coming to arrest him. The Spencers have produced several eccentric members, like all great English families: one John Spencer would not soil his hands with silver coins and died at thirty-eight because, as Horace Walpole said, 'He would not be abridged of those invaluable blessings of an English subject, brandy, small beer, and tobacco.' His son fought an election at Northampton that cost him £120,000 and he set two footmen at the front door of his house with sandwiches in which were hidden two golden guineas. He won the election and ruined his rivals; Lord Halifax had to sell his house and Lord Northampton had to sell the contents of Castle Ashby. How seriously profitable politics must have been in those days for people to want to get into it so keenly.

The Spencers have never been poor and they might at some times have been richer than others but Charles Spencer, the third Earl of Sunderland, married Anne Churchill, heiress of the great Duke of Marlborough, who was a huge help to him in his political work as a Whig leader. Sarah, Duchess of Marlborough, a favourite of Queen Anne, made her grandson John Spencer her heir, with the result that her pictures and other works of art are here, as is a lot of the Marlborough plate. Charles did a lot of work on the Act of Union between England and Scotland and when he returned from his time as Ambassador in Vienna he returned to politics, but Queen Anne disliked him, for she was very jealous of her favourites and she possibly resented his connection with the Churchills. She had him dismissed from office, offering him £3,000 a year to soften the blow. He refused the money and said that if he could not have the honour of serving his country he would not plunder it. Thereafter, he did nothing but hunt by day and gamble by night and loved nothing more than to adorn his house. As it was he who had spent all that money on his election, it is perhaps unfortunate that he was then removed from politics.

We all know the story of Princess Diana and her tragic death and I felt a little sad when I went to Althorp because all the Spencers, historically, lie on a rather cosy little canopy, huggermugger in the church, except for poor Diana, their one real connection with royalty and power, who lies in her mausoleum on her lonely little island, but what do I know?

One of the other places I have visited in Northamptonshire is Nassington, by the River Nene, which has now virtually been proved to stand on the site of an earlier manor house that belonged to King Canute. I have always been something of a fan of Canute, who was a very shrewd king, the son of Sweyn Forkbeard who took England by conquest. And I have always loved the story of how, when he got so sick of the flattery and sycophancy of his courtiers, he put his chair on the beach because somebody had said that he was so powerful that he could even hold back the tide and he proved to them very firmly that he wasn't. I remember at a very young age learning a poem that began 'King Canute in his bathing suit went down to the sea one day', so perhaps that was the cause of my affection.

Of course I have been to visit the battlefield at Naseby where Cromwell successfully and finally defeated the Royalist forces and brought the English Civil War to an end, which led to the death of the King. Curiously it is a watershed for rivers that go to either side of the country, truly the Mid-Lands; the Avon rises here and there are two springs, one travels east and one west, one finding the Avon and the Severn and the wide Atlantic and the other the Nene, the Wash and the North Sea. Naseby, which was fought about a mile away from the village, was really the first test of Cromwell's New Model Army, which was still untried and held in contempt by the Royalists. On the day in question, 14 June, Charles was so sure of his victory that he was away hunting at Fawsley Park and Cromwell was addressing his troops, and then Charles came late to the battlefield with his cousin Prince Rupert of the Rhine and 7,000 of his men. The actual field of battle is a small stretch of open pastureland with gorse and rabbit warrens, and the enemies were so close together that they could actually call out to each other. Cromwell had ridden out the night before from Ely and had only just arrived in time. He had been waiting for Parliament to free him from the restraints of the self-denying ordinance that forbade any member of the House from holding any military office.

Prince Rupert's opening charge went right through the left wing of the Parliamentary army, but the Cavaliers were then distracted by the baggage wagons and went off to loot them, and this was their fatal mistake. Cromwell reformed his infantry and routed the King with the loss of all his artillery, his carriages, his colours and 5,000 of his men. Charles fled and Rupert returned from the baggage hunt to find that the battle was lost. It would appear that Puritanical righteousness triumphed over Royalist greed. With Charles's baggage train was found correspondence that revealed that far from being a knightly figure of chivalry, he was seeking to buy foreign armies to destroy the English Parliament.

Also in Northamptonshire is the town of Corby, perhaps best known as the home of the Corby Trouser Press. Corby had large deposits of iron ore but it was quite heavily infected by phosphorus which made the steel brittle and fairly useless. An almost forgotten solicitor's clerk, a student of chemistry in his spare time, overheard a lecturer's comment that the man who eliminated phosphorus by any means would make his fortune. Sidney Gilchrist Thomas set himself to solve the problem. He discovered that there was something flawed in the Bessemer converter, which allowed the phosphorus to re-enter the metal, and what was wanted was a lining that would absorb the phosphorus. He found a way of doing this which revolutionised the steel industry and brought prosperity to Corby. Thomas became famous and made a fortune but died at the age of thirty-five. Having made provision for his mother and sister, he put the rest of his money in solemn trust that his fortune should be spent on bringing comfort to the lives of working folk. I think he deserves a mention.

The county town is, of course, Northampton, which as I said is a great centre for the shoe industry and has an interesting church built by returning Crusaders on the model of the Holy Sepulchre in Jerusalem. As proof that the shoe industry has been here for a very long time, King John is reputed to have bought a pair of boots here for nine pence. Given the habits of King John, one wonders if he paid the bill. Henry VIII wore a pair of Northampton boots at the Field of the Cloth of Gold and the town supplied 1,500 pairs of shoes to Cromwell's Parliamentarians. Northamptonshire boots have marched with Marlborough and Wellington and right through to the Second World War. In the 1930s it was said that there were 2,000 shops in England belonging to Northamptonshire shoe firms. One of the town's claims to fame is that Spencer Perceval was its Member of Parliament and was Prime Minister when he was shot dead in the lobby of the House of Commons in 1812.

This, I am afraid, concludes all I really know about Northamptonshire, except that it is a bonny, rural land for all its industry in the north.

Durham

No matter what angle you come at Durham from you will see a notice saying 'Land of the Prince Bishops'. Most people would probably look at it and shrug, but it does make Durham unique among all the counties of the British Isles in that it is a palatinate county; that is one where power, although nominally belonging to the King, was devolved, if you like, on to the bishops. This was not uncommon in central Europe and in the states of Germany but it is unique in the British Isles. This came about very early on after the Norman Conquest. The Conqueror had outlawed the Saxon Bishop Aethelwine for speaking out against him and had appointed William Walcher of Lorraine, a canon of Liège, described as an amiable and honourable man, who was a friend of Waltheof, the new Earl of Northumberland. Walcher had persuaded Waltheof to build a new, stronger castle of stone, and when Waltheof died Walcher succeeded him as Earl, a title for which he is supposed to have paid £400. The bishopric was thus endowed with political sovereignty over a vast domain.

For centuries the bishop was the representative of the sovereign, though not always of one mind with the sovereign, and he was the Prince Palatine of the county. In 1080 Walcher was killed by a Gateshead mob for condoning the murder of Liulf, a Saxon, and was succeeded by a priest from Bayeux. He conspired with William the Conqueror's son Robert, Duke of Normandy, to overthrow Robert's brother William Rufus as King of England, and was banished to Normandy. This went on throughout the centuries with the monks falling out with the bishop, the bishop falling out with the King, but basically the status quo continued until it came to an end in 1836 with the death of the last Prince Bishop, William van Mildert. He had founded the University of Durham and had decided that the time had come to abolish the medieval privilege that still lingered on. Future bishops were to have a fixed income and the palatinate powers were to pass to the crown.

If you were coming down the A1 from the north you will know when you reach Durham because you will see the Angel of the North, that strange, huge sculpture created by Antony Gormley, which I, among others, have become very fond of over the years, although there was much outcry when it was first put up. Dr Johnson remarked of Gateshead that it was a dirty little back lane out of Newcastle, and now it is a sprawling Tyneside town made rich over the centuries by engineering and allied industries. There are various bridges joining Gateshead to Newcastle, the most famous, historically, of which, the Swing Bridge, can be swung round on the central pier through ninety degrees to enable deep-sea vessels to travel further up the river. Robert Stephenson built a six-arched bridge which was opened by Queen Victoria in 1849, and the latest road bridge is the Tyne Bridge, opened by George V in 1928 as the pride of Tyneside. The roadway is suspended 84 feet above the river from a gigantic arch containing 4,000 tons of steel, and has a span of 531 feet and a rise of 710. The foundations go down seventy feet below the water level. It is the second largest steel single-span bridge in the world, the only one longer being that in Sydney Harbour, Australia.

The western side of Durham where it joins Cumbria and Northumberland is high moorland and fairly unpopulated. It is the east coast which over the centuries has been a prosperous area for coal, iron and shipbuilding.

Sunderland, the biggest town and chief port of the county covers an area of thirteen square miles. Its fortunes were founded on coal and shipbuilding and at the height of its boom it was extremely rich indeed. The original port here at the mouth of the Wear was called Monkwearmouth because of the monastery that had been founded at the same time as the one at Jarrow. There has been a port here for ten centuries, and for eight of those it has been called Sunderland because it is the part sundered from the monastic lands by the river. There is a rather charming statue of a small barefoot boy nailing up a flag using the butt of a pistol for a hammer which commemorates Jack Crawford, the sailor who heroically nailed Admiral Duncan's flag to the main topgallant mast of HMS *Venerable* in the Battle of Camperdown in October 1797. The *Venerable* was the admiral's flagship and received heavy enemy fire and its colours were shot away, finally crashing down with part of the mast. Up went young Jack, since lowering the flag was a sign of surrender. He was born in Sunderland in 1775 and died as a victim of cholera at the age of fifty-seven, having survived his dramatic climb. His medal from the people of Sunderland, which he wore at Nelson's funeral, is in the museum. His statue is considerably smaller than the rather large statue to Sir Henry Havelock of Indian Mutiny fame who was born nearby in 1795, but it is infinitely more delightful.

In the late seventeenth century, Sunderland was a haven for glass and pottery and the Sunderland Company of Glassmakers began operating on the banks of the Wear in 1698. If you love old glass as I do, it is well worth going to the National Glass Centre to see the beautifully engraved glass goblets showing full-rigged ships, and there is quite a lot of painted glass as well. There is a history of glassmaking because in 1674 Bishop Benedict Biscop built a church here and brought masons and glaziers from Gaul. The church was believed to have been the first in England to have had glass in its windows. He was a Northumbrian noble who, tired of worldly ways, after various pilgrimages, finally returned home to promote Christianity in his own land. Bishop Biscop went on to establish the monastery at Jarrow, which was, of course, the home of the Venerable Bede.

The name of Jarrow is heavily associated with the Venerable Bede. How I used to laugh at that when I was a child, wondering why a bead should be venerable, thinking of the beads you put on strings and gave as unwanted presents to relatives. Bede, who was born in 673, entered the monastery at Jarrow as a boy and remained there with occasional visits to Monkwearmouth until his death in 735. It is curious that for a man who never left Northumberland and barely ever left Jarrow, he should have written such extensive chronicles about the comings and goings in the wider world. It was he who translated St John's gospel into English. When he lay dying he turned to the boy who was his scribe and said, 'Have we finished yet?' The boy replied that there was one more sentence to translate, so Bede held himself together, translated it and then expired as it was finished.

Jarrow was often raided by the Danes and sacked several times, and in 1069 the rebuilt parts of the monastery were razed by William the Conqueror. It became merely a cell of the great house at Durham and something of a holiday destination for the priors of Durham. Jarrow became extremely prosperous in the world of shipbuilding and, even after the shipbuilding, had ceased it carried on a flourishing repair business for ships, some of which it had built. During the Great Depression the workers at Jarrow, who had nothing to occupy their time because there was no business for them, marched to London wearing their ordinary working clothes and tackety boots and Barbara Cartland, the authoress, as a young woman described how she was at the Savoy Hotel when the marchers came past and looked in on the diners in all their jewels and furs. Today, with the decline of shipbuilding and coal mining, this whole area of the Durham coastline is suffering from a lack of jobs and opportunity and is just dismal.

One pleasant town in Durham is Barnard Castle, with the

ruins of the old castle looking down on to the River Tees and its High Force waterfall, but the particular reason for going there would be to visit the Bowes Museum. The Bowes had long held Streatlam Castle and other estates in the neighbourhood and John Bowes, when he was in Paris, met his wife, a French actress named Joséphine Benoîte. They were both fascinated by the arts and she encouraged her husband in his hobby of collecting works of art; she always said that the idea of creating a museum and a gallery was hers. Originally this was going to be at Calais but they then decided to make it at Barnard Castle and the foundation stone was laid in November 1869. However, Mrs Bowes died at the age of forty-nine and her husband died some eleven years later, and it was another seven years after his death before the museum actually opened. Built of local stone, the museum is 300 feet long and covers nearly an acre, with 10,000 or so beautiful objects on display and a public park of twenty-one acres.

The entrance hall is hung with sixteenth-century Flemish tapestries depicting country sports – you can guess what took me there – and also many other beautiful tapestries. There are sedan chairs, a Japanese lacquered palanquin and lots of other fascinating items. Two rooms are devoted entirely to porcelain, one to English porcelain with Worcester, Chelsea, Derby and so forth, and the other to German pottery, mainly Dresden. One room has pieces entirely dedicated to the surrounding county such as fossil fishes from prehistoric periods, a heavy stone hammerhead from nearby Egglestone from the Stone Age, little stone arrowheads found by a man fishing in the Tees at the foot of Cronkley Scar, and a Bronze Age axe found at Middleton-in-Teesdale. One of the artefacts that I have always loved is the silver swan which swims over a sea of glass rods and when wound up bends its neck to gather fish. It is an eighteenth-century piece and at one time was bought by the Emperor Napoleon III as a toy for the Prince Imperial.

The jewel of the county is the City of Durham itself, which is magnificent. If you are travelling north on the train, or indeed south on the train, you get the most wonderful view of Durham Castle and Cathedral and I admired this for quite a long time in my life before I actually ever went to Durham. The occasion that took me to the city was the Woodcock Dinner, where Johnny Scott and I were asked to speak, and it was at the dinner that I bought my dear little gun; it is only a sixteen bore with an under lever action, and is not really terribly suitable for the driven shooting of today, but I picked it up and fell in love with it. Nobody bid against me so it didn't make the reserve and I had to ask what the reserve was so that I could bid it and make the purchase.

The *Anglo-Saxon Chronicle* records the consecration of a bishop in 762 at a place called Aelfet Ee, which various pundits have translated as Swan Island; but as the other name for the place is Elvet, it seems far more likely to me that it has something to do with eels. Anyway, whatever it means it lies in the loop of the river to the east of the cathedral, and became a village served by St Oswald's, the mother church of Durham. The mists closed round it and we don't hear of it again until 995, when the monks were taking St Cuthbert's body back from a procession to Ripon towards Chester-le-Street, where it had been enshrined for 113 years. Because of the incursions of the Danes and the Scots they were anxious to try to find a new and more secure base for it. The story goes that when the party arrived at Elvet the hill, Dunholme hill, which we now call Durham, seemed to them an excellent place to settle. Legend of course tells us a different story: that the coffin suddenly became unmovable and incredibly heavy, as if the saint were announcing his intention of staying there.

For three years the body remained in something called the White Church, until Aldhun, Bishop of Chester-le-Street, persuaded his son-in-law Uchtred, later Earl of Northumberland, to levy the people between the River Coquet and the River Tees to build a more fitting shrine. This proved to be a good investment for the area because, by 998, the first part of the Saxon cathedral was dedicated, and the coffin was duly placed there. Durham became a place of pilgrimage, which it remained for many years to come. The money then had to be diverted to build fortifications against the Danes and the Scots and it was twenty years before the cathedral was finally finished. King Canute, newly converted to Christianity, came on a barefoot pilgrimage from Garmond's Way near Trimdon, bringing with him deeds concerning gifts of land. As the *Chronicle* said:

> Relicks innumerable
> Which perform many miracles
> As the Chronicles tell us
> And which await with them
> The judgement of the Lord.

These sacred relics included the bones of the Venerable Bede which were stolen from Jarrow and placed in the cathedral. William the Conqueror's destruction of the north caused the monks to flee back to Lindisfarne with the much transported relics, but in 1072 William the Conqueror came to Durham to confirm the privileges granted by Canute. The great visionary and builder of Durham was a man called Ralph Flambard, who was a favourite of William Rufus and who was made bishop. He constructed better city walls of stone in place of earthworks, a wall from the choir of the cathedral to the castle keep, dug a moat and built the Framwellgate Bridge. In 1104 Cuthbert, and presumably the intermixed bodies of the Venerable Bede, were transported to the new cathedral and its new shrine, and the annual fair of St Cuthbert was started to raise money for the cathedral in those periods when it was not being supplemented by pilgrimage. The cathedral is fantastic and well worth a visit, but the bit I particularly like is Durham Castle.

Rather uniquely, the entrance to Durham Castle is at the corner of Palace Green, the bishop's principal residence from 1072, which has been part of the university since 1837. It was William the Conqueror himself, a great man for spotting good places for castles, who inspected the site high above the river and determined to make it the centre of the buffer state he was establishing as a protection against the Scots. The Scots never succeeded in taking the castle, and the palatinate scheme that was set up worked because the head of it was a bishop appointed by the King and not a powerful and possibly treasonous hereditary noble. Of particular interest to me is the rather splendid early sixteenth-century kitchen, which is next to the castle hall and has huge fireplaces and a high chestnut roof. It used to be the guardroom until Bishop Fox transformed it. It was certainly in daily use in the 1930s, and when the Duke of Wellington and Sir Walter Scott had dinner with the last of the Prince Bishops, William van Mildert, in 1827. It is a kitchen where I would be really happy to cook.

You will by now have gathered that St Cuthbert spent a lot of time being carried about. The last time he was dug up was in 1827 when the coffin was once more unearthed – I must say they built 'em good back then; the bones were reburied and the coffin was reassembled on to new oak boards. It measures five feet six inches long, St Cuthbert being a small man, and is completely covered with energetic carvings and is the earliest and only specifically dated piece of early Christian carving in the country. Also found when he was dug up was his pectoral cross, a fifth- or possibly sixth-century piece of gold torsini work set with garnets and beautifully worked with delicacy and obvious durability; by the time St Cuthbert got it, it had already been considerably patched and mended. In the coffin too was the earliest piece of English embroidery ever found, which is made of gold thread and is dated as ten or fifteen years after the death of King Alfred. Its Latin inscription shows that it was made on command of

Queen Aelflaed of Mercia for Bishop Frithestan of Winchester in 909 and was presented to St Cuthbert's shrine by Athelstan in 934. I think it is rather wonderful that poor old Cuthbert in all his journeys, being carted around willy-nilly ahead of invaders, still managed to preserve about him all these really early objects while people who led much quieter lives after their deaths have not.

Another place I should mention while dealing with these very ancient monastic memories is Hartlepool. According to Bede, the first we know of it is in 640 when St Aidan, Bishop of Lindisfarne, gave permission for a religious house for men and women to be established there. This was set up and placed in the charge of Heiu, the first woman in the Northumbrian province to give her life to take up the habit of a nun, Bede says, and set upon the Headland, north of the harbour, which is still the centre of modern-day Hartlepool. Heiu is believed to have been an Irish princess who presided over the monastery for many years and was succeeded by St Hilda, who remained in charge for eight years before moving south and founding Whitby Abbey. From fairly early on it was a religious house for women only, quite unique in those days, and of great prestige, but in 800 it was destroyed by the Danes so completely that the site was lost for about 1,000 years. The settlement that grew up around the monastery after the Norman Conquest came into the possession of Robert de Bruce, who was the ancestor of the Bruces of Annandale and the family of Robert Bruce himself. There is actually a plaque on the Headland that says: 'The place whereon thou standest is holy ground. Around lie buried the monks and nuns of the ancient Saxon monastery of Hartlepool founded circa 640 AD and destroyed by the Danes. This cemetery was discovered in 1833.'

In more recent times, in the eighteenth-century Napoleonic Wars, a monkey was shipwrecked in Hartlepool; it was apparently wearing a French military jacket. The inhabitants of Hartlepool, who had never seen a monkey, assumed that this was what Frenchmen looked like because he was little and dark – he was possibly a chimpanzee – and they hanged him. It remains one of the more embarrassing stories about Hartlepool. Why am I minded to think that in later years they got as their Member of Parliament Peter Mandelson?

What fascinates me about the county of Durham is that amid all this industrial history you constantly come across some of the earliest religious history of England. Chester-le-Street, for instance, where I once went electioneering with my friend Matthew Palmer, who was standing as a Conservative in an unwinnable seat – there are some parts of the British Isles where the Hartlepool monkey, as long as it was a member of the Labour Party, would be elected regardless – looks quite ordinary really and slightly run down, and yet it has this amazing early Saxon history with its resting place of St Cuthbert and safe haven for the monks of Lindisfarne who would come here when fleeing the Vikings. The church that Bishop Elgrec built twenty years before the Norman Conquest is still there, although much altered in the fourteenth century, and has a fine stone spire and a thirteenth-century tower with an eight-sided belfry.

Against the north wall of the tower is a stone building, erected about the same time to be a cell or anchorage for a hermit, and it is one of the best preserved anchorages of the very few remaining in England. There is a slit through which the inhabitant could see the altar and another that enabled food to be passed in. After the Reformation this became an almshouse for poor widows and I rather like the story that in 1626 a curate, who thought he would quite like to live in it, obtained a warrant from Durham to eject the poor widows and give them a ducking, as if they were witches. However, with the help of three strong men and a bar to the inner door, the ladies held their end and remained.

Durham is a county that, I realise while writing this, I have perhaps spent too much time driving through to get to my beloved Yorkshire, and really warrants more time to discover further treasures.

Oxfordshire

Oxfordshire is a small county of only 750 square miles and nowhere is it wider than about thirty miles, but it is a rich, fertile county and has a longer stretch of the Thames than any county other than Berkshire, the river winding for about eighty miles along its boundary. I do not intend to deal in any depth with the university, since there are people better placed than me to talk about it and they have done so at some length. In its beginnings the university was not the elitist establishment it has become; anyone could study there, and nobody was too poor or indeed too rich to study with the monks. I'm really quite glad my father wouldn't pay for me to go there because among my contemporaries I look at those who did and there is a particular mindset and an air of superiority that they must be right because they went to Oxford. Good old UCL was fine by me, the first university to take in women and people of colour, but in my youth I went to the May Balls in Oxford, I watched the bumping on the river, I was punted down in the dawning light by handsome young men and it was all great fun but, rather like a holiday, not something that you wanted to last for ever.

So I am only going to tell you one story about Oxford, which was during the days of the run-up to the hunt ban and I went to speak at the Oxford Union on the subject. With me was Robin Page and against me was the government's rural tsar, whose name I cannot at this stage remember, and all I can tell you about him is that he thought that the 'f' in Defra stood for 'farming' when it does of course stand for 'food'. With him was a rather handsome young man in white tie who actually voted with us at the end of the day, the only time I have ever seen this in a debate, and I used to do a lot of debating when I was young. I should tell you that the motion was carried for our side unanimously. The rural tsar abstained, I think rather overcome by the vehemence of the audience, and every other single person voted in favour of continuing hunting. Oh, you will shout, that proves that Oxford is full of toffs, but I have to tell you that this audience was not made up of toffs. The intellectuals who flocked to the Union and only a generation earlier had voted that 'this House would not fight for King and Country' were not the people I expected to turn out in favour of hunting, so well done Oxford!

Anyhow, that's not the story I wanted to tell you. As I was going up to the President's room, a voice from a group of people standing to one side said, 'Would you like to come and have a drink with some proper people, madam?' It was the 'madam' that gave it away, because that is a term very much used in hunting circles, and when I looked at them I had the impression that they were hunting people, so I said yes and went into the bar. After the Union Bar had closed I said to them, 'Oh, well, come upstairs to the President's rooms and we'll carry on.' They were from the Christ Church and Farley Hill Beagles and they asked me if I would like to have a day out with them. So I smiled sweetly and said that my days as a beagler were long since over, as I couldn't run from one end of the cot to the other very successfully these days. They said, 'No, no, on a quad bike.' So there I found myself, on a bright Oxfordshire morning, with a quad bike in fields that were growing horse hay for the racing stables of the country, having the most beautiful day. The young man who had first approached me had arranged for me to stay in Christ Church that evening, so after a lovely day with fit young men hanging on to my quad bike and taking a lift off me from time to time, many of whose fathers I had known when I was their age, I went to dine in Christ Church Hall.

The hall was as magnificent as one might expect from anything founded by Cardinal Wolsey; think Hampton Court. He founded the college in 1525, four years before he fell from power, and he spent his money lavishly on his new foundation. Always referred to as 'the House' by its old alumni, its chapel is Oxford's cathedral, because when Henry VIII took it over on Wolsey's fall, he moved his new see to Oxford from Osney. The college is a conjunction of quadrangles such as Peckwater Quad and Canterbury Quad. Great Tom, the bell that tolls the hours, was brought to the college from Osney Abbey and was re-cast in 1680. It is seven yards round the rim and weighs over seven tonnes and has pealed the curfew every night at five minutes after nine for 250 years. The tower in which it is housed was built by Christopher Wren. Nearby stands Fell's Tower. Dr Fell was a brave man who fought, sword in hand, for the Royalists, but will be remembered as the result of an encounter he had with a farmer's son, Tom Brown. Young Brown had clashed with Fell and was on the point of being expelled. He wrote a penitent letter to the dean and Dr Fell told him that he would be pardoned if he could translate on the spot Martial's epigram on Sabidius:

> I do not love thee, Sabidius
> Nor can I say why
> I can only say this
> I do not love thee.

Tom was equal to the occasion and his famous reply was:

> I do not love thee, Dr Fell,
> The reason why I cannot tell;
> But this I know, and know full well,
> I do not love thee, Dr Fell.

However Dr Fell was not universally disliked and it was at his suggestion that the Sheldonian Theatre was built, and he was one of the group that kept the Church of England services going in Oxford all through the Civil War.

For all its magnificence, I know something about Christ Church Hall that makes me love it all the more, which is that when the magnificent hammerbeam roof was being repaired, one of the students shinned up the scaffolding at a point where it was about to be taken down and placed a little yellow rubber duck on one of the beams. So up there it sits, who knows where, and one day posterity will wonder what on earth it was doing there and what strange ritual it represented.

I spent the night in Christ Church, which I have to say was horrendously uncomfortable – obviously the aesthetic principle still prevails in the Oxford colleges – and although the view out of the window was wonderful, the room was sparse and the lavatories were a very long way down. I suppose that is fine if you are fit young students. The young man who had invited me, who I like to think of as my beagling boy, although as this was some years ago now he is no doubt grown up, said to me that his mother was very worried about his passion for beagling because he had been brought up in Peckham and had never known anything about hounds until he came up to Christ Church. I said, 'Why, is she an anti?' and he said, 'No, no, not at all, it is simply that my grandfather's patrimony was Surbiton and he was so passionate for hunting that he blew the lot.' So I said, 'Well, tell your mother that beagling is rather cheaper than hunting.' I won't give you his name because I know that he has in mind a political career and I'll let him tell his own story.

I always find it curious for a university that would not allow women students for most of its existence that Christ Church was established by St Frideswide, who is the patron saint of Oxford. She was a king's daughter who fled from another king who wanted to marry her and took refuge here, setting up a church which was burned down in the year 1000. Ethelred the Unready had the church rebuilt and so the whole story of Oxford began.

One of the best places, to me, in Oxfordshire is Blenheim Palace at Woodstock. Woodstock is mentioned in the Domesday Book as a forest and we know that Henry I had a zoo there, but it is nowadays famous as the home of John Churchill, first Duke of Marlborough. It is also, curiously, the birthplace of that other great soldier, the Black Prince. One is given the impression that Blenheim, built by the renowned architect John Vanbrugh, with grounds later laid out by Capability Brown, was supposedly planned in such a way that the avenues and trees represent a battle plan of Blenheim. The lake was formed by damming the River Glyme and spanned by a bridge 300 feet long with a centre span of over 100 feet. The Column of Victory that you can see from the bridge is crowned by the heroic figure of the Duke as a Roman and around the base is a record of his battles.

People like to say that Blenheim was built as a gift from the nation in recognition of the heroism and victories of John Churchill, but actually it was really built because Sarah Jennings, the Duke's wife and Duchess, was a friend, to put it mildly, of Queen Anne. Like all the royal Stuarts, Queen Anne was ambiguous in her sexuality, and Sarah ruled the Queen like a tyrant, reducing her to abject submission. Poor old Anne didn't have a happy life really, when you think that she had seventeen pregnancies with her husband Prince George, which produced only one child who survived infancy, William, Duke of Gloucester, and he died of a mastoid abscess at the age of eleven. Then at the height of the Duke's fame, and while Blenheim was being built, the Queen switched her affections to a cousin of Sarah's, Abigail Hill, Lady Masham, and the palace was only finished slowly and laboriously with increasing coldness and impatience from Parliament. The rent paid annually on the anniversary of the Battle of Blenheim is a hand-embroidered banner lavishly made with gold thread. God knows what has happened to them all over the centuries, but perhaps nowadays the same one just goes back and forth.

There is obviously something in the soil at Blenheim because the other person born there was the great Winston Churchill, whose mother was at a ball when her waters broke. She was carried to a small room off the ballroom and there the baby arrived. Churchill's grandmother was an American Vanderbilt heiress who was married to the seventh Duke purely as a business proposition. All those in the vestry after the marriage had to wait while the Duke's man of business and the Vanderbilts' man of business counted the gold that was the price of the union. Another person associated with Blenheim Palace is Charles II's poet, the second Earl of Rochester, who ended his extremely wild and dissolute life in one of the bedrooms.

My favourite story about Blenheim was forty-odd years ago, when I had a part-time job as a tourist guide and I worked for a company that brought choirs and bands and college orchestras over from America, Australia and Canada. It was a lovely job because not only did you take them to see the sights, but also you made the arrangements for them to sing at eisteddfods and play at Coventry Cathedral and places like that so it was really interesting. One sunny day, we were standing on the steps of Blenheim Palace waiting for the tour and, because that is what they did, they started to sing and they sang very well. The Duke must have heard them because he came out and invited them to come in and sing in the chapel. So we all went into the beautiful white marble chapel at Blenheim and, while we were waiting for our tour, they sang various pieces from their repertoire and we all enjoyed ourselves enormously.

The other place in Oxfordshire where I have spent many happy times was Henley, the home of the world's most famous regatta, the Henley Royal Regatta. When I was quite young I had an admirer who was coxing the Winchester boat and he gave my mother and me a couple of vouchers to go and watch him row; I thought my mother would probably find it rather dull, forgetting that my mother's brother used to row when he was at both Beaumont and Oxford. Henley is so quintessentially British, it really couldn't exist anywhere else. You see men of all ages wearing the blazers, caps and badges that marked their rowing fame in their heyday. You might get somebody wearing a Leander blazer which is salmon pink (the Leander Club is the elite rowing club), with perhaps a British badge on it and a university cap adorned maybe with a school badge and the victor's salmon-pink socks. It is the English male at his peacock best. Anyway, no sooner had we got through the gates, with me slightly worried about what my mother would do while I went off and talked to my friends, when a man, attired in the way I have described, came up and said, 'Tubs, it's never Tubs.' I had never heard my mother referred to as Tubs before, and she was an elegant woman, but her maiden name was Bath. He said, 'Come on, come on, come to the Leander and we'll have a Pimm's; all the gang's there.' Well, this must have been a gang that my mother hadn't seen for fifty or sixty years. Anyway, off they went and she had the most lovely day linking up with old friends while I went off and watched the young man row. They did rather well so I spent a lot of time without my admirer on that first visit to Henley.

I've been there many times over the years since then at different stages of my life, and I can't say that I saw all that much of the rowing. Usually one would have quite a lot of Pimm's then go and sit in a deckchair in a nice haze in the sunshine and the boats would go past and every so often you would see a colour you recognised and clap enthusiastically. Rowing is not really a sport that I am terrible knowledgeable about, but it was a magical time there. I haven't been to Henley for many years and I don't think I'll ever go again. I expect like everything else it has got an awful lot of corporate hospitality now. The story I love is that Princess Grace of Monaco's father, who was a brilliant rower in America, was refused permission to row at Henley because he was a common working labouring man, but then his daughter married Prince Rainier of Monaco. The people at Henley got very excited and remembered that he was a rower and invited him to attend and I can only imagine with what enormous pleasure he must have declined the invitation.

Banbury comes to mind simply because when I was a child everybody knew the nursery rhyme, the bumping rhyme for babies, about Banbury Cross that went 'Ride a cock-horse to Banbury Cross to see a fine lady upon a white horse'. Unfortunately there is not a lot to see in Banbury nowadays; the cross of the nursery rhyme was pulled down while Queen Elizabeth was still in power and the new cross is barely a hundred years old. The church at Banbury, which was known as Banbury Cathedral because it was so beautiful, was blown up by the citizens of Banbury at the end of the eighteenth century. They quite literally blew it up by laying gunpowder under it. They did so because they were not prepared to pay for the repairs and the new church is not something one would really go out of one's way to see. Oxfordshire is fine hunting country and has among its packs the Heythrop and Bicester, both of which I have had the pleasure of going out with.

Pat Llewellyn, that great perfectionist when making *Two Fat Ladies*, sieved through 600 cricket grounds searching for a venue for us to film a cricket match and a cricket tea, and settled finally on Wallingford in the south of the county as the perfect example of John Major's England, with women going to evensong on sit-up-and-beg bicycles and the click of leather on willow in the evening air. One of the dishes I cooked was a very lush Hungarian cake named after a louche Hungarian musician called Rigo Jancsi, who brought down a government with his sexual misbehaviour. The cake was invented by a Budapest pastry chef, and consists mainly of chocolate and cream. It was very popular with the cricket club and was adopted by them as their club cake; I love the thought of this perfect model of an English village having adopted a cake named after a Hungarian male prostitute.

Turn due west and you will come to Wantage, the birthplace of King Alfred, readily identifiable by the fine statue of him standing in the centre of the town. I always find it fitting that the town contains such a splendid educational establishment as St Mary's Wantage (now Heathfield St Mary's) for the education of women. It should be here because it was Alfred's mother who was so keen that her younger son should learn to read and write that she promised to give him her Book of Hours if he could read it. Wantage is obviously still excelling in the education of women because among others Judith Keppel, the first ever winner of £1 million in *Who Wants to Be a Millionaire?*, was educated here. It used to be the case, and I hope it still is, that the old grammar school, on the anniversary of Alfred's birthday, would offer burned cakes to their chief guest in memory of Alfred's culinary disaster.

You might like to continue inland and visit Uffington, the supposed burial place of Uther Pendragon, father of King Arthur, and admire the oldest of the chalk white horses cut into the Downs here. Legend says that it was created to mark the victory of Alfred over the Danes at Ashdown, but the first mention of it by any chronicler is 200 years later in the records of the Abbey of Abingdon in the reign of Henry II. It is an etiolated, phantasmagorical horse, 374 feet from nose to tail and 120 feet from ear to hoof and with such a strange head you could almost think it was a dragon. It used to take four men three weeks to scour it clean of weeds. You can climb up on to the Ridgeway and visit Wayland the Smith's workshop: this is a ruined cromlech in a ring of beeches, with one great stone resting on five others with lesser ones scattered about. Once an underground chamber, perhaps a sepulchre of some chieftain, centuries have linked it with the legend of Wayland the Smith, who made swords 'none could resist' and winged armour that carried one over the land like an eagle. Here it is said that if a traveller left a horse that had lost a shoe overnight, with money on top of the cromlech, Wayland Smith would come back from wherever it was that he rested and shoe it. A number of legends say that it was Wayland the Smith who was responsible for making Excalibur.

Keep going north-eastwards along the Ridgeway and you will come to the town of Abingdon. Not much remains of the Saxon Abbey of Abingdon, but the town of Abingdon is pleasant enough and was home to one of our strangest Archbishops of Canterbury, a man called St Edmund Rich, whom people have described as scholar, patriot and saint. A virulent xenophobe, he was an odd man, whose father had retired to a monastery leaving him to be brought up by his mother. She induced him to wear sackcloth next to his skin, to fast frequently and never to eat on Sundays and festivals until he had sung through the whole Psalter. In the grip of poverty, he begged his way from Oxford to Paris and remained there until he had gained all the knowledge he thought he could from French scholarship.

He returned to England as the most eloquent and learned teacher of the day. Without parade or ostentation he became renowned for austerity and self-denial. Clothed in sackcloth and iron plate, knotted thongs and horsehair, 'he lay but daily among his flock' and spent all his revenues on the poor, so that during the second half of each year he was dependent upon charity for

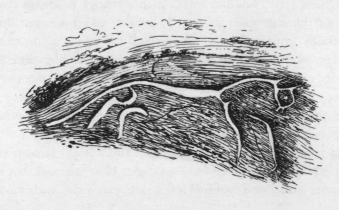

his bread. He was made Primate of all England at the age of sixty-three, much against his own preferences, and he stood adamant again King and Pope, insisting that the provisions of Magna Carta be implemented by Henry III. He threatened the King with excommunication unless he dismissed his foreign favourites, but unfortunately he took too stubborn a stance and was deserted by the King and insulted and flouted by the Pope. He retired, heartbroken, to France where he died in 1240, a funny place to go for such an adamant xenophobe.

Yorkshire

So finally we come to the county that holds the brightest place in my heart; it is a shining star from whence my ancestors left just over 500 years ago and where I often think I may end my days. I would quite like to have one of those houses on the cliffs south of Scarborough, the ones that are falling into the sea. You can't get a mortgage on them but you can buy them quite cheaply. I think it would be rather exciting in my old age to go to bed at night not knowing whether I would wake up in the morning or just wake up as I slid into the sea, but then I have very strange ideas on the subject of death.

Yorkshire is the largest of all the English counties, and in my youth it was divided into three ridings, the North Riding, the East Riding and the West Riding, terms that are no longer used. There was no South Riding, although it is the title of a 1930s novel. I have always loved the dry wit of Yorkshire people; it is so dry, rather like drinking a good Chablis, but so well concealed that if you don't know what to look for you might think that they are actually being somewhat dour and offensive. I also love their indomitable intractability and their incredibly practical attitude to authority as a whole. I remember being at the Great Yorkshire Show shortly before the hunting ban, during the marching days, and there were hounds in the ring. Over the loudspeakers came a Yorkshire voice saying, 'And 'ere we 'ave the North York and Anstey 'ounds and they've just finished a cracking season 'unting and they'll 'ave a cracking season 'unting next season and if any say owt 'e'll not be welcome in Yorkshire.'

There are eighteen hunts in North Yorkshire alone and I recall a former Chief Constable of the county saying that if he had any men left over after sending them out to deal with crimes in the major cities and football hooliganism he might consider sending them out to inspect the most law-abiding core of all the people in his allocated area.

Originally my father's family came from Richmond, the capital of Swaledale. The main dales are Swaledale, Wensleydale and Teesdale with the smaller dales running into them such as Coverdale, Bishopdale, Raydale and Arkengarthdale. The Dales are magnificent, with their fine river scenery and splendid waterfalls – a waterfall is known as a 'force' in this part of the country, such as High Force at Aysgarth – and do not have the barren isolation of the moorland area. Richmond itself has the remains of a castle built on sheer walls of rock by Earl Allan ten years after the Conquest, and is probably the loftiest Norman keep in England. Easby Abbey is nearby and both were painted by the artist Turner in his heyday. This, not its London equivalent, is the Richmond of the song 'Sweet Lass of Richmond Hill'. She was a young woman by the name of Frances I'Anson and the poet Leonard McNally fell in love with her and wrote the song for her. The town has a great feel of the Middle Ages about it. There are passages between the houses on ledges of rocks, the cobbled streets have names such as Friars Wynd, and many of them afford glimpses of the castle, while the Market Place is steep and roughly cobbled.

The only reason I know of my connection with Richmond was that we had a portrait in the hall at home of a man by the name of Sir Edmund Wright who was Lord Mayor of London and held London for the Commonwealth during the English Civil War. I discovered that he was one of the band of merchant adventurers based in Richmond, as well as one of the founding members of the Muscovy Company, and that he moved south to look after his fortune. You can just see it, can't you, a sort of thick-set Yorkshire man deciding, ''Ere, those buggers in London aren't looking after my money properly, I'll go and sort it.' It was he who built Swakeleys House in Ickenham and married the woman who burned her little page boy – hopefully by accident.

So I went to Richmond to find out more about him and here is one of the things I love in Yorkshire. The warden of the Merchant Adventurers' Company who told me about them sat talking to me at great length about Sir Edmund and, just as I was preparing to go, he sucked his teeth and said, 'Here's something you might admire to know,' and I said, 'What's that?' He replied, 'Those are the Wrights that financed Guy Fawkes.' Of course, while I knew that Christopher and James Wright had died with Guy Fawkes, I had never actually connected them to my own Wrights before this. They wouldn't half have annoyed my grandmother, my father's mother, who was so Protestant that when my father said that he was engaged to a Catholic she wrote back: 'I would rather she were a black, naked, heathen whore.' She would have been appalled to discover that there were Catholic martyrs in her own bloodline. I am very taken with the fact that the nearby military camp at Catterick, which must be the coldest and most inhospitable of all the military camps in England, was probably a Roman marching camp.

There are possibly more ancient ways crossing the North Yorkshire Moors than there are modern roads. These were set up, as was always the way, for purposes of trade, and of course there are Roman marching roads across the moors, going not only to make war but to bring back salt and dried fish from the coast. Otherwise they are mostly drovers' roads. If you ever have cause to watch afternoon television, as I did when I was ill a couple of years ago, there is a programme called *Helicopter Heroes* about the work of the Yorkshire Air Ambulance Service. I was amazed to discover how many properties there are up on the moors that are actually not reachable by any made road, and if you don't have a four-wheeled-drive vehicle you'll never get there, hence they have such an efficient helicopter service for when disaster strikes.

One of the aspects of the Yorkshire character I particularly like is its stubborn refusal to accept the impossible, which reminds me of Northallerton, the home town of a woman I greatly admire, called Anne Willan, who took on the French. She is a bit younger than me, I suppose, and went to the Cordon Bleu in Paris, where even to this day they are not particularly keen on women, and then set up a cookery school and a hotel and restaurant in Paris, followed by another one in Burgundy. Despite every adversity she was greatly admired by the French who had to admit that she was a very good cook indeed. It is the sheer scale of this achievement at that time that is beyond measure. Her *Complete Guide to Cookery* was my desert island book because when I went to Scotland and all my books were packed, I could only grab one to take with me of the 1,000-plus cookery books that I own. Without a moment's hesitation I grabbed that book.

Northallerton in its own right is another symbol of the Yorkshire indomitableness. Just outside it stands a stone obelisk to the Battle of the Standard fought in 1138. The name comes from the rather curious standard that the English forces raised against the Scots, which was the mast of a ship fastened to a carriage on four wheels having, at the top of the mast, a pyx containing the host. It was here that the barons of the north met the Scots, who they were determined to drive out of England, and they left their horses a mile behind the lines so that they could not retreat. The Scots gave a great roar and battle was joined, but the English archers shot high in the air and destroyed 12,000 of the enemy, resulting in a complete defeat of the Scots.

The north-east coast of Yorkshire, as I said, is an area of cliffs falling into the North Sea and beautiful beaches. I never spent my holidays on the Yorkshire coast and for that, to a certain extent, I am grateful, because it would have to be a rare day indeed when the wind didn't come from the east and it wasn't icy cold, but they are hardy folk in Yorkshire. There are some remarkable places along this coast, one of which is Staithes. It is the highest point along the English coast and the land runs steeply down to the sea with narrow passages and small alleys right to the water's edge. Sixteen houses were swept away from a ledge under Penny Nab, including the grocer's shop where James Cook had been sent by his father, a mason, who had found a Mr Sanderson who was to train James up to be a grocer and draper. He was a poor apprentice and his master flogged him because instead of performing his duties he would stare idly out of the window at the ships passing by set to the wind. One day James had had enough and he wrapped his only possessions, a shirt and a knife, in his handkerchief and set off for Whitby. Here he lodged with two Quaker brothers whose house still stands in Grape Lane, and is now the Captain Cook museum. It is an old fifteenth-century building and it was in the brothers' Whitby-built ship that he set off on the first of his three voyages of discovery. It is an interesting fact that all Cook's voyages to the Antipodes were made in what is known as the Whitby Cat, a sturdy vessel used more for inshore trading than for long journeys, but they certainly served Cook very well.

Whitby no longer builds ships, but the ones it used to build were originally used on the Greenland whaling grounds. One of the pioneers of whaling was William Scoresby, who for thirty years brought home oil worth about £100,000 every year. He is said to have captured more whales than any other man and to have sailed the furthest north of any of his day. It was he who devised what we know as the crow's nest as a lookout at the masthead for spotting whales. Whitby was clearly all about shipping. In one of churches there is a three-decker pulpit with square lower deck and a many-sided top deck.

Whitby was the birthplace of the first ever poet of the English language, Caedmon. The Abbess of Whitby at the time of Caedmon's 'Song of Creation' was St Hilda; we have already met her in Northumbria. Caedmon was called upon to sing a song when the harp was being passed around, but he was unable to sing because he was unlettered and afraid. That night he dreamed a song and brought it to the nuns in the morning; this was 'The Song of Caedmon'. Caedmon's work was really quite remarkable; let me give you this Victorian attempt at putting it into understandable English. These are some lines from his first poem, 'Song of Creation':

> There had not here as yet,
> Save Cavern-shade,
> Aught been;
> But this wide Abyss
> Stood deep and dim,
> Strange to its Lord,
> Idle and useless;
> On which looked with his eyes
> The King firm of mind,
> And beheld those places
> Void of joys;
> Saw the dark cloud
> Lower in the eternal night,
> Swart under heaven,
> Dark and waste.

Good stuff for an illiterate swineherd, don't you think?

And it was at the Synod of Whitby that the early Church was persuaded to choose the way of the Romans over that of the Celtic Church. The main debates, ironically, in those days were over whether the tonsure should be worn as a circle in the Roman manner or as a crescent in the Celtic manner and how to calculate the date of Easter.

Whitby is also known for its jet. There has been a trade in jet from Whitby since time immemorial and there have been some exquisite pieces of this strange coal-like stone produced here. Whitby jet really took off in Victorian times when, following the death of Prince Albert, Queen Victoria favoured it as mourning jewellery and it became extremely fashionable indeed. Apparently there is a vampire buried at Whitby which might explain why twice a year they appear to have a festival of Goths. I know this because Jennifer and I were filming there when it was on and we got some very strange looks, and vice versa I dare say.

Kippers have long been associated with Whitby. There is a wonderful, slightly old-fashioned, kipper smoking firm that has been in the same family for many generations, and funnily enough I discovered this when talking about the herring road with my own fishmonger David Clarke in Musselburgh. Their kippers were excellent, having been smoked on tenterhooks over oak chippings. The owners were fighting hard with Europe which, having already banned kippers being sent by post within the United Kingdom, was attempting to do away with the kipper altogether. Until the Women's Institute stepped in, that is, and won another victory. The family were proper fisher-folk, and as a gull screamed on the roof of the building, the woman said to me that her father had died not very long before and that the fisher-folk believed that the newly departed souls inhabited gulls to come back and visit the homes where they had lived in their lifetimes. There was no doubt in my mind that she believed it and why not?

When you go into churches around rural Yorkshire, especially in the north in what was the North Riding, you will come upon the most lovely Saxon carvings. There are some particularly good hogback tombstones in the church in Brompton which feature bears. Everyone makes such a fuss about the fact that the wolves are now extinct in this country and there are various schemes to reintroduce them, but of course not only did we have wolves but we also had bears. These charming tombstones are about 1,000 years old and the two by the chancel have a bear at each end, which are stretching out their paws along the sides and in their mouths hold the strap running along the top. The one in the aisle has the bears lying on their backs, feet in the air, and the strap in their mouths.

A particularly attractive little Saxon sculpture is in the church at Newburgh Priory in Coxwold. There is a mystery about this church, which is believed to be the place where Oliver Cromwell's body finally came to rest. His daughter was married to Lord Fauconberg who owned the priory at that time. Charles II had dug up Cromwell's body and had it hanged at Tyburn and then placed his head over London Bridge from where it was stolen, but Lady Fauconberg is believed to have got hold of the body and brought it to Newburgh. There is a room in the house called Cromwell's Room where he is rumoured to be walled up, but it is probably more likely that he is hidden somewhere in the church. The tomb has never been opened and it is perfectly possible that Cromwell's body does lie here.

The Cistercian monks who invented sheep farming found the perfect location to pursue this in Yorkshire. They had decided that the order, the Benedictine Order, had become too corrupt and distanced from its original ideals, and so they sought a different life of hardship and meditative work in remote places. Yorkshire was perfect; inland it was away from the marauders, whether Danish or Scottish, who came in from the sea, and so the whole area is littered with the ruins of the once great abbeys. Clearly the idea of poverty – surprise, surprise – passed on fairly quickly. You will find the remains of Jervaulx, Rievaulx and Fountains Abbeys, and of course Bolton Abbey. Somebody once said that Bolton Abbey was for artists, Fountains Abbey for historians and Rievaulx Abbey for poets. Rievaulx was founded by Walter Espec, Lord of Helmsley, and flourished so well that it sent out its monks to found other sister houses. Rievaulx, in a very short space of time, had 140 monks and 600 lay brothers.

All these ruins are beautiful and evocative and the transepts and the remnants of the windows in the sacristies are such that one has a very clear idea of what they must have looked like in their heyday. Set in these remote places they must really have brought the locals to thoughts of God. A monastic life offered employment and food and shelter to many, and I am quite certain, looking at monastic records, that poverty, chastity and obedience were in short supply among a great many of their followers. The Catholic tradition of forgiveness by confession does, in some people, encourage a less than perfect lifestyle. There are ruins of abbeys and priories all over Yorkshire and, given the time that has elapsed following the Reformation after the Dissolution of the Monasteries, it says a very great deal for the honesty of Yorkshire people that the stone has not been taken away to a much greater extent than it has been. Yorkshire was devoutly Catholic, and at the time of the Reformation the Pilgrimage of Grace set out to march to London to protest to Henry VIII for the actions of his commissioners. It was actually a very real threat to the Tudor monarchy and it was turned back by deceit and lies. Ain't it always so?

What the moors of Yorkshire mean to me, apart from hunting, of course, is coursing under National Coursing Club rules. I saw my first coursing meeting when I was in my teens and we went to stay with my mother's great friend from school who lived at Brough. We went out to the moors with, presumably, the Old Yorkshire or the Ryedale Club and I have loved it ever since. It is therefore appropriate that it was in Yorkshire that the League Against Cruel Sports brought a prosecution against myself and Sir Mark Prescott, which was to be tried in Scarborough Magistrates Court. I remember the Chief Constable saying that he could not guarantee my physical safety and had I had to go to court, I had been promised a bodyguard of thirty stalwart terrier-men, and they don't come much tougher than them. In the event I received an absolute discharge in my absence, so I didn't cause any fighting in the streets of Scarborough, which is one of the North Sea holiday towns and is very pleasant.

One cannot leave this part of Yorkshire without mentioning the magnificence of Castle Howard. Built as the stately home for the third Earl of Carlisle by Sir John Vanbrugh, the builder of Blenheim Palace, it is a palace in itself surrounded by wonderful grounds. Horace Walpole declared it to have 'the noblest lawn in the world fenced by half the horizon'. It is almost amazing in its splendour, even more so than Blenheim in some ways because of its setting. I once went to a dance at Castle Howard and it is a place that lends itself to a good party. Interestingly, the chef James Martin's father was head gamekeeper there, so James must have learned a lot about game.

If Castle Howard is pure grandeur, then Middleham Castle is pure power. For centuries it was the home of the Neville family, coming into the family when Ralph FitzRanulph's heiress married Robert Neville of Raby. It is a ruin now, but Richard III, as Governor of the North, ruled Yorkshire and the north from there. It gives one a sense of the power of the Neville family. Had the son of Richard III and his Neville wife survived, the Nevilles would possibly have ruled England as well. It's another of history's what ifs.

While all the Cistercian monasteries are in ruins, there is one remaining abbey in Yorkshire that still carries the Catholic faith, only in this case of the Benedictines, who in England seem to have outlived pretty well their Cistercian brothers. This is Ampleforth Abbey, which runs the Roman Catholic boys' school of Ampleforth College, an extremely impressive building up on the high moors. If you carry on beyond Ampleforth westwards, you will go down the massive Sutton Bank, which is forbidden to caravans and other such vehicles, and you will come to the market town of Thirsk. Once a famous mail coach posting station, Thirsk has a large number of old inns, some of which offer extremely good hospitality, and there are still traces of the bullring in the square and the site of a castle built by Roger de Mowbray. Then you can head south to York itself.

York is the capital of the north, the Roman Eboracum, the Viking Jorvik and home to many very good museums with interesting objects that have been found. Of particular note, I think though, is the Viking museum. It was really the excavations and research done in York that taught us that the Vikings were so much more than just marauders coming in from the sea to rape, loot and pillage; they had come to settle and they were farmers, weavers and makers of artefacts of considerable skill. It was one of those bits of history that should have been obvious in a way, because why else would there have been the Danelaw, that area of the kingdom settled by the Danes; the whole story is very well set out in the Jorvik Viking Centre. Once a year, York has a Viking Festival, when Viking galleys come up the Ouse as they would have done long ago. Much drinking takes place, but not much in the way of pillage and very little in the way of rape these days.

York is a very fine example of a medieval city and the Shambles by the Petergate, which dates back before the Domesday Book and was where the livestock were brought into the town and killed, still has an incredibly good pork butcher. It is said that it was the shavings and sawdust from the construction of York Minster that gave rise to the very good quality smoke of the York hams, and certainly pork is much favoured in Yorkshire. I once went into a little café and asked, as I invariably do, usually receiving a negative response, whether they kept the fat on the ham, and the woman looked at me in astonishment and said, 'Aye, but this is Yorkshire, of course.'

The pride of York, it seems to me without doubt, is its minster, one of the greatest pieces of architecture in England. There is a story told of a South African soldier who saw the minster for the first time and stood in a fixed salute before its marvellous west front, so impressed was he. There was a wooden church here in 627 and a stone church in 633. The present church was built between 1220 and 1472. It is immense, the largest church in England apart from the Anglican cathedral in Liverpool, and the widest Gothic church in England. The flanking towers rise to 200 feet and from east to west the church is 525 feet and the transepts are 250 feet wide. Three of the 128 windows are nearly eighty feet in height. When, not long ago, it was struck by lightning and caught fire, one really did feel that perhaps God had turned against us. At the east end the minster has the biggest window area of stained glass in England and probably in the world, large enough for a tennis court. In the crypt there are some wonderful carvings. The one I particularly liked when I was young was the 'hell cauldron', which showed the souls that had gone to hell being heated up in a cauldron stoked by grinning devils. You see I was interested in cookery even then!

York is now the only town outside London that has its own butchers' livery, and I have the great honour of being a member of the York Butchers' Guild as well as of the Worshipful Company of Butchers in London. The York butchers have one big feast a year on Shrove Tuesday, where the new incumbents are sworn in in the chapel of the Merchant Adventurers' Hall, followed by an excellent dinner. It is the lot of the Master for the year to provide the baron of beef that is carried around the hall and then sliced to be eaten; it is the only place I have ever seen this. On the high table were little dishes of grated horseradish, a bowl of cream and a bottle of vinegar and you mixed your own horseradish sauce, which I think is an excellent idea but is something I have never come across before.

York is not the only minster in the county; the other is at Beverley, which I once had quite a good opportunity to visit after my car broke down outside it, and I was waiting for the AA to fix the car. Beverley made its fortunes out of sheep and from the high-quality woollen cloth that was woven in the town. I don't know what it is with sheep men and towers, but it is a beautiful minster, although rather large for the town that surrounds it, and a fine example of the Perpendicular style. I had plenty of time to admire the capitals of the nave and they are curiously carved indeed. There is one of a fox preaching to a flock of geese, another of a goat holding a sheet on which are two women, so presumably the goat represents the devil and sin, and a carving of a serious man with a book and a bell, as well as all sorts of grotesques and animals fighting and bears. I love the carvings in these medieval churches. In the centre of the church is the huge tomb of the Earls of Northumberland, among them Henry Percy known as 'the Magnificent', who was one of the most resplendent figures at Henry VIII's Field of the Cloth of Gold. Also buried in the Percy Canopy is his father, who was killed by the rabble as he was collecting taxes for Henry VII. Henry the Magnificent was the father of the Earl whom Cardinal Wolsey did not allow to marry Anne Boleyn, another of the what if moments in history. So if your car breaks down in Beverley, you will know how to occupy your time while it is fixed.

The southern dividing line of Yorkshire is the mighty Humber. Hull sits on its wide estuary and has been a port certainly since the time of Edward I. With its access to both the Ouse and the Trent, Hull was in an ideal position for trade in England, and then further afield to the Continent as trade increased. Hull has many things going for it, but there are two that spring to my mind, the first being that it was the birthplace of William Wilberforce, the man who was responsible for the successful campaign to abolish slavery. When this finally did happen, it was brought about by a very clever use of parliamentary practices and actually went through not on yet another bill to abolish slavery, all of which had been dismissed because of pressure from the members from the slave ports, but on a seemingly innocuous bill about the transportation of cargo. Most MPs had gone off to the races at Epsom, and by the time they realised that this bill was being put through it was too late. The other thing is the Black Hut on the Humber at its mouth, which was owned by the Humber Wildfowlers. It was where the Wildfowlers Association of Great Britain and Ireland (WAGBI), the first conservation organisation in this country for the preservation of stocks of wildfowl, was founded by Stanley Duncan from Hull in 1908. WAGBI grew and grew and in 1981 became BASC, the British Association for Shooting and Conservation.

There used to be an old saying about Yorkshire which was 'Hell, Hull and Halifax'. Halifax, in what was the West Riding in the old days is part of the great industrial conglomeration that is West Yorkshire. Halifax was one of the centres of the cloth industry, and to this day it still has a factory that produces Melton cloth for hunt coats and riding coats and also produces baize for snooker tables. Another of these towns is Leeds where, among other traditions, John Aspdin perfected the manufacture of Portland cement. Leeds has the wonderful old Victorian Kirkgate market, which is still there, although I don't really think the town makes enough of it, for some reason being much keener on the fact that they have the only Harvey Nichols in the north. I visited the market and thought what a wonderful place it is, with all its curlicue wrought-iron work; it was where I first came across stotty bread, which is Northumbrian in origin, and is no doubt eaten in Leeds with much joy and presumably ham and pease pudding just as it is in the north. Sheffield, which was for so long the centre of the Sheffield Plate industry (silver-plated copper), turned from manufacturing silver cutlery and artefacts to making them out of a material more financially acceptable to the emergent middle classes in Victorian times.

What is remarkable about all these towns is that they are within easy access of the moors, the dales and the wolds of the county, so that you can get away from what would have been the dirt and the unpleasantness of the factories and into the fresh air and walk on green grass. It is a complete mystery to me why this current coalition government, given that Nick Clegg is Deputy Prime Minister and Member of Parliament for Sheffield, refused the loan to Forgemasters, which is probably one of the few large companies manufacturing in Sheffield, that would have ensured a cast-iron contract building bunkers to store nuclear waste. Mrs Thatcher might have killed the north or at least the industry in the north, but I have to say that all those years of Labour rule didn't do much for it either. It is such a tragedy to see so much energy and brains going to waste while everything is manufactured abroad.

Also in this part of Yorkshire is Harrogate, a wonderful place to go, if only to visit Bettys Tea Rooms, which has all the efficiency and industry of a well-run establishment while preserving the pleasure of an old-fashioned atmosphere, looking out on to gardens filled with flowers of the type that a friend of mine refers to as 'civic pride'. Near Harrogate is Knaresborough, which I used to be fascinated by, because in a cave there they hung various artefacts which over the years have become petrified by limestone, and I used to love that.

Yorkshire, as you probably know, has a great tradition for pork pies, which in Yorkshire are actually eaten warm. One of the most terrifying things I ever had to do, on three separate occasions, was to judge the Great Yorkshire Pork Pie Competition which also contains categories for sausages and black pudding. If I had got it wrong, imagine, I would never have been able to go into Yorkshire again. I stood there looking at this great array of some 140 pies entered for the competition. I have a friend called Peter Ibbotson who is a Yorkshire butcher, and I think the funniest man it has ever been my privilege to meet, and there I was standing feeling not very well – I think I'd just got over a bout of bronchitis – and he kept me going all day with this burble of humour like a little stream trickling over rocks. I thought we would never find a winner. Obviously quite a lot of them were disqualified fairly early on because of soggy bottoms, or not enough jelly, or you could tell just by looking at them, until finally I came to the best pork pie I have ever eaten, and I have eaten quite a lot of pork pies. It was made by a shop called Gledhills of Stanley which is on the edge of Wakefield, and I said to the young woman who'd made it, 'This is the best pork pie I've ever eaten,' and she said with true Yorkshire modesty, 'Aye, I thought they came nice out of the oven this morning.' I always keep meaning to go to Stanley to buy some, but somehow I haven't got round to it yet.

Judging things reminds me of one of the most charming letters I have ever had, which came from the organisers of the Bugthorpe Show. Bugthorpe is near Stamford Bridge and is so small that I think the last tourists to go there were probably Harold of Hastings on his way to the battle, but let me show you the letter:

> Dear Clarissa,
> We would like you to open the Bugthorpe Show. It's not a very big show but you would eat your traditional Roast Beef and Yorkshire pudding to the mellifluous tones of our local brass band. It's not a very big brass band but it's very mellifluous. Lest you should lose your name in Yorkshire we would not ask you to judge cakes, jams and biscuits but we would leave that to Lady Halifax but we would like you to open the show and present prizes. Do hope you can come.

This stands out in my mind as one of the loveliest days of my life. I had driven across from Lancashire on the A59 on a beautiful day with the roof of my car down, and I had found this pub that mentioned hunting in its blurb about three times. Sure enough, I hadn't been in the bar more than ten minutes when someone came up and said, 'Hounds are meeting tomorrow morning at six at the Hall' (it was cubbing time). 'Would you like to come?' It was the Bedale Hunt and I had the most lovely morning driving around with the terrier-men and a small girl who assured me that the only reason she was in the terrier-men's Land Rover was the fact that her pony had trodden on her face the previous week, and her cheek was still quite bruised. Her mother had said that the pony's foot might not be fully recovered so it was best if she went with the terrier-men. Afterwards I set off and got to Bugthorpe in time for my traditional lunch and just had the most delightful day.

In order to persuade the BBC to film hunting in the second series of *Clarissa and the Countryman*, I volunteered to get back on a horse, this in Yorkshire with the Saltersgate Hunt. I hadn't been on a horse for twenty years and everybody, including Johnny and the BBC for some reason, seemed to think that I would not go through with it, but of course I did, beautifully attired in all the clothes that we had collected over the course of the programme. I went out on this nice cob called Killarney, which for reasons you will understand I had renamed Nemesis. I had a great morning hunting the Fylingdales Moor, and it was after the BBC had finished with me that my metal instep locked solid and I decided it was time to get down. So I came down

from the horse and, visualise this, there was me in full hunting apparel and bowler hat, on my knees on the cold Yorkshire hillside because my instep had collapsed. I was unable to get up and the farmer, whose land we were on and a former Master of the Saltersgate, came over. He put his hands under my armpits and lifted me straight up on to my feet; very strong, these Yorkshire farmers. I was pretty amazed, and when I got my breath back I said, 'Heavens, Brian, that was impressive.' He looked at me and said, 'Aye, I've lifted a lot of heifers.' Thank God he said heifers, I suppose. That really sums up to me all that I love about Yorkshire.

Acknowledgements

To Rowena Webb for commissioning this. To my friend and agent, Heather Holden-Brown, and her sidekicks, Elly James and Claire Houghton-Price. To Morag Lyall, my copy editor, and to Pauline Dinsdale, my redoubtable fingers. To Kipper, my cover companion, and not forgetting Kipper's hair by 'Prue'!

Picture Acknowledgements

© Alamy: 1 above/Nick Turner, 1 below/Gary Stones, 2 above right/Jeremy Pardoe, 3 above left/ World History Archive, 3 above right/William Edwards, 4 above/Angelo Hornak, 4 below/Mike Kipling Photography, 5 above left/Pictorial Press Ltd, 5 above right/Stephen Worth, 6 above left/The Art Gallery Collection, 6 above right/Mike Titterton, 6 below/David Keith Jones, 7 below Tim Graham. © The British Library Board/1485. pp.18: 7 above right. © Mary Evans Picture Library/The National Archives, London: 5 below left. © Getty Images: 2 above left DEA/M. Seemuller, 2 below, 3 below, 7 above left, 8.

Illustrations © Dan Williams

Map by Rosie Collins

Index